Teaching with the Internet:

Lessons from the Classroom

Third Edition

Teaching with the Internet:

Lessons from the Classroom

Third Edition

Donald J. Leu, Jr. and Deborah Diadiun Leu
University of Connecticut

Christopher-Gordon Publishers, Inc.
Norwood, Massachusetts

Disclaimer

The authors and the publisher assume no responsibility for errors or omissions in the resources identified in this book. Moreover, the authors and publisher assume no liability for any damages resulting from the use of any information identified in this book or from links listed at sites that are described. As we indicate in this book, the best way to protect children from viewing inappropriate sites or receiving inappropriate messages is to implement a sound acceptable use policy and to carefully monitor student use of the Internet in your classroom, at school, and at home.

We have devoted much time and energy to providing accurate and current information in this book. Nevertheless, in an environment as constantly changing as the Internet, it is inevitable that some of the information provided here will also change. Information provided at one location may move to another, sometimes without any indication it has moved. Updated links are maintained at the web site for this book, **Teaching with the Internet** (http://www.sp.uconn.edu/~djleu/third.html) as well as extensive, additional information about how to use the Internet in your classroom.

Christopher-Gordon Publishers, Inc.
1502 Providence Highway, Suite #12
Norwood, MA 02062
(800) 934-8322

Printed in the United States of America

10 9 8 7   06 05 04

ISBN 1-929024-20-7
Library of Congress Number 00132289

Credits

Every effort has been made to contact copyright holders for permission to reproduce borrowed material where necessary. We apologize for any oversights and would be happy to rectify them in future printings.

All e-mail correspondence, classroom web-sites and home pages used with permission.

Microsoft Explorer Images used with the permission of Microsoft ©.

Netscape Images used with the permission of Netscape Communications Corporation ©.

Chapter 1   Children's Literature Web-Guide reprinted with the permission of David K. Brown.
The After Reconstruction: Problems of African Americans in the South Web-Page from the Web-Site American Memory reproduced with permission of the Library of Congress, Washington, D.C.
The Journey Exchange Project Web-Site reprinted with the permission of Brian Maguire.
The Math Forum Problems of the Week Web-Site reproduced with the permission of The Math Forum, a virtual center for Math Education, housed at Swarthmore College and funded by the National Science Foundation.
Pi Mathematics Web-Site reprinted with the permission of Georgette Moore and Betty A. Ganas.

Chapter 2   The NASA Web-Site reproduced with the Permission of NASA.
The Spacekids Web-page on NASA's Web-site is reproduced with permission of John Lee at NASA.

Chapter 3   Microsoft Outlook Express Images reproduced with the permission of Microsoft©.

Chapter 4   BBC Online reproduced with permission.
Kids' Web Japan reprinted with permission of Japan Information Network, Illustration by Chitose Yamada ©.
The Particle Adventure Web-Site reproduced with permission and developed by the Lawrence Berkeley National Laboratory.
Internet Project Registry reprinted with permission of Global Schoolnet©.
Yahooligan is a registered trademark reprinted with permission.
Ask Jeeves for Kids reproduced with permission.

Chapter 5   AfROAmeric Myths and Fables web page reproduced with permission.
The Complete Works of William Shakespeare Web-Site reproduced with permission of CNRI.
The Children's Literature Web-Guide reprinted with the permission of David K. Brown.
The Cyberguides: Teacher Guides and Student Activities Web-Site reproduced with permission of Linda Taggart-Fregoso.

Chapter 6   The Hunger Site Web-Site reproduced with permission of The Hunger Site and Melissa Milburn of APCO Worldwide.
Image "Votes for Women" Suffrage picture at American Memory reproduced with permission of the Library of Congress.
History/Social Studies Web-Site reprinted with permission.
American Memory Web-Site reproduced with permission of the Library of Congress.

Chapter 7   SETI @ Home Web-Site reproduced with permission of David P. Anderson, Director of the SETI @ Home Project at the University of California, Berkeley, CA.
Women of NASA home page on the NASA Quest's Online Interactive Projects Web-Site reproduced with permission of NASA Quest, supported by the NASA Learning Technologies Project of NASA's Office of High Performance Computing and Communications.
The home page for the Eisenhower National Clearing House for Mathematics and Science Education reproduced with permission of the Eisenhower National Clearinghouse for Mathematics and Science Education.
The Earth Day Groceries Project, 2000 reproduced with the permission of Mark Ahlness.
DNA for Dinner Web-Site reproduced with permission of William E. Peace.

Chapter 8   The Math Forum Elementary Problem of the Week Web-Page and the Math Forum home page reproduced with the permission of the Math Forum, a virtual center for Math Education, housed at Swarthmore College and funded by the National Science Foundation.
The Sierpinski Triangle Web-Site reproduced with permission of Cynthia Lanius.

Chapter 9   The Aunt and The Grasshopper web page reproduced with permission.
The Nanoworld Image Gallery Web-Site reprinted with the permission of The Center for Microscopy and Microanalysis, The University of Queensland.
The Prince and I web page reproduced with permission of the National Film Board, Canada.
The Monarch Watch home page reprinted with the permission of Monarch Watch ©.

Chapter 10   Intercultural Classroom Connections reprinted with permission.
Bobby Approved icon is a trademark of the National Center for Accessible Media.
KIDPROJ Web-Site reproduced with permission of Kidlink.

Chapter 11   Selected Links for ESL Students reproduced with permission.
Seeing Disabilities Web-Site reproduced with permission.
Sign Language Dictionary Online web page reproduced with permission.
Special Education Resources on the Internet Web-Site reprinted with permission.

Chapter 12   Illustration on North Star Navigators reprinted with permission. Copyright © 1997 Peter Reynolds.

To our parents:

Rose, Anne, Don, and Dan.

Our first teachers, our best teachers.

Contents

Chapter 4
Effective Instructional Strategies: Internet Workshop, Internet Project, Internet Inquiry, and WebQuests 127

Chapter 5
English and the Language Arts: Opening New Doors to Literature and Literacy 165

Chapter 6
Social Studies: A World of Possibilities 201

Chapter 7
Science: Using the Internet to Support Scientific Thinking 235

Chapter 8
Math: Thinking Mathematically on the Internet 265

Chapter 9
Special Ideas for Younger Children: Using the Internet in the Primary Grades 285

Chapter 10
Using the Internet to Increase Multicultural Understanding 311

Chapter 11
Including All Students on the Internet 333

Chapter 12
Developing a Home Page for Your Classroom 351

Glossary 369

Index 373

About the Authors 387

Preface

This book is about teaching. Our focus on teaching is what distinguishes this book from others. We have found other books to emphasize the technical side of the Internet. Our approach is very different. Instead of emphasizing the technology of the Internet, we focus on how to use the Internet for teaching and learning. The Internet is fundamentally changing the nature of classroom instruction, enhancing students' opportunities to learn about the world around them. This book shows you how teachers are developing classroom communities filled with the excitement of learning and discovery.

We developed this book to save you time. Teaching is a profession that demands extraordinary amounts of time and we know you have little to spare as you explore this new context for learning. We seek to help you effectively integrate the Internet into your classroom in the shortest time possible.

One way to do this is to visit the new web site for this book, **Teaching with the Internet** (http://www.sp.uconn.edu/~djleu/third.html). We have many new resources for you at this site including updated links to each location mentioned in this book and more great classrooms on the Internet for you to visit. We regularly add information to this location to keep you up to date on the changes taking place. We invite you to take advantage of this resource as you read.

Assumptions That Guide our Work

Several assumptions have guided our work. First, *we assume the active role you play in orchestrating experiences with the Internet will determine the extent to which your students gain from this resource.* Students left entirely on their own to "surf" the Internet will waste much time and learn little from their experiences. Students guided in their explorations of the Internet by a knowledgeable and thoughtful teacher will understand the world in new and powerful ways. We share useful ideas about how best to guide students in these explorations.

Second, *we assume that understanding something as powerful, complex, and constantly changing as the Internet requires us to learn from one another; socially constructed learning is central to success with the Internet.* Our writing is guided by this assumption in several ways. We begin each chapter with a story of a talented teacher using the Internet in the classroom and then discuss the lessons each of us can learn from this experience. These classroom episodes were developed from multiple sources: e-mail conversations we have with teachers around the world, descriptions of Internet experiences posted on various listservs, ideas posted by teachers at Internet Project sites, classroom observations, and our own experiences as teachers. Each story represents a fusion of multiple sources; no story represents a single teacher's experiences. We feel, however, that each story faithfully reflects the many outstanding classrooms we have encountered in our travels on the Internet.

We also include over 40 e-mail messages to you from teachers around the world, describing the lessons they have learned from using the Internet. These teachers are the new researchers of the Internet world, exploring these new contexts for teaching and learning and reporting on what works. Their insights are critical to your success.

Each chapter also includes a visit to one outstanding classroom web page, showing you important lessons we can learn from this classroom.

Finally, many chapters provide listservs and newsgroups to put you in touch with other teachers facing the same challenges as you. We all learn from one another in this new electronic environment. We hope to support this learning so that you and your students may benefit.

Third, *we assume that child safety needs to be paramount as we consider the use of this new tool for instruction.* Throughout this book, you will find ideas to ensure the appropriate use of Internet technologies in your classroom.

And finally, *we assume that critical literacies become increasingly important as students begin to use the Internet.* We must help students develop new and more critical stances toward the information they encounter on the Internet. In this edition, we show you how to do this and provide you with the new resources on the Internet that can support your work in this area.

> We also include over 40 e-mail messages to you from teachers around the world, describing the lessons they have learned from using the Internet.

Changes Appearing In This Edition

You will see many important changes in this third edition, many of which were suggested by teachers through their thoughtful e-mail messages to us.

> Each chapter takes you on a tour of an outstanding teacher's classroom home page in a new feature called "Visiting the Classroom."

- *Classroom Models for Internet Use.* Each chapter takes you on a tour of an outstanding teacher's classroom home page in a new feature called "Visiting the Classroom." These talented individuals can teach all of us important lessons about how to use the Internet for teaching and learning. We explore these lessons in each chapter.

- *Expanded K-12 Coverage.* We have expanded our coverage to include an even more comprehensive discussion of instruction at all levels. You will find resources and instructional strategies that immediately apply to your elementary, middle school, or high school classroom.

- *New Instructional Models for Teaching with the Internet.* In this edition we have expanded our coverage to include WebQuest models for instruction. Since the quality of WebQuests varies so greatly, we also show you how to evaluate a WebQuest to determine its utility for your classroom. In addition, we share a developmental sequence of models for instruction that we have developed: Internet Workshop, Internet Project, and Internet Inquiry. Chapters 4-11 will show you how to begin with easier instructional models and move to more complex and richer models as you feel increasingly comfortable with using the Internet in your classroom.

- *Great, New Central Sites.* Teachers tell us one of their greatest challenges is locating information quickly on the Internet. We have included the best central sites from earlier editions and added many new ones. Start your search at one of these locations. It is much faster than using a search engine.

- *Expanded Coverage on How to Save Time With Effective Search Engine Strategies.* Search engines are often frustrating to new users looking for information. In Chapters 2 and 6 we show you a number of useful ideas to save you time.

- *An Updated Section on Citing Internet References.* Many teachers have told us that students need to know how to cite Internet resources in their reports and writing. We show you how to do this in Chapter 4.

- *Expanded Coverage of Child Safety Strategies.* Throughout the book, we show you effective ways to protect children as they use the Internet. Chapters 4 and 9 have special sections about this important issue.

- *New Classroom Scenarios.* As we communicate with teachers around the world, we continually learn new lessons. We share these lessons through new stories about how teachers are using the Internet in their classrooms.

- *An Expanded Discussion of Strategies to Avoid the Growing Commercialization in the Classroom.* Chapters 2 and 9 explore a new controversy being discussed in schools—the growing commercialization of the Internet and other information resources. We show you how to reconfigure your browser to minimize commercially motivated links. We also provide you with specific strategies to avoid the commercialization of your classroom in Chapter 9. Moreover, our selection of sites minimizes much of the growing commercialism since we avoid those with extensive commercial messages.

- *Many New Internet Resources for Teachers and Children.* And finally, of course, we have included many new sites that have appeared on the Internet to help you and your students. The Internet is changing quickly, providing many new opportunities for each of us to explore this exciting world for teaching and learning. Because this book is frequently revised, we will continually bring you the most recent Internet resources we believe are useful to the important work you do to prepare students for their future.

The People Who Have Contributed to the Third Edition

We could not have completed a complex project like this without the assistance of many individuals. To each, we are profoundly indebted. We would like to thank as many of them as possible.

Many educators shared their experiences with the Internet, providing us with important insights that appear in this book. These include teachers from across the U.S. and Canada as well as teachers from Argentina, Australia, Ecuador, Finland, Japan, Germany, Great Britain, New Zealand, South Africa, Sweden, and The Netherlands. Most are only known to us through their insightful e-mail messages and the descriptions they shared of their classes. We hope someday to have the opportunity to actually meet each person and personally express our gratitude for his or her important contributions.

We especially wish to thank the following educators who were kind enough to share their insights through the e-mail messages we include in this book: Lisa Brayton, Dana Eaton, Barbara McInerney, Susan Silverman, Elizabeth Rohloff, Terrie Gray, Ruth Musgrave, Maggie Hos-McGrane, Peter Lelong, Cindy Lockerman, Jeff Scanlan, Jeanette Kenyon, Emily Buchanan, Jill Newcomb, Susy Calvert, Linda Shearin, Beverley Powell, Cindy Ross, Linda Taggart-Fregoso, Karen Auffhammer, Maureen Salmon-Salvemini, Marjorie Duby, Tammy Payton, Richard Strauss, Gary Cressman, Linda Swanson, Linda Hubbard, Jodi Moore, Doug Crosby, Isabelle Hoag, Cathy Lewis, Angeles Maitland Heriot, Bill Farrell, Anne Nguyen, Nicole Gamble, Janice Smith, Terry Hongell, Patty Taverna, and Sharon Hall.

As we write this list, each name brings back an important memory of e-mail exchanges with a very knowledgeable educator. We thank each of you for sharing your wonderful lessons with us. Each of you is an outstanding educator, contributing in important ways to our increasingly global community. We have learned from your insights and we know our readers will too!

We also wish to thank our students and colleagues at Syracuse University who provided us with useful ideas as they responded to the second edition. Others at Syracuse also supported our work: Joan Simonetta, Roberta Hennigan, and Isabelle Glod assisted with important aspects of communication and production; Jessica Bevans provided valuable assistance in obtaining permissions; and Mike Hardt obtained several important images for us at the last minute.

Dr. Michael Hillinger of LexIcon provided important initial feedback about central ideas in this book. He has also been a valued colleague over the years as we have explored issues in digital learning together.

Lynne Schueler of OutSide Services assisted in important ways to the final stages of this third edition. Her work in layout and formatting can be seen on each page. We greatly appreciate her many contributions.

We especially wish to thank our good friends at Christopher-Gordon Publishers, Inc. without whom this third edition could not have been completed: Hiram Howard and Susanne Canavan. Hiram and Susanne shared our enthusiasm for this project at the beginning and have given us the freedom to complete this third edition in the way we envisioned it. They also picked up our spirits at several important points with their kind deeds and words. Behind the scenes, others at Christopher-Gordon have also contributed to this project in important ways: Colleen Brown, Karen Gates, Laurie Maker, Paula Mazzone, Linda Nevins, and Noelle Robinson. Authors could not ask for a more considerate and helpful publisher.

Finally, a special word of thanks is due our two daughters. Without the assistance of Caity and Sarah this project would not have happened. Caity contributed in central ways to previous editions of this book. In this edition, Sarah identified a number of important sites that have proven to be especially useful for high school content areas. We greatly appreciate our daughters' many important contributions.

To everyone, our deepest thanks!

— Don Leu and Debbie Diadiun Leu
  Manlius, New York

Welcome to the Internet

 ## E-MAIL FOR YOU

To: Our readers
From: djleu@syr.edu (Don Leu), ddleu@syr.edu (Debbie Leu)
Subject: Welcome!

Welcome to the third edition of *Teaching with the Internet*! So much has happened on the Internet since we wrote the second edition. We'll update you on all of these changes in this third edition.

Teachers new to the Internet tell us that time is their biggest concern: time to learn about the Internet and time to incorporate it into an already busy schedule. All of our changes have tried to keep this concern in mind. This new edition will help you to quickly learn the essentials of teaching with the Internet. It will also show you how to integrate the Internet into your schedule in ways that actually save time as you integrate reading and writing with content area instruction. Your time is precious and we keep this in mind with all that we do.

This is a book about teaching and not about technology. That is what makes this book different. We emphasize effective teaching practices in the classroom while limiting the technical discussion of the Internet to basic essentials. We show you how other teachers are using the Internet in their classrooms and then discuss the lessons we can learn from these experiences. We show you how to use the Internet thoughtfully, enabling you to make a powerful difference in the lives of your students.

We regularly update our web site containing links to each of the locations mentioned in this book: http://web.syr.edu/~djleu/teaching.html Many readers use this site as they read each chapter, quickly linking to each site we discuss. If an address listed in this book doesn't work, come visit our web page!

This first chapter will introduce you to the Internet and show you some of the wonderful resources that are available. While the Internet is just another tool for teaching and learning, we believe it will quickly become the most powerful one in your classroom as you prepare your students for the futures they deserve.

Don and Debbie

Teaching with the Internet: Venita Rodriguez's Eighth-Grade Team

The new state standards made Venita Rodriguez and the other members of her eighth grade team wonder how they could accomplish everything in only nine short months of school. They faced new state assessments in English, math, and science. At the same time, their district had updated curriculum requirements in history, technology, and several other areas. While expectations were increasing each year, time in the classroom certainly wasn't. Sometimes it seemed overwhelming.

During the summer, Venita attended a workshop on teaching with the Internet with two other team members, Yolanda Mathews and Jackie Thomason. Venita taught English, Yolanda taught math, and Jackie taught science. The workshop showed them amazing instructional resources on the Internet and described effective teaching strategies such as Internet Workshop, Internet Project, Internet Inquiry, and WebQuests. They came back excited about using the Internet to help them integrate more of their curriculum as they prepared students for their state English, math, and science proficiency exams.

"Not another thing on top of everything else we have to do!" Clearly, not everyone on the team agreed. Still, Venita and her colleagues convinced the remaining members about the potential the Internet provided. Having the school wired last year and finding new Internet computers placed in all the labs and classrooms after the summer certainly helped. So, too, did the technology coordinator's offer to assist them. She wanted this team to succeed and become a model for all of the other teams in the school. What convinced Venita's team, though, were the amazing resources available at central sites on the Internet for content areas. Venita and her colleagues gave a tour of some of these sites during the planning meeting before school started:

- **American Memory—**
  http://lcweb2.loc.gov/ammem/ammemhome.html
  The location where the US Library of Congress was putting its priceless collection of historical artifacts and documents online, making them available to anyone with an Internet connection.

- **Inkspot for Young Writers Under 18—**
  http://www.inkspot.com/young
  A wonderful resource for young writers interested in learning from experienced authors and getting writing tips and feedback on their drafts.

- **History/Social Studies Web Site for K–12 Teachers—**
  http://www.execpc.com/~dboals/boals.html
  An exhaustive collection of links to resources for K–12 social studies education organized by topic and maintained by a social studies educator.

- **The "Action" section of the Eisenhower National Clearinghouse for Mathematics and Science Education—**
http://www.enc.org:80/classroom/index.htm
Looking for immediate resources to use in your K–12 math or science classroom? Here's the place for you. Be certain to visit the "Action" section of this site for teaching resources and ideas.

- **Children's Literature Web Guide—**
http://www.acs.ucalgary.ca/~dkbrown/index.html
If you are interested in children's and young adult literature, this is the place for you. This location contains an extensive collection of the best resources in children's and young adult literature including links to stories, teaching ideas, and the sites of award-winning authors (see Figure 1-1).

- **The Math Forum—**http://forum.swarthmore.edu
An exhaustive collection of hands-on resources for immediate use in math classrooms, K–12 (see Figure 1-2).

Figure 1-1
Authors and Illustrators on the Web (http://www.acs.ucalgary.ca/~dkbrown/authors.html), part of the **Children's Literature Web Guide** (http://www.acs.ucalgary.ca/~dkbrown/index.html). This site contains links to award-winning authors and illustrators for both children's and young adult literature including: Avi, Jan Brett, Eric Carle, Virginia Hamilton, Lois Lowry, Patricia Polacco, and many more.

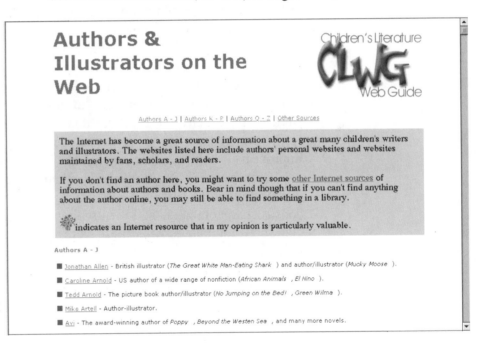

These Internet locations feature easy-to-use teaching tools that any teacher can use immediately to make a difference in the classroom.

These Internet locations feature easy-to-use teaching tools that any teacher can use immediately to make a difference in the classroom. During their quick review, the Technology Coordinator showed them how to set bookmarks to each location on the Internet computers they had in their classrooms. She also showed them how to set any computer to open first to the web site you want to use in your class by setting the preferences for a home page. Both strategies, she pointed out, cut down on random surfing and made it easier for students and teachers to find useful material quickly.

"Better visual descriptions. It needs better visual descriptions. I just don't see the things that are happening in this story." Tanika was sharing her critique of a draft of fictional narrative, "Australia 3000," written by Rob Johnson, a student in Melbourne, Australia. Rob was looking for revision suggestions from other student writers. He had posted his work at the **For Critique** (http://www.inkspot.com/young/crit/) site of **Inkspot for Young Writers** (http://www.inkspot.com/young) in hopes that other students might read his work and provide suggestions before his assignment was due.

Venita Rodriguez was using this location where young writers can post their work and receive feedback from other students over the Internet. There were 30 works available for review this month. That was plenty. She wanted to help her students develop constructive feedback strategies during revision conferences while they read interesting works written by students from around the world. She knew that looking critically at someone else's writing would also improve their own writing. She set a bookmark for this site on her classroom computers. She also printed out multiple copies of several works. In class, she wanted her students to work in small groups to critique these drafts as they practiced making effective revision conference suggestions.

Venita didn't want to begin revision conferences with works by students in her classroom until everyone felt comfortable with this activity and knew how to provide constructive suggestions. This activity was perfect, and it put her classes in touch with other students from countries such as England, France, and Australia. A bit later in the year, Venita planned to have her students post their own drafts at this site and receive revision comments from other students. It was a great way to use the Internet to help her students improve their writing, connecting them with student writers around the world.

Venita's first period English class had broken up into small groups and was critiquing the several drafts. Each group was deciding upon the most constructive comments and then typing these into a file on one of the four classroom computers. After these were approved by Venita, each group sent their comments to their author using Venita's e-mail account. The district had a policy that only teacher's e-mail accounts could be used at school. This enabled each teacher to monitor any e-mail correspondence. The policy was designed to protect students when using the Internet.

Venita's class was also involved in a literature discussion group with classes from New Zealand, Arizona, and Florida using **Book Raps** (http://rite.ed.qut.edu.au/oz-teachernet/projects/book-rap/). Here, classes reading the same work of literature could exchange responses to what they read via e-mail. The daily messages that flowed in from classes reading Lois Lowry's *The Giver* engaged her students in thinking more deeply about this important work and expanded their literary responses. It also helped her students to discover new cultural perspective and meet students from other parts of the world. In order to save time, while also ensuring child safety, Venita had appointed a highly responsible student, Tanika, to print out all of her incoming e-mail messages each morning. That way, Venita could quickly read them during her second period planning time. Venita monitored outgoing messages in the same way.

"Ms. Rodriguez, Ms. Rodriguez!" Tanika said from the computer. "Rob liked the ideas we gave him about his story and his teacher wants us to send his class some of our stories so they can give us revision ideas. They live in Melbourne, where the Olympics will be. That's phat!"

Venita smiled, knowing her students were really on their way this year.

"I know they're gonna be the same. They gotta be. The cylinders use the same size paper so they gotta be the same volume." Tiffany was explaining her thinking to her group in her science class. The problem they were discussing came from a wonderful site, **The Math Forum Problem of the Week** (http://www.forum.swarthmore.edu/pow/). Each week, challenging problems were posted for students at every grade level to solve (see Figure 1.2). This problem had students use two pieces of paper the same size to make cylinders by rolling one paper lengthwise and the other widthwise. They had to predict if the volume inside these two cylinders was greater in one cylinder compared to the other. They also had to explain the thinking behind their hypotheses and then conduct an experiment to test their predictions. Finally, they had to write up a report of their experiment with their results.

Figure 1-2.

Problems of the Week (http://www.forum.swarthmore.edu/pow) is a set of challenging math problems for students at all levels. New problems appear each week. Answers are provided and mentoring classrooms are available for assistance with problem solving strategies.

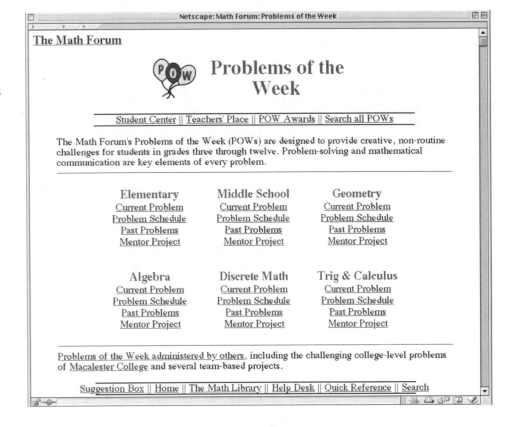

Yolanda Mathews, the math teacher, saw this activity on the Internet and showed it to Jackie Thomason, the science teacher. They decided to use it as a team-teaching activity for students in their math and science classes. Jackie was starting the activity in her science class to introduce the method of scientific inquiry at the beginning of the year. Yolanda was going to follow-up with a unit on measuring volume. It was a great problem to get students thinking about both the scientific method and the mathematics of volume. Yolanda planned to use this site every week for Internet Workshop in her math class, giving her students important opportunities to think systematically about a complex problem during the week and then discussing their thinking during a Friday workshop session. This Internet resource really got her students to think deeply about mathematics and use what they were learning in highly engaging ways.

"Write up your predictions along with your explanation for why you think this will be the result," Jackie told her students. "Make sure you explain your hypothesis clearly because afterwards you are going to conduct an experiment to see if your hypothesis is correct."

"Ms. Thomason? We gonna do science and math like this all year?" Jason asked.

American Memory is a gold mine for the primary source documents of American history. Even more importantly, there are complete instructional units, designed by teachers, and just waiting to be used in a classroom.

In another example of incorporating the Internet into the classroom, Bob Richter, the team's social studies teacher, had been a bit dubious about the Internet. At least until he saw the resources at **American Memory** (http://lcweb2.loc.gov/ammem/ammemhome.html), an extensive collection of historical documents placed on the Internet by the Library of Congress. Here, he discovered Civil War photos by Mathew Brady, the papers of George Washington, an Abraham Lincoln Virtual Library, as well as extensive collections of on-line videos, recordings, and documents from all periods of American history. It is an amazing resource for social studies educators, especially with the recent emphasis placed on the classroom use of primary source documents for critical thinking. American Memory is a gold mine for the primary source documents of American history. Even more importantly, there are complete instructional units, designed by teachers, and just waiting to be used in a classroom.

"Mr. Richter, look at this. Remember when we did the unit on the Civil War and all of the pictures by Mathew Brady. Here's my newspaper article. Remember. We shared our work with that class in California. That was cool!" Armand was cleaning out his locker at the end of the year, recalling the many experiences in Bob Richter's class with primary source historical documents they found at American Memory and other locations.

Armand's comment prompted Bob to remember the wonderful lessons and instructional ideas he had discovered that year at a great location with the American Memory site: **Lesson Ideas, the Learning Page of the Library of Congress** (http://learning.loc.gov/ammem/ndlpedu/lesson.html). This location got him started with the Internet since it provided everything he needed, from units and lessons developed by teachers for other teacher, to links to historical documents located at American Memory. During the year, Bob had completed many units: **Historian's Sources** (http://learning.loc.gov/ammem/ndlpedu/lessons/psources/pshome.html), an introduction to using primary source documents; **Turn of the Century Child** (http://

NuevaSchool.org/~debbie/library/cur/20c/turn.html), a project studying what it was like to be a child in 1900 using artifacts and diaries from children and families at that time; **Learning About Immigration Through Oral History** (http://learning.loc.gov/ammem/ndlpedu/lesson97/oh1/ammem.html), a project about the immigrant experience through archived oral histories; and **After Reconstruction: Problems of African Americans in the South** (http://memory.loc.gov/ammem/ndlpedu/lessons/rec/rhome.html) an exciting project designed for high school that Bob liked so much he adapted the lessons for his eighth graders (see Figure 1-3). Each had fit in perfectly with his curriculum and provided wonderful opportunities for cross-curricular collaboration with his team members in English, math, and science. Many provided opportunities for his class to exchange work and share projects with other classrooms around the world. Yes, it had been a great year with everyone learning new things, including himself.

Figure 1-3

After Reconstruction: Problems of African Americans in the South (http://memory.loc.gov/ammem/ndlpedu/lessons/rec/rhome.html) is a teaching unit available for you at American Memory, the collection of historical documents being developed for teachers and students by the Library of Congress.

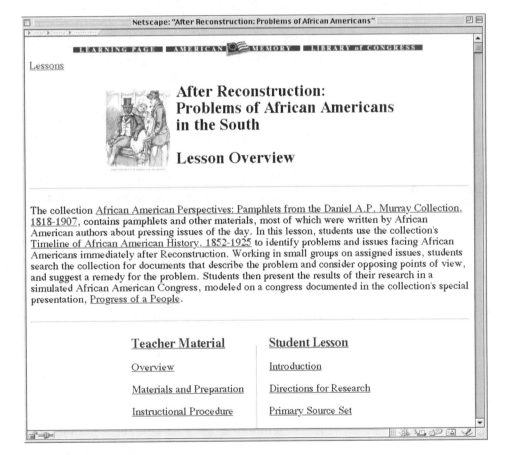

At the final team meeting that year, there was talk about the summer that lay ahead. Venita and Yolanda were taking a summer course on the use of web video cameras for video conferencing between classrooms around the world, Jackie was taking a workshop on designing classroom web pages, and Bob, the person most cautious about the Internet when they started, had been accepted into the summer fellows program at the Library of Congress.

He was going to be working with another social studies educator from Colorado to develop a unit on the westward migration. Their classes had worked together on this unit during the year after they discovered one another on the Internet. Now they would have a chance to refine their work and post it at the American Memory site for others to use. Everyone was going to stay in touch over the summer by e-mail so they could exchange the new ideas and resources they discovered. It really had been an amazing year for everyone.

Lessons from the Classroom

Teachers around the world report the biggest change they see with the Internet is a new enthusiasm and excitement for learning among their students, and among themselves.

These episodes illustrate a number of important lessons; lessons that will guide us throughout our journey together. First, they illustrate how resources available to students on the Internet may be used in your classroom to get your students excited about learning. Teachers around the world report the biggest change they see with the Internet is a new enthusiasm and excitement for learning among their students, and among themselves. That is what happened in these classrooms every day. Tanika's excitement about sharing responses to drafts with students in Australia, Jason's new-found enthusiasm for math and science, and Armand's fond memories for the unit on the Civil War photographs are examples of what nearly every student felt that year. Every day, students came early and left late because they wanted to continue their work on their Internet projects. This same enthusiasm swept across the entire team of teachers. Even Bob Richter, the team member who was least excited about having to use the Internet in his class, ended up its most ardent advocate. The Internet brings new enthusiasm for both teaching and learning.

Looking through the new windows of the Internet develops greater appreciation for the benefits that diversity bestows as others outside our classrooms contribute to the learning that takes place within.

We also learn a second lesson from these stories, one we hear from nearly every teacher we meet on the Internet: The Internet opens wonderful new windows to the world for your students. Being able to exchange drafts of your writing with students in England, Australia, New Zealand, Japan, or Canada, helps your students to see the world in new ways. Exchanging responses to *The Giver* and other literary works prompts a deeper understanding of how people in other parts of the world see things from their special cultural perspective. Exchanging solutions to math problems with a mentoring class helps students to discover new ways of thinking. And, reading the diaries of children in the year 1900 at American Memory enables your students to go back to another time and listen to the voices of children their own age. Looking through the new windows of the Internet develops greater appreciation for the benefits that diversity bestows as others outside our classrooms contribute to the learning that takes place within. The Internet provides a powerful new tool for you and your students to access information and then communicate with others about what you have learned. Throughout this book you will find other sites on the Internet just as powerful for supporting your students' learning. The Internet opens many new windows for all of us.

These episodes also illustrate how an insightful teacher can use book-marks and preferences to efficiently direct students to information and help them avoid endless "surfing." By setting the computer to open to a location on the Internet, Venita and her colleagues made a number of resources immediately available to their students. Later, we will describe additional techniques to help students use their limited time wisely.

In addition, these episodes show how the Internet can be easily integrated into your current classroom activities. Using the Internet in your class does not need to take additional time. We will show you how Internet resources may be used with any of your current teaching practices: activity centers, writing process activities, author chair experiences, thematic units, cooperative learning groups, response journals, jigsaw grouping, and K-W-L, among others. We will also show you how you to use several new instructional models in your class: Internet Workshop, Internet Project, Internet Inquiry, and WebQuests.

Finally, these scenarios show how the Internet brings together new communities of learners who engage in socially constructed learning experiences. Venita's team discovered this principle in the new exchanges they had during team meetings about great Internet resources and teaching ideas. Many, like Yolanda Mathews and Jackie Thomason, developed collaborative units during the year across curriculum areas, increasing the learning opportunities for their students. Just as important, though, each teacher discovered the powerful potential of collaborative relationships with other teachers and classrooms beyond the walls of their school. Bob's class became experts in US history when they received inquiries about their work from classes in England and Finland. Yolanda's class was mentored by another class in Wisconsin as they sought solutions to the math Problem of the Week. In January, they volunteered to mentor classes in Hawaii and Oregon. Venita's class joined with several classes during the year to exchange drafts of writing at Inkspot for Young Writers and to share responses to works of literature at Book Raps. The Internet provides very special opportunities to learn from one another about the world around us. We will show you other ways in which you can assist your students to safely develop new learning communities with Internet resources, an excellent lesson for life.

The Times, They Are A-Changin'

These stories are not the first you have heard about the Internet. In just a few years, the Internet has become a central part of popular culture. Every day we encounter stories in the press about the Internet and how it is changing our lives; ads in magazines and on television now carry World Wide Web addresses; we hear radio talk-show hosts mention the live "chat-rooms" where listeners can continue their conversations "online"; and we hear colleagues talking about all the e-mail they had to answer before going to bed last night.

Using the Internet in your class does not need to take additional time.

The Internet provides very special opportunities to learn from one another about the world around us.

In just a few years, the Internet has become a central part of popular culture.

You have also seen the changes taking place in your own school. Your classroom may already be connected and you are trying to better understand these new resources for your students. Perhaps your district has recently completed a technology plan and new Internet connections have been placed in each of your classrooms this year. Like many of us, you probably can recall the day when a student first showed you a print-out with Internet information for a class assignment and you began to wonder about the new world all of us are entering. Bob Dylan certainly had it right when he wrote, "The times, they are a-changin'."

Undoubtedly, you have many feelings about these changes. You may be excited, skeptical, nervous, or, like us, you may experience all of these feelings, sometimes at the same time. We get excited when we discover a site like "American Memory" and think about how it can be used in the classroom. We become skeptical when we read about politicians who advocate higher standards for student achievement, but disappear when it comes time to fund the new costs these will require. We become nervous when we think about the speed of these changes and whether we can ever know everything there is to know about new technologies. After all, who had even heard of the Internet just a few years ago? And who can tell what new technologies will show up as soon as we begin to understand this one? Yes, the Internet prompts all of these thoughts.

What is the Internet?

It is sometimes hard to figure out what the Internet really is. We can't see it; we just use it. Sometimes it is a place to buy a car with a computer. Sometimes it is a place to send and receive e-mail. Sometimes it is a place to read the newspaper. Sometimes it is way to talk with someone while you view them on your computer screen. It is all of these things, and more.

> At heart, the Internet is simply a set of computers around the world that are connected to one another.

At heart, the Internet is simply a set of computers around the world that are connected to one another. You can go to one computer in Texas to check the price for a car, send e-mail to another computer in Tokyo, and read a newspaper that appears on yet another computer in London. When you visit a site, your computer sends a message to another computer asking it to put their web page onto your computer screen. When you think about what happens, sending a message to a computer across the world that sends a web page back to you in an instant, it is really quite amazing.

Initially, only large computers at universities were connected to one another. Now, anyone with a desktop computer and a telephone can get connected and become a part of the Internet. This is how the first connections were made in many school districts. Increasingly, though, schools are moving away from separate phone connections and are wiring classrooms directly to the Internet. Either strategy allows you and your students to link up with any computer, anywhere in the world.

E-MAIL FOR YOU

To: Colleagues
From: Lisa Brayton <Lisa.Brayton@MSB.Mat-Su.k12.ak.us>
Subject: Using the Internet at our School

Greetings!

My name is Lisa Brayton. I am a fifth grade teacher at Cottonwood Creek Elementary School in Wasilla, Alaska. Our school has been using technology for a long time. We are making a natural progression to using the Internet in our classrooms. Our principal, Marie Burton, is the visionary!

In just a few years, Cottonwood has gone from having one terminal with Internet access (in our lab) to having a shared line for 4th and 5th grade classrooms, to now having our own free line in each classroom! We also have four lines in the computer lab and one in the library. At this point, our Internet access is unlimited! This has made a positive impact in many ways.

I started this year by entering my class in an Internet contest . . . **Cybersurfari** (http://www.cybersurfari.org). This was an excellent way to teach students how to surf for information. It was, in a sense, a scavenger hunt. Students went from site to site through links, looking for clues. This contest is held annually in October, although you can practice at other times. My students learned navigational skills, neat facts and felt excited and successful. We also participated in several other great projects at the **Global Schoolhouse** (http://www.gsn.org)

My students also use the Internet as an information tool. During our Colonial study we've gathered historical information about Jamestown, Plymouth, John Smith, Ben Franklin . . . the list is exhaustive! This is exciting for the students because the information is there to find, and they're very skilled at locating it!

Finally, my students use the Internet as a communication tool. We have key-pals from all over the world. We write to friends and relatives. Our current project is our web page. Students are now creating their own web pages. We are putting together a Fifth Grade Newspaper which will be published on our web page. We hope to inform, entertain and include links to other sites. Please visit our school's new web site (http://www.CWE.Mat-su.k12.ak.us) and send your ideas or comments to us. Talk to you soon!

Lisa Brayton
5th grade teacher
Cottonwood Creek Elementary School
Wasilla, Alaska

There are many different ways in which you may access information on computers linked to the Internet.

There are many different ways in which you may access information on computers linked to the Internet. You may use an e-mail program to send messages or documents back and forth. Most computers linked to the Internet have this ability because it is relatively simple. Other, richer sources of information are also available on the Internet including: music, video, audio, animation, color graphics, and even free software programs you can download to your computer. These are located on computers that are a part of the World Wide Web (WWW or, simply, the Web). You access the WWW through special software called a web browser. A web browser, like Internet Explorer or Netscape Navigator, allows you to read text, listen to music, watch a video clip, and view color graphics. The WWW of the Internet is an especially useful source of information for classroom learning since many educators are now sharing the curriculum resources they develop with others.

Figure 1-4, for example, shows you the home page for **Journey Exchange** (http://www.win4edu.com/minds-eye/journey) a location on the Web developed by a teacher in upstate New York for grade 3–12 social studies. Small groups of students in one classroom develop a 5-day journey to different locations around the world, providing clues from their Internet research to another group of students somewhere in the world. Students in the other classroom then research the clues in a scavenger hunt, attempting to follow the trip that has been planned for them. When they think they have figured

Figure 1-4
Journey Exchange (http://www.win4edu.com/minds-eye/journey), is just one of many resources available on the Internet for you to use in your classroom.

Internet FAQ

Who pays when I use my computer to communicate with another computer somewhere else in the world? We pay for telephone calls. Why don't we pay for using the Internet to visit places around the world?	With a few exceptions, no individual really pays for traffic on the Internet since everyone agrees to let everyone else travel through their network to get to other, connected networks of computers. The only fee you pay in many countries is a monthly access fee charged by Internet Service Providers (ISPs) like ATT, America Online, Time-Warner Cable, or other ISPs in your community. These organizations charge people to connect to their computers in order to connect to the Internet. Your district will probably pay a fee to an Internet Service Provider who provides Internet access for your school. Recently, however, Congress and the FCC have determined that schools only have to pay a percentage of the costs for network hardware and fees for Internet access, depending upon the percentage of students receiving free or reduced lunches. The remainder will be provided by a small fee on costs we all pay for using the phone or other telecommunication systems. This subsidy program, known commonly as the "e-rate program," provides an annual pool of more than two billion dollars to subsidize Internet costs for schools in the US. This program is quickly increasing the number of schools connected to the Internet. To find out more about federal support for schools interested in getting connected to the Internet, visit the WWW site set up to keep schools informed about new policy initiatives, **LearnNet** (http://www.fcc.gov/learnnet). Information about the e-rate program for schools, is available at the **Schools and Libraries Division** (http://www.sl.universalservice.org) of the Universal Service Administrative Company, the not-for-profit corporation set up by the FCC to manage this program.

out the entire trip from the clues, they check with the classroom that posted it. This simple activity puts children in touch with one another around the world in wonderful ways as they study different geographical regions. You could use this today in your classroom. No special skills are required.

Being a part of this large network of computers allows you and your students access to information at any other computer located on the Internet. This is what makes the Internet such a powerful instructional tool for you and your students. It connects your classroom to the information treasures of the world. There are many, many things you can do when your class gets connected to the Internet:

Being a part of this large network of computers allows you and your students access to information at any other computer located on the Internet.

- **Send an E-Mail Message to Anyone in the World.** Students in a classroom in New Jersey were each doing an Internet Inquiry on a European country. They followed a K-W-L (Know, Want to Know, and Learn) model developed by Ogle, (1989). During their study, one student discovered **Web 66** (http://web66.coled.umn.edu/schools/Maps/Europe.html), a location where you can locate web pages for schools from around the world, including most countries in Europe. The students quickly discovered they could send e-mail to schools in Europe from the web pages they located. Noticing this, their teacher decided to have each student write to students in their project country, asking them to describe what took place during a typical day in their part of the world. Students followed traditional process writing procedures as they developed their letters: brainstorming, drafting, revising, editing, and publishing (sending). Because their teacher was sensitive to child safety issues with the Internet, messages were only sent out through her classroom e-mail account. This allowed her to monitor every message that was sent and received. Within a few days everyone was receiving e-mail from Europe describing "typical days." They printed out the "typical day" stories and displayed these on a bulletin board for parents to see during the school's Open House. The experience provided a very special window into the many cultural traditions of Europe. It was also highly motivating. Students couldn't wait to check their mailboxes each morning to see if they had e-mail from their foreign friends. Many new understandings were developed about life in other cultures.

- **Discover Great Lesson Plans and Teaching Ideas.** There are many locations with lesson planning resources and complete teaching units. If you are interested in integrating the Internet into literature experiences, for example, pay a visit to **CyberGuides** (http://www.sdcoe.k12.ca.us/score/cyberguide.html). Here, you will find an extensive set of links to outstanding works of children's literature organized by grade level. Each link contains lesson plans, instructional ideas, links to other Web resources, and suggestions for how to use those resources. This location should be familiar to every teacher with an Internet connection in the classroom. Set a bookmark!

- **Acquire Content Area Information.** You may go to any other computer on the Internet and look for information put there for your use. You can read the complete works of Shakespeare, view a map of the world displaying earthquakes recorded during the past month, take a guided tour of the White House, view videos of different penguin species in the Antarctic, read the news and view news videos at sites operated by CNN, ESPN, or USA Today, obtain photos of ancient Egyptian artifacts recently discovered in the Valley of the Dead, and even read information about each country in the world provided by the CIA. The list of information resources available to you and your students is nearly endless. Most importantly, the information on the Internet is almost always more recent than any textbook in your classroom.

Most importantly, the information on the Internet is almost always more recent than any textbook in your class-room.

- **Communicate With Others Who Share a Similar Interest.** You can join a mailing list and receive messages from others who share a common interest. Are you interested in discussions with other teachers about science education, math education, music education, art education, literacy education, social studies education, ESL education, or special education? Mailing lists exist for each of these areas where teachers exchange teaching ideas and instructional resources. In addition to mailing lists, there are Newsgroups, and an increasing number of real-time, "chat" locations appearing on the Internet for teachers. At these locations, teachers can share ideas about instruction with other teachers around the world and immediately read what others think.

- **Acquire New Software.** A new teacher in Olympia, Washington, was looking for a better way to keep track of grades in her social studies class. She heard about a free software program for the Macintosh called **Eagle Gradebook** that she could download onto her computer and then use to record and average her grades. She went to the site at Virginia Tech (http://tac.elps.vt.edu/htmldocs/Software/Macintosh/TeacherUtilities.shtml) a friend had located, downloaded the software, and found that it met her needs perfectly. She also noticed programs at the same location for keeping track of attendance, making banners for the classroom, and making calendars. She downloaded these free programs and used them often during the year. Many locations on the Internet provide free and very useful software for classroom needs. Visit **Softseek** (http://enternet.softseek.com/Education_and_Science/) to see many other free programs that can be downloaded to either your Windows or Macintosh computer for immediate classroom use in all subject areas.

- **Conduct a Video Conference.** Do you want to have a discussion between your class and a class in a foreign country about a book you have both read or an issue you have both studied? No problem. All you need is the right software and an inexpensive video camera for your computer. The interchange could provide your students with special insights into another culture. Or, conduct a video conference with an expert on the topic your students are studying. This might be a member of Congress, a scientist, a historian, or the author of a book they have recently read. Have your students do their research in advance and prepare their questions for this expert. If you would like to find out more about this technology visit one of several sites explaining how to use this in your classroom:

> **The Global Schoolhouse Classroom Conferencing—** http://www.gsn.org/cu/index.html
>
> **Pacific Bell Videoconferencing for Learning—** http://www.kn.pacbell.com/vidconf
>
> **Videoconference (Advantages, Types, Resources, Directories . . .)**—http://www.marshall-es.marshall.k12.tn.us/jobe/videocon.html

- **Publish A Page on the WWW for Your School and Your Class.** Many teachers are finding the WWW to be a useful location for publishing their students' writing and presenting other information about classroom activities. They find that publishing writing for the entire world to read motivates students to produce exceptional work. See, for example, the wonderful homepage developed by **Ms. Hos-McGrane's Grade Six Class** in the Netherlands (http://www.xs4all.nl/~swanson/origins/intro.html). Teachers like Ms. Hos-McGrane quickly discover that other students, parents, and grandparents visit their classroom page to read their work and learn about classroom activities. Schools and classrooms with web pages also present an image of education that is different from the many critical images portrayed in the press. The importance of this positive image should not be overlooked by our profession.

Schools and classrooms with web pages also present an image of education that is different from the many critical images portrayed in the press.

These are just a few of the things you can do on the Internet in your classroom. While we will try to present a balanced view of the Internet and not get carried away with the hype of this new technology, it is easy to see why some people do get a bit excited. The information and communication resources available on the Internet are the beginning of a radical departure in the nature of information available to us and our students. Without trying to hype the technology, it is probably fair to say the Internet is fundamentally changing the nature of teaching and learning as it enters our classrooms (Leu, in press a; Leu, Karchmer, & Leu, 1999). Our response to these important changes will determine our students' ability to succeed in the world that awaits them. New challenges and new opportunities await us all.

Our response to these important changes will determine our students' ability to succeed in the world that awaits them.

Why Is the Internet So Important to My Students?

The rapidly changing nature of technology affects each of us. More than anyone else, though, these powerful changes affect our students and the opportunities they will have in life. Let's think for a moment about the world our students will enter when they complete their formal education. This is where we should begin our plans for their education. As we think about this, let's make at least one assumption: Let's assume that many of our students will complete four years of education after completing high school, a consideration that is increasingly becoming a requirement for effective employment in a post-industrial society.

To begin our "thought experiment", let's add 17 years to the current year. This is the time when children who started kindergarten this year will enter the workplace to seek employment. For example, a student beginning kindergarten in 2001 will enter the workplace in 2018. What will it take to be successful in the world of 2018? While we cannot tell with absolute preci-

E-MAIL FOR YOU

To: Colleagues
From: Dana Eaton dana_eaton@nhusd.k12.ca.us
Subject: A window to the world

Sometimes I wonder whether the Internet has opened up the world to our classroom or if it has opened up our classroom to the world. Perhaps it's a bit of both.

The Internet is a communication tool between my class and the wider world. A poem that might have been shared only inside the classroom is now instantly published to the world. We have had City Council members e-mail students about their publications because they were able to view them on the Internet. Publishing to a worldwide audience is also great motivation for students who are attempting to do their best work. Visit this example from one of my students: http://www.nhusd.k12.ca.us/Searles/Homepage_40/juan.html

The Internet is also a communication tool between the world and our classroom. With the help of our local Iditarod expert, Diane Douglass, we embarked on a two-week long thematic unit on the Iditarod. Students were able to get hourly reports about the position of dog sled teams, read Alaskan newspapers, view weather reports, and read diaries of mushers. They did this all from the comfort of sunny California. We were also able to research local animals and cities that were checkpoints along the way. We found this resource really useful: http://www.dogsled.com

The Internet is quickly entering every classroom, becoming as common a classroom resource as a dictionary, encyclopedia, or a thesaurus. Come visit our classroom homepage (http://www.nhusd.k12.ca.us/Searles/HomepageEaton/38SearlesEaton.html) and see how we are using the Internet! Let us know what you think.

Dana Eaton
Grade 4
Searles Elementary
Union City, CA
dana_eaton@nhusd.k12.ca.us

sion, there are several trends that give us a reasonable chance to anticipate the broad outlines for successful entry into society 17 years from now.

First, it is clear that economies around the world will be engaged in a competitive struggle for markets, jobs, and business. We see the beginnings of this now as areas of the world join regional economic groupings, as barriers to trade are lowered, and as companies compete for global markets. Successful societies will be those with individuals who can compete effectively in a global economy because their educational system prepared them for these economic realities.

Second, to succeed in an increasingly competitive global marketplace, organizations will have to change the way they work. In the past decade, many organizations have worked to transform themselves into "high-performance" workplaces. In most cases, this means changing from a centrally planned organization to one that relies increasingly on collaborative teams at all levels in order to assume initiative for planning ways to work more efficiently.

There is also a third trend underway. Increasingly, problem-solving skills will be critical to successful performance. As collaborative teams seek more effective ways of working, they will be expected to identify problems important to their unit and seek appropriate solutions. Thus, when students leave school, they will need to be able to identify central problems, find the appropriate information quickly, and then use this information to solve the problems they identify as important.

Fourth, in "high performance" settings it appears that effective collaboration and communication skills will be central to success. The changes from a centralized to a decentralized workplace will require collaboration and communication skills so that the best decisions get made at every level in an organization and so that changes at one level are clearly communicated to other levels. Our students will need effective collaboration and communication skills when they leave us.

Finally, there is a fifth trend—effective information access and use will be increasingly important to success. Individuals who can access information the fastest and use it effectively to solve important problems will be the ones who succeed in the challenging times that await our students. This will make informational literacy a crucial determinant of success. We must prepare our students for the new information technologies that will become increasingly available as we change from an industrial to an information society.

> We must prepare our students for the new information technologies that will become increasingly available as we change from an industrial to an information society.

What does all of this mean for our students? How can we support them to become effective individuals who make important contributions to society? We believe in the truth of the following maxim:

> In the information age in which we all live, the race will be won by individuals, groups, and societies who can access the best information in the shortest time to identify and solve the most important problems and communicate this information to others.

This is why the Internet and other electronic technologies are so important. We need to prepare our students to use these new information and communication technologies because they enable us to identify and solve important problems in the shortest time and communicate our ideas to others. Nothing is more important for the future of our students. This is the challenge we face as educators in the new world we are all entering. This is what we must prepare our students for as we think about their futures.

Internet FAQ

I have heard a lot about children visiting sites on the WWW and seeing things they shouldn't be seeing. I have also heard stories about children being contacted by strangers for inappropriate purposes. Is this true? How can we protect our children from these things?	Schools have always taught children safety related to drugs, fire, earthquakes, school bus travel, strangers on the street, and other matters. As the Internet enters our worlds, schools are constructing and teaching safe Internet practices, developing "Acceptable Use" policies, and implementing other strategies to protect children. Internet safety will be an important part of the curriculum as we seek to prepare children for their futures. We will describe more specific strategies to protect children in later chapters. If you wish to consider this issue now, visit the location at the Global School Network, **Protect your Students** (http://www.globalschoolhouse.com/web/webproj/define/protect/index.htm). This site contains many useful resources and strategies for developing an appropriate child safety policy for your school.

Internet safety will be an important part of the curriculum as we seek to prepare children for their futures.

Like every other area of education, it is not what the instructional materials are but what you do with them that determines the extent of your students' learning.

How Can I Use the Internet To Help My Students?

Throughout this book, we will help you to answer this important question. The Internet is an extensive resource of information and communication, but its effective use in the classroom will ultimately depend upon how *you* take advantage of this resource. Like every other area of education, it is not what the instructional materials are but what you do with them that determines the extent of your students' learning. No packaged set of materials can compete with a teacher who cares about students, understands their unique needs, and responds in effective ways to support their learning. As you begin to consider how to use the Internet with your students, it may be helpful to see specific examples of what is possible on the WWW of the Internet:

- **The Read In**. Join award-winning authors of children's and young adult literature and hundreds of thousands of teachers and their students during a special day in the spring to celebrate reading. **The Read In Foundation** (http://www.readin.org/), a non-profit group, organizes this special day to culminate several weeks of preparatory activities around the reading of important works of literature. Many exciting activities are listed at this site for your class to do as you prepare for the day of the read in. You may also join in monthly conversations with famous authors throughout the year.

- **Science Resources.** The Science Learning Network is a group of museums and schools devoted to improving science teaching through the Internet. Use the **Science Learning Network** (http://www.sln.org/) to access descriptions of science units taking place in classrooms around the world based on the National Science Standards and inquiry learning. E-mail teachers who have classes working on the same units as you to share ideas and resources. Have students use e-mail to discuss their results and compare them with the results from other students. Post science ideas and questions on a bulletin board and receive replies back from other teachers and students. Have your students complete interactive, multimedia units on topics such as: the physics of water, storm science, dissecting a frog or a cow's eye, using a scanning electron microscope (students can see the photos of objects they request), and much more.

- **Whales: A Thematic Web Unit.** This incredibly rich resource (http://curry.edschool.virginia.edu/go/Whales) provides all the resources you will need for a cross-curricular thematic unit using cooperative grouping as your students study whales. Assign small groups to research a particular area and then report back to the whole class. After preliminary reports, decide upon additional questions to explore and develop new groups to explore these issues. Along the way, students can actually hear the voices of many different whale species, study the physics of echolocation, track several whales by satellite, and download a software program that provides basic information on all of the great whale species.

- **Pi Mathematics.** As students learn about Pi, use this site (http://www.ncsa.uiuc.edu:80/edu/RSE/RSEorange/buttons.html) to supplement your lessons (see Figure 1-5). Have groups select an activity from this location and then share the results with the class: some may choose to research and report on the history of Pi; others may wish to use Pi to determine the best deal at a pizza shop; others may wish to complete an activity measuring Pi using common objects; others may wish to calculate Pi out to one hundred decimal places and then show the class how this can be memorized by singing a popular tune; still others may choose to calculate the circumference of planets and then check their answers at other locations on the Internet. These activities are all clearly matched with standards from the National Council of Teachers of Mathematics. Set a bookmark!

- **Learn About Popular Authors.** Are your students looking for information about a favorite author? Have them visit **The Author Page** (http://ipl.sils.umich.edu/youth/AskAuthor) at the Internet Public Library. This site provides biographies and interviews with many popular authors of children's and adolescent literature. It also provides links to many of the best author sites available on the Internet. Ask students to share the results of their discoveries with your class.

Figure 1-5.
Pi Mathematics: A great location on the WWW for math classes (http://www.ncsa.uiuc.edu:80/edu/RSE/RSEorange/buttons.html).

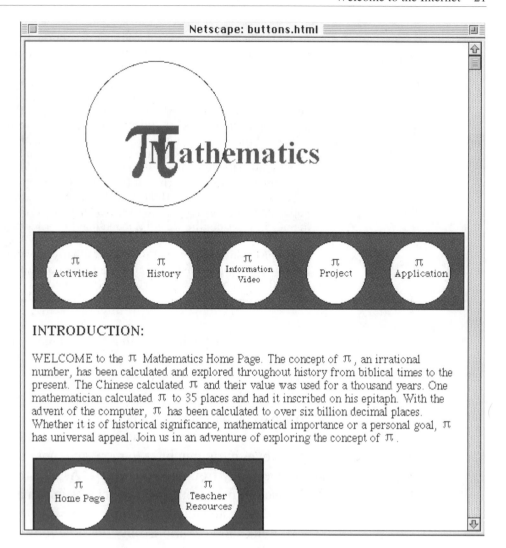

Using the Internet Effectively With Your Students

Teaching and learning are being redefined by the communication technologies that are quickly becoming a part of the information age in which we live (Leu, in press a; Leu & Kinzer, in press; Negroponte, 1995). We are experiencing a historic change in the nature of learning as digital, multimedia resources enter our world. The many resources available on the Internet are the beginning of a radical departure in the nature of information available to you and your students. How we respond to these important changes will determine our students' ability to succeed in the world that awaits them.

How we respond to these important changes will determine our students' ability to succeed in the world that awaits them.

Internet resources will increase, not decrease, the central role you play in orchestrating learning experiences for your students. Each of us will be challenged to thoughtfully guide students' learning within information environments that are richer and more complex than traditional print media, presenting richer and more complex learning opportunities for both us and our students.

TEACHING TIP	Many teachers find the most powerful aspect of the Internet is the opportunity it provides them to learn about successful activities and resources from other teachers. Sometimes these are ideas related to Internet use, but more often they are ideas about traditional instructional issues: good works of literature for an upcoming unit, an idea about teaching radicals in mathematics, a great science demonstration on gravitational force, or an upcoming PBS video for social studies. The Internet eliminates traditional walls that have prevented us from sharing the wonderful things happening in each of our classrooms. In Chapter 3 you will see how to participate in these conversations by using mailing lists, newsgroups, and chat rooms. However, to see a preview of the exchanges taking place every day, visit the archives of either **RTEACHER** (http://listserv.syr.edu/archives/rteacher.html) or **K12ADMIN** (http://listserv.syr.edu/archives/k12admin.html), two popular mailing lists. The first is a mailing list devoted to conversations about literacy instruction; the second is a mailing list for K–12 administrators interested in teaching and learning issues. Notice how educators use these resources to ask questions about instructional issues and discover new ideas for their schools and classrooms. The Internet is a very social environment, putting teachers in touch with other teachers so that all children benefit.

As one example of how the Internet will make our role even more important, consider recent concerns raised by Healy (1999), Birkerts (1995) and Stoll (1995). These authors worry that electronic information environments like the WWW of the Internet will encourage students to "surf" many unrelated topics on only a superficial level. Left on their own, students may be seduced away from reading and thinking critically about a single topic as they discover intriguing links to more and more locations and move farther and farther away from the initial topic. As a result, students will only skim the surface of many, unrelated, pieces of information, never integrating or thinking deeply about any of them.

We think this scenario is only possible, however, in classrooms where teachers do not actively guide the use of Internet resources and, instead, leave decisions about Internet use entirely to students. When students always determine their own paths through this rich and intriguing information resource there is a powerful tendency to search for what students refer to as "cool", highly interactive and media-rich locations that quickly attract their attention but are unrelated to important learning tasks (Leu, 1996). These often include video, sound, animation, and other elements. As students search for "cool" sites, they are less likely to explore important topics in depth or think critically about the relation of this information to their own lives. Students end up viewing much but learning little.

On the other hand, when students are guided to resources and provided with important learning tasks to accomplish, they quickly focus on important information related to the issue at hand. This is not to say that students should only be limited to Internet resources that you select to complete tasks that only you devise. Clearly, if we wish students to become effective users of the Internet, we want them to develop independent strategies for searching and analyzing information. And, in order to do so we must provide them with learning experiences which they direct. Still, it points to the central role

Internet FAQ	
How can I get my school connected to the Internet without spending a lot of money?	In addition to the subsidy provided by the "e-rate program" mentioned earlier, you might also wish to consider the cyber version of a traditional barn raising. A national organization, Net Day, is a grassroots volunteer effort to wire schools so they can network their computers and connect them to the Internet. Labor and materials come from volunteers and support from companies, unions, parents, teachers, students, and school employees. This organization has been remarkably successful at coordinating efforts to get schools wired inexpensively with the support of the business community and others. Visit their WWW site and find out more about **Net Day** (http://www.netday.org) resources and their inexpensive wiring kits.

you will play with this new resource as you support their ability to independently acquire and evaluate information on the web.

In this book, we will show you an integrated set of instructional models for teaching with the Internet. These include: Internet Workshop, Internet Project, Internet Inquiry, and WebQuests. You will see how to begin with easier instructional models and move to more complex and richer models as you feel increasingly comfortable with using the Internet in your classroom.

> In this book, we will show you an integrated set of instructional models for teaching with the Internet.

Teachers who understand the Internet and thoughtfully integrate its many resources into their classroom curriculum will see students expand their understanding of important concepts and communicate these ideas more effectively to others in their class and around the world. Teachers who simply allow students to explore the Internet on their own after their regular work is completed will see little change in student learning. In fact, this type of Internet experience may actually take students away from thinking critically about important ideas as they search for surface level "cool".

> A central assumption of this book is that your role in orchestrating experiences with the Internet is central to your students' futures.

A central assumption of this book is that your role in orchestrating experiences with the Internet is central to your students' futures. Your instructional decisions will determine the extent to which your students gain from this resource. That is why we focus on effective teaching practices while limiting the technical discussion of the Internet to essential basics.

The Social Nature of Learning With the Internet

Much recent research suggests learning is best accomplished through social interaction in supportive social contexts. When students work together, they often are very effective at "scaffolding", or helping, one another on the way to important insights (Meyer, 1993). Theoretical perspectives established by Vygotsky (1978), Bahktin (1981), and others are often used to explain this process. Method frameworks such as cooperative learning (Johnson & Johnson, 1984), peer conferences (Graves, 1983), jigsaw activities (Aaronson, 1978), literature discussion groups (Leu & Kinzer, 1999), text set activities (Short, 1993) and others are thought to be particularly useful because they create situations where students help one another to learn important concepts.

E-MAIL FOR YOU

To: Colleagues
From: Barbara McInerney <bmcinern@freeside.scsd.k12.ny.us
Subject: Using the World Wide Web of the Internet

Hi!

I am really excited about the new doors opening to me as a high school teacher through the use of the Internet. However, that excitement is tempered by some reservations and concerns. One of my biggest concerns is the application of the sources on the Internet. Will I be able to make the use of the Web integrated and meaningful to my students? Will I be able to instruct them correctly and completely in the use of the Web? Will their use of the Internet add to the completeness of the curriculum or just be a casual aside? I feel teachers need to be fully trained and capable in the workings of the Net before attempting to guide students in its use. We do so many "hit and miss" procedures in education—but this technology is here to stay and will be an integral part of their future so students need to learn its use completely and correctly to really enhance classroom experiences.

One of my students, when asked about the feelings they had about our school becoming hooked up to the Internet and what possibilities it presented for them, answered in this manner, "I think it's going to be really cool! I mean, if you are studying, say China, and you could communicate with students in China to really see what it is like there, that would be so cool! Or, if you needed to know some stuff about a topic and all your books were old, then you could go to the Internet and it could tell you new stuff."

Even students with no experience to date on the Internet have a general idea of what they would like to try to do with it—it shows they are thinking about the possibilities, as I am.

I am excited about using this in my class next year!!!!

Barbara McInerney

This socially mediated learning may be especially important within the Internet and other electronic information resources. Because these information resources are powerful, complex, and constantly changing, they often require us to communicate with others in order to make meaning from them. No one person knows everything there is to know about the Internet; each of us has useful information that can help others. I may know something about how to search for information but you may know a really good location for students who want to publish their work. By sharing our information, we can help one another learn about these rich information resources. Learning about the Internet is best accomplished through social interactions with others, perhaps even more naturally and frequently than in traditional print environ-

Learning about the Internet is best accomplished through social interactions with others, perhaps even more naturally and frequently than in traditional print environments.

ments. This is one reason we have asked other teachers to share their insights with you through e-mail messages that appear throughout this book.

The instructional episodes at the beginning of this chapter illustrate how insightful teachers can take advantage of socially mediated learning with the Internet. Corresponding with other students about their drafts, exchanging responses to literature with other classrooms around the world, working with mentors on challenging math problems, are all examples of this important principle. You will find many additional opportunities described throughout this book.

We will also show you a powerful instructional model, Internet Workshop, to support students learning from one another. With a little encouragement from you, you will discover students helping one another and discovering new aspects of the Internet to share with still other students. This can make Internet use an effective tool for community building as well as for learning.

If you seek new ideas about integrating the Internet into your own classroom, visit the classrooms of other teachers who use this tool in exemplary ways.

E-MAIL FOR YOU

To: Colleagues
From: Celia <cbmg@MIDWEST.NET>
Subject: You are NEVER too old!

One should never, ever feel lacking when it comes to knowledge about computers and the net, no matter how old you are. I say this because, there is so terribly much out there to learn. I sincerely do not believe that any one can know all or even approach knowing all because it is ever changing and growing. I think it is important to liken your quest for knowledge about cyberspace to how a kindergartner or 1st grader must feel when the doors begin to open up to the masses of knowledge one must have in order to be a reader. Or when a child first realizes that there is so much to learn out there about anything and everything. Just think we give them a minimum of 12 years to learn it! Technology creates that same feeling in us older folks!

My advice is to sit back, relax, and feel good in the knowledge that the cruise ship you are on is full of individuals on the same quest! There are tons of caring individuals out there that are more than willing to help. And just think how exciting it is every time you find out something new!! That "Aha" feeling is really cool. Good luck and keep up the good work.

From a kindred spirit!

Celia Godsil
Title I Teacher
Nielson School,
Galesburg, Il.

Visiting the Classroom: Sharon Hall's First Grade Class in Ohio

If you seek new ideas about integrating the Internet into your own classroom, visit the classrooms of other teachers who use this tool in exemplary ways

We have seen how the Internet opens new windows for each of us, enabling us to learn from one another. If you seek new ideas about integrating the Internet into your own classroom, visit the classrooms of other teachers who use this tool in exemplary ways. Take a look, for example, at Sharon Hall's homepage for her first grade classroom at South Lebanon Elementary School in South Lebanon, Ohio (see Figure 1-6). Even if you do not teach at this level, her site contains important lessons for each of us.

Figure 1-6.
Sharon Hall's classroom web site for her First Grade Class (http://mrshall.cjb.net)

Sharon uses her classroom web page in many ways, but the most important lesson it teaches us is how to use a classroom web page to communicate effectively, forging a tighter relationship between home and school. Sharon has a special section for parents with a calendar, pictures of classroom work, and ideas about how to help their child at home. Parents may even work with their children to review high frequency sight words important for early reading. Sharon has the entire set appearing on interactive flash cards at her sight. There is a section with lesson plans, showing parents what their children will be learning and there are locations to show the wonderful work her children have completed with other classrooms around the world: Alphabet Across America, the Brown Bear project, and many others. She also has a section describing her entire curriculum in every subject area and a slide show of a typical day's schedule. One gets the idea these are resources she also uses during "Back to School Night" in the fall to orient parents to her classroom program. This classroom web page is a wonderful demonstration of how the Internet may be used in powerful ways to support teaching and learning. It communicates an important message to parents about the professional nature of Sharon's important work at the same time it provides guidance in how they can support their child's development. As more families obtain Internet access, this will be an increasingly important function of a classroom web page.

Notice, too, Sharon also provides resources for other teachers. The best example of this is a "First Grade Web Ring" she has developed, with links to the web pages of many other first grade classrooms. This is a wonderful resource and shows us how the Internet can put us together with others who share similar professional interests. Sharon also includes a series of pages with wonderful tips for teachers who are interested in creating their own web pages.

Visiting classrooms like this can inform all of us in important ways. Being able to see what teachers are doing around the world has the potential to change our instructional lives, providing us with many new and exciting resources for teaching. By sharing effective resources and strategies on the Internet, we are quickly developing rich curriculum networks that transcend materials previously available for instruction. This is an exciting and potentially powerful development for education. It shows how, once again, we all learn from one another in these new contexts for teaching and learning.

Welcome to the Internet!

> By sharing effective resources and strategies on the Internet, we are quickly developing rich curriculum networks that transcend materials previously available for instruction.

References

Aaronson, E. (1978). *The jigsaw classroom.* Beverly Hills, CA: Sage Publications.

Bahktin, M. M. (1981) *The dialogic imagination* (C. Emerson & M. Holquist, Trans.). Austin, TX: University of Texas Press.

Birkerts, S. (1995). *The Gutenberg elegies.* New York: Ballentine Books.

Graves, D. (1983). *Writing: Teachers and children at work.* Portsmouth, NH: Heinemann.

Healy, J. (1999). *Failure to connect.* New York: Simon & Schuster.

Johnson, D. W. & Johnson, R. (1984) *Circles of learning: Cooperation in the classroom.* Alexandria, VA: Association of Supervision and Curriculum Development.

Leu, Donald J., Jr. (in press a). Developing new literacies: Using the Internet in content area instruction. In M. McLaughlin & M. E. Vogt, (Eds.) *Creativity and innovation in content area instruction.* Norwood, MA: Christopher-Gordon.

Leu, D. J., Jr. (1996). Sarah's secret: Social aspects of literacy and learning in a digital information age. *The Reading Teacher, 50* (2), 162–165.

Leu, D. J., Karchmer, R., & Leu, D. D. (1999). The Miss Rumphius Effect: Envisionments for literacy and learning that transform the Internet. *Reading Online*. [Reprinted from *The Reading Teacher, 52*, 636–42.] [Online serial]. Available: http://www.readingonline.org/electronic/RT/rumphius.html

Leu, Donald J., Jr. & Kinzer, C. K. (in press). The convergence of literacy instruction and networked technologies for information and communication. *Reading Research Quarterly*.

Leu, D. J., Jr. & Kinzer, C. K. (1999). *Effective literacy instruction, 4th edition*. Upper Saddle River, NJ: Prentice Hall.

Meyer, D. K. (1993). What is scaffolded instruction? Definitions, distinguishing features, and misnomers. In D. J. Leu, Jr. and C. K. Kinzer (Eds.) *Examining central issues in literacy research, theory, and practice*. Forty-second Yearbook of the National Reading Conference. Chicago: National Reading Conference.

Negroponte, N. (1995). *Being digital*. New York: Knopf.

Ogle, D. M. (1989). The know, want to know, learn strategy. In K. D. Muth (Ed.) *Children's comprehension of text* (pp. 205–223). Newark, DE: International Reading Association.

Short, K. (1993). Intertextuality: Searching for patterns that connect. In D. J. Leu, Jr. & C. K. Kinzer (Eds.), *Literacy research, theory and practice: Views from many perspectives*. Chicago: National Reading Conference.

Stoll, C. (1995). *Silicon snake oil: Second thoughts on the information highway*. New York: Doubleday.

Vygotsky, L. S. (1978) *Mind in society: The development of higher psychological processes*. (M. Cole, V. John-Steiner, S. Scribner, E. Souberman, Eds.). Cambridge, MA: Harvard University Press.

Teaching Navigation Strategies

E-MAIL FOR YOU

To: Our readers

From: djleu@syr.edu (Don Leu), ddleu@syr.edu (Debbie Leu)

Subject: Supporting Navigation Strategies

Navigation is central to success on the Internet. Knowing how to find the best information in the shortest time will quickly advantage your students when they use the Internet to acquire important information.

You already teach navigation strategies in traditional print materials. Showing students how to use the library reference system to locate a book, to use a book's index to find information inside, or to use a dictionary to find a correct spelling are all examples of teaching navigation strategies. As important as navigation is within traditional school tasks, it is even more important on the Internet because information is richer and more complexly networked.

This type of knowledge is acquired as we have experiences on the Internet and as we learn new strategies from our students. As with other aspects of the Internet, we learn best by sharing our experiences with others. It is likely your students will teach you as many things as you teach them about navigating the Internet. All of us can learn much from one another.

This chapter will explain how to use the two most powerful Internet browsers: Internet Explorer and Netscape Communicator (Navigator). We will also explore several important issues related to navigation on the Internet: avoiding excessive commercialism on browsers and web locations, developing child safety policies, teaching navigation strategies in your classroom, learning how to use search engines, and developing research strategies.

Don and Debbie

Teaching With the Internet: Joe Montero's Class

"Hey, cool! We can send our names to Mars on the Internet! Look at this!"

"No way!"

"Way! Right there. Let's send our names to Mars and tell everyone at Workshop."

Julio and Davíd were students who had struggled a bit at school. Actually, they had struggled a lot. They found life outside of school much more interesting than life inside school. As a result, they found themselves further and further behind in reading, math, and other areas. However, this was the beginning of a new school year and both Julio and Davíd felt the possibilities in that important first week of school.

They were completing an activity developed by their teacher, Joe Montero, for Internet Workshop (see Figure 2-1). This workshop activity developed Internet navigation strategies as it introduced a unit on space exploration during the first week of school. NASA has such wonderful resources for teachers available on the Internet. Joe was using these along with a number of reading and writing activities to begin the year.

NASA has wonderful resources for teachers on the Internet.

Figure 2-1.
Nasa for Kids
(http://www.nasa.gov/kids.html),
the location used by Joe Montero for Internet Workshop.

Figure 2-2.
The NASA site, **Send Your Name to Mars** (http://spacekids.hq.nasa.gov/2001), discovered by Julio and Davíd in Mr. Montero's class.

"Cool! Let's write this place down, so we remember."

They wrote the name and address of the site on their worksheet.

Julio and Davíd had discovered **Send Your Name to Mars** (http://spacekids.hq.nasa.gov/2001). Here, you could type your name and have it put on a CD-ROM disk. The disk would be carried to Mars on a lander to be launched in April, 2001 (see Figure 2-2).

Figure 2-3
The official certificate from **Send Your Name to Mars** (http://spacekids.hq.nasa.gov/2001), printed out by Julio using Adobe Acrobat Reader.

Figure 2-4.
An activity for Internet Workshop used to develop navigation knowledge at the beginning of the year.

Navigating: Beginning our Unit on Space Exploration

Pilot:_____ Date: _____

Co-pilot: _____

Goals

1. To learn about the many space resources at NASA for Kids. You will share at least one great location you found during Internet Workshop.
2. To practice navigation strategies on the Internet.
3. To learn at least one new strategy and share it during Internet Workshop.

Evaluation

1 point	You explored the NASA sites and wrote down at least one great location.
1 point	You shared your location during Internet Workshop.
1 point	You practiced navigation strategies we learned on the Internet.
1 point	You learned at least one new navigation strategy and wrote it down.
<u>1 point</u>	<u>You shared the new navigation strategy you learned.</u>
5 points	Total

Exploring NASA

1. Begin your journey at **NASA For Kids** (http://www.nasa.gov/kids.html). The computer should begin with this page.
2. Travel around this site, exploring the many resources. Be certain to use the "Back" button if you want to move back to an earlier page.
3. Find an activity you think our class would enjoy during the next few weeks. Print out a copy of the page. Below, tell us the name of your discovery and why you think it would be fun to do.

What I found: _____
_____

Why it would be fun to do: _____
_____

Space Team Online

Visit **Space Team Online** (http://quest.arc.nasa.gov/shuttle) by using the bookmark I have set. Explore as many resources here as you have time. Pay special attention to the opportunities to chat with space engineers and scientists about this shuttle flight. Also note the many projects we could do. Write down your best ideas about which of these activities you would like to do during the next two weeks. Bring your ideas to Internet Workshop and be prepared to share them with the class.

What New Strategy Did You Learn?

Did you learn something new about using the Internet today? What was it? Write it down and share it with us at Internet Workshop.

If You Have Time: Look through the Hubble Space Telescope (HST) into Deep Space

1. Let's take a look at deep space with the Hubble Telescope. Select the bookmark for (http://oposite.stsci.edu/pubinfo/pictures.html).
2. View some of these pictures from the Hubble telescope. Print out your favorite. Write a description of what you can see on the back and attach it to this page. Bring it to Internet Workshop to share.

"Hey, only use your first name when you give it to anyone on the Internet. Remember what Mr. Montero said about safety?"

After entering their names into the database, they saw how to print out official certificates of their achievement (see Figure 2-3). Each letter had a unique ID number and their name in red. It was signed by a NASA executive.

"Look, there's the letter. Print that out. Where does it say 'Print?' . . . Oh, at the top. That does it."

"How cool is that? Our names are going to Mars!"

Joe Montero's new computer was connected to the Internet and loaded with both Netscape Navigator and Internet Explorer, browser programs enabling his students to navigate through the World Wide Web and other resources on the Internet. He also had loaded a plug-in from the Internet called Adobe Acrobat Reader. This was a program that lets you print out documents, like the letter from NASA, with images, signatures, and other graphic elements just as they appear on the Internet. He downloaded it for free from **Adobe Acrobat Reader** (http://www.adobe.com/products/acrobat/readstep.html).

This was the first year all classrooms in the district had an Internet computer. Joe was teaching his students navigation strategies at the beginning of the year. He knew this was an important first step. Joe had used **Yahooligans** (http://www.yahooligans.com) and **Ask Jeeves for Kids** (http://www.ajkids.com), search engines that screened selections for child appropriateness. He used these sites to discover resources to include on his activity page (See Figure 2-4). Joe knew anything he found at Yahooligans and Ask Jeeves for Kids would be appropriate for students.

> Joe knew anything he found at Yahooligans and Ask Jeeves for Kids would be appropriate for students.

He also used a feature called "bookmarks" on Netscape Navigator ("favorites" on Internet Explorer). Each bookmark (or favorite) took students to a location he wanted them to visit on the World Wide Web. This made navigation very easy since students simply selected items Joe had set and these took them to the correct location on the web.

Thus, the activity taught navigation strategies at the same time that it introduced important resources for the unit. Because it limited random searching and surfing, the activity also accomplished a third goal: it supported child safety in his classroom. This was important in Joe's district. In fact, the district used a filter program as part of its child safety strategy. Filter programs deny access to web pages deemed inappropriate for students to visit.

Another part of the district's child safety strategy was to follow an acceptable use policy. Over the summer, the district had developed an acceptable use policy with a committee of parents, students, and teachers. The policy described the Internet, defined the "Do's" and "Don'ts" of Internet use, and defined sanctions for unacceptable use. At the end of the form there was a location for everyone to sign, indicating they had read and understood the policy: student, parent/guardian, and teacher. The district based their policy on one they located at a site organized by the Houston Independent School District, **Acceptable Use Policies** (http://chico.rice.edu/armadillo/acceptable.html).

On the first day of class Joe introduced the computer and the Internet. He went over the acceptable use policy with his students, explaining each item. Then he had his students sign the form and take it home to obtain the signature of their parent or guardian, permitting them to use the Internet at school.

As students returned the forms, Joe introduced small groups to the fundamentals of navigation using Netscape Navigator. First, he showed his students how to connect to the Internet by launching this program. Then he showed them how to go to a site on the Internet by using a preset bookmark. Next, he showed his students how to move to locations with related information by clicking on a hypertext link. These colored, or underlined words, take you to additional locations on the Internet. He also showed students how to use the "Back" button to move back to the previous location they had just visited and the "Forward" button to move ahead. Finally, he introduced the activity in Figure 2-4, designed to be completed in pairs.

During his small group lessons, Joe discovered that some students knew more than he did about navigating on the Internet and that others knew very little. He wanted students to support one another as they developed initial navigation skills. Before they began, he set the home page location on Netscape Navigator to **NASA For Kids** (http://www.nasa.gov/kids.html). This would always be the first page to appear when students connected to the Internet and started their Internet activity (see Figure 2-4). Setting the home page location like this was an important new strategy Joe recently discovered from another teacher at school. This saved time and helped to ensure students only visited appropriate locations. It also avoided some of the commercialism at the Start Up Page on Netscape Navigator.

> Setting the home page location like this was an important new strategy Joe recently discovered from another teacher at school.

At the end of the week, after students completed the space navigation assignment, Joe organized an Internet workshop session with the entire class. Students shared additional navigation strategies they had learned as a result of their tour, teaching each other new ways of navigating on the World Wide Web. They also shared information they discovered about space as they completed the activity. Everyone was excited as they talked about the people at NASA they had met, the upcoming Space Shuttle flight, and the incredible photos from the Hubble Space Telescope they printed out to share during the workshop session.

Perhaps because school success had been rare for them, Julio and Davíd held their surprise until the very end of the workshop session. Finally, they told everyone how their names were being sent to Mars on the next Mars Lander. They explained details about the mission and showed the letters from NASA with their names on them, information no one else had found. Everyone wanted to know the name of the location and how to get there. They wanted to send their names to Mars, too, and obtain an official letter, documenting their accomplishment.

"Let's go over to the computer and you can show us how to do it," said Mr. Montero.

They all watched while Julio and Davíd gave them a tour of the site and talked in great detail about the mission to Mars. Then they showed everyone how to have their names included on the CD and how to print out the official letters from NASA. Julio and Davíd had become the experts in class with this information, a new position for them at school. It felt good.

Joe Montero had never seen this location before. He was amazed how quickly two of his students found such a useful resource for his class that engaged all of his students. And, these were two of his students that most concerned him. Clearly, the special moments possible during that first week of school had opened the school doors for Julio and Davíd and they had jumped right through. Joe was certain this experience was going to be a turning point for them. He could feel it in the confidence they demonstrated as they showed everyone this wonderful location.

As he stood thinking about this, Joe also recalled the words he heard at a workshop on Internet use in the classroom, "You will become the guide on the side, not the sage on the stage." As he stood watching Julio and Davíd teach his class about these new resources, the meaning of those words was suddenly very clear. His role as a classroom teacher was changing.

"Set a bookmark, Mr. Montero! We want to send our names, too."

It was a wonderful start to the new school year. Everyone learned important lessons that day.

Lessons From the Classroom

What lessons might we learn from this episode as we consider navigation issues in the classroom? First, is the important lesson of child safety on the Internet. Limiting search engines to those, like **Yahooligans** (http://www.yahooligans.com) or **Ask Jeeves For Kids** (http://www.ajkids.com/), that screened sites for children helped Joe to ensure his students didn't explore inappropriate locations on the Internet. Also, Joe's district used a software filter to prevent inappropriate sites from appearing on any of the district's computers and worked carefully with parents, students and teachers to develop an acceptable use policy for Internet use. Developing an acceptable use policy heads off a number of problems including the viewing of inappropriate sites, using inappropriate language on the Internet, and receiving inappropriate e-mail from strangers. Since it was sent to both students and parents/guardians, everyone received important information about the Internet and how it was going to be used at school. We will discuss acceptable use policies later in this chapter.

This episode also illustrates a second lesson—how important it is to systematically develop navigation strategies at the beginning of the year. Joe realized that navigational strategies were important; students gather more information in a shorter time when they know how to navigate through the Internet. Time was precious in Joe's class with only one computer connected

---

Julio and Davíd had become the experts in class with this information, a new position for them at school.

Limiting search engines to those, like Yahooligans (http://www.yahooligans.com) or Ask Jeeves For Kids (http://www.ajkids.com/), that screened sites for children helped Joe to ensure his students didn't explore inappropriate locations on the Internet.

Developing an acceptable use policy heads off a number of problems including the viewing of inappropriate sites, using inappropriate language on the Internet, and receiving inappropriate e-mail from strangers.

to the Internet. As a result, he wanted students to know how to use their time efficiently. He developed a thoughtful plan to accomplish this and started with teaching essential navigation strategies through Internet Workshop.

Another important lesson is how Joe strategically combined two elements within a single lesson: an introduction to the first thematic unit of the year and experiences designed to practice navigation strategies. Again, this saved time in a busy classroom; students were learning background information important for the upcoming unit at the same time that they developed important navigation strategies.

> Students were learning background information important for the upcoming unit at the same time that they developed important navigation strategies.

TEACHING TIP	Some teachers like to use Internet scavenger hunts at the beginning of the year to develop navigation skills. If you are interested in exploring a number of scavenger hunts, visit these locations:

- **Scavenger Hunts: Searching for Treasure on the Internet**—http://www.education-world.com/a_curr/curr113.shtml

- **A Collection of Scavenger Hunts**—http://www.crpc.rice.edu/CRPC/Women/GirlTECH/Materials/scavhunt.html

- **Internet Scavenger Hunts**—http://edservices.aea7.k12.ia.us/edtech/classes/internet101/scavenger/

This episode also illustrates how Joe saved time by designating a home page location on his Internet browser. Designating the NASA site as the home page location took students immediately to the location he wanted them to visit. Time was not wasted looking for the right page. This strategy also helped to prevent inappropriate surfing to other sites on the Internet.

> Designating the NASA site as the home page location took students immediately to the location he wanted them to visit.

There is also another lesson: the social learning opportunities that are critical to classroom use of the Internet. Joe used three methods (group introduction, paired learning, and whole class workshop) to teach navigation skills. These worked in a complementary fashion to take advantage of social learning opportunities inherent with Internet use. His initial group presentation explained essential elements for students to practice as they completed the tour in pairs. Working in pairs after the group presentation led to many new learning experiences as students helped one another when they were stuck, discovering new ways of navigating the Internet. Sometimes other students would even stop by the computer to assist a pair having difficulty; this saved Joe time as he worked with students in other areas of the classroom. Finally, having Internet Workshop at the end of the week tied everything together for his class, allowing each student to share new navigation strategies with the others.

Internet Workshop led to many new ideas for navigating the Internet. Someone, for example, had discovered the "Home" button and explained how this worked to take you back to the home page location, **NASA for**

Kids. Someone else had discovered how the browser saved a list of the locations visited during each session. This student took the class to the computer and showed them how they could return to any site that had already been visited, even one without a favorite (or bookmark), by looking under the menu item labeled "Go" or by clicking the "Back" button and holding it down. Someone else had noticed that only single clicks were necessary with the mouse to activate any link; double clicking was unnecessary. In fact, double clicking often caused the program to be confused about what you wanted. All of these new strategies were shared and discussed. It was a very productive session.

This episode also demonstrates how Internet technologies may create spaces for students who have met with failure in the past. The lesson Julio and David teach us is important; each child in your room can become an expert, showing others an especially useful resource on the Internet. The Internet creates new spaces in which each of your students may succeed, providing them with important opportunities to grow and develop. Anyone may become an expert in some aspect of the Internet, showing us something we did not know before. You will see these opportunities in your classroom, reminding us of the potential in each and every student.

Finally, we learn another important lesson: as teachers we need to anticipate the changes in our role. Because Internet technologies are increasingly powerful, complex, and continually changing, our students quickly become more knowledgeable than us in many aspects of information technologies. No teacher can keep up with all of the changes. As a result, our role is changing from being the central source of information in the classroom to becoming a facilitator and guide, putting children together with other children who possess different types of expertise in order to exchange information and solve common problems.

Joe Montero's classroom contains many lessons for us to consider: using child safety strategies, the importance of helping students develop navigation skills on the Internet, saving time by simultaneously teaching navigation strategies and introducing an upcoming instructional unit, designating a home page location to also save time, the importance of social learning opportunities inherent with Internet use, and especially the spaces Internet use creates for children who may be struggling in school. Each is important for us to consider.

> The Internet creates new spaces in which each of your students may succeed, providing them with important opportunities to grow and develop.

> As teachers we need to anticipate the changes in our role.

Important Tools for Navigating the Internet

How, exactly, do we navigate through the Internet? Many books have already been written on this topic and many online tutorials can provide assistance. You may wish to explore some of these:

- **Learn the Net: An Internet Guide and Tutorial—**
  http://www.learnthenet.com/english/

E-MAIL FOR YOU

To: Colleagues
From: Susan Silverman <susansilverman@yahoo.com>
Subject: A Tip for Busy Teachers

You have Internet access in your classroom but are not sure how to integrate it into your curriculum. You would like to take a course but your family obligations don't allow you the time to do so. Well, you can relax now because I am going to share a program that is easy, impressive, practical, and free. You can learn this program by yourself in just a few minutes!

If you would like to post homework assignments on the web or have a place to showcase student work, **School Notes** is the place for you! You may find it at: http://www.schoolnotes.com

Once you register at their web site you will be given a user name, password, and web address. Your web address will include your school's zip code so parents and students can easily find your site.

Last year I posted weekly spelling assignments on School Notes. They have a wonderful feature that allows you to create flash cards to reinforce skills. My students really enjoyed studying for their spelling tests and math quizzes online. School Notes offers a choice of backgrounds and font colors. You can edit your page at any time. You can also include your e-mail address, allowing students and parents to communicate with you outside of the classroom.

School Notes allows you to link to web sites that are relevant to your assignments. Students can take an active role in finding resources for online research. Some educators use School Notes to highlight a "Student of the Week." The possibilities are endless!

Be sure to print out copies of your page to distribute to students without Internet access at home. Provide these students time to do their research on the school computers. Once your students and parents see your classes on School Notes, they will think that you're a techno wiz!

Susan Silverman
Clinton Avenue Elementary School
Port Jefferson Station, New York
Come visit the work we do in my class at: http://kids-learn.org

- **Beginners Central**—http://www.northernwebs.com/bc
- **Surf the Web: Web Browsers**—
  http://www.learnthenet.com/english/html/12browser.htm

The best way to learn, however, is to just get out and explore the Internet. Our discussion can help this exploration, especially if you are just beginning and are at your computer as you read this chapter. It will focus on the most important navigation elements for teachers and students in busy classrooms. As you become more adept at using the Internet in your classroom, you may wish to explore this issue in greater detail. We list a number of sites on the WWW at the end of this chapter to provide you with additional information.

A browser is a software program on your computer allowing you to connect to locations on the Internet. The two most popular browsers are Internet Explorer and Netscape Navigator.

The most important tool for navigating the Internet is a browser. A browser is a software program on your computer allowing you to connect to locations on the Internet. The two most popular browsers are Internet Explorer and Netscape Navigator. Each comes in at least two flavors: Windows and Macintosh.

This section will explain the essential elements of Internet Explorer 4.5 for Macintosh and Internet Explorer 5 for Windows-based computers. The following section will explain the essential elements of Netscape Navigator 4.7 (Communicator), for both types of computer systems. You only need to read the section that applies to the type of browser on your computer.

Internet Explorer and Netscape Navigator are the most powerful browsers available because each allows you to access multimedia information (graphics, audio, video, and animations) on the WWW. In addition, each comes packaged with a number of components such as e-mail. The other nice thing is that both are free. You simply download them from the Internet to load them onto your computer. The latest version of Internet Explorer may be downloaded at Microsoft's home page for Internet Explorer (http://www.microsoft.com/ie). The latest version of Netscape Navigator (Communicator) may be downloaded at Netscape's Download page (http://www.netscape.com).

A Few Thoughts at the Beginning

Before you read the section appropriate for your needs, we wish to share three important thoughts with you. The first is that the images you see here may be slightly different from the images you see on your computer screen. New releases for each browser appear frequently, making minor changes in the appearance of windows the browser displays. New releases also appear frequently for your operating system (Macintosh or Windows), resulting in even more changes. Between changes in browsers and changes in operating systems, it is impossible to visually keep up with each permutation. Fortunately, even if the images change slightly, the main functions of each browser are remarkably stable, at least for periods of up to several years. Thus, you will be able to follow along just fine, even if the images are slightly different from what you see on your computer.

Learning new ways of exploring the Internet is one of the exciting aspects of the journey ahead of you.

Second, in the upcoming description of browsers we will only present basic fundamentals to get you started using the WWW quickly and effectively in your class. With these basics firmly in hand, you will discover many more useful features and functions as you explore on your own and as you learn from colleagues and students. Learning new ways of exploring the Internet is one of the exciting aspects of the journey ahead of you. Take full advantage of these moments. Exploring new features of a browser, e-mail, or a web site is how all of us learn to navigate on the Internet. Be certain, too, to share your discoveries with others. They will appreciate it and share their own discoveries with you.

The final thought is an important one. It concerns a developing controversy within the educational community. You will need to decide, perhaps with guidelines from your district, about the amount of advertising you wish to expose your students to. This happens through the choice and configuration of your browser and the locations you ask students to visit for classroom assignments. Increasingly, browsers use links to commercial sites favoring their products and companies with which they have formed strategic alliances. Increasingly, sites on the WWW include banner advertising along with the information they provide.

Some see this as inevitable and worthwhile. Exposing students to commercial messages helps initiate conversations about how best to critically view information on the Internet. Commercial images are seen as tools for teaching students about the increasingly commercial nature of the information they will encounter in their lives. Others see the intrusion of commercial images as inconsistent with the traditional, commercial-free nature of most educational materials.

We tend to favor exposing students to fewer, not more, commercial images. We believe it is important to engage students in discussions about these matters, but not when we have other educational goals in mind. As a result, we have tried to avoid commercial sites in the recommendations and examples of WWW locations we provide. In some cases, this is not always possible. Nevertheless, as we made decisions about which WWW locations to include in this book, we have favored those developed by professional organizations, governmental organizations, non-profit organizations, federally funded sites, and others who limit or exclude advertising at their locations. In some cases, you will find the WWW locations we mention contain advertising or commercially motivated links. In these cases, we decided the information resources were much more important than the advertising. You will need to make similar decisions as it is difficult to be entirely commercial-free in the locations you select for classroom use.

This issue also affects your choice of browser in important ways. Both Internet Explorer and Netscape Navigator have commercially motivated links. Often these appear in subtle ways, ones you would not immediately consider. We have found Internet Explorer to be especially problematic in this area. This is a shame since Internet Explorer has several nice features. Our presentation will show you how to remove most of the commercially motivated links built into this browser. If you choose to use Internet Explorer, this should enable your students to focus more on the information at a web location and less on commercially motivated links that appear as part of the browser.

Internet Explorer: A Powerful Internet Browser

One popular browser for the Internet is Internet Explorer and another is Netscape Navigator. If you are reading this section, we will assume you will be using Internet Explorer. If you use Netscape Navigator (Communicator), you should read the following section.

If you have not loaded Internet Explorer onto your computer or you do not know how to obtain Internet access, seek the assistance of a person at your school who can provide technical support. If you are at your computer, launch Internet Explorer by double clicking on the icon for this program. If not, simply follow along by using the illustrations in this section.

A Few Words At The Beginning

When you connect to the Internet, you will see a screen similar to that in Figure 2-5 for Macintosh or Figure 2-6 for Windows. If you have a different version of Internet Explorer, or if your system administrator has configured your system at school in a special fashion, some of the buttons at the top may be slightly different. It will be similar enough, though, to follow our discussion. Take a close look at these screens and let's go over several navigational elements that appear there.

The very top bar contains the title of the page on the WWW you are currently viewing. In Figure 2-5, you are looking at the home page for Internet Explorer 4.5.

Figure 2-5.
The Home Page for Internet Explorer 4.5, a WWW browser (http://www.microsoft.com/mac/ie /) on a Macintosh System.

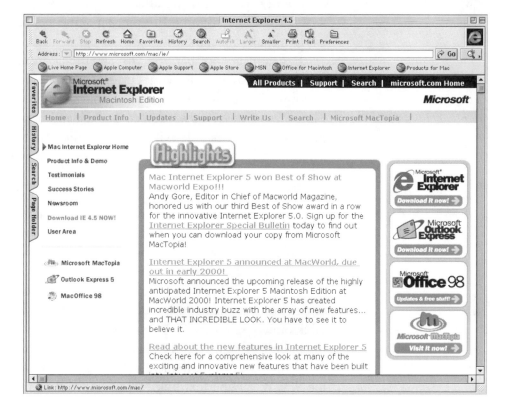

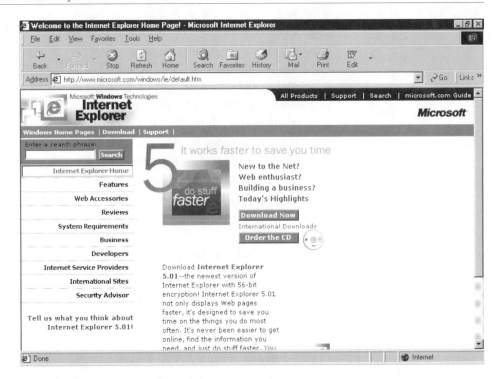

Below the title bar (or beneath the menu bar in Windows) you will find a tool bar. Items in the tool bar allow you do things with your browser. The tool bar for Internet Explorer includes items such as (from right to left) "Back", "Forward," "Stop," "Refresh," "Home," "Favorites," "History," "Search," "AutoFill," "Larger," "Smaller," "Print," "Mail," and "Preferences". This tool bar may be slightly different on some systems. Don't worry. We will explain each in just a bit.

Beneath the tool bar you will see the address bar with a narrow white window. The address for your current location on the Internet appears in this window. The address in Figure 2-5 (http://www.microsoft.com/mac/ie /) or Figure 2-6 (http://www.microsoft.com/windows/ie/default.htm) is the initial screen most people will see when they first launch Internet Explorer. This will be different if someone has already installed Internet Explorer on your computer.

Below the address bar may be a favorites bar. These contain buttons that can take you to favorite locations on the Internet. As you can see in Figure 2-5, this aspect of your browser contains commercially motivated links. It is possible to change the buttons on this bar to locations you plan to use in class assignments instead.

Now look at the window containing the home page for Internet Explorer just below this final row of buttons. This is the viewing window. When you click on words or images in the viewing window that are underlined or distinctively marked, you will notice that Internet Explorer takes you to another location related to the item you clicked. This is a key navigational feature on the WWW, a hypertext link. If you single click on an underlined or distinctively marked element with your mouse, a hypertext link will take you to the site on the Internet linked to that item(s). If you are at your computer, try clicking (only once) on any hypertext link you can see.

Notice how a new screen appears with information related to the word(s) or picture you selected. You may wish to also note the new address in the address window. You are now at this new location on the Internet and this location probably contains several more hypertext links. You could keep clicking on hypertext links and travel to different locations throughout the Internet, seemingly forever.

Also notice the tabs on the left side of the viewing window. Clicking on any of these locations will open up a folder for each item. You may wish to explore these. Several of these items have commercially motivated links. A little later we will show you how to limit the effect of commercially motivated links within your classroom.

The Toolbar

Take a look at the items in the toolbar (Figures 2-7a for Macintosh and 2-7b for Windows). These tools allow you to do things as you navigate through the WWW. The first button, **Back**, allows you to move back one location from where you are currently. Note that this is active only after you move to a location beyond the first page. If you haven't already tried moving to another location by clicking on a hypertext link, do this now. Take a look at the page you see on your computer and try to locate hypertext links by clicking on them. Then, try clicking on the Back button on the toolbar and note that you return back to the previous location.

The first button, Back, allows you to move back one location from where you are currently.

Figure 2-7 a.
The Toolbar for Internet Explorer 4.5 (Macintosh).

Figure 2-7 b.
The Toolbar for Internet Explorer 5.0 (Windows).

The next button, **Forward**, moves you forward one location in your travels through the Internet. Note this is only active if you have moved back at least one location and can really move forward to places you have visited. Try moving backwards and forwards. You may also wish to try using the hypertext links at some of these pages. As you navigate, note the changes in your current location in the address window.

Stop will abort any transmission to your computer that is in progress. This is helpful when it is taking too long to get into a web site; sometimes too many people want to go to the same place at once. If you don't wish to keep waiting to connect, press Stop. Then move on to another location. Come back in a few minutes and the line may be open.

The next button, **Refresh**, is helpful when you are having problems accessing a popular location on the WWW because everyone else wants to get there, too. When this happens, you will receive a message indicating you were unable to connect to your desired location. Press Refresh and try again. Sometimes, a screen will not transmit completely to your computer for one reason or another. Press Refresh when this happens and you should receive a complete screen. Refresh also works well for locations that are regularly updated, such as newspapers.

Home is the next button on the toolbar. This button always takes you back to the location you have designated as the first one to show in your viewing window. This saves time in a busy classroom. Right now, "Home" will probably take you to a Microsoft location, perhaps your start page. We will show you how to change the home location to one more appropriate for your students. More on this later.

Favorites is the next button. Clicking on this button will open the favorites folder on the left side of your viewing window. The favorites folder contains a list of links to favorite sites on the Internet. Clicking the favorites button a second time (or the favorites tab on the left side of the viewing window with Macintosh, version 4.5) will close this folder. You will find that your list of favorites will be very useful. It makes it easier for students to find important locations during your instructional units. It may also be used to limit the sites children may visit. Some teachers only allow students to visit sites on the favorites list. The next section will explore the favorites feature in greater detail.

The next button, **History**, will open the history folder on the left side of your viewing window. This folder keeps track of the locations you have visited in the past. If you wish to return to any of these locations, simply click on them. You will also notice a series of folders organized by date. If you click on any folder, the places you visited that day will appear. This is a very useful feature. It helps you get back to places if you have forgotten the addresses.

TEACHING TIP	Are you interested in knowing the locations your students visit during the day? The History button on Internet Explorer is very helpful. At the end of each day, just open the History folder and quickly skim the locations that are listed. If you are worried about any of the locations, just click on them and take a quick peek. This shouldn't take more than a minute or two. It will help you to keep track of locations that students in your room are visiting and let you know if any problems arise.

Search engines are programs on the Internet that search for sites containing words or phrases that you specify.

Often we need to search the Internet for very specific information. Clicking on the button **Search** will open the search folder on the left side of the viewing window. A search engine will appear in this folder. Search engines are programs on the Internet that search for sites containing words or phrases that you specify. Clicking the Search button a second time will close the search engine folder.

Are you looking for information about origami for next week's unit on Japan? Click on the Search button and the search engine window will appear on the left side of your window. You will find that one of several search engines has been selected for you. There will also be a white box at the top with the words "Choose provider." You may click here and select one of several other search engines. Whichever search engine you select, look for a small box in which to type a keyword for a search. Click inside this box to activate your cursor. Then type in the word "origami." Press return or click the Search, Find it, or Go get it! button next to the keyword window. A list of sites on the WWW will appear, each with information about origami.

Often, the locations found by the search engine will also contain short descriptions of the contents for each location. You may find a great location, **Joseph Wu's Origami Page** (http://www.origami.vancouver.bc.ca), with directions for creating many wonderful paper objects as well as information about this Japanese art form. To go to this location, all you need to do is click on the hypertext link that takes you there. If you do not find this location from your search, you may need to do a more precise search. Type all of the words "Joseph Wu's Origami Page" in the search engine's keyword box and do another search. When you find this location, pay a visit. It is an amazing location if you are interested in this art form from Japan.

If you selected the "Choose provider" button you will have noticed there are several different search engines available to you such as MSN, Altavista, GoTo, InfoSeek, Lycos, and others. Each searches in a slightly different fashion. If you develop a preference for one, all you need to do to select it at the top and leave it in this window. We will explore search engines a bit later. For now, just play around a bit at the search engine site and notice the types of features you will find.

AutoFill, the next button, will automatically complete a personal page with information about you. First, though, you must complete a master form containing your name, address, phone number, and other personal information. We recommend you do not complete this form or use this feature for classroom safety purposes. It is useful if you use the Internet at home for shopping.

You may also find buttons called **Larger** and **Smaller.** These allow you to display information in your viewing window in a larger or smaller sized font. Each time you click one of these buttons, the print will quickly be set to a different font size. Setting the print to a larger size is especially helpful for children experiencing vision difficulties. It makes information in the viewing window easier to read.

Print, simply prints out a copy of whatever is displayed in the viewing window if you are connected to a printer.

Mail is a button that will take you to the e-mail program used with Internet Explorer. We will show you how to use this in the next chapter.

Finally, there may be a button on your toolbar called **Preferences**. Go ahead and click on this button, opening the preferences window. (With some

Windows systems, changing preferences may be accomplished by choosing "Internet Options" from the Tools menu.) You will see a number of options here. These allow you to configure the browser to satisfy your individual needs. Go ahead and explore this area to see some of the features you may set. Don't change any settings yet, though. We will come back to this in a moment.

The Address Window

Your current location on the Internet is indicated in the address window. This contains the "Uniform Resource Locator" (URL), or address, of the site that appears in the viewing window. Note in Figure 2-8, for example, the URL for **Harriet Tubman and the Underground Railroad**, (http://www2.lhric.org/pocantico/tubman/tubman.html), an exceptional resource for your classroom.

> Your current location on the Internet is indicated in the address window.

Figure 2-8.
The address window for Internet Explorer, showing the address for **Harriet Tubman and the Underground Railroad**, an outstanding resource developed by Terry Hongell and Pam Taverna, teachers at Pocantico Hills School in Sleepy Hollow, New York.

You may use the address window to travel to any location on the Internet, as long as you know its address. Perhaps, for example, you were reading an article and came across the web site called **Franklin D. Roosevelt Library and Digital Archives.** The article listed the URL, or address: http://www.fdrlibrary.marist.edu/index.html. You want to review this resource for your upcoming unit on presidents. How do you visit the site? Simply highlight the current address in the address window with your mouse, type in the new address, and press return. This will open any location on the WWW as long as you know the address in advance. Be careful though! The address must be typed exactly as you find it. A missing period or even the wrong case for a letter (e.g., upper case instead of lower case) will give you an error message. If this happens, go back and double check the URL, making certain you have typed it in correctly.

> Favorites are very useful in a classroom. During a unit, you may set favorites for sites you wish students to use in their studies. This saves time finding resources and also limits the possibility of extensive "surfing" to sites you do not wish students to visit.

Using the Favorites Feature With Internet Explorer: An Important Navigational Aid for Your Class

Internet Explorer has a useful feature to assist you and your students as you navigate the Internet: the favorites folder. If you are at your computer and Internet Explorer is running, click on the Favorites folder on your toolbar. Clicking on this button (or the tab for the favorites folder on the left side of your viewing window) will open the favorites folder on the left side of your window (see Figure 2-9). Inside the favorites folder is an item that says "Add Page to Favorites." Clicking on this will add a link to your current location on the WWW into your folder of favorite sites. If you wish to return to the same location at a later time, open your favorites folder and select this location.

Figure 2-9.
Here you can see the favorites folder as it appears on the left side of your viewing window in Internet Explorer. Notice the favorites tab. This opens the folder.

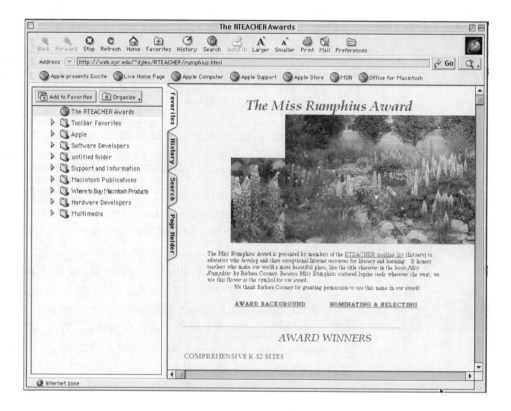

Favorites are very useful in a classroom. During a unit, you may set favorites for sites you wish students to use in their studies. This saves time finding resources and also limits the possibility of extensive "surfing" to sites you do not wish students to visit.

You may add new folders to your favorites window and rearrange favorite sites. Simply use the option in the Favorites menu item at the top of the screen to add new folders. Once you have established a new folder, use the Favorites menu item and select "organize Favorites" to open up a window listing all of your favorites. This is where you can rearrange the organization of your Favorites folders (see Figure 2-10). You may move items into new folders by simply clicking and dragging them to the desired location. You may also delete items by clicking once on the item and then selecting "Clear" from the "Edit" menu item.

Favorites are very useful in a classroom. During a unit, you may set favorites for sites you wish students to use in their studies. This saves time finding resources and also limits the possibility of extensive "surfing" to sites you do not wish students to visit. Simply make a rule that students may only visit sites where you have set a favorite, or sites that are no more than one, two, three, or four links away.

Figure 2-10.
The Favorites window with Internet Explorer on a Macintosh. This helps you to organize your list of favorite sites on the WWW and to find favorite sites.

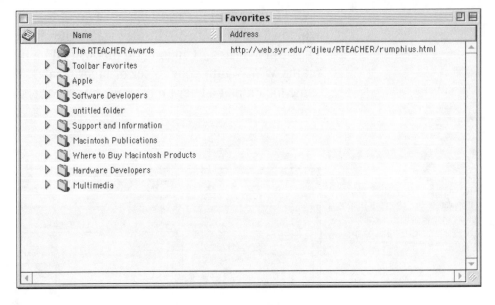

Designating a Home Page Location

It is helpful to designate a home page location for the content your class is studying. A home page location is the page that shows up first on your screen each time students connect to the Internet with Internet Explorer. As Joe Montero discovered, this saves time in a busy classroom; students begin immediately with the site you want them to visit first, one with important content for your unit. To change the home page location from the one that first appears on Internet Explorer, click on the "Preferences" folder in the toolbar and then select "Home/Search." (With Windows systems, changing preferences may be accomplished by choosing "Internet Options" from the Tools menu.) This will take you to a window that looks like Figure 2-11. Simply type in the URL of the location you wish to designate as your home page location. Note that you may also use this window to designate the URL for a search engine, if you have a preference. The search engine you designate will appear whenever you click the "Search" button in the toolbar. Later, after you have had a chance to try out various search engines, note the URL of your favorite and enter it here.

It is helpful to designate a home page location for the content your class is studying.

Content Advisor: Censoring Web Sites Based on Content

Internet Explorer also contains a feature enabling you to block student access to web sites with inappropriate content. If you wish to explore this feature you may find it by selecting Preferences from your toolbar and then choosing "Ratings." (In Windows, you may need to choose Internet Options from the Tools menu, click the "Content" tab of the Internet Options dialog box, and click "Enable" in the Content Advisor section. Then create a password, confirm it, and click "OK".) In both systems, a window appears containing settings for the RSAC Ratings Service. You may set each content filter to different levels. Then, if your students visit a site that includes a rating from the RSAC service, it will determine whether or not to allow access, depend-

Figure 2-11.
Opening the preferences window and setting the home page location in Internet Explorer. This saves your students time and helps them to begin their work at a useful location.

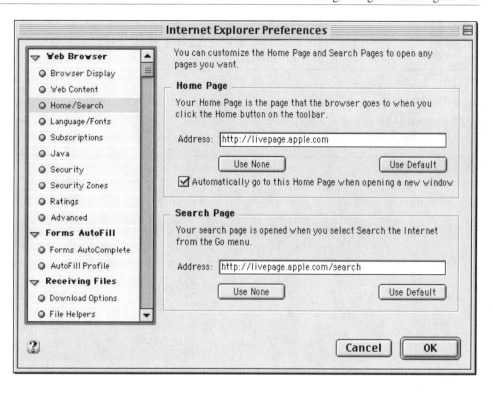

ing upon the levels of access you have set. If the site has not been rated, this feature will block access. Thus, your students will be unable to access many inoffensive, and potentially useful, sites. You may provide access to unrated sites by selecting "Options" and turning this feature off. However, this tends to defeat the purpose of the screening function. You should explore the Content Advisor on Internet Explorer and decide if you wish to use it. Your district may also have established a policy about this feature.

We believe the best solution to viewing inappropriate content is a solid acceptable use policy at your school that is consistently applied and a teacher who carefully monitors student use of the Internet.

We feel Internet Explorer's Content Advisor is more problematic than helpful. We believe the best solution to viewing inappropriate content is a solid acceptable use policy at your school that is consistently applied and a teacher who carefully monitors student use of the Internet. In an upcoming section we will explore these alternatives.

Removing Commercially-Motivated Aspects of Internet Explorer

It is possible to remove several aspects of Internet Explorer containing commercially-motivated links without limiting students' ability to navigate the Internet and access resources important to classroom learning projects.

It is possible to remove several aspects of Internet Explorer containing commercially-motivated links without limiting students' ability to navigate the Internet and access resources important to classroom learning projects. If you are concerned about commercial aspects of this browser, we suggest you do the following:

- Set your home page for an appropriate content page, not the Microsoft page.

- Remove all commercial items from the favorites toolbar, replacing these with your own favorites for classroom learning.

E-MAIL FOR YOU

To: Colleagues
From: Elizabeth Rohloff <erohloff@teleport.com>
Subject: Inspiration

My experiences with new ideas in the field of education have been many and varied. With each swing of the pendulum I have tried new curriculum plans, taken classes, shared with teachers and presented what I learned to an eager group of young faces. But few ideas have had as great an impact as my exposure to the use of technology in the classroom. Entering a school that is fully connected and wired to the Internet, is an eye-opening experience. Plunk a few computers down in front of children and be prepared for another awakening. Inspiration is easy from that vantage point.

I realized as a teacher that I could either plunge ahead with the inspiration from this or slowly observe the process. My students were already involved, I might as well join in. Rarely fearing new ideas, I embraced technology the first time I saw another teacher communicating to our classroom over a CU-See Me Camera. This was connecting, this was networking, and this was sharing!

My enthusiasm spread the first time I completed a web page of our students' poetry. We were studying a science unit on weather. Using the Internet, my teaching partner and I were able to share weather data with the students. Included in the unit were some rare (for our region) snow and ice storms and a series of wind storms. My literary focus for the 7 and 8 year-old was the use of rhyming words. With my focus intact, they produced a collection of poems and drawings.

My task was to put it all together for use on our Home Page. It was so inspiring to take a project from the very beginning of process, the study of a science/literature unit, to an end product, an art product that linked and integrated many subjects. I was hooked on technology and it's use with the kids. I'm not sure who was more excited, the students or I.

I have this newfound source to use with my students when I teach. I do my homework and research the information I plan to use; previewing sites and coordinating written material with the skills I want to teach. Technology (the Internet) does not replace my other outstanding resources, but its connections to the "big world" are empowering for all of us. We can communicate with our neighbors in the city and talk to someone in another part of the world. We can see the world as a smaller place and feel connections with others doing the same or different things. As for myself, it is an opportunity to be a learner along with my students pioneering this vast new arena. Visit our work at http://buckman.pps.k12.or.us/room100/room100.html

Good luck on your journey!

> Experience is not what happens to you;
> experience is what you do with what happens to you.
> Aldous Huxley

ElizaBeth Rohloff
Buckman Elementary School
Portland, Oregon   http://buckman.pps.k12.or.us/room100/room100.html

E-MAIL FOR YOU

To: Colleagues

From: tgray@pepperdine.edu (Terrie Gray)

Subject: Using the WWW in my classroom

Hi! My 7th and 8th-grade students and I were fortunate to work in a classroom with 15 Macintosh computers and a teaching workstation all connected to the Internet via an ISDN line, which means we have fast access. We used Netscape Navigator for our browser.

Using the web for research requires navigation skills. When we first started, the search engines weren't as easy to use as they are now, nor were the resources available to the degree they are currently. Nevertheless, even at this date, I still find that students of this age tend to become easily frustrated. Many have not developed skills for selecting likely sites from a long list. They are not patient readers. Or, they get distracted by something that looks intriguing, but is off topic.

Because of this response to my early web projects, I tried to steer students first to a page I've created which contains links to sites that will most likely be useful. In the spring I involved the students in a research project on an animal of their choice. They were required to search multiple resources, including the Internet, for information. The page I created for this assignment (the first one I ever made!) is located at http:// www.chicojr.chico.k12.ca.us/staff/gray/animals.html

Since its original creation, students and contacts from all over the world have contributed links to this collection. 8th grade students studying the weather were involved in multiple web-based activities this last year. Our most successful was one involving lessons and resources located at: http://athena.wednet.edu/curric/weather/index.html

This site contains directions for activities as well as the links to up-to-date weather maps for collecting data about current conditions. The project we focused on required the students to choose 3 cities, read and chart the weather for those cities over a period of a week or two. Then they researched the topology of the surrounding areas, drew in the nearby land forms and water bodies on their maps, and tried to figure out what caused the weather patterns or changes. As students worked through this project, I moved from group to group asking, "What are you learning from this project?" Most responded that while they had learned to read weather maps, they were learning much more about how to use the Internet. That surprised me, but reinforces the idea that using a tool like the web outside of a content area or disassociated from real work—like just having kids browse through "fun" sites—is not as powerful as using it to get what they need for a complex project.

This year I am directing ED's Oasis (http://www.EDsOasis.org), a site that seeks to support teachers new to the Internet. Be certain to pay us a visit and say hello. Good luck with your own Internet experiences!

Terrie Gray
Director, ED's Oasis
Former Science Teacher, Chico Jr. High School Chico, California
tgray@pepperdine.edu http://www.EDsOasis.org

Where you will find education treasures, share effective strategies, and build community . . .

We will explain how to take each of these actions and make your classroom browser a little less commercial.

The homepage designated by Microsoft to appear when you first launch Internet Explorer contains many commercial links. As a result, we believe it is more appropriate to designate a home page on the WWW related to current work in your classroom, your classroom home page, or your school's home page. You will recall the strategy for designating your home page location: click on the "Preferences" button in your toolbar, and then select "Home/ Search." (With Windows systems, changing preferences may be accomplished by choosing "Internet Options" from the Tools menu.) Type in the address for the page on the Internet you wish to appear when you first launch Internet Explorer and you should be all set. For suggestions, see some of the best central sites listed in Figure 2-18.

Netscape Navigator: A Powerful Internet Browser

If you are reading this section, we will assume you have selected Netscape Communicator on your computer and your computer is connected to the Internet. Communicator is a suite of several programs that work together. Navigator is the web browser and Composer is the tool used to develop web pages. Communicator also includes an integrated e-mail package called Messenger.

Figure 2-12 and Figure 2-13 shows the Welcome page for Netscape Navigator. Something like this will appear when you first start this program.

Figure 2-12.
The Welcome page for Netscape Navigator, a WWW browser (http:// my.netscape.com/home/ su_setup.html) if you use a Macintosh system.

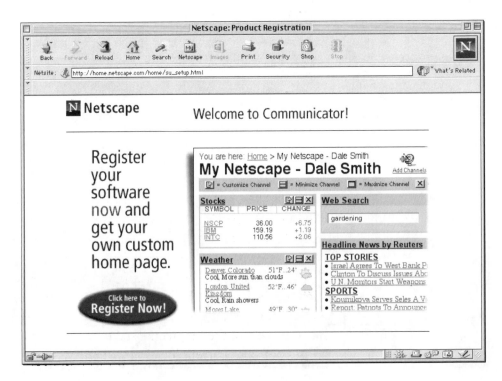

Figure 2-13.
The Welcome page for Netscape
Navigator (Communicator), a WWW
browser (http://home.netscape.com/
home/su_setup.html) if you use a
Windows system.

If you have not loaded Communicator onto your computer or you do not know how to obtain Internet access, seek the assistance of a person at your school who can provide technical support. In many schools, this may be a colleague in the room next door who is already connected and beginning to explore the Internet. Sometimes you will be fortunate and have a technology specialist to assist you.

Launch Netscape Navigator by double clicking the icon for this program on your computer or follow along by using the illustrations in this chapter.

A Quick Orientation

At the top of Figure 2-12 and 2-13, you see a title bar with the words: "Product Registration: Netscape". The label on this bar will change as you navigate through the Internet. It will always tell you the title of the page on the WWW you are looking at. Right now, it indicates you are looking at the "Product Registration: Netscape" page.

Beneath the title bar you will see a toolbar, a row of objects with labels underneath each object. Items in the toolbar let you do things with your browser. The toolbar includes items such as "Back", "Forward", "Reload", "Home", "Search", "Netscape," "Images", "Print", "Security", "Shop," and "Stop". We will explain each below.

Beneath the toolbar is the address window. In this white window, you will see the address for your current location on the Internet. The location showing in Figure 2-12 and Figure 2-13 (http://home.netscape.com) is the address for Netscape's "Welcome" page. There is no need to know the technical aspects of the language used to mark locations now. Just note that the address of your current location will appear here.

Now, look at the viewing window containing the Welcome Page just below this final row of buttons. Note how some words are underlined and written in a distinctive color (usually blue). Words that are underlined and/or marked in a distinctive color signal a key navigational feature on the WWW, a hypertext link. If you single click on an underlined or specially colored word with your mouse, a hypertext link will take you to the site on the Internet linked to that item(s). The same is true for many of the pictures and graphic elements you find on the Internet. If you are at your computer, try clicking (only once) on a hypertext link and notice how a new screen appears with information related to the word(s) or picture you selected. Also note the new address in the address window. You are now at this new location on the Internet and this location probably contains several more hypertext links. You could keep clicking on hypertext links and travel to different locations throughout the Internet, seemingly forever.

The Toolbar

Now, let's take a closer look at items in the toolbar as seen in Figure 2-14. These tools allow you to do things as you navigate through the WWW. The first button, **Back**, allows you to move back one location from where you are currently. This is only active after you move to a location beyond the first page, the Netscape Welcome Page. If you haven't already tried moving to another location by clicking on a colored hypertext link, do this now. Then, try clicking on the Back button on the toolbar and notice how you return back to the previous location. Hold down the Back button for a second and you will notice that previous locations are listed in a new window. You can go to any of these locations simply by selecting it.

The first button, Back, allows you to move back one location from where you are currently.

Figure 2-14.
The Toolbar for Navigator.

The next button, **Forward**, moves you forward one location in your travels through the Internet. Note this is only active if you have moved back at least one location and can really move forward to places you have visited. Try using the Back and Forward buttons. You may also wish to try using the hypertext links at some of these pages. As you navigate, note the changes in your current location in the address window.

The next button, **Reload**, is helpful when you are having problems accessing a popular location on the WWW because everyone else wants to get there, too. When this happens, you will receive a message that says Netscape was unable to connect to your desired location. Press Reload and try again. Sometimes, a screen will not transmit completely to your computer for one reason or another. Press Reload when this happens and you should receive a complete screen. Reload also works well for locations that are regularly updated, such as newspapers. To receive a completely fresh version of news

Sometimes, a screen will not transmit completely to your computer for one reason or another. Press Reload when this happens and you should receive a complete screen.

screens that are regularly updated, just hold the Shift key down while you press reload.

Home is the next button on the toolbar. This button always takes you back to the location you have designated as the first one to show in your viewing window. Right now, this has been designated as the Welcome to Netscape page. Your home location is an important feature. You may designate another location, such as a content site central to an instructional unit, as your home location. This is what Joe Montero did to save time in a busy classroom and to avoid the commercially motivated links at the Netscape home page. More on this later.

Often we need to search the Internet for very specific information. The button **Search** will take you to a location with "search engines", computers on the Internet that search for sites containing words or phrases you specify. Are you looking for information about origami for next week's unit on Japan? Click on the Search button and the search engine window will appear. Click in the white, keyword window and then type in the word "origami". Press return (or click the Search, Find, or "Go get it!" button next to "origami") and a list of sites on the WWW will appear, each with information about origami. Often, they will also contain short descriptions of the contents at each location.

You may find a great location, **Joseph Wu's Origami Page** (http://www.origami.vancouver.bc.ca), with directions for creating many wonderful paper objects as well as information about this Japanese art form. To go to this site, or any other location the search engine found, just click on the appropriate hypertext link. If you do not find this location from your search, you may need to do a more precise search. Type "Joseph Wu's Origami Page" in the search engine's keyword box and do another search. When you find this location, pay a visit. It is an amazing location if you are interested in this art from Japan.

After clicking the **Net Search** button you will notice there are many different search engines available at this location: Netscape, Excite, GoTo.com, HotBot, Lycos, and others. Each searches in a slightly different fashion. If you develop a preference for one, just click on the hypertext link to the search engine you prefer. We will explore search engines a bit later. For now, just play around a bit with one of the search engines and notice the types of features you will find.

The **Welcome** button takes you to the home page (http://my.netscape.com/). At this location you can set up a personalized home page.

Images is a button to open up images that have been turned off. Why would you turn images off? Sometimes teachers will turn off images in order to speed up the transmission of text information. To see the pictures on any page when they have been turned off, simply press the Images button and the graphic images will appear after a short time.

Print does pretty much what it says. You may print out pages on the Internet that appear in your viewing window with this button. This is often

---

The button Search will take you to a location with "search engines", computers on the Internet that search for sites containing words or phrases you specify.

You may find a great location, Joseph Wu's Origami Page (http://www.origami.vancouver.bc.ca), with directions for creating many wonderful paper objects as well as information about this Japanese art form.

Sometimes teachers will turn off images in order to speed up the transmission of text information.

Internet FAQ	
How do I turn off images to speed up the transmission of information?	You may turn images off by selecting the Edit menu (with both Windows and Macintosh systems) and selecting "Preferences". Click on the item "Advanced" and then uncheck the box, "Automatically load images and other data types." This will turn off images. Recheck the box in your preferences or options window if you wish to turn images back on.

helpful in scavenger hunts when students need evidence they have found a location you specified. It also comes in handy in other situations as well. Need a lesson plan for tomorrow? Find a nice collection at **AskERIC Lesson Plans** (http://ericir.syr.edu/Virtual/Lessons) and print out ones that meet your needs.

You will also see a button on your toolbar called **Security**. Go ahead and click on this button, opening the security window. You will see a number of options here. Basically, this area allows you to set up Navigator to send and receive confidential information so others may not see it. While this is becoming increasingly important for businesses, the security area is probably one you will not immediately use in your classroom.

The **Shop** button takes you to commercial sites. We suggest you develop a rule in your classroom never to use this button. We wish we could eliminate it.

Stop will abort any transmission to your computer that is in progress. This is helpful when it is taking too long to get into a web site; sometimes too many people want to go to the same place at once. If you don't wish to keep waiting to connect to a web location, press Stop. Then move on to another location. Come back in a few minutes and the line may be open.

> Sometimes too many people want to go to the same place at once. If you don't wish to keep waiting to connect to a web location, press "Stop".

Address Window

Your current location on the Internet is indicated in the address window. This contains the "Uniform Resource Locator" (URL), or address, of the site that appears in the viewing window. Note, for example, the URL for **The Quill Society** (http://www.quill.net) in Figure 2-15, one of the finest locations for students 12 years old and older who are serious about their writing.

Figure 2-15.
The address window, showing the address on the Internet for The Quill Society, an outstanding resource for high school English classes.

You may use the address window to travel to any location on the Internet, as long as you know its address. Perhaps, for example, you were reading an article and you came across the web site called **Franklin D. Roosevelt Library and Digital.** The article listed the URL, or address: http://www.fdrlibrary.marist.edu/index.html. You want to review this resource for your upcoming unit on presidents. How do you visit the site? Simply highlight the current address in the address window with your mouse, type in the new address, and press Return. This will open any location on the WWW as long as you know the address in advance. Be careful though! The address must be typed exactly as you find it. A missing period or even the wrong case for a letter (e.g., upper case instead of lower case) will give you an error message. If this happens, go back to double check the URL, making certain you have typed it in correctly.

Internet FAQ	
Why does my computer sometimes "freeze" when students are using Netscape Navigator or Internet Explorer? The computer won't respond to commands or the cursor is stuck in one position.	There are several possibilities when something like this happens. There may be a conflict between different software programs on your computer, for example. This type of problem will usually require technical assistance to resolve. Often, however, we have found a simple cause to the problem: students freeze the cursor because they click the mouse too often and too quickly, trying to get something to happen on the screen, without allowing Netscape Navigator or Internet Explorer a chance to keep up with their commands. Students are used to the double-click techniques and rapid response typical of most computers. Navigator and Internet Explorer usually require only a single click to activate a hypertext link. When students use double-click strategies and click quickly on multiple items, it sometimes causes the computer to "freeze" as the computer they are trying to reach on the Internet, say in Australia, can't keep up. We have found it is important to explain this to students, reminding them to only click once on a hypertext link and encouraging them to wait until it says "Done" at the bottom of the browser window before clicking on a new item.

Using Bookmarks: An Important Navigation Aid for Your Class

Navigator uses bookmarks to assist you and your students as you navigate the Internet. The menu item, Bookmarks, allows you to set a bookmark when you are at a useful location on the WWW. At a later time, you can use this bookmark to quickly return to your location.

If you are at your computer and Netscape Navigator is running, look at the top of your screen on the menu bar. With a Macintosh you will find a menu item called "Bookmarks;" on a Windows machine, this will be inside the menu item, "Communicator." If you open this menu item with your mouse, you will see several choices. Selecting "Add Bookmark" will set a bookmark for your current location. The bookmark will be listed inside the Bookmarks menu item at the top of your screen. At a later time, if you wish to return to this location on the Internet all you need to do is to click on this menu item and select the location where you wish to return.

Bookmarks are useful in a classroom. During a unit, you may set bookmarks for sites you wish students to visit and use in their studies. This saves time finding resources and also limits the possibility of extensive "surfing" to sites you do not wish students to visit. Simply make a rule that students may only visit sites where you have set a bookmark or sites that are no more than a few links away.

You may manage the organization of your bookmarks by creating folders for different curriculum projects and placing your bookmarks in the appropriate folder.

You may manage the organization of your bookmarks by creating folders for different curriculum projects and placing your bookmarks in the appropriate folder. How do you do this? First, select the Bookmark menu item and then choose "Edit Bookmarks." A window will open similar to the window in Figure 2-16 listing all of your bookmark folders. You may do a number of things once this window is open. You may create a new folder for a unit by selecting File in the Menu Bar and then choosing New Folder. You may delete a bookmark by selecting it and pressing the delete key or selecting Clear in the Edit menu. You may also move bookmarks around in the list in your bookmark window by dragging them with your mouse and dropping them to another location in your list. Other features and functions may be explored on your own by looking at each of the menu items at the top of your screen when you have the Bookmarks window open. When you finish, close the Bookmarks window.

Figure 2-16.
The Bookmark window in Netscape Navigator.

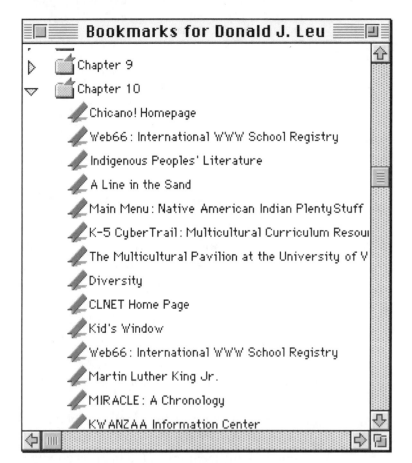

Bookmarks for Donald J. Leu

▷ 📁 Chapter 9
▽ 📁 Chapter 10
  Chicano! Homepage
  Web66: International WWW School Registry
  Indigenous Peoples' Literature
  A Line in the Sand
  Main Menu: Native American Indian Plenty Stuff
  K-5 CyberTrail: Multicultural Curriculum Resour
  The Multicultural Pavilion at the University of V
  Diversity
  CLNET Home Page
  Kid's Window
  Web66: International WWW School Registry
  Martin Luther King Jr.
  MIRACLE: A Chronology
  KWANZAA Information Center

TEACHING TIP

It is often very useful at the beginning of the year to have a workshop session devoted to the use of bookmarks (favorites with Internet Explorer). At one session, share information about how bookmarks/favorites work. Then, encourage students to try out some of the additional features described there. At the next workshop session have students share what they have discovered. Teachers in older grades with a single classroom computer, will develop a separate bookmark folder for each student in the classroom.

Designating a Home Page Location

It is important to designate a home page location on your classroom computer related to content your class is studying. A home page location is the page that shows up first on your screen each time students connect to the Internet with Netscape Navigator. As Joe Montero discovered, this saves time in a busy classroom; students begin immediately with the site you want them to visit first. To change the home page location from Netscape's Home Page, go to the menu item "Edit" and select "Preferences". In the left column of this window, select the item labeled "Navigator." A window similar to that in Figure 2-17 will appear.

In the middle of this window, type in the Internet address you wish to designate as your home page location or click the "Current Page" button. In this example, Joe Montero has designated the site called **NASA for Kids** (http://www.nasa.gov/kids.htm) as the home page location.

Also note several other options in the "General Preferences" window in Figure 2-17. Selecting any of the items at the left will take you to windows where you may set preferences for other items: Appearance, Mail & Groups, Composer, Fonts, Roaming Access, Offline, and Advanced.

A home page location is the page that shows up first on your screen each time students connect to the Internet with Netscape Navigator.

Figure 2-17.
Open the Preferences window and set the Home page location in Netscape Navigator. This saves time and helps your students begin their work at a useful location.

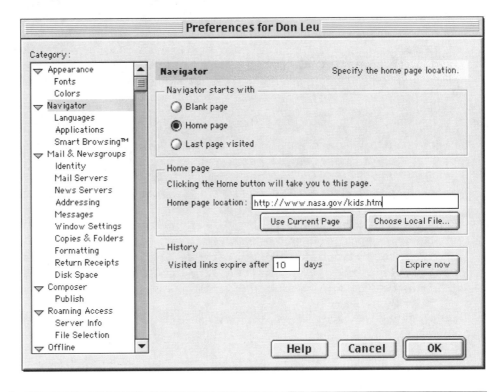

TEACHING TIP

A useful preference setting in Netscape Navigator is located in the "Appearance" window. If you wish to save a bit of space on your screen, select the button "Show Toolbar as Text Only ". This will eliminate the pictures in the tool bar, take up less room on your screen, and display more information in the viewing window. Often this is helpful with the smaller monitors purchased for classrooms; every bit of extra space in the main window helps your students to see more information without having to scroll down the window.

E-MAIL FOR YOU

To: Colleagues
From: Ruth Musgrave (whaletimes@whaletimes.org)
Subject: Developing Navigation Skills

Hi! My first bit of advice is, "Play, play, play and play some more, on the Internet first before you do anything." If you're "playing" you'll relax, take all sorts of twists and turns, and find many exciting sites.

Try the various search engines like Yahoo, Lycos. . . . etc. You'll find that the search engines vary in style and content. Our favorite is "AltaVista"; we've found it to be by far the most comprehensive search engine available. Using key words or phrases you can find just about anything.

Now you're ready to allow your students access. Be certain to allow your students time to play, too. If you feel you need to structure the "play" (due to time limitations or other concerns), create a scavenger hunt that encourages students to use the various search engines. Take them all over the world (with a tie-in to geographic studies by pairing with a world map). Have them find locations like **The White House for Kids** (http://www.whitehouse.gov/WH/kids/html/kidshome.html), **USA TODAY** (http://www.usatoday.com), or visit a computer in France and take a tour of the Louvre at the **Virtual Tour of the Louvre** (http://www.smartweb.fr/louvre/globale.htm). Once they're comfortable traveling via the computer they can begin to use it effectively.

The biggest challenge is to allow students room to explore without allowing too much freedom. The Internet is this amazing open world. Scientists, authors, and artists . . . from all over the world allow students to send them questions directly—the minute they think of it. Because of this freedom, we also suggest you teach your students Internet etiquette (sometimes students take advantage of the anonymity of the computer). Scientists and others who provide e-mail addresses or forms will answer student's letters, but become disenchanted when they begin to receive silly or inappropriate notes. You may want to visit one of the sites on the web that discuss Internet etiquette like **The Net: User Guidelines and Netiquette** (http://www.fau.edu/rinaldi/net/index.htm). Good luck and enjoy this wonderful tool for classrooms!

Ruth Musgrave, Director
WhaleTimes SeaBed
www.whaletimes.org
whaletimes@whaletimes.org

TEACHING TIP

How do I know when I see a good web site for my classroom? The answer is not always obvious. Visit the two locations below to see how to evaluate web sites. The first is for teachers and parents. It is from the American Library Association and describes the set of criteria used at their web site. The second has great ideas for web site evaluation and activities for your students to help them develop these important critical thinking skills.

Selection Criteria—http://www.ala.org/parentspage/greatsites/criteria.html
ICYouSee: T is for Thinking —http://www.ithaca.edu/library/Training/hott.html

Multimedia Tools for Your Computer: Using All of the Resources on the Internet

OK. You are all set. Your computer is connected to the Internet with Netscape Navigator or Internet Explorer, you have figured out the essentials for navigating around the world and visited the **Galileo Project** at Rice University (http://es.rice.edu/ES/humsoc/Galileo) to discover a vast amount of historical material about this famous scientist. You have also found **Poetry HiFi** (http://www.poetryhifi.com) to hear modern poets read their work and discovered the nature of a poetry "slam." Increasing numbers of great resources like these are available on the Internet. At some locations, the pages even contain audio and video, in addition to graphics. Sometimes, these came through and sometimes they didn't. Why?

First, a little background. Each location on the Internet may require slightly different tools to read its graphics, audio, and video information. Netscape Navigator and Internet Explorer have plug-ins and helper tools that let you read many items. Often, though, you reach a site where the person wasn't very thoughtful and used a multimedia tool you do not have. As a result, you discover you can not hear the audio or view the video or graphic without adding the appropriate tool to Netscape Navigator or Internet Explorer.

When this happens, a message will usually appear directing you to extend your capabilities by adding a new plug-in tool to your plug-in file. You may be directed to a central location for plug-in programs and be encouraged to download the appropriate program. Go ahead and follow these directions, restart your computer, and visit the multimedia site you had located earlier. You should then be able to view, read, or listen to the appropriate multimedia element.

Developing Acceptable Use Policies

Because the Internet is so powerful it has the potential for accomplishing wonderful things in the classroom. At the same time, however, this power may be abused. Students may travel to sites that are inappropriate for them to view, they may send out an offensive e-mail message, or they may interfere with the running of a computer system.

Because the Internet is so powerful it has the potential for accomplishing wonderful things in the classroom. At the same time, however, this power may be abused.

Internet FAQ	
I have heard that some Internet sites collect information about me. Can I prevent this?	Some sites on the WWW collect information about you with what are called "cookies." Cookies are requests for information from web site administrators who may record and request information about you whenever you visit their site. Sometimes this is information they collect to direct you to locations you visit most often. Sometimes web sites gather information about you for statistical purposes in order to determine how many people visit their site.
	Internet Explorer and Netscape Navigator may be set to warn you when a cookie is being requested. Here are the directions for Internet Explorer:
	Select Preferences from your tool bar and then select "Cookies" under "Receiving Files." A window will appear showing all the cookies that have been set. You may remove any you wish. You may also set your preferences for when you receive cookies. Select from the options at the bottom of this window "Never ask," "Ask for each site," "Ask for each cookie," and "Never accept."
	Here are the directions for Netscape Navigator:
	Select Preferences from Edit in the menu bar. Then select Advanced from the bottom of the list on the left of the Preferences window. You will see an option for setting cookies at the bottom. Select the cookie setting you prefer.

To respond to the viewing of inappropriate sites, some schools use software filters that deny students access to certain Internet sites, especially in the younger grades. These filters deny access to locations where certain words appear.

To respond to the viewing of inappropriate sites, some schools use software filters that deny students access to certain Internet sites, especially in the younger grades. These filters deny access to locations where certain words appear. Teachers and parents may edit the list of words used in the blocking software. You may find out more about these software programs and download evaluation copies for free at the following commercial locations:

Cyber Patrol—http://www.cyberpatrol.com

Net Nanny—http://www.netnanny.com

SurfWatch—http://www.surfwatch.com

Whether your system uses a software filter or not, it is important for your district to develop an acceptable use policy as part of a comprehensive program of Internet navigation.

Whether your system uses a software filter or not, it is important for your district to develop an acceptable use policy as part of a comprehensive program of Internet navigation. An acceptable use policy is a written agreement signed by parents/guardians, students, and teachers which specifies the conditions under which students may use the Internet, defines appropriate and unacceptable use, and defines penalties for violating items in the policy. Parents/guardians, teachers, and students all need to be aware of the consequences for misusing the privilege of Internet access. Developing an acceptable use policy and then asking all parties to sign it helps to ensure that everyone understands these important issues.

What does an acceptable use policy look like? Most contain the following elements:

- *An explanation of the Internet and its role in providing information resources to students.* It is important to explain to parents/guardians and students why the Internet is important to include in the curriculum. It is also important to explain that students will be taught proper use of the Internet.

- *A description of acceptable and unacceptable behavior which emphasizes student responsibility when using the Internet.* It is important to supervise student use of the Internet but ultimately each student must take responsibility for his or her own actions. This section describes what is appropriate and inappropriate behavior.

- *A list of penalties for each violation of the policy.* Often this will describe increasing levels of penalties: a warning letter to parents/guardians for a first violation and a suspension of privileges for a repeated violation. A panel may sometimes be established to review cases.

- *A space for all parties to sign the agreement.* After discussing each element carefully with students, the form is usually sent home for parents and students to sign.

Teachers will also sign this form before it is carefully filed in an appropriate location. You may find out more information, print out sample acceptable use policies, and read about other teachers' experiences by visiting the following Internet sites:

Houston Independent School District's Acceptable Use Page—
http://chico.rice.edu/armadillo/acceptable.html

Acceptable Use Policies—http://www.erehwon.com/k12aup

Child Safety on the Information Highway—
http://www.safekids.com/index.html

Global School Network's Guidelines and Policies for Protecting Students—
http://www.gsn.org/web/webproj/define/protect/aup.htm

Internet FAQ	
It takes a long time to repeatedly click the Back button when I need to go back more than one or two locations. Is there a faster way to go back to a site I visited a while ago?	Sure! There are two ways. First, click and hold down the back button or find the "Go" menu item and then click and hold this down. In both cases, you will see a list of sites you have already visited since you launched your browser. Just highlight a location you wish to return to and you will go there immediately. Internet Explorer will even show you a list of places you have visited many days ago, a nice feature.

E-MAIL FOR YOU

To: Colleagues
From: Maggie Hos-McGrane <mhos-mcgrane@isa.nl>
Subject: Collaboration

Hi!

I teach at the International School of Amsterdam (http://www.isa.nl/main_site/~root/index.html). When I began using the Internet three and a half years ago, I had no idea that it would become the centre of my teaching. At that time I had no link to the Internet at school, but was fortunate to work with a wonderful colleague, Linda Swanson, who encouraged both myself and the students to learn about publishing on the world wide web.

Our first published projects were the students' grandparents' stories which tied in with our topic on origins. At this stage we had no graphics, but later when we got hold of a digital camera we started taking photos of the students and models they had made to go with their writing. However as we still couldn't visit the site at school we had to download the pages students had created onto disks so they could view them off-line.

Shortly after our first projects were published, Linda moved back to California. By this time we were so enthusiastic that we agreed to continue our collaboration via e-mail. During the last 3 years, although Linda and I have only met each other twice, we've communicated (almost daily) by e-mail to develop the site.

Once I had Internet access in my classroom the computer became one of my major tools for research. Linda found sites for the students to use and created web pages with links to the sites. As I've moved into teaching younger children the site has also grown in scope, to include not just social studies projects but also math and language arts activities. This year I've taught science for the first time, and my only question was "What science projects can we work on now using the Internet?"

This year has also been the first year that I decided to publish an on-line newsletter for my students and parents. The site is updated weekly and contains photos of what the students have been doing that week, details of current projects, an overview of the work covered in the various subjects, a homework timetable for the week and information about upcoming events.

It has been wonderful to become a "student" again to learn something new and I'm constantly amazed at how my whole style of teaching has changed. It has been a tremendous effort, but certainly very worthwhile. Come visit the work Linda Swanson, my students, and I have done at our home page: http://www.xs4all.nl/~swanson/origins/intro.html We would love to hear from you!

Maggie Hos-McGrane
Grade 5 Teacher

Instructional Strategies for Developing Navigation Skills

Learning to navigate on the Internet is important for our students. Finding information quickly and then using it appropriately will be central to their futures. We see the reality of this statement in many ways. One of the most visible is the rapid appearance of national web sites for educators. Nations around the world are taking bold policy initiatives to prepare their children for the future. While each country is responding to the educational challenges of global competition in a distinctive fashion, many nations are developing Internet locations to support the important work teachers do to prepare children for Internet use:

> **EdNA** (Australia)—http://www.edna.edu.au/EdNA

> **ScoilNet** (Ireland)—http://www.scoilnet.ie/homeframe.asp

> **The National Grid for Learning** (UK)—http://www.ngfl.gov.uk/ngfl/index.html

> **SchoolNet** (Canada)—http://www.schoolnet.ca/home/

> **Te Kete Ipurangi** (New Zealand)—http://www.tki.org.nz

How do we begin to teach our students navigation skills? If you are just starting to use the Internet in your classroom and only have a single computer linked to the Internet, begin each week with short, small group instruction at the computer on an important navigational strategy such as one of the following:

- The use of search engines
- How to use directories
- Printing strategies
- How to use graphic elements from the WWW in your writing projects
- Using the address window to type in a new address
- Using the "Go" menu item
- Helping others effectively

Nations around the world are taking bold policy initiatives to prepare their children for their future.

If you are just starting to use the Internet in your classroom and only have a single computer linked to the Internet, begin each week with short, small group instruction at the computer on an important navigational strategy.

- Understanding the meaning of addresses on the Internet
- Strategies for staying on task

During this time, show five to six students a new aspect to navigating the Internet. Introduce the strategy, show students why it is useful and when it might be used, and then give one or two students an opportunity to practice it while others watch. As you move through the year, you may wish to turn this responsibility over to the groups themselves. Each week, make a different group responsible for teaching the other groups a new skill they have discovered recently.

During the week, students can integrate the new strategy as they complete content work in one of the subject areas or on a thematic unit. While some schools may have sufficient computer resources to allow students to work alone on the Internet during the week, it is often preferable to have students work together in pairs since this provides more teaching/learning opportunities. Seldom do two students know the same navigation strategies for using the Internet. When students work together, they exchange information and teach each other navigation skills. Rotating partners each week or so ensures that all students have a chance to learn from every other student in the class. This increases opportunities for sharing information about navigation strategies.

At the end of each week, an Internet Workshop will help to consolidate the navigation strategies you introduced at the beginning of the week. It will also raise new navigation issues that you may then explore in subsequent weeks, again in small groups at the beginning of the week, in pairs during the week, and with the whole class at the end of the week.

It is important to note that time used to develop Internet strategies need not be great. Small group sessions at the beginning of the week should take no more than 5-10 minutes. The learning that takes place as students work in pairs occurs during regular content learning experiences; this also takes little time. Finally, Internet Workshops need not take more than 15-20 minutes as you share navigational experiences and raise questions that came up during the week. You will find that time devoted to developing navigation skills at the beginning of the year pays rich dividends as your students develop confidence and expertise at navigating the Internet on their own.

As your students become more experienced on the Internet, you should think about modifying this initial structure for developing navigation knowledge. Spend a little time observing students working together on the Internet, looking for those students who have not acquired all of the basic navigational strategies. Then, gather these students together in small group sessions at the beginning of each week according to the strategies they need to refine. One group may need additional assistance on using search engines while a second group may need additional assistance on using the address window to go to a known address. This additional small group work ensures that all of your students develop the essential skills of navigation. It probably won't

> At the end of each week, an Internet Workshop will help to consolidate the navigation strategies you introduced at the beginning of the week.

> It is important to note that time used to develop Internet strategies need not be great.

Within a short period of time your students will have all of the basic navigation strategies in place.

take more than a week or two to accomplish this. During this time, students may continue to work in pairs on classroom assignments, helping one another. Within a short period of time your students will have all of the basic navigation strategies in place. When this happens, new strategies may be successfully handled during content projects using Internet Workshop, with the entire class sharing ideas they have discovered.

As students develop the ability to navigate on their own you will find yourself devoting less time to this area and more time on content projects. Questions during Internet Workshop, for example, will gradually and naturally move from navigation issues to useful content locations that students have discovered on the Internet for classroom work. As you move through the year, you will find less and less time devoted to navigation and more and more time devoted to useful information students have discovered on the Internet.

Internet FAQ
When I try to go to a location on the WWW it sometimes gives me a message that the server is not responding. What should I do?	The server (computer) where this web page is located may be down for servicing, someone may have turned it off, or too may people may be trying to get in at once. Our strategy in these cases is to try a location three times; often you can sneak in, even if it is very busy. If this fails, try again at a later time, especially if it sounds like a good site.

Search Engine and Other Research Strategies: Saving Time in Busy Classrooms

The three most important things in Internet use are time, time, and time.

As the saying goes, the three most important things in Internet use are time, time, and time. We hear this concern expressed in several ways:

- How do I find the time to learn about the Internet?

- How do I find the time to teach the Internet in addition to everything else?

- How do I quickly locate good sites on the Internet?

Often, our students will teach us as much about navigation as we will teach them. This is the one of the new realities of life with the Internet.

The answer to the first question is one each of us must determine in our own way. Clearly, you are taking time out of your busy schedule to learn about the Internet as you read this book. It is important to recognize, though, that we can not possibly keep up with all the changes taking place by ourselves. We need to organize our classrooms to take advantage of opportunities for each of us to learn from one another. By making Internet Workshop a part of your instructional program, you can help everyone in your class learn from one another. Often, our students will teach us as much about navigation as we will teach them. This is the one of the new realities of life with the Internet. In Chapter 4, we will show you how to use Internet Workshop along with several other strategies to help you learn together with your students.

The second question is also important: How do I find the time to teach the Internet in addition to everything else? The answer to this is to be certain you make the Internet a resource, not a subject. The Internet is just a tool that provides you and your students with information resources. It is no more and no less than a book, a library, an encyclopedia, or a video. The Internet should not become a permanent, separate subject for your students. Except for initial instruction at the beginning, the Internet should not require extra instructional time during the day. Even Internet Workshop should be seen as a time to learn about subject areas, not a time to focus exclusively on the Internet, especially after students develop beginning navigation skills.

The third question is important, too: How do I quickly locate good sites on the Internet? We need to learn to become efficient in finding useful resources on the Internet. There are two types of strategies that should assist you in this area: central site strategies and search engine strategies.

Locating Information With a Central Site Strategy

As you begin your journey with the Internet, consider using a central site strategy. A central site is a location on the Internet with extensive and well-organized links about a content area or important subject. Some people may refer to these as "portals" since they are entryways to rich sources of information. Most are located at stable sites that will not quickly change. Most are not commercial sites. As you explore the Internet, you will discover these well-organized treasure troves of information. They will become homes to which you will often return. We take this approach in this book. Each of the content area chapters will share the best central sites we have found. Set a bookmark or a favorites marker and begin your explorations at these central locations. This will save you much time and frustration until you develop effective strategies for using search engines. In fact, you could use only central sites and find everything you require for your class.

We have found the locations in Figure 2-18 to be the most useful central site locations for different subject areas. You may wish to visit some of these now and set a bookmark (favorites) for those you find useful. We will discuss each in upcoming chapters.

The Internet is just a tool that provides you and your students with information resources. It is no more and no less than a book, a library, an encyclopedia, or a video. The Internet should not become a permanent, separate subject for your students.

As you begin your journey with the Internet, consider using a central site strategy.

TEACHING TIP

Set bookmarks for each of the central sites listed in Figure 2-18 right now. This will save you important time when you, or your students, are looking for good resources in a content area. You might also wish to designate one of these sites as your home page location. You will recall that your home page location is the first screen to appear each time you launch your Internet browser. With most browsers, this can be set from your preferences window. See the earlier discussions for Navigator or Internet Explorer to see how this may be done with either a Windows or a Macintosh system.

Figure 2-18.
Central sites on the Internet for teaching and learning.

Area	Central Internet Sites
Science (general)	**Eisenhower National Clearinghouse: Action** (http://www.enc.org:80/classroom/index.htm) **Science Learning Network** (http://www.sln.org/index.html)
Math (general)	**Eisenhower National Clearinghouse: Action** (http://www.enc.org:80/classroom/index.htm) **The Math Forum** (http://forum.swarthmore.edu/)
Social Studies (general)	**History/Social Studies Web Site for K-12 Teachers** (http://www.execpc.com/~dboals/boals.html) **Nebraska Department of Education Social Science Resources HomePage** (http://www.nde.state.ne.us/SS/ss.html)
Literature (all ages)	**Children's Literature Web Guide** (http://www.ucalgary.ca/~dkbrown/index.html)
ESL	**ESL: Study Lab** (http://www.lclark.edu/~krauss/toppicks/toppicks.html)
Multicultural Curriculum	**Cultures of the World** (http://www.ala.org/parentspage/greatsites/people.html#b) **Multicultural Pavilion** (http://curry.edschool.Virginia.EDU:80/go/multicultural/)
African American Culture	**Multi-Cultural Paths: African American Resources** (http://curry.edschool.Virginia.EDU:80/go/multicultural/sites/afr-am.html)
Chicana/o Latina/o Culture	**Latin American Network Information Center** (http://www.lanic.utexas.edu/la/region/k-12/)
Native American Culture	**Native American Indian Resources** (http://indy4.fdl.cc.mn.us/~isk/mainmenu.html)
Special Education	**Family Village** (http://www.familyvillage.wisc.edu/)

Locating Information With a Search Engine Strategy

Each search engine seems to have its own style, its own strengths, and its own weaknesses.

There are many, many search engines on the Internet to help you find information you require. A search engine locates sites on the Internet containing the key word(s) you enter. Each search engine seems to have its own style, its own strengths, and its own weaknesses. You should become familiar with how each engine searches for information and displays the information it finds. As you use search engines, you will develop a favorite for your work. When this happens, be certain to set a bookmark/favorites so that you can return to this search engine whenever you require it.

For now, it is useful to be able to match one of several search engines with the needs you might have in a search. If, for example, you wish to search a broad topic and gradually narrow down the resources you find, you should begin with the search engine **Yahoo** (http://www.yahoo.com/). Yahoo organizes information hierarchically, providing you a general category as well as a specific site for each match of the key word(s) you entered. This is useful as you explore different broad categories, looking for specific treasures.

Sometimes, though, we know the exact phrase or a very narrow key term we wish to find and we do not wish to explore higher-level categories. Perhaps, for example, you wish to find the home page for the Smithsonian Institution and you know it is called The Smithsonian Institution Home Page. For narrow searches, the best search engines are **AltaVista** (http://www.altavista.digital.com/) or **HotBot** (http://www.hotbot.com/). Be certain to take advantage of some of their advanced search features to refine your search. Each will quickly find your key word if it exists on the Internet.

If you are interested in the quality of sites found by a search engine, you should use either **Magellan** (http://www.mckinley.com/), **Lycos** (http://www.lycos.com/), or **WebCrawler** (http://webcrawler.com/). Each of these search engines reviews sites and ranks them in terms of quality. This is often helpful for busy teachers who are looking for central sites in a particular area.

If you are most interested in reading summaries of sites located in your search, you should probably use **Excite** (http://www.excite.com/). This search engine is known for providing a more limited number of items containing very descriptive summaries of the information at each location. When you find a site that interests you, you can then link to additional locations like the one you found.

TEACHING TIP	Most search engines only search through a small percentage of the resources on the Internet, often as little as 20 percent of the available web pages. This means that you will miss many good resources using a single search engine. To increase the Internet locations evaluated in a search you may wish to use a meta (or mega) search engine. A meta search engine is a search engine that searches multiple search engines and deletes duplicate results. This approach yields a more thorough search. Try these meta search engines:

Ask Jeeves—http://www.askjeeves.com
Dogpile—http://www.dogpile.com
Metacrawler—http://www.metacrawler.com/index.html
MetaFind—http://www.metafind.com
Chubba—http://www.chubba.com

If you use a Macintosh, you could also try a feature called Sherlock. This is also a meta search engine.

A Central Site for Internet Research and Search Engine Use

At the Research (http://www.nueva.pvt.k12.ca.us/~debbie/library/research/research.html) page of the Nueva School Library, Debbie Abilock and Marilyn Kimura have developed an outstanding resource for helping you and your students understand more about effective research and search engine strategies.

These suggestions, though, just provide you with the beginning steps in your journey as you discover effective research and search engine strategies. If you wish to explore this topic more thoroughly, pay a visit to a computer at Nueva School in the San Francisco Bay area. At the **Research** (http://www.nueva.pvt.k12.ca.us/~debbie/library/research/research.html) page of the Nueva School Library, Debbie Abilock and Marilyn Kimura have developed an outstanding resource for helping you and your students understand more about effective research and search engine strategies. Stop by and explore the wonderful work they have accomplished. Drop a note, too, and let these good folks know how useful the work they are doing is for all of us.

Visiting the Classroom: Steve Heffner's 9th Grade English Class in Pennsylvania

Regardless of the grade level or the subject you teach, we can all learn important lessons by exploring the web page for Steve Heffner's 9th grade English class (http://www.pipeline.com/~sheffner/classroom.html).

Regardless of the grade level or the subject you teach, we can all learn important lessons by exploring the web page for Steve Heffner's 9th grade English class (http://www.pipeline.com/~sheffner/classroom.html). Steve teaches at Conrad Weiser High School in Robesonia, PA. His stated goal for this class: "Every student will leave my class a better reader, writer, thinker, and speaker. I strive to foster an atmosphere in which EVERY student can succeed."

Perhaps the most impressive aspect of this location is the comprehensive and integrated manner in which Steve has developed this web page, providing everything for his students to succeed (see Figure 2-19). It is a wonderful model for all of us to follow and one that will be increasingly common for classrooms. Steve provides, for example, a clear description of each of his course requirements along with a description of how grades will be determined. He also has developed a Progress Report section, an on-line data base so that students, with their individual passwords, can obtain a current record of their grades for all class assignments.

In addition, all of the handouts and materials distributed in class are available for students at his class web page. Steve uses Acrobat Reader so that when students open up one of the files for these handouts, they can print out an exact copy of the material. Included in this section is a copy of the letter he sends home to parents, a form for recording books each student has read, portfolio requirements, the requirements for Reading Workshop, a form that must be completed and signed in order to publish any student work on the Internet, a scoring rubric for response journals, and much more. Every assignment is carefully described.

Steve also provides his students with links to many Internet resources for all of their major reading assignments. He has separate sections for each of these authors with links to related resources in each area: Edgar Allan Poe,

Figure 2-19.
The home page for Steve Heffner's 9th grade English class, an exceptional model for any classroom.

Romeo and Juliet, Scott O'Dell, *A Tale of Two Cities, The Chocolate War, The Effect of Gamma Rays on Man-in-the-Moon Marigolds, The Adventures of Tom Sawyer,* as well as links to grammar and composition resources and many other topics covered in his class.

Steve also includes a section where student writing is published. His students select one work of exceptional writing each month to be featured at this location. The work receives a "Golden Pen Award." Take a look at some of this exceptional work. The nicest part of this award is the selection process. Students can nominate their own work which is then reviewed by all of the students in class. This process facilitates critical evaluation of your own writing as well as the writing of others. He includes, in another section, tips from his students on good writing.

This is really an impressive classroom home page. We invite you to take a look. Be certain, too, to drop Steve a note and let him know how much you appreciate his contribution.

Navigation Resources on the Internet

Adam Rosen's Quick Guide to Viewing the World Wide Web—
(http://www.cgicafe.com/~ajrosen/guide.html)
> Have you been working hard trying to figure out how to navigate in the WWW and need of a little humor? Visit this (very) quick guide to viewing the WWW and enjoy the joke. Cute.

Beginners Guide to the Internet—http://www.pbs.org/uti/begin.html
> Developed by NPR, this provides a quick and easy overview of navigating around on the Internet. There is a self-checking quiz, too, to see how you have done.

AskERIC Virtual Library: Educational Questions—
http://ericir.syr.edu/Qa/userform.html
> At this location you may ask any question regarding educational research or practice and receive a personalized response back via e-mail within 48 hours. The "Educational Questions" site is a part of the Educational Resources Information Center (ERIC), a federally-funded national information system. Many other useful resources are also located here. Take advantage of this important resource.

Beginners Central—http://www.northernwebs.com/bc
> This is an outstanding guide to the Internet, especially if you are just starting out. It takes you through everything you need to know to successfully navigate the Internet. This guide is updated regularly, a real bonus. This might also be a useful location to direct your class to at the beginning of the year. Set a bookmark/favorite!

Ed's Oasis—http://www.EDsOasis.org/
> Here is a wonderful location for all teachers who are using the Internet in their classroom. Stop by for a visit with Terrie Gray and her outstanding colleagues whose work supports us all on our journeys. They will show you great ideas about using the Internet in your classroom. E-mail Terrie and let her know what important work she is doing.

Exploring the Internet—http://www.screen.com/start/guide
> If you are just beginning your travels on the Internet, this is a good location to assist you with information about navigation issues. In addition to an easy-to-read style, it includes many useful links to locations that will be helpful as a new user.

From Now On—http://www.fno.org/
> This is a free electronic journal with some of the best ideas on using the Internet and other technologies in the classroom.

Global Connections Online—http://www.nsglobalonline.com/
> This is a free web-based Internet training course designed specifically for K-12 teachers. A great series of tutorials for effectively using the Internet with your students.

Glossary of Internet Terms—http://www.matisse.net/files/glossary.html
> This is an extensive set of Internet terms, precisely defined for your use. A nice resource.

Internet 101—http://www2.famvid.com/i101/internet101.html

Here is a good on-line guide to the Internet we have discovered. It covers everything you need to know. Be certain to visit this location. Set a bookmark/favorite!

Introduction to Communicator—http://help.netscape.com/products/client/communicator/IntroComm/Introcom.html

Here is the official Netscape introduction to your Netscape browser containing all kinds of useful information. Learn new tricks and tips by exploring this document.

K-5 Cyber Trail—http://www.wmht.org/trail/trail.htm

This is a great location to develop navigation skills as you see how other teachers are using the Internet in their classrooms. Developed in the Albany, NY, area it is a wonderful resource for every teacher. Set a bookmark/favorite!

Learn the Net: An Internet Guide and Tutorial—

http://www.learnthenet.com/english/

A comprehensive set of explanations about how the Internet works and how to use the two major browsers.

Net Lingo—http://www.netlingo.com

Here is a great location if you want to find out about all the new vocabulary the Internet is generating. Need to know the meaning of a word you came across. Here is the location for you!

RealNetworks—http://www.realaudio.com/

This is a commercial site but we find it very useful. You can download most versions of their wonderful plug-ins for free. These will allow you to listen to radio stations around the world (see Chapter 12), or receive audio and video from an increasing number of locations on the Internet. This is wonderful technology that everyone should download to their browser. Currently, you only have to pay for the latest version of their software. We hope this continues! The older versions work just fine. Best of all, they are free!

Surf the Web: Web Browsers—http://www.learnthenet.com/english/html/12browser.htm

A quick and to-the-point explanation of the functions in both Netscape navigator and Internet Explorer. This quickly explains each of the major functions in both types of browsers.

Teacher Talk—http://www.mightymedia.com/talk/working.htm

A useful discussion area for teachers to talk about issues of instruction and technology. If you have a question, post it here and you will receive answers from other teachers. You will be asked for your name and a password to enter. Do not use your e-mail password or another password you use on a computer. Use a different one to prevent anyone from accessing your accounts.

The Internet Index—http://www.openmarket.com/intindex

Here you will find a collection of interesting Internet statistics. Interesting reading.

The Librarian's Guide to Cyberspace for Parents and Kids—
> http://www.ala.org/parentspage/greatsites/guide.html
> A wonderful resource for both parents and children containing child safety strategies and information on how to best use the Internet. Send this one home with parents on Back to School Night.

The Net: User Guidelines and Netiquette—
> http://www.fau.edu/rinaldi/net/index.html
> This Internet book provides a useful discussion about socially responsible ways of using the Internet. It provides useful background before developing an acceptable use policy. It is also useful as required reading for older students at the beginning of the year. Included is a list of Ten Commandments for Computer Ethics from the Computer Ethics Institute. This might be printed out and posted next to each computer in your classroom.

Communicating on the Internet: E-Mail, Mailing Lists, and Other Forms of Electronic Communication

 E-MAIL FOR YOU

To: Our readers
From: djleu@syr.edu (Don Leu), ddleu@syr.edu (Debbie Leu)
Subject: The Power of Communication

Not only is the Internet a powerful tool for linking and locating information, but it also links people. In fact, electronic communication is probably the most familiar use of the Net for many people, and it is certainly one of the most popular. Communicating via the Internet is usually cheaper, quicker, and more efficient. It allows us to communicate one-to-one with family, friends, and colleagues both locally and globally. Moreover, it serves as the basis for group communication through mailing lists, newsgroups, and real-time interactions.

This chapter will show how electronic communication lends itself to various purposes through a variety of activities for both teachers and students. For example, teachers can access the expertise and experience of educators around the world while students may conduct peer interviews in another language. At first it may seem as if some Internet activities are no more than renamed older techniques—penpals become keypals, for instance—but take a closer look. Internet versions often expand the scope of traditional lessons and activities while helping students toward more independent learning. Most importantly, electronic communication exposes us to a variety of people and a wide range of views from all over the globe. This has great potential to broaden perspectives and develop critical thinking as students integrate new and diverse ideas with their own experiences.

Using e-mail is not just another way to get information; it is an opportunity to increase our understanding and share our ideas.

Don and Debbie

Internet FAQ	
What exactly are e-mail, mailing lists and newsgroups?	E-mail is electronic mail, messages sent electronically from one computer to another. Special software programs allow any person who has an e-mail address to send and receive messages to any other individual who has an e-mail address. Mailing Lists are a kind of group e-mail in which sending and receiving messages is limited to individuals who are listed as members of a particular group formed to discuss a specific area of interest. Newsgroups are also a kind of group e-mail focused on a specific topic. However, there are no membership lists; anyone can read and reply to messages.

Teaching With the Internet: Marilyn Campbell's Classroom

Marilyn Campbell was especially excited about the upcoming school year. The first major unit for her social studies class was Latin America. She and the other eighth grade teachers were working together so students could study various aspects of Latin American culture in all of their classes. As in the past, Marilyn was searching the Internet for information related to the unit; in addition, she decided to expand her electronic communication skills by exploring a variety of e-mail uses. It was easier than she had expected.

She started by sending an e-mail message to Gary Diaz, the high school Spanish teacher. Although they lived in different towns, e-mail made it easy to communicate. Marilyn didn't have to call at a certain time or leave messages on an answering machine. In addition, she felt more comfortable asking for help since e-mailing wouldn't interrupt Gary's schedule in the way that telephoning might have. Gary sent a reply including some of his favorite sites and also suggested that she check out some keypal sites on the Net.

Marilyn thought international keypals would be great. The students could ask questions, conduct interviews, and maybe exchange photos. They could learn a lot about other cultures. When she did a search for "keypals", Marilyn found several sites. She was pleased to find that not only could her students look for individual keypals, but also she could request a partner class. She did this by subscribing to a mailing list at one of the sites, **Intercultural E-mail Classroom Connections** (http://www.stolaf.edu/network/iecc/ index.html). She then posted an e-mail message introducing herself and her class and asking if there were any teachers from South American countries who might want to partner their class with hers in the fall. It would be convenient to have keypals all from one class and another teacher to share ideas with.

Next, Marilyn sent a message to other teachers on **MIDDLE-L** (listserv@postoffice.cso.uiuc.edu), a mailing list she first discovered and then joined during an in-service for the district. Although she had subscribed to the list for some time, she had never posted a message. She had read many helpful replies to others, however, so she wasn't surprised when she received many e-mail responses over the next few days. Several teachers sent information about Latin American sites and Internet activities that their students had done the previous year. One teacher recommended working on a project with a partner class, and mentioned several project sites. He also gave Marilyn the address for a projects discussion group. Another message suggested checking out newsgroups on related topics. Two teachers mentioned how they had used Internet resources to help their students begin to develop research skills. Another teacher gave information about how she had arranged for her students to e-mail questions to a professor of Japanese history, and suggested that Marilyn might be able to do the same with an expert on some aspect of Latin American culture.

As Marilyn read her e-mail messages, she began thinking about the best way for her class to present their ideas to a partner class in order to make full use of e-mail's capabilities. Just exchanging facts that could easily be found in an encyclopedia wouldn't be very effective. Perhaps she could get two partner classes from different countries. Then, the students could get information on specific topics and compare different viewpoints. They might be able to use the data they collected to do some sort of analysis in math class. In fact, maybe their other teachers could also give specific assignments for the students to complete on the Internet. Marilyn kept notes about the best ideas on index cards so that she could share them with the other eighth-grade teachers in their planning meetings. She would also share ideas with her students once school started in order to get their input before final decisions were made.

In addition to thinking about content, Marilyn had been working with the other teachers to develop a plan to help the students expand their computer skills and manage their time on the computer. Each classroom had only one computer, but this year, students would have their own individual e-mail accounts. This would be a big change from last year when they had sent their messages from their teacher's account. Last year's teacher had kept an electronic folder for each student in his account, so he could easily monitor what was sent and received. Marilyn would need a different system. She didn't want to print out all the students' messages, but she wouldn't have time to read each one as it was sent either. She decided that she and her students should have a discussion about manners on the Net, relating to themselves and their keypals. Perhaps she would do a workshop and include role plays about how they would feel if they received a mean message. It was a good beginning, and Marilyn was looking forward to the new year, but there was still a lot to do.

Lessons From the Classroom

This scenario illustrates several lessons for using electronic communication effectively. First, Marilyn used e-mail, mailing lists and newsgroups to get suggestions on sites, resources, and activities from other teachers. This is

Having e-mail is almost like having access to an individualized in-service program anytime you need it.

one of the most powerful ways for teachers to expand their knowledge and learn from others' experiences. Many lists have hundreds of members, and newsgroups may have thousands of readers; together, their composite expertise covers almost every topic and point of view. Having e-mail is almost like having access to an individualized in-service program anytime you need it.

Second, Marilyn had clear goals and purposes. She didn't see the Internet as an end in itself but as a tool whose use could be incorporated into the district's curriculum and her lessons to help students develop certain skills and meet desired standards. In this case, electronic communication would help increase understanding of other cultures, provide practice in collaborative teamwork, develop critical thinking, and encourage tolerance and respect for others.

Third, her students' ages and previous computer experience played a large role in Marilyn's planning. She planned age-appropriate activities which included student participation in choosing activities. This would expand their e-mail skills and foster better decision-making, both of which would help prepare them to use electronic communication more independently in the future.

By planning activities and projects that involved not only obtaining information, but also analyzing and synthesizing it, Marilyn was helping her students develop their critical thinking skills.

Fourth, by planning activities and projects that involved not only obtaining information, but also analyzing and synthesizing it, Marilyn would help her students develop their critical thinking skills. The new state standards emphasized reading and critical thinking, and e-mail experiences seemed to fit very well into the program her district was developing to help students reach the goals in these areas.

Finally, Marilyn planned lessons on netiquette. As an e-mail user herself, she knew the importance of good Internet manners. With a younger group of students, she would have posted a list of rules. However, because she recognized the eighth graders' developing ability to understand the need for order and safety, she would have them participate in discussions to formulate their own netiquette guidelines.

Getting Started With E-Mail

In order to use electronic communication effectively, it is important to integrate Internet knowledge and skills with your own beliefs and teaching practices. You will want to reflect on which types of communication—individual e-mail, mailing lists, newsgroups, and real-time interactions—fit in with your approach to education, state and national standards, your district's curriculum, and the particular students you teach. If you haven't used e-mail before, allow yourself extra time to practice various functions before trying them out with your students in the classroom. The more proficient you are, the easier it will be to anticipate your students' needs and develop effective teaching and learning strategies.

In the next sections, we provide an overview of electronic communication from a classroom perspective. We will focus on the basics and use as little technical jargon as possible. Our goal is to help you get started, serving as a jumping off point for your own future exploration. We encourage you to work cooperatively with other teachers, and when necessary, to seek help from technical resource people for more detailed information.

We will begin with e-mail, the basis of electronic communication on the Internet. Once you have a computer and Internet access, you need two things to get started: an e-mail account and an e-mail software program. Then, identify yourself to the program, and you are ready to receive and send electronic messages.

Your E-mail Account

The first step is to request an e-mail account from your Internet service provider (ISP), who will then give you an e-mail address and an e-mail password. E-mail addresses follow a standard, three-part format:

userid@host.domain

1. **userid** (pronounced *user I.D.*) is the name or identifying number of the account user.
2. @ is the "at" sign.
3. **host.domain** is the name and location of the computer that handles the user's account and the type of group which hosts the account.

Here is an example: ddleu@mailbox.syr.edu

The last part of the address (.edu) means that the host is an educational institution. Other common categories are: .com for commercial; .gov for government; .org for organization, and .net for network. Some addresses, especially those outside the U.S., are followed by a country code such as .ca for Canada or .au for Australia.

Your e-mail password will be a number, word, or some combination of these. It is known only to you, somewhat like a PIN number for your bank account. Most programs allow you to change your password, but do not choose an easily guessed word or number since your password provides security for your account. For this reason, you should memorize it and keep it secret. We recommend never letting anyone else use your password.

TEACHING TIP	**E-Mail Security in the Classroom** Unless you have your own computer in a secure place, it's a good idea to shut it down, or at least log off your e-mail account, when you leave the terminal. That way, no unauthorized person can read your e-mail files or use your account. If your students will send and receive e-mail through your account rather than have their own individual accounts, it is also a good idea to discuss security and privacy issues with them.

E-mail Software

Your second step is getting an e-mail software program. There are several different programs, so check with your technical resource person for information about which ones are supported by your service provider. We will explain e-mail using examples from Internet Explorer (IE) and Netscape Communicator, two popular browsers available in both Mac and Windows platforms, which include e-mail software. Don't be concerned if you notice some differences between your screen and our examples, or have another version of these browsers. Companies are continually improving their software, which results in small changes between upgrades (version 4.5 vs. 4.7, for example). Even if you have a different version or use a different software program altogether, you should be able to follow or adapt the procedures described in this chapter since most programs perform the same basic functions and use similar terminology.

We will explain e-mail using examples from Internet Explorer and Netscape Communicator, two popular browsers available in both Mac and Windows platforms, which include e-mail software.

Identifying Yourself by Setting Preferences

Before you actually communicate via e-mail, you must let your software program know who you are and where to get and send your mail. This is done by "setting preferences". Most programs offer many options for organizing your mail, but there are only a few which must be set in order to begin sending and receiving messages. Later, when you are more familiar with e-mail, you can customize your system. For now, you will need the information listed in the box below. You may wish to write it down here for easy reference. Contact your technical resource person or service provider for any information you do not know.

Read one of the following two sections about using e-mail with either Internet Explorer or Netscape Communicator. Then continue with the section: Moving On.

Now, depending upon which Internet software you use, read one of the following two sections about using e-mail with either Internet Explorer or Netscape Communicator. Then continue with the section called "Moving On" later in this chapter.

E-Mail Information

Your name: _____

Your "reply to" address: _____

Your organization: _____

Your outgoing (SMPT) mail server: _____

Your incoming mail server: _____

(usually the same as the outgoing server)

Your POP ID: _____

(usually the same as your userid)—some providers may use IMAP instead of POP)

Internet FAQ	
There are so many different e-mail programs and hosts. Do I need different kinds of software to communicate with everyone?	No, any e-mail software will allow you to communicate with anyone else who has an e-mail address, regardless of their location or software program. There may be some minor differences, particularly regarding the way attachments are handled. Generally speaking, however, all e-mail systems are compatible.

Using Internet Explorer for E-Mail

Microsoft's Internet Explorer contains an integrated program which handles mail and news functions through its Outlook Express component.

Microsoft's Internet Explorer (IE) contains an integrated program which handles mail and news functions through its Outlook Express component. The examples in this section are from Internet Explorer 4.5 for Macintosh systems and 5.0 for Windows, the most current versions available at the time of writing. The basic information should be similar to other versions you may be using. When Internet Explorer is first opened, it may give users an opportunity to set all preferences; thus, you may already have set your e-mail preferences when you set your browser preferences, or they may have been set by your technical resource person. If so, move on to the next section: Receiving and Reading Messages. If you haven't set your e-mail preferences, or aren't sure whether they are set, continue reading here.

Setting Preferences

The first time you want to use e-mail, open Internet Explorer. Be patient—depending on your computer and the type of connection you have, it may take several seconds for the machine to respond to your click. Then, in Macintosh systems, click on the **Preferences** button in the IE toolbar. This brings up a Preferences dialog box showing a category frame on the left. Click on General under the E-mail category in the left frame, which will display the identity box on the right as in Figure 3-1.

If you can't see the General subcategory, it means the E-mail category is collapsed. This is a common feature in e-mail and newsgroup programs. To reveal the hidden categories, click on the small triangle to the left of E-mail. When the triangle is pointing down, all the categories are revealed. When the triangle is pointing to the right, categories are hidden. When you see the Identity box, enter your name, e-mail address, organization, your incoming and outgoing servers, and your account ID (usually the same as your userid). Then click OK to close the Preferences window. This is all that is necessary for now, but you can change or further customize your preferences later by clicking the Preferences icon. Now click the **Mail** button in the IE toolbar to open Outlook Express and go on to Receiving and Reading Mail.

In Windows systems, you click on the **Mail** button in the Internet Explorer toolbar and select Read Mail. This opens the Outlook Express component. Click on Tools in the menu and select Accounts. Then click on Add and select Mail. This brings up the Internet Connection Wizard which

Figure 3-1.
In Internet Explorer, with Macintosh systems, you set your e-mail preferences by clicking the Preferences button in the IE toolbar and then completing the information in the Preferences window.

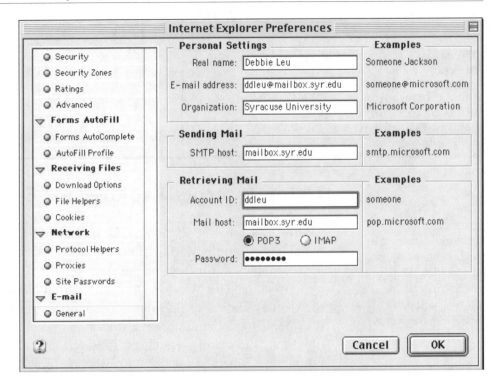

will help you set your preferences step by step. The first box is shown in Figure 3-2.

Fill in the required information; then click Next to go to the next screen. You will need to enter your name, your e-mail address (usually the same as your userid), your incoming and outgoing servers, and your password. Click Finish in the final dialog box, then click Close in the Accounts window. This

Figure 3-2
In Internet Explorer with Windows systems, you set your e-mail preferences in a series of Internet Connection Wizard boxes such as this.

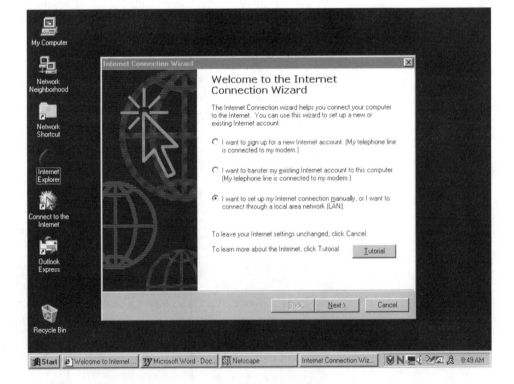

is all that is necessary for now, but you may change or further customize your preferences at another time by choosing Tools and selecting Accounts or Options.

Receiving and Reading Messages

Now you are ready to communicate using your e-mail account. If your Outlook Express window is not open, click the **Mail** button in the IE toolbar and select Read Mail. In order to receive new messages you must be connected to the Internet. Since Internet Explorer allows you to use some features offline, make sure that you are working online. You can check this by clicking File in the main menu and selecting Work Online.

Depending on your default settings, Outlook Express may automatically check with the mail server to see if you have any new mail every time it is launched. However, before retrieving your mail, it will ask for your password by opening a dialog box. Type your password to allow your mail to be received.

The dialog box may also offer you a Remember Password option. If you want Outlook Express to enter your password automatically each time, click this box. (You should only do this, however, if you have your own computer in a secure location since the Remember Password feature retrieves and displays your mail for anyone who clicks Send/Recv in the Outlook Express toolbar.) You can also initiate retrieval of new messages yourself at any time by clicking the Send/Recv button in the Outlook Express toolbar. Figures 3-3 and 3-4 show the Outlook Express window for Macintosh and Windows systems respectively.

Notice that the Outlook Express Mail window is divided into several sections. The top section contains the Outlook Express toolbar. The middle left section shows a list of your Outlook Express folders; the middle right section, the listing pane, lists messages you have received together with their subject headers, senders and dates; and the bottom section, the display pane, displays the text of a highlighted message.

We will return to the folder list later. For now, look at the listing pane on the right. The first time Outlook Express is opened, a welcome message from Internet Explorer will be listed here. Any other messages you may have been sent will also appear in the listing pane together with their subject headers, senders, and dates. New messages always appear in bold type, while previously read messages are in the usual typeface. To read a message, click on its header in the right pane, which will show the message text in the display pane below.

Notice the two additional icons in the listing pane: an exclamation point icon will appear if a message has been prioritized as urgent by its sender, and a paper clip icon if the message includes an attachment. (An attachment is an additional document included with an e-mail message.) In Windows there is also a flag icon, which you may use to mark a message for yourself. You can do this by clicking in the space under the flag next to the message you want

Figure 3-3.
The Outlook Express window in Internet Explorer, as it appears in a Macintosh system.

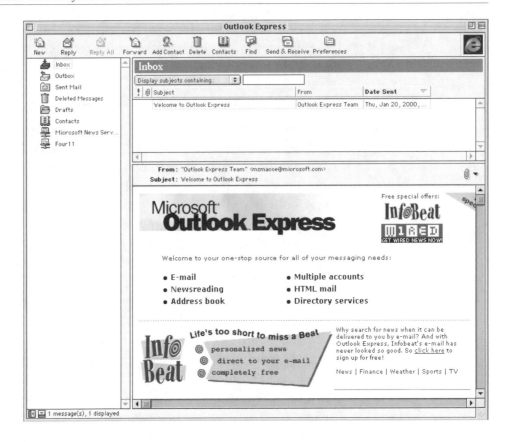

Figure 3-4.
The Outlook Express window in Internet Explorer, as it appears in a Windows system.

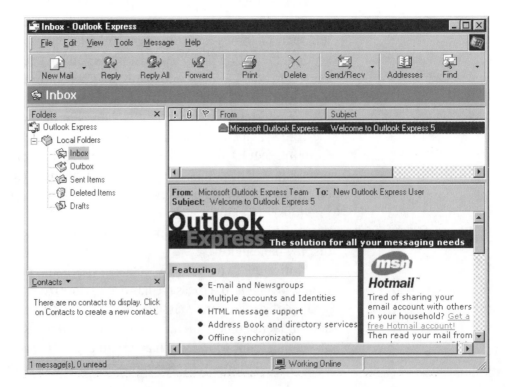

to mark. Windows users will also see either an open or closed envelope icon next to each message indicating its status as read or unread.

Depending on your default settings, messages may be grouped by topics, or "threads." In Macintosh systems, threads may be collapsed using the triangle icon. Click the triangle to point down, which will reveal all messages; or to point right to hide all but the first message. In Windows, the collapse icon is a box with a plus or minus sign; click to show the minus sign, which reveals all messages; or the plus sign, which shows only the first message in the thread.

Also depending on your default settings, Outlook Express may automatically check for new messages at regular intervals in each session. If you don't receive new messages automatically, or want to check between intervals, you can get new messages at any time during a session by clicking the Send/Recv button.

Replying to a Message

After reading a message, you may wish to respond. First, make sure the message you are replying to appears in the message display pane. Then, if the message was sent by one person and has only one address, click the Reply button. If the message contains multiple addresses, and if you want to reply to all of the addressees, click the Reply All button. This opens the Message Composition window as shown in Figure 3-5. Notice that the subject and address are already entered. However, you may edit any entry by moving the cursor to the appropriate box and deleting or adding information. To type your reply, simply move the cursor to the bottom pane of the Message Composition window and type your message.

Internet FAQ

Sometimes I have seen e-mail software with symbols in a toolbar directly below the subject line of the Message Composition window. What are these and how do you use them?	This is the Formatting toolbar. It will appear in more advanced e-mail programs, allowing you to add color and images to your email message. These programs are based on the same programming language used to develop a web page, HTML (see chapter 12). Sometimes they are referred to as HTML e-mail. You can use these word-processing features to customize your messages in many ways using the icons that appear below the Message Composition window. You may make letters bold, underline words for emphasis, add images and animations, and even insert a web page within your e-mail message. Before you click on the icons to use these features, keep in mind that not all e-mail programs support different type faces and layouts. Check to see if the recipient of your message uses HTML e-mail or plain text e-mail. It may be better to forego these features unless you are certain that your recipient's e-mail software can handle them; otherwise, your message may be unreadable.

Figure 3-5.
The Message Composition Window in Internet Explorer's Outlook Express showing a reply, ready to be sent.

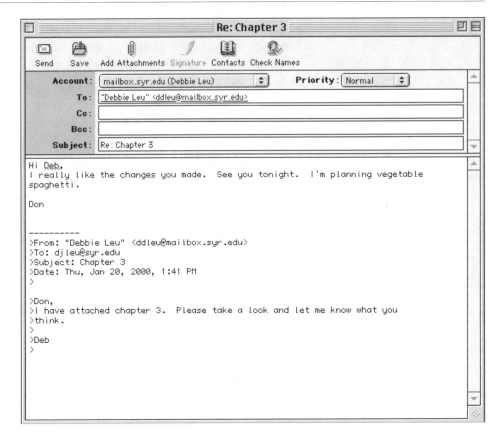

After typing your message, it is a good idea to read it over, confirming both the contents and the recipient(s). When you are sure your message is the way you want it, click the Send button. This immediately sends your message to the server if you are working online.

If you aren't ready to send a message at the end of a session, you can save it by clicking the Save button or selecting Save from File in the main menu. This moves your message to the Drafts folder and holds it until you are ready to finish it. When you want to work on your message again, you can retrieve it by clicking the Drafts folder in the left pane folder list. Then in the listing pane, click the message which you want to work on. This brings the saved message up in the Message Composition window where you can continue working on it. When you are finished you can send it or save it again for further editing.

Including Original Messages With Your Reply

By default, Outlook Express automatically quotes and includes the original message with any reply. Depending on the settings of your program, the quote of the original author and text may be shown with a greater-than sign (>) at the beginning of each line or a vertical line (|) along the left side (see Figure 3-5). Some people like this automatic feature. They always include the original message in their replies to provide context for the recipient. Other e-mail users prefer not to repeat the original message because it takes up additional Inbox space for recipients and adds extra charges for those who pay for e-mail by the line. Some people prefer to quote only a few important lines. If you prefer not to include the original message, you can delete part or all of it by editing with the cursor while you are working in the Message Composition window.

Forwarding Mail

Sometimes you receive a message that you think would be useful for a colleague. It's easy to share these messages by using the Forward button. Before forwarding a message, however, consider whether the original sender would want the message relayed to other people. You may want to ask for permission.

To forward a message, you must be in Outlook Express with the message you want to forward in the display pane. Then click the Forward button on the toolbar. This will bring up the Message Composition window with the subject box filled in, and the forwarded message in the lower pane of the window shown as a quote. All you need to do is enter the recipient's e-mail address on the To: line. If you wish, you may also type a message of your own above or below the quoted message. Then click Send.

Composing and Sending a New Message

Composing and sending a new message is basically the same as replying. To begin, you must be in the Outlook Express window. Go to the toolbar and click the New (Macintosh systems) or New Mail (Windows) button. This will open the Message Composition window, but unlike a reply message, the subject and address boxes will be empty. You must enter the name and e-mail address of the person to whom you are sending the message. You may send your message to more than one person by typing additional names and addresses on the same line, separating each person's e-mail address with a comma, or by clicking the To: button to bring up additional lines. You may also enter addresses for others to receive a carbon copy (Cc) or blind carbon copy (Bcc). You can see these options in the message composition window in Figure 3-5.

It's also a good idea to type in a subject. A subject isn't required, but it is considered good net etiquette and it's helpful for recipients who want to skim their messages in order to prioritize their reading. After entering the name(es), address(es), and subject, proceed in the same way as for a reply message.

Printing

Printing a message is very easy. Make sure the message you want to print is displayed in the bottom pane of the Outlook Express window. Then click the Print button or choose File from the main menu and select Print. Although it probably isn't necessary to have paper copies of all your messages, you may

Although it isn't really necessary to have paper copies of all your messages, you may want to use this feature to print out e-mail messages for posting on a bulletin board for the whole class to read or to share with parents at home or at an open house.

want to use this feature on occasion to print out e-mail messages for posting on a bulletin board for the whole class to read. It's also nice to print out some student messages to share with parents at home or at an open house.

Attaching

At times you may want to include additional information such as a Microsoft Word document (file) or an Internet site with your messages. To attach a file from your computer, begin in the Message Composition window. Either before or after typing your message, click the paper clip icon in the toolbar. This will open a dialog box which allows you to select the file you want to attach. If the file you want appears in the box, highlight it and click Add. If the file you want is inside a folder, first highlight the folder and click Open (this is because you can attach only individual files, not folders), then select and highlight the file and click Add. Click Done to close the window. Finish your message and send it. When the message is received, the recipient will be alerted to the attachment by a paper clip icon next to the message header.

To attach an Internet site, you must begin in the Internet Explorer (IE) window with the site you want to attach on the screen. In Macintosh systems, select Mail and release on Send Link. This will add the address of the open web page (only the URL, not the page itself) to the message which is currently displayed in the Message Composition window. If the Message Composition window is not open, IE will automatically open it and add the address of the web page in the message pane. Add whatever information you want and send the e-mail. (When IE 5 becomes available for Macintosh systems, it is likely the web page itself will be shown in the message pane, since this is how version 5 operates in Windows systems.) In Windows systems, from the Internet Explorer screen, go to File, select Send, and click on Page By E-mail. This brings up a new Message Composition window with the site shown in the message pane. (You may see only the address, not the page in your Message Composition window, but depending on individual settings, the recipient will see the page when the message is read.) Finish your message and send the e-mail.

Managing Your Mail and Working with Folders

Now that you understand the basic e-mail functions of receiving and sending, and are familiar with most of the buttons in the toolbars, you can manage your mail by using folders. Outlook Express initially creates and displays several default folders. These may be seen in Figures 3-3 (Macintosh) and 3-4 (Windows). In general, clicking on a folder once will display a folder's contents. The basic management folders are:

- The *Inbox*, which stores new incoming messages as well as any old messages which you have not deleted or filed elsewhere.

- The *Outbox*, which holds finished messages for sending at a later time.

- The *Sent Mail* (Macintosh)/*Sent Items* (Windows) folder, which holds copies of messages which you have sent or forwarded.

- The *Deleted Messages* (Macintosh)/*Deleted Items* (Windows) folder, which temporarily holds deleted items until you are ready to remove them permanently.

- The *Drafts* folder, which saves unfinished messages which you intend to work on later.

After you read a message, it remains in your Inbox folder until you move or delete it. As a result, over time your Inbox may become crowded and disorganized, and if it gets too full, you can't receive new messages. Therefore, it is a good idea to get in the habit of moving messages out of your Inbox as you read them.

Deleting Messages

If you don't need to keep a message after reading it, simply click the Delete button in the toolbar. This deletes the message appearing in the display pane and transfers it to the Deleted Messages/Items folder. If you want to delete any other message, highlight it by clicking its subject header in the listing pane; then click the Delete button. If you have several messages you don't want to save, you can "block delete" them as a group by clicking on each one while holding down the keyboard shift key. This highlights a group of messages. Click the Delete button and the whole group will be removed from the listing pane and transferred to the Deleted Messages/Items folder.

The Deleted Messages/Items Folder

At this point, although you have deleted your messages, they are not really gone. They are sitting in the Deleted Messages/Items folder as if you had thrown them in a wastebasket. This can be a convenient feature if you have accidentally deleted a message that you need. To retrieve such a message, click the Deleted Messages/Items folder, then highlight the message you want to retrieve in the right listing pane, and drag it to the folder in which you want to save it. It's a good idea to then open the folder to make sure that the message has appeared there.

In order to actually remove your deleted messages, you must empty the Deleted Messages/Items folder which is equivalent to taking out the trash. To do this, highlight the Deleted Messages/Items folder, choose Edit from the main menu, and select Empty Deleted Messages/Items. Be careful; once you click, all messages in the Deleted Messages/Items folder are permanently removed.

Saving Sent Messages

Outlook Express automatically saves copies of messages that you send, including forwarded messages, to the Sent Mail/Items folder (unless you have changed the default setting in Preferences or Tools). This provides a convenient record of your messages and allows you to easily re-send a message if necessary. However, this folder can become very large if you are an active e-mailer. Therefore, you may wish to create additional folders (by month or topic, for example) and then transfer your sent messages accordingly. Or if you do not need to save them, simply delete as explained above.

Saving Received Messages

The easiest way to save a message after you have read it is to drag its subject header from the right listing pane to the folder in which you want to save it. You can "block save" messages just as you block delete them by clicking each message while holding down the keyboard shift key. Then drag this group of messages to the folder where you want to save them. The whole group will be removed from the listing pane and transferred to the selected folder.

Up to this point, any messages you have saved have been kept in one of the default folders mentioned above. Since these folders do not offer much flexibility, it is likely that your mail is not organized as effectively as possible. You can improve the situation by creating new folders to suit your individual needs.

The easiest way to save a message after you have read it is to drag its subject header from the right listing pane to the folder in which you want to save it.

Creating New Folders

The procedure for creating new folders is a little different, depending on which platform and version you use. For Macintosh users, choose File from the main menu, select New, and release on Folder. This creates a new folder in the left pane folder list. Type the new folder's name in the highlighted box next to the folder. You can now add messages to this folder. For Windows users, choose File from the main menu, select New and click Folder. This displays a dialog box. Type the name of the new folder in the name box and then click OK. This adds the new folder to the folder list in the left pane. You can now add messages to this folder.

If you have younger students, or only one computer in your classroom, student mail will probably be sent through your e-mail account. To help manage these mail messages, you may want to create folders labeled with each student's name. Depending on the age of your students, you can keep track of their messages and monitor their correspondence or teach them how to save and delete messages for themselves. In addition, you will most likely want to discuss privacy issues and remind students to read and use only their own folders.

Deleting Folders

To delete a folder, highlight it and click the Delete button in the toolbar. Or go to File in the main menu and select Delete Folder. This deletes the folder as well as any messages it may contain.

Using Netscape Communicator for E-Mail

Netscape Communicator is an integrated program which handles mail and news functions through its Messenger component. The examples in this section are from Communicator 4.7, the most current version available at the time of writing. As mentioned earlier, however, the basic information should be similar to other versions you may be using. Figures in this chapter may show an example from only one platform, since screens in Macintosh and Windows are often very similar. However, if there are significant differences, examples will be given from both platforms.

When Netscape Communicator is first opened, it gives users the opportunity to set all preferences; thus, you may already have set your e-mail preferences when you set your browser preferences, or they may have been set by your technical resource person. If so, move on to the next section: Receiving and Reading Messages. If you haven't set your e-mail preferences, or aren't sure whether they are set, continue reading here.

Setting Preferences

The first time you want to use e-mail, open Netscape Communicator. Be patient—depending on your computer and the type of connection you have, it may take several seconds for the machine to respond to your click. Next, set your e-mail preferences by choosing Edit from the main menu and selecting Preferences. This opens the Preferences window and shows a Category frame on the left. Look for the item Mail and Newsgroups in the list. Click on the subcategory called Identity. If you can't see the Identity subcategory, it means the Mail and Newsgroups category is collapsed. Collapsing is a common feature of e-mail and newsgroup programs. In Macintosh systems, click on the small triangle to the left of Mail and Newsgroups to reveal the hidden items. When the triangle is pointing down, all the categories are revealed. When the triangle is pointing to the right, categories are hidden. In Windows systems, the icon is a small box containing a plus or minus sign. Click on the box to choose the minus sign, which reveals all the categories, or the plus sign which hides them. Clicking the Identity subcategory opens the Identity Preference box. Enter your name, e-mail address, reply-to address and organization in the appropriate boxes. Leave the other boxes empty for now. Then click OK. An example is provided in Figure 3-6.

Next, return to the category list and click Mail Servers within the Mail and Newsgroups category. This opens the Mail Servers dialog box. Enter your mail server user name (your userid); also enter your outgoing and incoming mail server addresses (these are usually the same). Select the type of server (which is usually POP3) by clicking the appropriate button. Click OK to close the Preferences window. Your required mail preferences are now set, but you may change or further customize them by returning to the Preferences window at another time.

Figure 3-6.
Setting Preferences in the Mail and Newsgroups Identity box for Netscape Communicator.

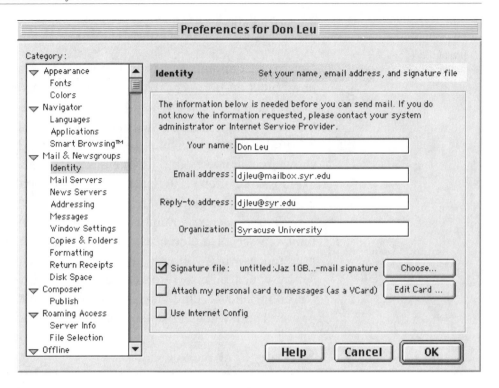

Receiving and Reading Messages

Now you are ready to communicate using your e-mail account. To receive new messages, you must be connected to the Internet. Since Netscape Communicator allows you to use some features off-line, make sure you are connected. You can check this by clicking File in the menu and selecting Work Online. Then, begin by clicking the Messenger Inbox icon in the Component Bar as illustrated in Figure 3-7. The Messenger Inbox icon contains a small image of letters in an inbox. The Component Bar is located in the lower right corner of the Netscape Communicator window.

Figure 3-7.
The Component Bar in Netscape Communicator showing the icons, in order: Navigator, Messenger Inbox, News Server, Address Book, and Composer.

The first time the Inbox is clicked in any session, Netscape Communicator will attempt to check with the mail server to see if you have new mail. In order to retrieve your new messages, it will ask for your password by opening a dialog box. Just type your password and click OK. This opens the Messenger window as shown in Figures 3-8 and 3-9, for Macintosh and Windows respectively.

Figure 3-8.
The Messenger Inbox window in Netscape Communicator, as it appears in a Macintosh system.

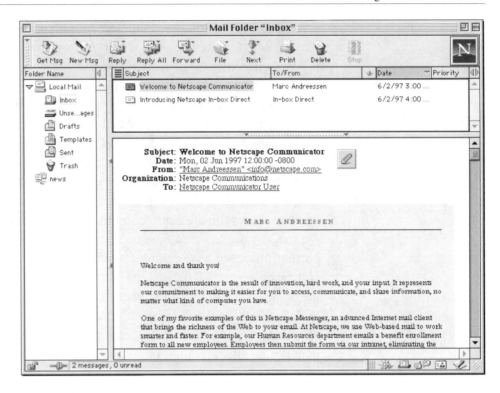

Figure 3-9.
The Messenger Inbox window in Netscape Communicator, as it appears in a Windows system.

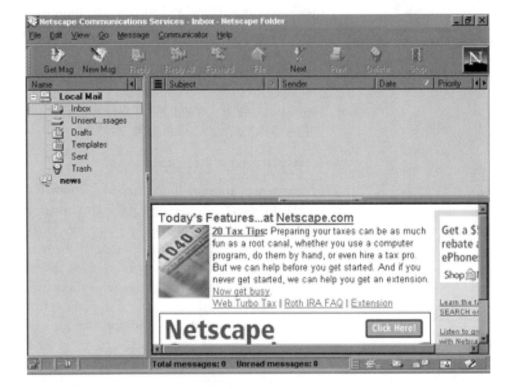

Notice that the mail screen is divided into several sections. The top section contains the Messenger toolbar. The middle section, the listing pane, lists your folders on the left and your messages with their subject headers, senders, and dates on the right. The bottom section, the message pane, displays the text of the message which is highlighted in the listing pane.

We will return to the folders list later. Now, look at the pane on the upper right. The first time Messenger is opened, a welcome message from Netscape will appear in the message listing pane. In addition, if any other messages have been sent to you, they will be retrieved from the server and also appear in the listing pane. New or unread messages always appear in bold type. Additional message information can be found in various columns on the right. A green diamond next to a message indicates the message is unread. The diamond disappears when a message is read, but you may return it by clicking under the diamond column next to the message you want to mark. Do this if want to remember to re-read a message. You may also mark important messages by clicking under the red flag column next to a message you want to mark. The Priority column indicates the sender has given the message a particular priority level, shown by different colors: highest is red, high is purple, normal is black, low is blue, and lowest is green). A small blue paper clip on the letter icon next to message indicates that the message includes an attachment. (An attachment is an additional document included with an e-mail message.)

After your first use of Messenger, it will automatically check for new messages the first time in each session that you open the Inbox window (unless you have changed the default settings in Preferences). Follow the procedures mentioned above, and enter your password if you want to read your messages or click Cancel if you don't. Remember, you may also get your mail at any time during a session by clicking Get Msg in the toolbar. If you have more than one message, click on a succeeding or preceding message to display and read it in the bottom pane. You may also move to the next unread message by clicking the Next button in the toolbar.

Replying to a Message

In many cases after reading a message, you will want to respond. First, make sure that the message you want to reply to appears in the message display pane. Then if the message was sent by one person and has only one address, click the Reply button in the toolbar. If the message contains multiple addresses, and if you want to reply to all of the addressees, select Reply All. Either selection opens the Message Composition window as shown in Figure 3-10. Notice that the subject and address are already entered. However, you may edit any entry by moving the cursor to the appropriate box and deleting or adding information. Next, move the cursor to the bottom pane of the Message Composition window and type your message.

After typing your message, it is a good idea to read it over, confirming both the content and the recipient(s). If you are sure your message is the way you want it, click the Send button. Once you click this button, if you are working online, it is impossible to stop or retrieve your message; it is immediately sent to the server. If you click Send while you are working offline,

After typing your message, it is a good idea to read it over, confirming both the content and the recipient(s). Once you click the Send button, if you are working on-line, it is impossible to stop or retrieve your message.

Figure 3-10
The Message Composition window with the "To" and "Subject" items already entered for a reply message.

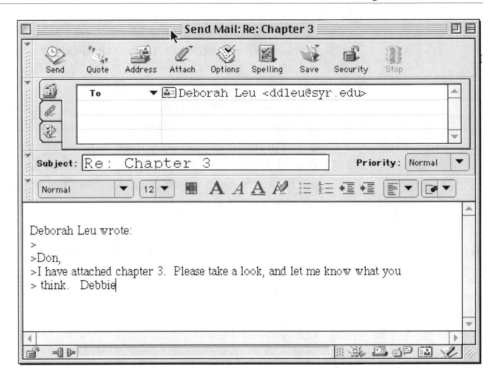

Internet FAQ

People forward jokes and what look like chain letters to me. Is it correct to pass these on to a mailing list or to other people I know?	Jokes and chain letters should never be sent to a mailing list. Hundreds of members usually subscribe to a mailing list. Most would be upset with you for flooding their inbox with information they did not request. Chain letter e-mails are not usually passed along to friends for the same reasons regular chain letters are not sent. Jokes are sometimes sent to friends, but not if they are offensive or insensitive.

your message will be put in the Unsent Messages folder for later delivery. The next time you come online, Messenger will ask if you want your unsent messages sent.

If you aren't ready to send your message, you can save it by clicking the Save button. This will hold it in your Drafts folder until you are ready to finish it. When you want to work on your message again, you can retrieve it by clicking the Drafts folder and selecting the message you want. When you are finished you can send it or save it again for further editing.

The Quote Button

The Quote button in the toolbar of the Message Composition window (See Figure 3-11) can also be useful when replying to a message.

The Quote button can also be useful when replying to a message. Whether to use it, however, is a matter of personal choice. Some people like to always include the original message within their reply message to provide context for the recipient. (You may set up your mail to automatically quote the original message every time you reply by selecting that option in Preferences.)

Other e-mail users prefer not to quote the original message because it takes up Inbox space for recipients, and adds extra charges for those who pay for e-mail by the line. Some people quote only a few important lines. When you click the Quote button, it adds the original message which is shown in the display screen to your reply message (see Figure 3-11). Depending on the default settings of your program, the quote will be shown with the original author's name and either a greater-than sign (>) at the beginning of each line, or a vertical line along the left side of the quoted message. You may edit the quote by moving the cursor and adding and deleting information as in any message.

Figure 3-11
The Message Composition window, showing the use of the Quote button when replying to a message.

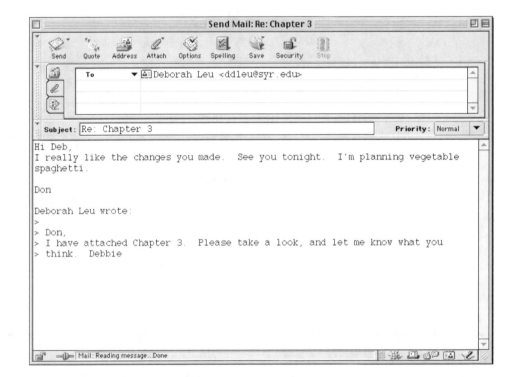

Forwarding Mail

Sometimes you receive messages you know would be useful for colleagues. It's easy to share these messages by using the "Forward" button in the Messenger Inbox toolbar.

Sometimes you receive messages you think would be useful for colleagues. It's easy to share these messages by using the Forward button. Before forwarding a message, however, consider whether the original sender would want the message relayed to others. You may want to ask for permission. If you decide to share a message, click the Forward button while the message you want to forward is in the message display pane. This will bring up the Message Composition window with the subject box filled in, and the forwarded message may be shown as a quote in the lower pane of the window (similar to Figure 3-11). All you need to do is enter the recipient's e-mail address on the To: line. If you wish, you may also type a message of your own above or below the forwarded message. Then click Send. The message will be forwarded to the person you have designated.

Composing and Sending a New Message

Composing and sending a new message is basically the same as replying, but you begin in a different way. Start by clicking the New Msg button in the Messenger Inbox toolbar. This will open the Message Composition window (see Figure 3-10), but unlike a reply message, the subject and address boxes will be empty. You must enter the name and e-mail address of the person you wish to contact on the To: line. You may send your message to more than one person by typing additional To: lines. You can choose other options by clicking on To:, which will show a sub-menu for choices such as Cc (carbon copy) and Bcc (blind carbon copy).

It's a good idea to type in a subject for your messages. A subject isn't required, but it's helpful for recipients who like to skim their messages to prioritize them before reading. After entering the name(s), address(es), and subject, proceed with your new message in the same way as for a reply message.

> It's a good idea to type in a subject for messages. A subject isn't required, but it's helpful for recipients who want to skim their messages and prioritize them by subject.

Printing

Printing a message is one of the easiest features. Just click the Print button in the Messenger Inbox toolbar while the message you want to print is shown in the display screen. Although it probably isn't necessary to have paper copies of all your messages, you may want to use this feature to print out e-mail messages for posting on a bulletin board so that the whole class can read them. It's also nice to print some e-mail messages for students to share with their parents at home or at an open house.

Attaching

At times you may want to include additional information such as a Microsoft Word document (file) or an Internet site with your messages. To attach a file from your computer, begin in the Message Composition window. Either before or after typing your message, click the paper clip icon in the toolbar. This will open a dialog box which allows you to select the file you want to attach. If the file you want appears in the box, highlight it and click Attach. If the file you want is inside a folder, first highlight the folder and click Open (this is because you can attach only individual files, not folders), then select and highlight the file and click Attach. Click Done to close the window. Finish your message and send it. When the message is received, the recipient will be alerted to the attachment by a paper clip icon next to the message header.

To attach an Internet site, you begin in the Netscape Communicator/Navigator window with the web page you want to attach displayed on the screen. Then go to File in the main menu and select Send Page. This will bring up a new Message Composition window with the hotlinked address of the site in the message display pane. (You may see only the address, not the page in your message screen. However, depending on individual settings, the recipient will see the page when the message is read.) Add whatever information you want and send the e-mail.

Managing Your Mail and Working With Folders

Now that you understand the basic e-mail functions of receiving and sending, and are familiar with most of the buttons in the toolbars, you can manage your mail by using folders. Netscape Communicator initially creates and displays several default folders. These may be seen in Figure 3-8 (Macintosh) and 3-9 (Windows). In general, it is necessary to double click to display a folder's contents. The basic management folders are:

- The *Inbox,* which stores new incoming messages as well as any old messages which you have not deleted or filed elsewhere.
- The *Unsent Messages* folder, which holds finished messages for sending at a later time.
- The *Drafts* folder, which saves unfinished messages which you intend to work on later.
- The *Sent* folder, which holds copies of messages which you have sent or forwarded.
- The *Trash* folder, which temporarily holds deleted items until you are ready to remove them permanently.

After you read a message, it remains in your Inbox folder unless you move or delete it. As a result, it may become crowded and disorganized, and when it gets too full, you can't receive new messages. Moreover, if you want to refer back to a message, it can be difficult to find it in a long list. Therefore, it is a good idea to get in the habit of moving messages out of your Inbox as you read them.

Deleting Messages

If you don't need to keep a message after reading it, simply click the "Delete" button in the toolbar. This removes the current message from the listing and display panes and transfers it to the Trash folder. If you want to delete a message at a later time, highlight it by clicking its subject header in the listing pane; then click the Delete button. If you have several messages, you can "block delete" them as a group by clicking on each one while holding down the keyboard shift key. This highlights a group of messages. Click the "Delete" button and the whole group will be removed from the listing pane and transferred to the Trash folder.

If you don't need to keep a message after reading it, simply click the "Delete" button in the toolbar.

The Trash Folder

At this point, although you have deleted your messages, they are not really gone from your mail service. They are sitting in the Trash folder as if you had thrown them in a wastebasket. This can be a convenient feature if you have accidentally deleted a message that you need. To retrieve such a message, click the Trash Folder, then highlight the message you want to retrieve in the right listing pane. Click on File and select the folder you want to save the message in. This moves the message to the selected folder. It's a good idea to then open the folder to make sure that the message does appear there.

In order to actually remove your deleted messages, you must empty the Trash folder, equivalent to taking out the trash. To do this, choose File from the main menu, and select Empty Trash Folder. Be careful; once you click, all messages in the Trash folder are permanently deleted.

Saving Sent Messages

Netscape Messenger automatically saves copies of messages that you send, including forwarded messages, to the Sent folder. This provides a convenient record of your messages and allows you to easily re-send a message if necessary. However, this folder can become very large if you are an active e-mailer. Therefore, you may wish to create additional folders (by month or topic, for example) and transfer your sent messages accordingly. Or if you want to remove them, simply delete as explained above.

Saving Received Messages

To save a message after you have read it, make sure it is highlighted. Then click the File button, which will bring up a menu of your folders. Release on the folder in which you want to save the message. This removes the current message from the listing and display panes and transfers it to the selected folder. If you want to save a message at a later time, highlight it by clicking its subject header in the listing pane; then proceed as above. You can "block save" messages just as you block delete them by clicking each one while holding down the keyboard shift key. Then choose File from the toolbar and select the folder in which you want to save the messages. The whole group will be removed from the listing pane and transferred to the selected folder.

Up to this point, any messages you have kept have been saved to one of the default folders mentioned above. Since these folders do not offer much flexibility, it is likely that your mail is not organized as effectively as possible. You can improve the situation by creating new folders to suit your individual needs.

Creating New Folders

To create a new folder, go to File in the main menu and select New Folder. This opens a dialog box. Type in a name for your new folder and click OK. The new folder will then appear in your list of folders and you will be able to save messages there. As you accumulate more messages, you can create additional folders to further organize your mail.

If you have younger students, or only one computer in your classroom, student mail will probably be sent through your e-mail account. To help manage these mail messages, you may want to create folders labeled with each student's name. Depending on the age of your students, you can keep

If you have younger students, or only one computer in your classroom, student mail will be sent through your e-mail account. To help manage mail messages, create an electronic folder labeled for each student.

track of their messages and monitor their correspondence or teach them how to save and delete messages for themselves. In addition, you will most likely want to discuss privacy issues and remind students to read and use only their own folders.

Deleting Folders

To delete a folder, highlight and click on the Delete button in the toolbar. Or go to File in the main menu and select Delete Folder. This deletes the folder as well as any messages it may contain.

Before going on, read the following e-mail message to hear about one teacher's long-term experiences with e-mail.

 # E-MAIL FOR YOU

To: Colleagues
From: Peter Lelong lelongp@fahan.tas.edu.au
Subject: E-mail Projects

Although many of us view the Internet and the use of electronic mail as somewhat recent developments I cast my mind back to 1986 when my class of Year Five students set up a Collaborative project with two schools in the United Kingdom. One in Newham a suburb in the east end of London and the other in Derbyshire. More recent projects that have been conducted with students in Indonesia have met with similar challenges as the ones we faced over a decade ago.

Those challenges can appear onerous at times although the rewards of a successful collaborative project with students overseas or in the next town have in my experience always made the efforts extremely worthwhile. Students in my Year Four class in Tasmania who worked with the Indonesian teacher, Ibu Wahyuni and her students in Malang, East Java learnt more from each other and their cultures through actively communicating via e-mail than I could possibly have taught in class. The sharing of poetry, stories, recipes, favourite sports, books, and television programs along with views on citizenship in our respective countries led to a prolonged three month collaboration with over sixty students involved.

I have found my students respond positively to the challenges and questions presented by their e-mail partners. They write clearly with greater attention to their use of grammar and with more care in their spelling. They want to "look good" in the eyes of their new found friends and look forward to each new email message.

If you have any doubts about the value of a collaborative project using Internet keep a scrapbook of all that your students have written and marvel at how much has been learnt and shared at the end of the day.

```
Peter Lelong      http://www.fahan.tas.edu.au
Fahan School      Mercury Newspapers 'Cyberclass' articles published
Fisher Avenue     each Monday can be found at;
Hobart 7005       http://www.fahan.tas.edu.au/mercury/cyberclass.html
```

Moving On

It would take too long to explain all the features of Internet Explorer and Netscape Communicator, but we hope that the information we've included has gotten you off to a good start. Now is the time to move on. Reading about e-mail can get tedious, and like swimming, you don't really know how to do it until you try it. So take some time for hands-on practice. Try one or two things at first and work at your own pace. You may wish to work with a partner. If your school doesn't have a media specialist or technology resource person, try to find someone a bit more experienced who can help out. Remember, everyone was a beginner once and no one knows it all, not even the experts.

As you become more familiar and confident with the basic features of e-mail, you can customize your mail service further. Explore other toolbar selections. Go back to Preferences or the Internet Connection Wizard and choose additional options. Create an automatic signature or a personal address book or learn how to reconfigure the mail window.

Using E-Mail in the Classroom

Learning how to use e-mail does take some time, but it is well worth the effort when you consider the many ways it can be used in the classroom. Perhaps the most common use of e-mail is to communicate with people you already know—just like a letter. This ordinary activity is easily extended to communicating electronically with new people, which can add special excitement to learning as it brings the world into your classroom and lets you and your students make new friends and interact with new cultures. It is not surprising then that many teachers begin with and continue to use e-mail activities as one way to integrate the Internet into their classrooms.

Keypals

In the past, one of the most common ways for students to interact with new people has been to write to penpals. The Internet equivalent, e-mailing keypals, or e-pals as they are sometimes called, is equally exciting and beneficial: it can provide motivation, improve writing skills, increase knowledge, and broaden perspectives. E-mail's greatest feature, however, is that it reduces the time between messages to just a few seconds or minutes. Because of this speed, students can do much more than simply correspond once or twice a month. Very quickly, they can get almost any kind of information by asking questions and conducting interviews with other students or experts in their own country or abroad; they can practice a second language; they can share cool web sites; they can collaborate on joint projects; they can even help each other with homework. It isn't always necessary to do an elaborate pre-planned project through a keypals site. Close-to-home activities can be productive, too, as this next message points out.

Reading about e-mail can get tedious, and like swimming, you don't really know how to do it until you try it. So take some time for hands-on practice.

Very quickly, students can get almost any kind of information by asking questions and conducting interviews with others in their own country or abroad; they can practice a second language; they can share cool web sites; they can work on joint projects; they can even help each other with homework.

E-MAIL FOR YOU

To: Colleagues
From: Cindy Lockerman <klocker@UNCC.CAMPUSCWIX.NET>
Subject: Keypal Project

About a year ago I was involved in a discussion on RTEACHER Listserv concerning keypals for the students that I teach. I am posting this experience because I feel it is important to see the connection between the theoretical and the life experience. The first decision was the selection of a keypal organization. I chose IECC, the listserv service out of St. Olaf College. I had a wide choice through them of prospective keypal partners. I teach ESL students in grades 3–5, many of whom are intermediate level ESL students and need written communication practice as much as any other area of instruction. Much to my delight, I found a group of Canadian children on a remote island in Manitoba called Wasagamack. They all learned English upon entering school and spoke Oji-Cree as their native language. Many of the Wasagamack students had never left the area of their birth, and were interested in learning about life in an urban American setting. Their students were all in the sixth grade.

We began our joint project after the Christmas break and continued until the end of school. I prepared my students previous to the break by reading literature about life in colder climates and by having them research the Wasagamack area of Canada on the Internet. The students were paired up as best we could, ground rules were set and goals were discussed before my students went home for the Christmas break. When they returned to school, we began. The students wrote back and forth approximately once a month. I did some grammar editing when necessary, but my students were given one or two writing areas to concentrate on perfecting with each new letter they composed. We also kept the whole school informed of our progress through a large bulletin board which was updated with each new batch of letters.

This project was a huge success. The teacher in Wasagamack and I agreed that not only did the children LOVE getting to know each other, but it offered a great incentive to them to work on the problem areas of their writing. Their children were fascinated with the concepts of multiple restaurants, theme parks, warm weather, big schools, and keypal partners with unpronounceable names! Our kids learned about ice highways, Canadian cities, hunting and fishing in the ice and snow, and ice hockey. Our students also learned the advantages of communicating on the Internet and now are "old pros" at Internet use. It was a wonderful experience. Many other teachers at our school now want to give it a try—which is, after all, the best success indicator of all.

Cindy Lockerman

E-MAIL FOR YOU

To: Colleagues
From: Paula Reber <preber@CSRLINK.NET>
Subject: Keypal project

   My class has participated in many Travel Buddy projects with other countries for the past few years and it's been very successful. This year, I wished to try something new. One of my best friends also teaches in my district but at another building (K-3 is in one school, 4-5 in another). My first graders became keypals with her fourth graders. We used a combination of e-mail and the district's LAN server to correspond with each other. In addition to writing back and forth the students also worked collaboratively on some book projects. For example, near St. Patrick's Day my student's wrote the first paragraph to a leprechaun story. Each student saved the work on the district server and the fourth grade buddies then finished the stories. After the stories were complete, my students created graphics in KidPix to correspond with the story.
   We plan to expand on this next year when I loop to second grade. We are hoping that the kids will also get to meet next year at some point.

   Paula Reber
   Visit Reber's Resources for K-6 Teachers
   http://www.geocities.com/Athens/8854

Central Sites for Keypals

There are numerous sites for locating keypals and partner classes.

There are numerous sites for locating keypals and partner classes. Some of them are commercial sites which charge fees, but many of the best sites are free. The sites included below are ones that we and other teachers have found to be especially useful for educational purposes. Although it is impossible to control every aspect of Internet use, these sites are also concerned with safety; nevertheless, it is best to think of them, and of all our recommendations, as starting points for your own exploration. The Internet changes quickly and often; some of these sites may disappear; certainly new ones will come online. Most importantly, you will know best which sites meet your needs. Therefore, we encourage you to move on from our sites and make your own list of favorites.

- **ePals Classroom Exchange**—http://www.epals.com/
  Teachers can look for class matches based on age, geography, and languages among other criteria. Currently there are classes from 108 countries.

- **ESD 105**—http://www.esd105.wednet.edu/kp.html
  Sponsored by the Educational Technology Support Center Program through Educational Support District 105 in Yakima, Washington; the Office of the Superintendent of Public Instruction; and the Washington School Information Processing Cooperative, this site allows teachers to search for matching keypal classes in the US and abroad through free subscription to current K–2, 3–5, 6–8, or high school groups. You can also access all previous messages on the web.

- **Gaggle**—http://www.gaggle.net/
  This site stresses safety and control by monitoring, blocking inappropriate messages and language, and only allowing sign-up through teachers and schools.

- **Heinemann Interactive**—http://www.hi.com.au/
  Located in Australia, sponsored by Heinemann publishing, this site is open to students and teachers who may post messages on lists for students from age 5–10 years; 11–13 years; and 14–20 years. They encourage responsible net use through (free) registration, a netiquette section, and their privacy policy.

- **Intercultural E-Mail Classroom Connections**—
  http://www.stolaf.edu/network/iecc/index.html
  Located at St. Olaf's College, this is a good site for linking with keypals and partners from different countries. They also host several discussion groups which teachers can subscribe to directly from their web page.

Many of the sites above will ask you to write a message giving details about your class and the kind of class you'd like to work with. Before you contact another teacher, you should consider what you would like your students to do and how you would like them to do it. Then you and the other teacher can discuss possibilities and decide on ground rules. The following two e-mail messages offer some good suggestions to help you get started.

E-MAIL FOR YOU

To: Colleagues
From: Jeff Scanlan <jscanlan@powerup.com.au>
Subject: Using E-mail in the Classroom.

Hi!

. . . Here are several ideas I would like to share with you. First, if you want to correspond with a school in another country, make contact with several schools. Teachers everywhere are busy people with lots of responsibilities and although they might not intend it, they may not get the time to organize the replies. (It can be quite a task in making sure that all kids get their replies away and you really don't want to disappoint anyone at the other end).

Also, think about how to integrate your total English program into an e-mail project before you begin to e-mail other schools. I am a great believer in getting children to write reflectively and express feelings. It is important that children in writing to other children know to write more than just basic information about their life circumstances. You really need to explain and show children how this can be done.

Finally, when you are corresponding with another classroom, don't be afraid to share snail mail addresses and telephone numbers. Kids get quite a buzz from an intercontinental phone call! A lesson or two on time zones and time differences does not go astray here! In any case it is something of which in future we will all need to be more aware. Best wishes with all your e-mail projects!

Yours sincerely,
Jeff Scanlan
Year 3 teacher (7-8 year olds)
Alexandra Hills State School
Queensland, Australia

E-MAIL FOR YOU

To: Colleagues
From: Peter Lelong lelongp@fahan.tas.edu.au
Subject: Project Challenges

. . .The greatest challenge many of us have when we contemplate a collaborative project is in finding a partner school to work with that shares the same goals as yourself. Unlike our first experience in 1986 when locating any school to communicate via electronic mail was difficult, today's classrooms in many schools have access to a wealth of educational sites such as the Global School House (http://www.gsh.org), the Aussie School House (http://www.ash.org.au), or EdNA—The Education Network of Australia (http://www.edna.edu.au). Projects such as the highly successful Travel Buddies (http://rite.ed.qut.edu.au/oz-teachernet/projects/travel-buddies/webs.html) all aim to stimulate ideas that will encourage students to dip their toes into the world of electronic communications.

The relationship that develops between the coordinating teachers has always been crucial in any of the projects I have been involved with. As teachers we share via e-mail our aims and objectives prior to commencing work with the students. Our topics for each week are planned ahead through regular e-mail contacts and a promise to communicate on set days if possible so that our students can expect responses to any questions asked are also scheduled.

Such planning has always been of importance to the success of a project. Not only does it provide teachers with a chance to become acquainted and plan a series of lessons together but it ensures that the students because of this prior contact between the teachers will not become disappointed through lack of interest or poor planning by either party to a project.

    Peter Lelong
    Fahan School
    Fisher Avenue
    Hobart 7005
    http://www.fahan.tas.edu.au

Signing up for keypals is a good way to get started with electronic communication. We hope you are getting excited about its potential for your classroom. You may be still be wondering, though, specifically what kind of activities your students can do, especially if they have never used e-mail before. The following message describes one teacher's plans.

E-MAIL FOR YOU

To: Colleagues
From: Jeanette Kenyon <jkenyon@ahoynet.com> <jkenyon@pen.k12.va.us.>
Subject: Using E-Mail in Third Grade

Dear Colleague,
   One of the first skills I taught to my 3rd grade children after becoming connected to the Internet was e-mail. This seems a logical starting point for teachers as well as students. We began by sending e-mail to the class next door to us. Even though my students have many friends in that class and they see each other daily, the e-mail they exchanged during our Computer lab time became a weekly "event." We composed collective messages where we chatted about what was going on in our room, interesting units we were working on, and general greetings to individuals from their friends. We often included the latest "knock knock" jokes and sometimes posed difficult math problems for the other class to solve. As the students became more skillful at sending e-mail we moved beyond our own school and began sending messages to family and friends. Parents love to receive messages at work from their children and far away relatives are thrilled to hear from their young family members. After becoming comfortable with the workings and etiquette of e-mail, the students were confident about sending messages to various people on the World Wide Web. They found that there were experts in almost any field who would gladly answer their questions, and they corresponded with a variety of students around the world whom they had located on the WWW. Many eight and nine year olds are reluctant letter writers but it is amazing how long they will sit at a keyboard painstakingly composing an e-mail message. This is also a great incentive and opportunity to improve keyboarding skills which are also an integral part of our curriculum.

   Jeanette Kenyon
   Moncure Elementary School
   Stafford, Virginia USA

Depending on the age and experience of your students, you might want to start out with a message composed jointly by the students, but entered by you.

This message shows how a teacher began simply within the classroom and gradually expanded her class's activities to include the world. Depending on the age and experience of your students, you might want to start out with a message composed jointly by the students, but entered by you. The message and any responses could be printed out and kept in a binder or put up on a bulletin board near the computer. Later, students could work in pairs or small groups to send their own messages to other students in their school. Then they could move into their community by e-mailing questions to local businesses and organizations. Finally, they might each have their own international keypal.

Netiquette

The previous message also brings up Internet etiquette, commonly referred to as netiquette. This is a very important issue particularly as students begin to use e-mail more independently and extensively. One concern about e-mail communication is the inability to share facial expressions, voice tone, and body language as we do with face-to-face oral communication. As a result, e-mail messages can lend themselves to miscommunication. Thus, it is important to help students develop good Internet manners and become sensitive to how their messages might be misinterpreted.

We are not talking here about actions that are dangerous or illegal (you can read more about these issues in the section on Acceptable Use Policies in Chapter 2), but about politeness and courtesy. Because the Internet is not run by any single group or government, there are no laws or official rules to teach, nor is there a single source of information about what constitutes acceptable behavior. Nevertheless, we need to help our students realize that the Internet, as a place of social interaction, has its own traditions and customs. We need to discuss Internet use as a privilege not a right, and together with our students develop guidelines that encourage tolerance and acceptance of the diversity of people, languages, and viewpoints that exists on the net.

People often talk about netiquette in terms of "common sense", but common sense varies depending on factors such as age, culture, and experience. Therefore, before you discuss this issue with your students, you may want get some background information from this excellent location: **The Net: User Guidelines and Netiquette** by Arlene H. Rinaldi (http://www.fau.edu/netiquette/netiquette.html). This is the most comprehensive site we've found on Netiquette. It's very detailed, giving netiquette advice on e-mail, lists, newsgroups and other areas of the net. It includes a question and answer section as well as a bibliography. Depending on the level of your students, you might choose various sections for them to read and discuss. For example, "The Ten Commandments for Computer Ethics" is a straightforward list of "thou-shalt-nots" which would probably be effective with all but the youngest students.

> We need to help our students realize that the Internet, as a place of social interaction, has its own traditions and customs.

> You may want get some background information from this excellent location: Users Guide to Netiquette by Arlene H. Rinaldi (http://www.fau.edu/netiquette/netiquette.html).

Mailing Lists

In addition to using e-mail for one-to-one style communication between individuals, an e-mail address also allows you to participate in one-to-many communication by joining mailing or discussion lists. (These are commonly referred to as listservs, a misnomer which comes from the name of one popular software program for managing lists.) You can think of lists as group e-mail, where a message sent to one address is automatically forwarded to a whole group of individuals without the need to make "old-style" photocopies. This is accomplished by a special computer program which maintains a list of people, the subscribers, who have joined a particular list in order to discuss a specific interest area. Subscribers participate by sending and receiving e-mail messages which come directly to their electronic mailboxes. Some lists are moderated by the owner or other designated person who screens and selects the messages that are sent out, but many lists are unmoderated, where all messages are passed directly on to the list members.

There are several thousand mailing lists covering almost every interest area. Most are intended for a specific audience, but are open for anyone to subscribe. There are some closed lists, however, so your subscription may be denied in a few cases, or you may realize after reading some of the messages that the list is not related to the topic you expected from its name. If this turns out to be the case, just unsubscribe. The amount of list activity varies; some lists have thousands of members and are very active. Others are quite small and generate only a few messages a month. One caveat: Do not oversubscribe. If you join several mailing lists, you may find hundreds of messages per day in your mailbox. It is possible to receive your messages in digest form, which saves them and sends them all at once each day; nevertheless, even in digest form, one hundred messages can still be too many. (You can find out how to request digest form in the Welcome Message received when you first subscribe to a list.) Initially, it is probably better to join only one list. You may want to check with colleagues about their favorite lists and subscribe to one of those. Later on, you can subscribe to additional lists as your time permits.

Many mailing lists can be very useful in education, especially for teachers. The members have subscribed to discuss topics that are particularly important to them and to interact with colleagues. As a result, mailing lists tend to develop a strong sense of community where members get to know one another. In short, mailing lists are great places to ask questions, get information, locate resources, share information, and meet new colleagues.

Another exciting aspect of mailing lists is that it is often possible to communicate directly with the experts in your field and with other people who are doing the most up-to-date research. It can be quite motivating, and wonderfully surprising, to read a response from the author of your favorite textbook or the keynote speaker from your last professional conference.

Although mailing lists can be useful for students as well as teachers, some care should be taken when deciding how to use lists in the classroom because there is no way to know in advance what will appear in individual messages. If a list is moderated, obvious problems such as bad language will probably be avoided, but there may still be topics or viewpoints which not everyone feels comfortable with. There are lists especially for kids and other education-oriented lists where kids can participate with interested adults. Still, almost anyone can subscribe to a list, and even when a list is moderated, the moderator may not be able to screen with 100% effectiveness. Thus, it is possible that even an appropriate list might occasionally have postings containing inappropriate material for some students. There is also the chance of encountering topics which you may considerable unsuitable, but which

---

There are several thousand mailing lists covering almost every interest area.

Do not oversubscribe. If you join several mailing lists, you may find hundreds of messages per day in your mailbox.

Mailing lists are great places to ask questions, get information, locate resources, and share information, and interact with the experts in your field.

Care should be taken when deciding how to use lists in the classroom because there is no way to know in advance what will appear in individual messages.

E-MAIL FOR YOU

To: Colleagues
From: Emily Buchanan <JEANS.BUCHANAN@worldnet.att.net>
Subject: Mailing Lists

For teachers in isolated areas, the Internet is a lifeline! My first teaching assignment was in a very small, private school where there was only one class at each grade level. I was the one and only 6th grade teacher. All my previous educational experience had been in larger public school settings. I missed the collaboration and cooperation with other grade level teachers. I felt isolated and worried about losing touch with mainstream educational practices.

In an effort to keep in touch, I joined a mailing list, or listserv, for teachers. Overnight the mailing list put me in contact with hundreds of other teachers. It was great! We shared lessons, recommended books, solved problems, and discussed issues. Finally, I could talk to other 6th grade teachers who faced the same challenges as me. In addition, it was reaffirming to see that, even as a new teacher, I could offer ideas and advice to other teachers. Since it was all through the Internet, I could read and send messages at any time that was convenient for me.

My mailing list colleagues helped me get through the first two years of teaching. I'm in a larger, public school setting now, with plenty of co-workers, but I still value my on-line teacher network.

Emily B. Buchanan
Camillus Middle School
Syracuse, New York, USA

P.S. Joining a mailing list is easy. If offered, choose the "Digest" mode. That way all your messages will arrive together, once a day, rather than in a constant stream of individual messages. You can then scroll through the list of subjects to select the messages you want to > read. Here are the addresses of two of the mailing lists I've joined:

MIDDLE-L, a listserv for middle school educators
<listserv@postoffice.cso.uiuc.edu>

RTEACHER, a listserv for literacy educators
<listserv@listserv.syr.edu>

the moderator views as worthwhile, and thus allows on the list. Despite these concerns, mailing lists are great resources and many teachers do use them effectively with their students. As always, it is best for you to check out the situation for yourself. Subscribe to a mailing list for awhile before deciding how it might be used in your situation with your students, and check with colleagues about any problems they may have encountered on various lists.

E-MAIL FOR YOU

To: Colleagues

From: Cindy Lockerman <cklocker@UNCC.CAMPUS.MCI.NET>

Subject: Using mailing lists or listservs

Hi!

I want to share with everyone two experiences using e-mail on the RTEACHER listserv that illustrate an important point: The opportunity to make important connections is useful, informative, and tremendously satisfying as I see concerns and opinions that I hold echoed by voices worldwide. It truly affirms the concept of a shrinking planet! I will try to relate concisely a couple of electronic experiences.

First, I needed some help with a biography on Marie Clay, the New Zealand educator. Clay's work is a mainstay at the school where I teach and so I am quite familiar with her work, but I needed some biographical information for a course I was taking. I posted my needs on the RTEACHER listserv and another member quickly sent me the e-mail address of Professor Yetta Goodman (another prominent literacy educator), suggesting that I ask her for the information. I sent a query and within an hour, she wrote back with biographical information from her personal experience with Dr. Clay. Not only was I able to get information "that inquiring minds want to know", but I was able to converse with Dr. Goodman about literacy issues on a level that would otherwise be impossible.

Second, I recently followed a discussion on RTEACHER concerning the Accelerated Reader computer program. Keith Topping, a professor in Scotland who has done extensive research on this area, shared a number of ideas. After some discussion back and forth with him and some evidence from his research, I decided to do my own research on intermediate proficiency ESL students (Gr. 4—6). While end-of-grade tests will ultimately tell me if there has been any marked score improvement, I have noted a new enthusiasm in most of my "experimental group" for reading. I have also been able to use the 10-question tests as a springboard to test-taking skill tips. I could probably go on and on, but let it suffice to say that without the discussion and expertise of the listserv participants, I would not have thought to try a program that has been readily available to first language students but untried (in our area) with L2 students.

You may wish to read the archives of this listserv or join it yourself. The archives are located at: (http://listserv.syr.edu/archives/rteacher.html). Good luck!

Cindy Lockerman

Central Sites for Mailing Lists

If you wish to try out the use of mailing lists, the first step is to find the name and e-mail address of a list you want to join. There are thousands of lists, so you might begin by checking with colleagues and professional organizations or looking through journals. There are also many Internet sites containing master lists of mailing lists. Go to one of the central sites below, select a list and follow their directions, or read on and follow the general steps in the next section on subscribing to a mailing list.

- **Liszt**—http://www.liszt.com/
  This is the most comprehensive site we've found. It contains over 80,000 lists managed by listserv, listproc, and majordomo, as well as independently managed lists. Liszt has a brief but useful introduction to lists with helpful tips for beginners. They tell you how to find out more about a list as well as how to subscribe, which you can do directly from their site. They also allow you to search by topic.

- **Reference.Com**—http://www.reference.com/
  Another very comprehensive list that allows advanced searches for thousands of mailing lists.

- **TileNet**—http://tile.net/lists/
  This list is also quite comprehensive. You can search for lists alphabetically by name, subject, or domain.

- **Publicly Accessible Mailing Lists**—http://www.neosoft.com/ internet/paml/subjects/
  This site is smaller but updates its list frequently, claiming to be the most accurate/up-to-date list of lists.

- **EdWeb**—http://metalab.unc.edu/edweb/lists.html
  This is a much smaller list that focuses on lists related to education, especially K–12 issues, educational technology, and education reform. It also has a little background on mailing lists and an example for how to subscribe.

- **ERIC Listserv Archives**—
  http://ericir.syr.edu/virtual/Listserv_Archives/
  This is not a list of lists for subscribing, but an archive of educational mailing lists. Here you can read previous messages to various lists to get an idea of the type of topics that are discussed.

Subscribing to a Mailing List

In order to subscribe to a mailing list, you need to send an e-mail message to the server that manages the list. It's very important to send your request to the correct address. Mailing lists have two addresses, one for administration, which begins with the name of the program and server that manage the list;

Mailing lists have two addresses, one for administration, which begins with the name of the server that manages the list; and another for posting contributions to the list members, which usually begins with the name of the list.

and another for "posting" (sending contributions to the list members), which usually begins with the name of the list. Make sure you subscribe to the administrative address. Most of these begin with "listserv@...", the most common server program, or "listproc@..." or "majordomo@..." Or, you may occasionally see another, independently managed program name. Do not subscribe by sending a message to the address that begins with the name of the mailing list.

To subscribe, type the administrative address in the address box of the message composition window. Leave the subject line blank. Then type a subscribe message in the first line of the message pane. (Upper and lower case is usually insignificant.) Your message should look like this, but with your name, and without the brackets:

subscribe [list name] [your first name] [your last name]

For example, if I wanted to subscribe to the MIDDLE-L list, it would look like this:

subscribe MIDDLE-L Deborah Leu

Do not put any other information, such as an automatic signature for example, in the message pane. Any extra information is rejected by the server and usually invalidates the request. Rarely a list has a different procedure, but this is usually indicated on the master list or on the list's web page.

The Welcome Message

Save the Welcome message. It contains important information about expectations for members, how to get help, and most importantly how to get off the list.

Shortly after you send your message, you should receive a return message that welcomes you to the group and details its procedures. *Save this message!* It contains important information about expectations for members, how to get help, and most importantly how to unsubscribe to get off the list.

Unsubscribing

You usually leave a list by sending a message similar to your subscription request. Some lists do have special procedures, though, so check the original welcome message if you are having trouble. The general process is to type "unsubscribe" and the name of the list. (If that doesn't work, try "signoff", which is also used occasionally.) It is not necessary to type your name. For example:

unsubscribe MIDDLE-L

Remember to send this message to the administrative address, not the posting address.

Mailing List Netiquette

Netiquette is especially important for mailing list subscribers because their messages may be read by hundreds or thousands of people from all over the world. In addition, a list is basically like a club where you may run into other

Internet FAQ	
I have tried to unsubscribe from a list several times, but I keep getting mail. I am using the administrative address. What's going on?	First, if you have more than one e-mail account, be sure to unsubscribe using the same account that you used to subscribe. The server is a computer, not a person, and it won't recognize you if you try to unsubscribe from a different address, use a nickname, or spell your name differently. Occasionally, there may be a problem even if you have only one account. If you access your account from different computers, at home and at work for example, this sometimes hinders successful unsubscription. The server seems to differentiate messages from the two computers, even if the address is the same. Therefore, it's probably safest to try to always subscribe and unsubscribe from the same account and the same machine. If you continue to have trouble, send a message to Help as explained in the original welcome message, which should put you in touch with the list manager or another resource person.

members at any time—you don't want to offend someone that you know you will be meeting (electronically) several times a week.

In order to get a feel for the culture and "personality" of the list it is strongly recommended that you just read the list for awhile without posting any messages, called "lurking." This will give you a chance to see how the group operates and find out answers to some of your initial questions. You can also check out **The Net: User Guidelines and Netiquette** by Arlene H. Rinaldi (http://www.fau.edu/netiquette/netiquette.html). Most group members are tolerant and helpful to beginners. However, the introduction of an inappropriate topic or yet another repetition of a basic question sometimes receives a nasty response, known as "flaming". Observing how list members interact before you post messages will help you get the most from your mailing list.

> In order to get a feel for the culture and "personality" of the list it is strongly recommended that you "lurk" for a week or two, that is, just read the list for awhile before posting any messages.

Posting a Message

When you feel ready to make a contribution to the discussion, you should send your message to the posting address which usually begins with the name of the mailing list, e.g. rteacher@listserv.syr.edu. The address for posting a message to a list is usually included in the welcome message—another reason to save it. If your message is a response to an individual's question, it is often better to send your reply directly to him/her rather than to the whole list. However, there are some lists which request that you always respond to the whole list in order to improve the discussion. Again, check your welcome message for information about what is expected, and pay attention to what others on the list are doing to see how they handle responses.

It is easy to reply to either an individual or the group because most e-mail programs give you the option of addressing your reply to either an individual or to the group. (Internet Explorer and Netscape Communicator offer these options as "Reply" to reply to an individual, and "Reply All" to reply to the group.

TEACHING TIP	**Double Check the "Reply-to" Address**
	It's a good idea to double check the "reply-to" address of any reply message before you actually send it. Make sure the address box contains the address you want, either an individual's name and address or the listserv name and address. There are a few mailing lists which are configured so that a reply message automatically defaults to the Reply All mode and sends messages to the whole list, even when you click the individual reply button.

Privacy

The issue of privacy is often overlooked by newcomers to the Internet. Perhaps because we often use e-mail in private, we believe it is private. In fact, it is actually less private than traditional mail. First, just as in the regular mail system, electronic communications occasionally get missent. In most cases, people do not read a letter which is not addressed them, and will probably try to have it forwarded to the addressee. With e-mail, however, the message will be displayed on the screen, and may likely be read before the recipient realizes it is for another person. Although, this does not happen frequently, it is a possibility.

Of more concern to many e-mailers, is archiving. Virtually all individual e-mail is archived somewhere by the service provider or perhaps the school district or the school; individuals may also save messages. These messages can be saved for an indefinite, long period of time. They are most likely in an out-of-the-way file, known only to a system administrator, so it is unlikely that someone would search through thousands of messages to see what you have written. It is possible, however. Recent TV news magazines have done programs on investigative firms which search e-mail archives to get evidence for court cases.

Postings to mailing lists are even more accessible and less private. Many lists are archived in easily accessed places. Some lists keep their own archives, which are available only to members, but that could be a number in the thousands. Several education lists are archived by ERIC/the Educational Resource Information Center (http://ericir.syr.edu/virtual/Listserv_Archives/), and are easily accessible through a net search. Other lists are posted and archived by Usenet newsgroups, which may be read by thousands of people around the world. Finally, there are search engines which can bring up an individual's postings when that individual's name is entered for a search.

This information is not meant to alarm you, but only to caution you to think about what you write. Think of an e-mail message as a postcard, not a sealed letter. We have heard that you should never write anything that would embarrass you if it happened to be read at your next town meeting. We think this is sound advice.

We have heard that you should never write anything that would embarrass you if it happened to be announced at your next town meeting. We think this is sound advice.

Internet FAQ	
What about viruses? I've heard that I can get them through e-mail.	Computer viruses are programs that can infect your computer with small annoying problems, destroy files, or even cause a major crash. You can "catch" them by transferring files from one computer to another. For example, using a program at school, saving files to a disk, and then using that disk at home can let a virus into your system. Viruses are not generally transmitted through e-mail messages themselves. However, if an e-mail message has an attachment which includes an infected file, you can release it when you open the attachment. You can reduce the problem by not reading attachments unless you have requested that someone send them to you. However, the best way to avoid problems is to invest in a good anti-virus software program, and then keep it updated to catch new viruses and methods of infection as they appear. In addition to real viruses, there are also virus hoaxes which appear with increasing frequency. You can find out more about viruses at the **CERT Coordination Center** (http://www.cert.org/other_sources/viruses.html) and at CIAC, the U.S. Department of Energy's **Computer Incident Advisory Capability** (http://ciac.llnl.gov/ciac/CIACHome.html).

Viruses are not usually transmitted through e-mail messages themselves, but it's a good precaution to install an anti-virus program to protect your work.

Useful Mailing Lists

It's difficult to recommend mailing lists because everyone's needs and expectations are different, but we have found the following lists to be useful while writing this book. In addition, there are addresses for mailing lists related to particular content areas given at the end of each of the chapters following this one.

- **ECENET-L**—listserv@postoffice.cso.uicu.edu
  This site is for those interested in early childhood education, ages 0–8.

- **EDTECH**—listserv@vm.cc.edu
  This is an active list about the use of technology in education. It's not for everyone as it is quite technical, but there seemed to be quick and friendly responses for more advanced set-up and equipment problems.

- **MIDDLE-L**—listserv@postoffice.cso.uiuc.edu
  This list is for classroom teachers, administrators, parents, and anyone else interested in middle schools and middle school students. People share ideas, resources, advice, and problems.

- **WWWEDU**—listproc@educom.unc.edu
  This very active list was created to, "…provide an online 'commons' where teachers, academics, web designers, students, and concerned citizens could voice their opinions and suggestions on how to better develop the Web as a pedagogical instrument." It is focused on discussion and informative postings with fewer requests for individual help than you may find on some other lists.

Usenet Newsgroups

Another popular use of e-mail is reading the postings of Usenet Newsgroups. Usenet is a world-wide network of distributed discussions. It consists of thousands of newsgroups which are organized hierarchically by category and topic. Like mailing lists, newsgroups are a one-to-many type of e-mail-based communication. However, they differ from mailing lists in several important ways.

First, access is different. While mailing lists are limited to individual subscribers, newsgroups are available to anyone whose server receives and stores them. Earlier we compared mailing lists to group e-mail, like copies of a letter being sent to each person on a list. Usenet is more similar to a bulletin board where anyone who is in the vicinity can post and read whatever is on the board over a period of days or weeks. The length of posting time varies by newsgroup, but many groups also archive their messages. This allows you to browse a large number of messages quickly and read at your convenience rather than having to check your inbox every day.

A second difference is that messages are not sent to individual mailboxes. They are sent and stored on computers at Usenet sites around the world, where they can be accessed by other computers. In a way, you can think of your service provider as a kind of subscriber since providers select the newsgroups which they will access and make available on their servers. This means you have access to hundreds or thousands of messages without worrying about subscribing individually or about your mailbox becoming too full.

There is also a different sense of community. Many more people from all around the world participate in newsgroups than in the average mailing list, but they may only read and not respond to messages. In addition, unlike mailing list subscribers, newsgroup readers are not necessarily reading and posting to their major interest groups; they may have been skimming newsgroups and come upon a group that sounds interesting. After reading some messages, they may respond, but often they move on. Even users who tend to read the same groups, often check messages infrequently. Thus, there is generally less chance to get to know other users well, but there is an incredible variety of topics and viewpoints to be found.

The wide open readership and diversity of views found in newsgroups makes them an excellent source of information and a great way to broaden horizons. These same characteristics, however, can cause serious concern in the classroom since there are sure to be some topics, language use, and discussions that are unsuitable for students.

Using Usenet Newsgroups in the Classroom

Most newsgroups are unmoderated. This, together with the wide open readership and diversity of views found there, makes them an excellent source of information and a great way to broaden horizons. These same characteristics, however, can cause serious concerns in the classroom since there are sure to be some topics, language use, and discussions that are unsuitable for students. Moreover, several newsgroup categories contain explicit discussions of sex-related topics. These areas may not present problems for you, however, depending on your service provider. If your provider is your school district or a state network, for example, chances are they will not carry or provide access to controversial newsgroups. On the other hand, even the unavailability of certain groups cannot totally guarantee appropriateness because it is still possible for almost anyone to post to any group, so even "appropriate" groups may post inappropriate messages from time to time.

Even though the number of obviously unsuitable newsgroups is relatively small compared to the total, our experience and many of the e-mail messages we have received indicate that many teachers have reservations about using newsgroups in class with their students. There are some teachers, however, who point out that having older students compare the diverse viewpoints presented in newsgroups can be very helpful in improving critical thinking skills. They do stress that there be suitable guidance and supervision, however.

In short, opinions on newsgroups vary. They can provide a large quantity of diverse information quickly, but it may be hard to find exactly what you are looking for. You may be concerned about the appropriateness of some sites for your students, or even for yourself. Therefore, as with all Internet activities, we encourage you to try out a few groups and then make your own decision. You are the best judge of what suits your situation and meets your and your students' needs.

Reading Newsgroups With Internet Explorer and Netscape Communicator

One of the benefits of using Internet Explorer or Netscape Communicator is that they have closely integrated mail and news functions. This means it is relatively easy to explore newsgroups using either platform once you have used their respective e-mail programs. We will give a brief overview here to help you get started.

First, just as with e-mail, before you begin to read Newsgroups, you must set preferences. This may already have been done by your technical resource person, or you may have set your news preference when you set your mail preferences. If you need to set your newsgroups preferences, go back to the sections on setting preferences at the beginning of this chapter, and follow the directions, but select Newsgroups or Read News instead of Mail. Both Internet Explorer and Netscape Communicator have built in news readers, but you may want to change to your provider's news readers. The only additional information you need to do this is the name of your provider's news server. If you don't know it, check with your service provider or technical support person. You can also try adding "news." before your provider's address; for example: news.syr.edu. You may wish to write your news server here for easy reference: _____

Newsgroup Names and Hierarchies

Before going on to explore newsgroups, take a moment to look at the format of their names. Names may appear confusing at first, but they are actually hierarchical categories and topics. They are written in lower-case letters with dots between the words. It is usually easy to figure out the topic of any group by reading its name from left to right as in the following examples:

news.newusers

This group is in the "news" hierarchy and its topic is information for "new users".

k12.ed.comp.literacy

This group is in the "k12 education" hierarchy and its topic is "computer literacy". Other common Usenet hierarchies include:

- alt   alternative (just about any topic)
- biz   business
- comp computers
- news   Usenet news

Newcomer's Groups

There are three groups especially for newcomers:

- news.announce.newusers
- news.answers
- news.newusers.questions

You should look over the postings in these three groups because they contain helpful information about participating in newsgroups and also answer FAQs (Frequently Asked Questions). Many of the messages in these groups are reposted on a regular basis, often monthly, so that they are always available to newcomers and others for reference. If you have trouble locating these groups on your server, go to the **Index of Usenet FAQs** (http://www.cis.ohio-state.edu/hypertext/faq/usenet/). This posts all the information from the newcomers groups as well as FAQs and welcome messages for hundreds of other newsgroups. It is recommended that you read this information, especially the information on posting messages, since experienced users often react negatively to redundant questions, and respond by "flaming" (sending nasty replies).

Reading Newsgroups

Begin as when reading mail: In Internet Explorer, click the Mail icon and select Read News. In Netscape, click on the Newsgroups icon in the Component Bar. This brings up the mail window. Try clicking on the News folder in the left pane. If this is the first time you have read News you may need to download the newsgroups. In IE go to View and select All Newsgroups. In Netscape double click the folder name, which open a dialog box. This should download the list of all newsgroups offered on your server. This process usually takes several minutes. When the list is complete, scroll down and skim through the names of groups. The groups may be collapsed to save space. If so, this will be shown by boxes with plus/minus sign icons (in Explorer) or triangles (in Netscape) next to the group names. Just as with e-mail, these icons indicate nested or collapsed sub-groups. Clicking the icons will alternately hide and reveal the sub-groups.

Subscription to Newsgroups

If you think you may be interested in reading a particular group's messages, you should subscribe. Actually, it is the service provider who subscribes by agreeing to carry various groups and providing access to them, but the same word is used when individuals identify specific newsgroups as ones they are interested in and would like to read again. It's a good idea to subscribe if you plan to read newsgroups often. That way, the next time you want to read them, you can click the News folder in the folder list and only the groups you have subscribed to will be downloaded. This saves considerable time. Of course, you can always select all groups if you want to view the whole list again or change your subscriptions. (In Explorer, go to View in the main menu and select either All or Subscribed. In Netscape, double click the news folder, and make the appropriate selection in the dialog box. Then click the gray dot in the subscribe column next to the newsgroup you want, which changes the gray dot to a check. To unsubscribe, click the check, which then becomes a gray dot again.) Another option with recent versions of both browsers is to select New Groups, which allows you to download only the new groups that have been added to the list since the last time you logged on.

Replying and Composing

Replying to messages is very easy since both platforms use the same Message Composition window for replying to mail and news. You can refer back to the Reply and Composing New Messages sections earlier in this chapter if necessary. If you are composing a new message, be sure to add an explanatory subject title. Remember, readers will be looking for messages in their interest area. There are so many messages on news servers that many readers ignore non-descriptive titles such as "question", so be as informative as possible in a few words.

Newsgroup Netiquette

In general, newsgroup netiquette is similar to that for e-mail and mailing lists. You can get more specific information, however, by reading the postings in the news hierarchies for new users mentioned above. Remember, if you have trouble locating these groups on your server, check the **Index of Usenet**

FAQs (http://www.cis.ohio-state.edu/hypertext/faq/usenet/). Another useful site for guidelines and netiquette is the previously mentioned: **The Net: User Guidelines and Netiquette** by Arlene H. Rinaldi (http://www.fau.edu/netiquette/netiquette.html). Finally, it is always helpful to lurk (just read without posting messages) for awhile until you have a good sense of the personality and culture of the new group.

Central Sites for Newsgroups

As we have said, the newsgroups that are available to you depend on your service provider. You can download that list as well as the list of newsgroups accessible from your browser e-mail program. Consequently, it is not really necessary to search the web for newsgroups. However, if you would like to see a list, check the following sources. If you find an interesting site which is not accessible through your service provider, you can ask your provider to consider adding it.

- **Liszt Select**—http://www.liszt.com/
- **TileNet**—http://www.tile.net/
- **Reference.com**—http://www.reference.com/

Real-Time Communication

E-mail, mailing lists, and newsgroups are non-synchronous forms of electronic communication. There are, in addition, several types of real-time communication available on the Internet. These include listening to radio broadcasts with software such as RealAudio (http://www.realaudio.com); live interactions on IRC (Internet Relay Chat) channels or through instant messaging (IM), where you "talk to" people by reading and writing simultaneous messages; or MOOs, where you "move around" and "converse" with other visitors in text-based virtual locations; audio conferencing (like a phone call); and video conferencing, where you interact while watching the participants on live video. We have heard and read about several positive experiences with real-time communication, but it is also a frequently debated topic on listservs and among teachers and parents. Therefore, as with other Internet activities, we recommend that you explore the possibilities and decide for yourself whether they are useful and appropriate for you and your students. Keep in mind that most of these applications require additional software, equipment, or special access, and they may be confusing at first, especially for new users. As usual, you may want to work with another teacher or get help from your technical resource person, who is familiar with your situation and equipment.

Real-time interaction is getting easier as various sites offer easier software with step-by-step instructions and click-on capabilities for participants.

On the positive side, real-time interaction is getting easier as various sites begin to offer better software with step-by-step instructions and click-on capabilities for participants. The following sites should be helpful:

For Chat

- **Teachers Helping Teachers Chat Area—** http://www.pacificnet.net/~mandel/ircinfo.html This site contains brief, but useful how-to information. You can also join real-time conversations with other teachers.

- **Tips for Conferencing with IRC—** http://www1.minn.net/~schubert/IRC.html Suggestions for using Internet Relay Chat for classroom conferencing.

- **The Teacher's Network**—http://www.teachnet.org/ You can join real-time discussions with other teachers.

- **IRCLE**—http://www.ircle.houseit.com/ Information and downloadable chat software for Macs.

- **mIRC**—http://www.mirc.co.uk/ Information and downloadable chat software for PCs.

For Instant Messaging

America Online—http://www.aol.com

One of the main problems with chat in the classroom has been safety. AOL's new Buddy Software allows teachers and students to set up their own private buddy lists, which should eliminate the problem because only those on the list can chat. Users are also notified which members of their buddy list are online as soon as they log on. It is not necessary to use AOL as your service provider to use this software.

For MOOs

- **Telnet Tips for Connecting to MOOs—** http://www.daedalus.com/net/telnet.html This site gives information on using Telnet, the most common ways to enter MOOs.

- **Moosetracks—** http://www.cc.gatech.edu/fac/Amy.Bruckman/moose-crossing/ This site is a MOO designed especially for 9–13 year olds. Originally only for Macs, they have just come out with a pre-release version for PCs. Both versions can be downloaded from the site.

Visiting the Classroom: Riki Peto's High School Social Studies Classes in Washington

Riki Peto demonstrates the power of cross-cultural communication and collaboration in the projects she develops with her students at Pasco High School in Pasco, Washington (see Figure 3-12). Riki has won numerous awards for her collaborative work with classrooms around the world as part of the Northwest History course she teaches. In these projects, her students study the history and culture of their area and share their work with classrooms that do the same for their area. These projects produce important learning outcomes about the history of the Northwest, of course, but they also broaden her students' insights into what it is like to live in other parts of the world. Moreover, they produce new communication skills via e-mail and teleconferencing skills using Internet web cameras.

Together, the teachers and students develop each of these projects, beginning with intensive periods of brainstorming and communication. Often they conclude with exchange parties where each class sends the other classes small boxes of traditional food along with directions for its preparation. When time zones permit, they try to have these simultaneously. When time zones and schedules conflict, photos are taken and posted on the web so that collaborating classrooms can see each class celebrate all their hard work together. One of these projects resulted in Riki's class winning the international grand prize in AT&T's Virtual Classroom competition and traveling to Japan.

Riki and her students have developed important insights into the potential of e-mail, the Internet, and communication with other classrooms in distant parts of the world. As she notes in a short article describing her work (available at: http://users.owt.com/rpeto/progress/),

> Schools must not use computers (merely) for drill and practice; this can be as deadly and time consuming as static textbooks. Students engaged in such projects as the unique and stimulating online environment called AT&T 'Virtual Classroom' not only learn valuable Internet skills, but also gain insights into different cultures, geography and history, and communicate about their ideas and dreams.

If you are interested in collaborative e-mail projects in your social studies classrooms, Riki and her students provide a wonderful model.

Figure 3-12
The home page for Riki Peto's social studies classes at Pasco High School in Pasco, Washington.

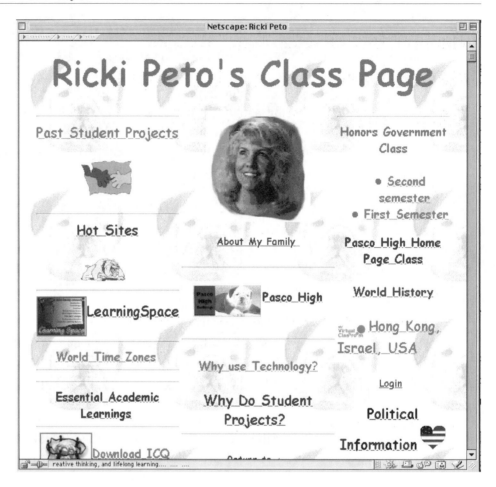

Effective Instructional Strategies: Internet Workshop, Internet Project, Internet Inquiry, and WebQuests

CHAPTER

4

We received an e-mail the other day from a teacher who wrote, "I was really surprised. Using the Internet isn't very different from what we already do in my class. I use Internet Workshop just as I use Reading and Writing Workshop. Internet Project was easy to do, too, especially when it has a website on the Internet with everything you need like **Earth Day Groceries Project** (http://www.earthdaybags.org/). I haven't used Internet Inquiry yet, but this shouldn't be very different from the inquiry projects my students already do. I am even making a WebQuest page now for my class."

Developing effective instructional strategies with the Internet is really not as difficult as it might seem. There are only a few major issues to consider. Once you consider these issues, Internet resources may be easily integrated with what you already use in your classroom.

On the other hand, the Internet will increase, not decrease, your central role in orchestrating learning experiences. You will be challenged to thoughtfully guide students' learning within information environments that are richer and more complex, presenting richer and more complex learning opportunities. Teachers who abdicate this responsibility will frequently find students "surfing" quickly from one location to another, not reading or thinking critically about information they find. Time spent will largely be time wasted. However, teachers who have thoughtfully considered how to weave Internet experiences into the curriculum will provide important learning opportunities for their students, opportunities their students would not be able to have otherwise. Moreover, they will have provided students with a better understanding of our increasingly interdependent and global community.

Don and Debbie

Teaching With the Internet: Sharee Mendoza's Class

Sharee Mendoza had a hard time sleeping each year during the first week of school; she was always filled with the excitement of new possibilities, new students, new ideas, and new challenges for her fifth grade class. Often, like this morning, she would come to school early to work, to plan, and to think.

Sharee checked the hamsters' water, she looked to see how Felix, their boa, was doing after yesterday's meal, straightened up the science books in the resource center, and checked her e-mail.

Sharee needed to pull things together for the dinosaur unit she was planning. It would start soon. She was gathering resources and ideas from a number of sources: her folder from last year's unit, the school library, and she was trying the Internet, too. Yesterday she posted requests for instructional ideas about dinosaurs at several locations:

- The **Dinosaur** mailing list—this is a mailing list for educators and others interested in exchanging information about dinosaurs. It is run by The Cleveland Museum of Natural History. Information about subscribing to this list is available at: http://www.cmnh.org/fun/dinosaur-archive/information.html

- The **RTEACHER** mailing list—this is a mailing list for literacy educators run in conjunction with the journal *Reading Teacher.* Information about subscribing to this list is available at: http://web.syr.edu/~djleu/RTEACHER/directions.html

- The **WWEDU** mailing list—this is a mailing list for educators interested in using the WWW. Earlier, Sharee had subscribed to this group by sending a subscription message (subscribe WWEDU Sharee Mendoza) to listproc@educom.unc.edu

- The **MIDDLE-L** mailing list—a mailing list managed by the ERIC Clearinghouse for middle school educators. Information about subscribing to this list is available at: http://ericeece.org/listserv/middle-l.html

- The message board at Classroom Connect's **ConnectedTeacher** (http://www.connectedteacher.com/home.asp)—a place where teachers post questions about using the Internet for teaching and hear what others are doing in their classrooms.

Many believe the best resources on the Internet for teachers are the other teachers you will meet in your journeys. They will provide you with many important ideas and resources for your classroom.

Now it was time to see if her inquiries had brought in any useful ideas.

The most amazing thing to Sharee was not the incredible resources on the Internet; it was the wonderfully supportive teachers she met. Sharee had several e-mail messages in her mailbox with great resources and ideas. None of these teachers knew her but they still took time to write lengthy notes, sharing their experiences and resources. Teachers had responded from California, Oklahoma, Arizona, Alberta, Manitoba, Florida, Washington,

Australia, New Zealand, and Great Britain. They provided a number of great ideas for her dinosaur unit:

Develop "healthy skeptics" in your classroom. A teacher in Texas used this phrase and it seemed to be a good one. She noted that anyone can publish information on the Internet and so one is never certain about the accuracy of information found there. She suggested Sharee have her students explore **ICYouSee Guide to Critical Thinking** (http://www.ithaca.edu/library/Training/hott.html) and learn how to critically evaluate Internet information through several guided experiences with web sites. She made other suggestions, too: require students to cross reference claims from several sources before accepting them as accurate and show students how to reference information found on the WWW by visiting **Citing Internet Resources** (http://www.classroom.net/classroom/CitingNetResources.html).

Conduct an Internet Workshop session. A teacher in New Zealand recommended this instructional model since it was consistent with more constructivist views of teaching and learning. He explained how to set bookmarks to specific sites rich in resources and then have students explore the sites as they record important information to bring to a workshop session and share with others. He had his class keep a "Digging for Dinosaurs" journal, writing down interesting information about dinosaurs and indicating where it was obtained. He used this activity as an introduction to the dinosaur unit.

Locate and bookmark central sites for dinosaurs. Several teachers sent along their favorite sites with extensive and well-organized links to dinosaur resources on the Internet:

- **Walking with Dinosaurs**—http://www.bbc.co.uk/dinosaurs
  There are so many incredible activities and resources for children at this site, developed by the BBC, it is hard to know where to begin (see Figure 4-1). Be certain to listen to the T-Rex and other dinosaurs! Lots of games, puzzles, and activities, too. Set a bookmark!

- **Dino Russ's Lair**—http://www.isgs.uiuc.edu/isgsroot/dinos/dinos_home.html
  An amazingly exhaustive set of links developed by a geologist working at the Illinois Department of Natural Resources.

- **Zoomdinosaurs.com**—http://www.zoomdinosaurs.com/subjects/dinosaurs/toc.shtml
  A commercial site with banner ads but this site contains amazing resources for the classroom study of dinosaurs.

- **The Museum of Paleontology at the University of California, Berkeley**—http://www.ucmp.berkeley.edu/index.html

Figure 4-1.
Walking with Dinosaurs from the BBC (http://www.bbc.co.uk/dinosaurs), a wonderful central site for dinosaur study in the classroom.

A sophisticated series of tours through the world of paleontology.

- **The Field Museum**—http://www.fmnh.org
  A great site with several useful areas related to dinosaurs including "Sue on the Web", a presentation explaining how a new T-Rex dinosaur is being conserved.

- **Dino-Roar**—
  http://www.sciam.com/explorations/121597dinosaur
  Where students can hear how duckbill dinosaurs may have sounded and read how scientists at Sandia Labs reached their conclusions.

- **Kenetosaurs**—http://www.childrensmuseum.org/kinetosaur
  A site developed at the Children's Museum in Indianapolis with interesting stories about many facets of dinosaurs including a location where students may dig for dinosaurs, as well as great ideas for making dinosaur models from classroom materials.

- **Dinosaur Eggs**—
  http://www.nationalgeographic.com/dinoeggs
  This location by National Geographic takes students on a hunt for dinosaur eggs, and then shows how these are "hatched" by researchers who wish to study the embryos inside. The

site includes many great stories about today's scientists and their work studying dinosaurs.

Provide time for students' independent exploration of the WWW for dinosaur resources. Direct this exploration by setting a bookmark to **Yahooligans** (http://www.yahooligans.com) and limit their search to this location. Yahooligans is a central site for children where information has been screened for child safety. Have students share their search strategies and the information they find about dinosaurs during Internet Workshop sessions.

Have students complete a WebQuest on dinosaurs. WebQuests are complete lesson experiences on the Internet, usually developed by other teachers following the WebQuest model. Visit WebQuest locations such as those found at:

- **Here Come the Dinosaurs**—http://www3.guilford.k12.nc.us/webquests/dinosaurs.html
- **Dinoriffic WebQuest**—http://tess.uis.edu/www/448sp99/dinoriffic.html
- **Dinosaur WebQuest**—http://www.lfelem.lfc.edu/tech/DuBose/webquest/Vaccarella/WQPS_VV.html
- **Dinosaurs**—http://www.lfelem.lfc.edu/tech/DuBose/webquest/reinhardt/dinosaur.html

Ask a paleontologist questions about dinosaurs. Have students visit the **Mad Scientists Network** (http://www.madsci.org) at the University of St. Louis and read answers to previous questions. If their question has not been answered, have them send it via e-mail. It will be answered by a paleontologist.

Have students generate and exchange puzzles. One teacher pointed Sharee to **Puzzlemaker** (http://puzzlemaker.school.discovery.com/) at the Discovery Channel site. Here, teachers and students could generate their own word searches, crossword puzzles, and many other different types of word games and then quickly print them out.

As she read these ideas, Sharee went to her web browser, found each location, and quickly reviewed the contents, determining if they would fit her goals for the unit. She made a bookmark for **ICYouSee Guide to Critical Thinking** (http://www.ithaca.edu/library/Training/hott.html) and decided to begin with an Internet Workshop around the critical thinking skills central to effective Internet use. She also decided to use Internet Workshop with the journal activity, "Digging for Dinosaurs". She set a bookmark for **Walking with Dinosaurs** (http://www.bbc.co.uk/dinosaurs) and for **Dino Russ's Lair** (http://www.isgs.uiuc.edu/isgsroot/dinos/dinos_home.html) for this experience.

Sharee set a bookmark for Yahooligans (http://www.yahooligans.com/) to provide independent exploration time in an area of the web that would be safe for her students.

Sharee also set a bookmark for **Yahooligans** (http://www.yahooligans.com/) to provide independent exploration time in an area of the web that would be safe for her students. One teacher had recommended a list of books on dinosaurs so she copied it into an e-mail message and forwarded it to the school librarian. She asked that any of these books in the school library be sent down to her class. Then, she set a bookmark for the **Puzzlemaker** location (http://puzzlemaker.school.discovery.com). This would come in handy during her unit.

Sharee liked the idea of having an Internet Workshop session where students could share the results of their dinosaur research. She would schedule a workshop period for 30 minutes each week. Students could share information they had acquired and the new locations they had found during Internet Inquiry. She would do this on Mondays.

Yesterday, Sharee had developed a schedule for students to use with the single computer she had linked to the Internet. Having only a single Internet computer limited access for students but her schedule provided equal access for everyone. Each week, every student in her class received half an hour alone on the computer and half an hour on the computer with a partner. If students needed more than an hour of Internet access, they would sometimes go down to the media center and use the lab there. While she always wanted more time on the Internet for her students, Sharee noted they quickly learned to use their Internet time efficiently. This appeared to help them develop useful strategies for navigation. You can see her schedule in Figure 4-2.

Each week, every student in her class received half an hour alone on the computer and half an hour on the computer with a partner. If students needed more than an hour of Internet access, they would sometimes go down to the media center and use the lab there.

Figure 4-2.
Sharee Mendoza's computer schedule posted next to her Internet computer.

	Monday	Tuesday	Wednesday	Thursday	Friday
8:30–9:00	Michelle	Michelle/Becky	Chris/Emily	Shannon/Cara	Cynthia/Jennifer
9:00–9:30	Chris	John/Peter	Jeremy/Dave	Kati	Patti
9:30–10:00	**Internet Workshop**	Ben	Aaron	Lisa	Julia
10:00–10:30	Shannon	**PE**	Paul	**PE**	Andy
10:30–11:00	**Library**	Mike	Scott	Faith	Melissa
11:00–11:30	Cynthia	Eric	James	Linda	Sara
11:30–12:30	**Lunch**	**Lunch**	**Lunch**	**Lunch**	**Lunch**
12:30–1:00	Jennifer	Dave	Peter	Cara	Emily
1:00–1:30	Becky	Jeremy	Ben/Sara	Mike/Linda	John
1:30–2:00	Eric/James	Aaron/Melissa	**Music**	Paul/Scott	**Class Meeting**
2:00–2:30	Kati/Lisa		Faith/Andy	Patti/Julia	

Yes, the unit was coming together. Now, she wanted to find another class on the Internet that would like to do a collaborative Internet project on dinosaurs. Maybe they could each share the results of classroom Inquiry projects. This would also help her students develop written communication skills. She would try posting a message again on each of the listservs to see if anyone was interested in joining her for this project experience. Things were coming together nicely as her class entered her room that morning.

Lessons From the Classroom

The episode with Sharee Mendoza provides us with a number of important lessons as we consider effective instructional strategies with the Internet. A central lesson is to recognize that the Internet will require us to rely upon what we call distributed learning. Increasingly, learning will require us to learn from one another since no single person can be expected to know everything that exists in a rich and complex world like the Internet. Sharee had learned this lesson; she relied upon many other teachers for their suggestions about the dinosaur unit. In a very short period of time, she mined the Internet and came up with many wonderful ideas to include in her unit. Sharee was going to pass along this lesson to her students, too. By engaging in Internet Workshop each student would learn something special they could bring back to the class during their workshop session and exchange with other students. Internet Project, another instructional model, also helps students develop the collaborative skills essential to distributed learning. By collaborating with another classroom, each class would exchange new ideas and resources with the other and develop new communication skills important for information exchange.

Teachers sometimes describe this change to us as moving from a "sage on the stage to a guide at the side." What they mean is that our role changes from being the only expert at the head of the class to being one of many members of a classroom community with expertise, each one knowing something very special and important to others.

Most of us first see this change when we have students in our classroom who begin assisting us when our computer freezes, when the printer isn't working, or when something else fails. Suddenly, a student's expertise becomes visible and critical to our classroom's success. As digital technologies become more important to our classrooms and as they repeatedly change, it is impossible for anyone to keep up with everything taking place. You will see each student becoming an expert in a particular area that interests him or her. One child might be an expert with knowing the best resources about Jan Brett, another with information about butterflies, and still others will become experts in other information areas or other aspects of technology.

This change reflects the changes taking place in the world of work today. The highly structured and top-down model of business and industry has

> Increasingly, learning will require us to learn from one another since no single person can be expected to know everything that exists in a rich and complex world like the Internet.

> Teachers sometimes describe this change to us as moving from a "sage on the stage to a guide at the side."

changed to a far more decentralized model in order for companies to successfully compete in a highly competitive global economy. Nimble, aggressive companies that take advantage of individual employee's expertise survive; inflexible and tightly structured companies that ignore their employees' special talents fail in a world of rapidly changing information and technology. Thus, it is important that we prepare children for these new worlds of literacy and life-long learning they will experience as adults.

Sharee's story also teaches us a second lesson: Developing a weekly schedule for Internet use in single-computer classrooms helps to ensure that all students receive access to this important resource. Sometimes, certain students will tend to dominate access to the Internet and other students will have their time curtailed. It is important to guarantee time for all students to use the resources on the Internet.

Third, Sharee discovered how easy it was to use Internet Workshop. Using Internet Workshop was a simple way to integrate the Internet into the curriculum. Setting a bookmark and then developing a short assignment was easy to do. Moreover, it focused student use of the Internet on important information. Sharee found this simple technique engaged students actively in their learning. She often noticed several students at the computer talking about the information for that week's Internet Workshop experience. It was a great suggestion. We have already mentioned the use of this procedure for developing navigation skills; it is also highly effective for sharing and discussing content information.

Sharee's story also reminds us how important it is to help students evaluate the accuracy of information they find on the Internet. Since anyone can publish nearly any information they wish on the Internet, it is hard to be certain the information you find is accurate. We need to help students become "healthy skeptics" if we wish them to become effective consumers of information on the Internet. We also need to show them how to reference the information they use in their writing.

It is also important to note the special opportunities on the Internet for Internet Project. Developing a collaborative project with classrooms in other parts of the world leads to important learning outcomes as information is shared and new questions are developed. Internet Project requires advance planning between teachers, but the rewards are often well worth the additional time.

Note, too, how Sharee provided opportunities for her students to search for information on their own. After students have developed initial navigation strategies, it is important to provide opportunities for independent navigation through the Internet. This encourages students to discover, and then share, even more useful strategies. Providing opportunities for independent research on the Internet, as Sharee did with Internet Inquiry, accomplished this.

It is also important to realize that Internet use may be easily integrated with other instructional practices with which you are already familiar. Sharee's

Developing a weekly schedule for Internet use in single computer classrooms helps to ensure that all students receive access to this important resource.

Using Internet Workshop was a simple way to integrate the Internet into the curriculum.

We need to help students become "healthy skeptics" if we wish them to become effective consumers of information on the Internet.

Developing a collaborative project with classrooms in other parts of the world leads to important learning outcomes as information is shared and new questions are developed.

It is important to realize that Internet use may be easily integrated with other instructional practices with which you are already familiar.

use of a journal for Internet Workshop is but one example of this. She also wove in a practice found in many classrooms, the use of an "author's chair." Nearly every instructional activity you currently use in your classroom may also be used with the Internet.

Finally, while the Internet is a tool to support students' learning, it is also a powerful resource for planning instructional activities. In a short session after school, Sharee quickly gathered resources and ideas for an extensive, thematic unit. As you become more familiar with the Internet, you will also develop efficient strategies for using the Internet to plan activities. After a short time, you will wonder how you ever taught without this resource.

 E-MAIL FOR YOU

To: Our readers

From: Jill Newcomb newcomb@voyager.net
      Cindy Ross jross@sunny.ncmc.cc.mi.us

Subject: My Hero Project

For our first experience using the Internet in the classroom, we decided to choose a small group to work on an activity called "Heroes." We used two web sites, **My Hero** (http://myhero.com/) and **The Giraffe Project** (www.giraffe.org/giraffe/).

The students first read about well known heroes described on these web sites. Then the students read about local heroes which were submitted by other students to these web sites. The group discussed qualities and characteristics of the heroes using the analytical skills of comparing and contrasting.

Students then chose their own personal hero and wrote an essay about this person. These essays were submitted to the **My Hero** web site to be published on the Internet for other students to read.

To further practice writing and communication skills, the students chose a hero from their school or community. Collaboratively they wrote interview questions. After practice and role playing, the students interviewed their hero. The interview was videotaped.

For a culminating activity we held a "Hero Celebration." Students invited their parents and the community hero. At the celebration, the students read their essays, introduced their hero, and all participants viewed the videotaped interview.

Using the Internet was highly motivating for these students. They eagerly shared their findings of heroes with their teachers and classmates. We noticed their enthusiasm carried over to other areas. For instance, when checking out library books, these students now choose biographies over easy-to-read fiction. We are looking forward to other activities using the Internet in the classroom.

Jill Newcomb newcomb@voyager.net
Cindy Ross jross@sunny.ncmc.cc.mi.us
Ottawa Elementary School
Petosky, Michigan

Management Issues in Departmentalized or Self-Contained Classrooms

It is essential to thoughtfully plan how to integrate Internet experiences into your classroom curriculum. Sometimes we abdicate this responsibility when we make Internet experiences available only after students' regular classroom work is completed, providing little direction for what should be done. Using the Internet like this makes it one of several "free choice" activities in the classroom. There are several problems with this approach.

First, making the Internet one of several "free choice" activities means that you abdicate your responsibility to prepare students for their literacy and learning futures. It is important for each of us to assume this new responsibility if we seek to adequately prepare them for a world in which we all are more closely connected to important information resources.

A second problem is that you implicitly communicate that the Internet is an activity for recreation, not for the important work of solving central problems, thinking critically about the information you encounter, or communicating with others around the world. When you integrate the Internet into a central position of your classroom curriculum you tell students the Internet is important to their lives and needs to be approached with respect and thoughtfulness as well as the interest and excitement it generates.

Finally, equity is an increasingly critical problem. Making the Internet available only when regular work is complete, ultimately results in more advanced students having greater Internet access. This ends up helping the rich get richer, as advanced students who finish their regular work first become more advanced in their ability to access and analyze information on the Internet. Meanwhile, weaker students, often last in completing work, are denied these opportunities to improve their abilities.

If you have a self-contained classroom with only a single Internet computer, equity becomes an important challenge. How do we provide all of our students with both sufficient and equal access to the Internet? One of the best solutions we have found is the one used by Sharee and illustrated in Figure 4-2. By developing a weekly matrix with 30-minute Internet periods and assigning students to one 30-minute period by themselves and one 30-minute period with a partner, you can ensure that everyone in your class receives at least on hour of Internet access each week. To do this, however, you must be willing to have 1–2 students working on their weekly Internet assignments while others in your class receive instruction in another area. Thus, many teachers in self-contained classrooms will assign students who are doing well in math to an Internet session that coincides with math, thinking that these students will be more likely than others to independently make up any missed instruction. Similarly, during science instruction they assign students to the Internet who are doing well in science.

If you adopt this plan in your classroom, you should keep several useful strategies in mind. First, be certain that you periodically rotate the assigned

Equity is an increasingly critical problem.

How do we provide all of our students with both sufficient and equal access to the Internet? One of the best solutions we have found is illustrated in Figure 4-2.

times on the computer schedule so that the same students do not miss their time because of regular conflicts with the school's special functions (e.g., regularly scheduled school assemblies, student council meetings, or special activity meetings). It would be unfair, for example, to have a student miss her Internet time on Monday of each week because she had to attend music class. To avoid this conflict, many teachers will change their Internet schedule once every two weeks.

Second, rotate partners regularly at the computer so that all of your students have an opportunity to work with many different individuals in your class. This increases opportunities for improving social skills at the same time it increases opportunities to learn new things from other students about Internet use.

Developing a regular schedule for Internet use in a self-contained classroom will help you to manage equity issues during school time. In the future, this problem will be resolved as additional connections are made to classrooms. For now, we need to develop strategies such as this to accommodate our students' learning needs.

What about teachers with a single computer classroom at the middle school or at the high school where instruction is typically departmentalized? Here you will be severely challenged to provide students with equitable access during a single 40 or 50 minute period each day. In fact, most teachers will not even attempt this with only a single Internet computer in their classroom. It is really only possible if you have a cluster of computers within your classroom, an unfortunate rarity, or a lab in your school.

Most teachers in departmentalized programs will schedule time for their entire class in an Internet lab, or provide assignments that are completed in the lab outside of regularly scheduled class time. In these contexts, it is important to provide students with the complete addresses of the sites you wish them to use in each assignment or to provide these at a school or classroom home page (see Chapter 12). It is not always possible to set bookmarks for all the computers in a computer lab.

> Most teachers in departmentalized programs will schedule time for their entire class in an Internet lab, or provide assignments that are completed in the lab outside of regularly scheduled class time.

| **TEACHING TIP** | If you develop a schedule like that described in this chapter for a single computer classroom, consider scheduling students who are strong at math during math time, students who are strong in language arts during language arts time, and so forth. This prevents students who really need assistance in a subject from missing important instructional time in that area. You may wish to read how Mark Ahlness uses this strategy in his classroom at Arbor Heights Elementary School in Seattle, Washington. Visit his spotlight page at **Ed's Oasis** (http://www.EDsOasis.org/Spotlight/Ahlness/Ahlness.html) to see how Mark uses the Internet in his class. |

Teaching With the Internet: Instructional Models

When the Internet is used without direction and guidance, it often takes students away from thoughtful integration and analysis of information in favor

Internet experiences should always have a purpose; they should always be an integral part of your instructional program.

Developing effective instructional strategies with the Internet is not difficult. It should include these models: Internet Workshop; Internet Project; and Internet Inquiry and WebQuests.

of random, unconnected surfing experiences. You will see this pattern, too, in your classroom unless students have a clear purpose each time they sit down to use the Internet. Internet experiences should always have a purpose; they should always be an integral part of your instructional program. This requires you to thoughtfully plan this integration.

How can you effectively integrate the Internet into your classroom? Developing effective instructional strategies with the Internet is not difficult. It should include these three models:

- Internet Workshop
- Internet Project
- Internet Inquiry

This sequence of instructional models is developmentally sensitive, so you can begin with Internet Workshop, a model that is easiest to use, and gradually build to more complex and powerful instructional strategies as you feel comfortable. You will probably find many similarities between elements in these models of Internet use and the instructional strategies you already use in your classroom. This should also make it easier to integrate Internet use into your classroom.

In addition, we will explore an instructional model often found on the Internet, a WebQuest. This, too, is easy to use in your classroom and it is made easier since so many teachers have developed web pages with this model. Thus, you can use their WebQuests for your own classroom.

Keeping it Simple: Using Internet Workshop in Your Classroom

Many teachers begin their instructional journeys on the Internet with Internet Workshop.

You just received an Internet connection in your classroom along with a new computer or perhaps your school just received a new Internet lab. How do you begin to integrate the Internet into your instructional program? Many teachers start by using Internet Workshop. This is the easiest way to begin using the Internet for instruction.

Internet Workshop has many variations. Generally, though, it contains these steps:

1. Locate a good site with content related to a classroom unit of instruction and set a bookmark for the location(s).
2. Develop an activity requiring students to use the site(s).
3. Assign this activity to be completed during the week.
4. Have students share their work, questions, and new insights at the end of the week during a workshop session.

The first step is to locate a site on the Internet with content related to the learning you have planned for that week in your classroom. As you consider which site on the Internet to use, it is helpful to begin your search at a central Internet site, a location on the Internet with extensive and well organized links about a specific topic. Visiting a central site such as those listed in Chapter 2 and in later chapters will often give you many useful resources for your instructional unit, some of which may be used for Internet Workshop. When you find a location you wish to use in your activity, set a bookmark.

The second step is to develop an activity related to the learning goals of your unit, using the site you have bookmarked. Sometimes this activity will introduce students to a site you will be using in your instructional unit. Sometimes the activity will develop important background knowledge for your unit. And, sometimes the activity will develop navigation strategies for Internet use. Often, teachers prepare an activity page for students to complete and then bring to Internet Workshop.

The third step is to assign the activity to be completed during the week. If you have only a single Internet connection in your classroom, you may wish to have students work in pairs to complete the assignment. If you have a departmental system at your school, you could take your class to the computer lab to complete the assignment or you could assign it as work to be completed on their own during the week.

The fourth step is to have students share their work, questions, and new insights at the end of the week during Internet Workshop. This is a time for the class to get together and share the learning they completed and to ask questions about issues that came up during their work on the Internet. It is also a time to plan and discuss the next areas to explore for the next workshop session.

Often, Internet Workshop is used by teachers to develop important background knowledge for a unit of a topic they will be exploring in class. These teachers will locate a central site about the topic and then develop an activity designed to explore the site, a location that will also be used throughout the unit. In these cases, the activity page invites students to explore the web site and bring their discoveries to Internet Workshop where they are shared and used to initiate important discussions about the topic. At other times, Internet Workshop is used during a unit to explore an idea or an issue that is central to your curricular goals.

The activity page in Figure 4-3 was developed by two teachers to develop background knowledge about Japan. They developed the activity to begin a unit for an interdisciplinary global studies course taught by a social studies teacher and an English teacher. These teachers located **Kids Web Japan** (http://www.jinjapan.org/kidsweb/) and set a bookmark to this central site on the classroom computers (see Figure 4-4). Notice how the tasks on the activity page are open-ended, inviting students to make their own discoveries at this location and bring these to Internet Workshop to share at the beginning of the unit. This is a critical aspect of any activity sheet prepared for Internet Activity. Open-ended questions invite students to bring many different types of information to Internet Workshop for discussion. If

---

Often, Internet Workshop is used by teachers to develop important background knowledge for a unit of a topic they will be exploring in class.

Notice how the tasks on the activity page are open-ended, inviting students to make their own discoveries at this location and bring these to Internet Workshop to share at the beginning of the unit. This is a critical aspect of any activity sheet prepared for Internet Workshop.

Figure 4-3.
A page developed for Internet Workshop to introduce a unit on Japan.

EXPLORING JAPAN

Internet Researcher: _____ Date: _____

Objectives

This Internet Workshop will introduce you to our unit on Japan. You will have an opportunity to explore an important resource on the Internet for our unit. You will also learn about recent news events and the national government of Japan.

News About Japan

1. Go to the bookmark I have set for **Kid's Web Japan** (http://www.jinjapan.org/kidsweb/) and scroll down to the bottom of this page. Now click on the button "Monthly News" (http://www.jinjapan.org/kidsweb/news.html) and read several recent news stories from Japan. Find out what is happening in Japan and be ready to share this during Internet Workshop. _____
   _____
   _____

Politics and the Constitution

2. Click on the button "Politics and the Constitution" and explore information about the national government Be certain to read answers to some of the questions at the bottom of this article. Write down what you learned about the politics and constitution of Japan. Be prepared to share this information during Internet Workshop._____
   _____
   _____

What's Cool in Japan?

3. Now let's find out what are some of the biggest fads among students in Japan your own age. Visit "What's Cool in Japan" (http://www.jinjapan.org/kidsweb/cool.html) and find out what students are doing. Write down notes about what you discovered is most popular among students and be ready to share this information during Internet Workshop. _____
   _____
   _____

Your Choice

4. Visit at least one of the many other locations at **Kids Web Japan.** You decide where to go! Write down notes of what you discovered and share your special discoveries with all of us during Internet Workshop. _____
   _____
   _____

Evaluation Rubric

8 points— You recorded important information for each item (4 x 2 = 8 points).
2 points— You effectively shared important information with us during our workshop session, helping each of us to learn about Japan.

_____

10 points—Total

Figure 4-4.
A portion of the screen at **Kids Web Japan** (http://www.jinjapan.org/ kidsweb/), a central site used to introduce a classroom unit on Japan with Internet Workshop.

you ask students to find the same factual answers, there will be little to talk about during your workshop session.

The workshop session is a critical element of Internet Workshop. The purposes of this session include:

The workshop session is a critical element of Internet Workshop.

1. To support students' ability to acquire information from the Internet.

2. To learn about the topic they are studying.

3. To think critically about the information they, and others, obtain.

During the session, students share what they have learned, ask questions about issues they do not understand, and seek information to guide upcoming work. As such, this time provides the perfect opportunity to make explicit the many "hidden" strategies we use to comprehend and analyze information, strategies that often apply in books, articles, and other traditional texts, as well as on the Internet. Engaging children in discussions about these matters during Internet Workshop should be a central part of your instructional program. It will provide important opportunities for each member of your classroom community to learn from one another.

The nature of the workshop session differs depending on the teacher and the students who use it. Often, however, it shares several common characteristics. First, it takes place during a regular time period, usually at the beginning or at the end of a week. A regularly scheduled time period allows all members to anticipate the session and prepare for it. Second, workshop sessions provide opportunities for both you and your students to share navigation strategies as well as content information. This time provides an important opportunity for everyone to learn from one another about the Internet and the information they find. Third, workshop sessions enable you to develop the cooperative learning and critical analysis skills that will be so important to your students' futures. Praising effective exchanges, modeling useful ways to exchange information and showing how to critically evaluate information resources are important strategies for teachers to use during these workshop sessions.

Teachers usually direct the first few workshop sessions to model what they wish to take place. After students understand the process, teachers turn over responsibility for the session to students. When you are modeling the first few experiences, workshop sessions might consist of these two steps:

1. What I learned.
2. What I want to learn.

During the first step, share with your students something you discovered while working on the Internet. This might be a navigational strategy such as how to contact an expert in colonial history to answer a question about the Boston Massacre. It might also be a content issue such as what you discovered about the Boston Massacre. Or, it might be a critical literacy skill you discovered such as checking a web page to see who created it and what might prompt their motives or interpretation of the information they place at this location. After you share what you have recently learned, invite students to ask questions or share their experiences related to your item. They might, for example, be interested in locations where they can contact an expert in the area they are studying (see Figure 4-5). They might also share their experiences with contacting experts and perhaps several new web locations where these experts are located. Or, they might share strategies they discovered about evaluating the extent to which a person is really an "expert."

During the second step, share something about the Internet (either navigation or content) that you want to learn but haven't quite figured out. After you share what it is you wish to learn, invite others to respond and see if anyone knows how to do this. If a student does know how to assist you, encourage him/her to share the information. This will allow others to try it out after the workshop session to see if it works.

Sometimes, the solution will not work as the student described it. When this happens, encourage students to bring their experiences to the next workshop to see if the problem can be solved by others or if the solution was misinterpreted. In either case, the discussion that occurs during the second step is often the most productive learning time about the Internet that take place in your classroom.

After one or two sessions modeling participation during workshop sessions, encourage students to follow the same procedures as you: What I learned; What I want to learn. Gradually, encourage students to assume ownership of Internet Workshop so the class is always focused on items which students find most helpful in their work.

Often teachers will add a rule for everyone to follow during Internet Workshop: each student may only respond twice until everyone else has had a chance to contribute a response. This rule prevents individuals from dominating the conversation and will encourage quieter students to contribute.

Several types of topics are appropriate for workshop sessions:

- Navigation (e.g., "What are the best strategies when using a search engine?")
- Content (e.g., "Has anyone found information about volcanoes.")
- Critical analysis (e.g., "How can I determine the stance taken by the person/group who developed this web page?")

Initially, you may find students more interested in navigation issues. As the year progresses, however, and they become more skilled at navigating the Internet, content issues will dominate. At this point, it will be important for you to introduce critical analysis issues.

There are many variations to how Internet Workshop takes place. Some teachers use an activity page like the one in Figure 4-3 and set a bookmark for the site(s) required for the activity. Others, however, ask students to record information in a journal and bring this to the workshop session. This is what Sharee Mendoza did with her "Digging for Dinosaurs" journals.

Still other teachers develop a web page for Internet Workshop. This is another way to organize this instructional strategy, one that is quickly becoming a popular approach. The advantage of this strategy is that your workshop materials will always be there for you when you wish to use it again next year. If you wish to see many more examples of Internet Workshop developed by teachers, pay a visit to **Internet Workshop** (http://web.syr.edu/~djleu/workshop.html).

There are many variations to how Internet Workshop takes place.

If you wish to see many more examples of Internet Workshop developed by teachers, pay a visit to Internet Workshop (http://web.syr.edu/~djleu/workshop.html).

TEACHING TIP

Often it is useful to vary the structure of Internet Workshop. There are probably as many ways to organize Internet Workshop as there are teachers with creative ideas. One way to increase social learning opportunities is to have several small groups engage in the workshop discussion at the same time. This gives everyone a greater chance to speak and share ideas. As you circle around, listen to the discussions. You will hear many new ideas being learned as students share their Internet experiences with one another. Have groups share their best ideas with the entire class.

... from
...ure (http://
...ure.org/), developed by
...e Lawrence Berkeley National
Laboratory and perfect for an
Internet Workshop experience for a
class in physics.

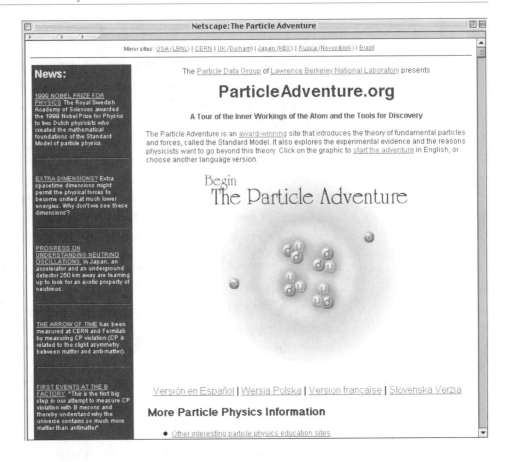

Using Internet Project in Your Classroom

Collaboration, so central to Internet Workshop, can also take place beyond the walls of your classroom. As you use the Internet in your class, there will come a time when you feel confident enough to explore collaborative learning possibilities with others at locations around the world. Collaborative projects may take place as you work with another class on a common project, with students and teachers communicating extensively about the topic both classes are exploring. Collaborative projects also take place when classes contribute data to a common site and then, after the data are analyzed, see how their data compare with others. Often there will also be discussion between participating classes about the meaning of the results and even opportunities to use the data for further analyses. Each leads to rich learning opportunities.

> Communicating with others around the world on a common classroom project provides special opportunities for your students, opportunities they will not experience without the Internet.

Communicating with others around the world on a common classroom project provides special opportunities for your students, opportunities they will not experience without the Internet. You should seek out these opportunities for your students and integrate them into your curriculum for several reasons.

First, communicating with students from a culture other than their own helps your own students to develop a greater appreciation for the diversity

E-MAIL FOR YOU

To: Colleagues
From: Emily Buchanan <JEAMS.BUCHANAN@worldnet.att.net>
Subject: Internet Workshop in the Not-Yet-Online Classroom

I was impatient to use the Internet to enrich a unit on Greek mythology, but faced one major problem: no Internet access at school! Here is how I integrated the Internet in my not-yet-online classroom.

By a show of hands, I found that one third of my students had Internet access at home. I went ahead and designed an Internet Workshop that explored mythology while providing web navigation practice for beginners.

Then I gave my students a choice. Each week they could write their usual journal entry or they could complete an Internet Workshop. Over the next few weeks, it was interesting to see the choices and cooperation that took place. Students with Internet access jumped at the chance to explore mythology on-line. Resourceful students suddenly discovered Internet access at the public library. Others worked on a friend's computer. Still others, some with access, some without, opted to write the Journal entry. The choice was theirs. At the end of each week, all students shared their work, either the Internet activity or the Journal writing.

By the end of the unit, these students learned a lot more than Greek mythology. They also learned valuable lessons in decision-making, sharing, use of community resources, and Internet navigation. Where there's a will, there's a way!

Emily B. Buchanan

that characterizes our world. Understanding diversity leads children to respect differences; a value increasingly important in a global community.

Moreover, writing takes on a different meaning as students learn that messages must be perfectly clear for others to understand what they mean. Communication in writing requires meaning to be very explicit; children come to learn this through misunderstandings from poorly written e-mail messages. This serves to help them learn important lessons about correct spelling, sentence structure, and organization since each may get in the way of effective communication.

In addition, reading information from other places in the world becomes an exciting way to learn. In fact, all of your curriculum will suddenly come to life when you are able to share work with students in another location who have similar interests. These special opportunities for communicating and learning from others comprise an important advantage of Internet use. You should seek them out as often as you can.

Website projects are more permanent projects, coordinated by an individual at a web site. They are a good starting point for teachers new to the Internet because they are often precisely defined with clear directions for participation and a complete package of instructional resources.

Spontaneous projects are increasingly common. These projects are created by an individual teacher who then advertises for collaborating classrooms at one of several locations.

There are two approaches to the use of Internet Project in a classroom: web site Internet projects and spontaneous projects developed by teachers who find one another on the Internet. Web site projects are more permanent projects, coordinated by an individual at a web site. They are a good starting point for teachers new to the Internet because they are often precisely defined with clear directions for participation and a complete package of instructional resources. There is not yet a central Internet site for website Internet projects. You will discover them in your explorations on the Internet. We will describe many of them throughout this book. Figure 4-6 lists several examples of website Internet projects. To participate, you simply need to visit the site and follow the directions.

A second type of Internet Project consists of spontaneous projects developed by teachers who find one another on the Internet. Spontaneous projects are increasingly common. These projects are created by an individual teacher who then advertises for collaborating classrooms at one of several locations. After teachers express their interest by e-mail, students in each classroom complete the project together and share their work. Spontaneous projects recently developed by teachers on the Internet include:

- **Neighbors to the North and South.** Posted by a middle school teacher in Illinois, this project sought collaborating classrooms in Canada and Mexico to learn more about each other's country and cultures. Each week, classes would exchange information on one topic: What is your school like? Which holidays do you celebrate and what is the significance of each? What is unique about the economy in your state or province? What are current political issues that people in your state/province do not agree on? How do you spend a typical weekend?

- **Passage to Hiroshima.** Developed by a teacher in Nagoya, Japan, this class sought other secondary classrooms interested in studying about the importance of peace and international cooperation. They proposed to begin by exchanging useful sites on the World Wide Web related to peace. This class also indicated they

Figure 4-6.Examples of Web-site Internet Projects and Their Locations

NASA Quest's Online Interactive Projects— http://quest.arc.nasa.gov/interactive/	Discuss issues of physics, engineering, space science, and many other topics with the women and men who make the Space Shuttle go and who are now building the International Space Station. Many other great projects are also at this site including: Women of NASA, Aero Design Team Online, and Space Scientists Online.
AT&T Virtual Classroom— http://www.att.virtualclassroom.org/	This location, for grades K–12, includes a wide array of great projects for your class, putting you immediately in touch with other classes around the world. Recent projects include Race Against Time, Global Clubhouse, and Global Water Study.
Earth Day Groceries— http://www.earthdaybags.org	Students decorate grocery bags with environmental friendly messages and distribute these at local grocery stories just before Earth Day. Classrooms report on their experiences. A great social action project for a unit on ecology and the environment.
Human Genetics— http://k12science.ati.stevens-tech.edu/curriculum/genproj/	Collect and analyze information to determine which traits are controlled by a dominant gene. Exchange your hypotheses, data, and conclusions with other students around the world.
The Albatross Project— http://www.wfu.edu/albatross/	A great biology project. Receive an e-mail each day with the coordinates of albatrosses being studied in the Pacific Ocean. Each has a small antenna that is being tracked by satellite. Follow their journeys around this enormous ocean. Plot their travels and formulate and test hypotheses about migration patterns with other biologists.
Global Schoolhouse Projects and Programs Main Page— http://www.globalschoolhouse.org/project/index.html	A number of popular projects are located at this site including Newsday, Geogame, Letters to Santa, and Global Grocery List.
Monarch Watch— http://www.MonarchWatch.org	Raise Monarch butterflies, tag them, release them, record observations about Monarchs in your area, then watch as your data and those compiled by others are used to track the annual migration of this wonderful creature!
Mind's Eye Monster Project— http://www.win4edu.com/minds-eye/monster/	Useful for primary grade classrooms for language arts. Classrooms and students are matched. Then one student draws a monster and writes a detailed description. The description is sent to the student's partner who must draw the monster from the description. Then, both pictures are posted in the monster gallery. Both reading and writing skills are supported. Much fun!
The International Boiling Point Project—http://k12science.stevens-tech.edu/curriculum/boilproj/	Boil water, collect data on several factors, and submit your results to a central database. Then, students can analyze all of the data to reach an answer to the question: What causes a pot of water to boil?
Journey Exchange Project— http://www.win4edu.com /minds-eye/journey	Classes research and develop a five-city journey around the world. Then they exchange clues to their locations with their partner class. Each attempts to discover the cities from the clues provided.

E-MAIL FOR YOU

To: Colleagues
From: Susy Calvert <scalvert@access.k12.wv.us>
Subject: Using The Mind's Eye Monster Project for Language Arts

Hi!

As the administrator for the Monster Exchange Project, I am responsible for answering any questions teachers have about the project and helping them out with the entire process for uploading monsters and their descriptions. I also assist teachers when they've made some minor mistakes and any other problems that may occur.

The Monster Project's greatest benefits to teachers and students are providing a so-called "real" audience for children's work including their original art work and creative expression. When students describe a monster they have drawn, they see the need for exact descriptions to allow someone who has never seen their monster to redraw the original as closely as possible to their artistic creation. The absolute delight in a student's eyes when they see the redrawing of their monster, especially when it is almost a twin of the original, is very special. The ability to print a copy of the description, original, and redrawn monster can become part of a student's portfolio for language arts. If students participate in both the fall and spring sessions, the teacher can see any progress the student has made. When students see their original monster and description with a redrawing that is so different from their original, it helps them see where they need to improve in the descriptive and sequencing process. The real difficulty is putting into words what the student can see with their own eyes so that another person can redraw a close duplicate.

Other positive aspects of the project include the chance to telecommunicate with students in another country to provide them with "real" age-level peers who respond to their messages. It's a wonderful Internet activity to incorporate all types of technology; i.e., Internet, e-mail, scanning, digital photos, and uploading files from a web page and one that doesn't demand an inordinate amount of time. When completed, students are delighted to find their monster descriptions, drawing, and redrawing accessible for everybody to view on the Monster Web Site. Sponsor of the Monster Project, Winstar, provides technical support through e-mail and a chat room for answers to any questions teachers may have. It's wonderful to have a sponsor who provides an excellent student project on the Internet without charge for as many teachers as want to join. Also included on the web site is an example of a successful grant written for technology equipment.

The Monster Project is an excellent Internet resource for teachers. It's a very comprehensive site with many features that teachers will truly find as "friendly" and one that promotes the publication of student work. Teachers with access to the Monster Project will find a perfect project for curriculum integration and lesson planning that they will continue to access every year.

Susy Calvert, Coordinator/Teacher of Gifted Programming
****
Raleigh County Schools, Beckley, West Virginia
scalvert@access.k12.wv.us
****

would be visiting Hiroshima in November and sought interview and research questions from a collaborative classroom. They volunteered to interview citizens of Hiroshima and then share the results, including photos, upon their return.

- **Culture and Clues**. In this project for 7–9 year olds, a teacher proposed exchanging boxes of cultural artifacts from the culture where each participating school is located. Students would use these artifacts to make inferences about what life was like at each location and then write descriptions of this culture. These would be exchanged by e-mail and then students would compare how close their guesses were.

Spontaneous Internet projects have many variations, but generally they follow these procedures:

1. Plan a collaborative project for an upcoming unit in your classroom and write a project description. The description should contain a summary of the project, a clear list of learning goals, expectations you have for collaborating classrooms, and a projected timeline for beginning and ending the project.

2. Post the project description and timeline several months in advance at one or several locations, seeking collaborative classroom partners.

3. Arrange collaboration details with teachers in other classrooms who agree to participate.

4. Complete the project, using Internet Workshop as a forum in your own class for working on the project and exchanging information with your collaborating classrooms.

The first step requires you to do some advance planning, at least several months before you wish to begin the project. A clear description with explicit goals and timelines will make it easier for everyone to understand what will be expected of them.

The second step is to post the project description and timeline at one of several locations of the Internet where teachers advertise their projects, seeking collaborating classrooms. This should be done several months in advance so that other teachers have time to find your project. Project descriptions may be posted at several locations, including:

- **Global SchoolNet's Internet Project Registry—** http://www.gsn.org/pr/index.cfm
- **SchoolNet's Grassroots Project Gallery—** http://www.schoolnet.ca/grassroots/e/project.centre/search-projects.html
- **Intercultural E-mail Classroom Connections—** http://www.stolaf.edu/network/iecc/

Figure 4-7 provides an example of a project description posted recently at Global SchoolNet's Internet Project Registry.

Figure 4-7.
An example of a project description posted at **Global SchoolNet's Internet Project Registry** (http://www.gsn.org/pr/index.html)

Project Name:	Latitude and Shadow Length
Contact Person:	Helen Schrand
E-mail Contact:	schrandh@ride.ri.net
Description:	Students will measure the length of the shadow of a 2 meter pole at three times during a school day on three dates over the course of the school year. We would like to receive similar data from schools in other locations so students can compare their findings with those from a variety of places.
How Long:	7 months
Objectives:	Students will:
	1. Learn to use meter sticks to measure accurately.
	2. Locate places on a world map or globe using latitude and longitude.
	3. Graph and analyze data.
	4. Determine the effect of latitude and time of day on shadow length.
Share:	We will compile a table of results we receive and e-mail it to participating classes.

The third step in an Internet Project is to arrange collaboration details with teachers in other classrooms who agree to participate in the project with you. Internet projects require close coordination. It is important to confirm procedures and timelines with everyone involved.

Finally, you complete the activities in the project, exchanging information with all of the collaborative classrooms. This step provides you and your students with opportunities to read, write, and critically evaluate information related to the project. Internet Workshop often provides a supportive forum for organizing and developing much of your classroom's efforts on the project.

TEACHING TIP

Are you interested in discovering more information about a project approach to Internet use? Pay a visit to **Collaborative Project-Based Learning** (http://www.gsn.org/web/pbl/index.htm). This site contains a wealth of suggestions and a number of great examples. Before developing your own project description and posting it to seek partners, you may wish to review the project description shown in Figure 4-8 at **Global SchoolNet's Internet Project Registry** (http://www.gsn.org/pr/index.cfm) or **SchoolNet's Grassroots Project Gallery** (http://www.schoolnet.ca/grassroots/e/project.centre/search-projects.html). You may also wish to participate in one of two Internet projects as a collaborating classroom before developing your own special project. This will help you develop insights about this approach as you seek to exploit its special opportunities for classroom learning.

Figure 4-8.
The home page for Global SchoolNet's Internet Projects Registry, a useful place to find examples of Internet projects developed by teachers around the world (http://www.gsn.org/pr/index.cfm)

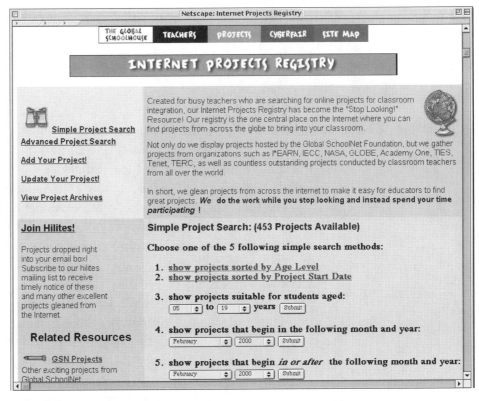

Using Internet Inquiry in Your Classroom

Once your students have become familiar with locating Internet resources, Internet Inquiry may be a useful means to develop independent research skills and allow students to pursue a question which holds a special interest for them. Internet Inquiry may be developed by small groups or by individuals. Inquiry units usually begin with students identifying a topic and a question they wish to explore related to the current unit. The question may be as specific as "What happened to Benedict Arnold after he betrayed his country in the Revolutionary War?" or as general as "What is it like to live in Japan?" The most important aspect of Internet Inquiry is that the students should do research on a question which they find to be important.

Internet Inquiry consists of five phases:

- Question
- Search
- Analyze
- Compose
- Share

During the question phase, students identify an important question they wish to explore. You can support this phase by engaging in group or individual brainstorming sessions or by setting a bookmark to a central Internet site for the general topic area and allowing students to explore the area, looking for an issue to explore.

> Once your students have become familiar with locating Internet resources, Internet Inquiry may be a useful means to develop independent research skills and allow students to pursue a question which holds a special interest for them.

Once students have decided upon a question they wish to explore, the second phase, search, begins. Students may search on the Internet for useful information related to their question. Students should also be reminded to use more traditional resources found in their classroom or school library during their search.

During the third phase, analyze, students should analyze all of the information they have located and respond to the question they initially posed. Sometimes, this will lead students to address another question they discover to be more important than their initial question. When this happens, they should be encouraged to repeat the search and analyze phases.

The fourth phase, compose, requires students to compose a presentation of their work. There are many ways to do this including a traditional written report, a poster session, a multimedia presentation, or an oral report.

During the final phase, share, students have an opportunity to share their work with others and respond to questions about their work. Some teachers set aside a regular time each week for sharing the projects students complete during Internet Inquiry. Sometimes this will take place during Internet Workshop. Sometimes a special science or social studies fair will be held where students have an opportunity to share their work with other classes at school.

Internet Inquiry can be an exciting part of your curriculum, allowing students important opportunities to read, analyze, and write within content areas such as English/language arts, math, science, and social studies.

TEACHING TIP	As you consider the use of Internet Inquiry, you may wish to direct your students to **StudyWeb** (http://www.studyweb.com/index2.htm) a very useful site to begin research explorations. Younger students may, of course, use one of the search engines that screens locations for their appropriateness for children such as **Yahooligans** (http://www.yahooligans.com) or **Ask Jeeves for Kids** (http://www.askjeevesforkids.com)

Using WebQuests in Your Classroom

A final instructional framework is what is called a WebQuest. WebQuests have quickly come to mean many things to many people. Originally, WebQuests were intended to be an activity in which some or all of the information students required came from resources on the Internet. They are usually developed on a web page for students to follow as they complete their learning experience. WebQuest pages usually contain the following sections:

- Introduction
- Task Definition
- A Description of the Process
- Information Resources
- Guidance in Organizing the Information
- A Concluding Activity

WebQuests may be developed by anyone but they are often developed by teachers to provide students in their classroom with an important learning experience using Internet resources. Because they appear on web pages, they are also available to other teachers.

WebQuests may be developed by anyone but they are often developed by teachers to provide students in their classroom with an important learning experience using Internet resources. Because they appear on web pages, they are also available to other teachers.

Often, the beginning of a WebQuest page contains an introduction, orienting students to the learning activity. Usually, this explains the purpose of the learning activity in a short paragraph.

Next, a WebQuest usually provides a description of the task students will complete. It will list each of the tasks they are to complete and do this in a manner that is clear to the student.

Then, a WebQuest usually describes the process to follow. This explains how each task should be completed.

The fourth part of a WebQuest page provides links to the information resources on the Internet that will be required to complete the activity. Because these links are provided, students avoid endless searching for information and are able to focus on the activity of the WebQuest.

The fifth section of a WebQuest page usually contains guidance about how to organize the information students acquire. This might direct students to answer guiding questions, or follow directions to complete a timeline, concept map, or other organizational framework.

WebQuest pages usually end with a concluding statement. This reminds students what they have learned and bring closure to the activity. Sometimes, this will invite students to explore related topics.

A recent addition to many WebQuest pages is information about how students' work will be evaluated. Often this appears in the form of a scoring chart or a rubric.

WebQuests are quickly appearing on the Internet as popular curriculum resources developed by many teachers. Examples of WebQuests for grades K–12 appear at **Example WebQuests** (http://edweb.sdsu.edu/webquest/matrix.html) and at other locations.

You will see many different varieties of WebQuests. Many tend to focus on specific learning tasks and do not always include the collaborative aspects found in Internet Workshop. They tend to focus on learning specific information and less often on evaluating information or constructing new problems to be solved, though you may find examples of WebQuests that also do this. You can find out more information about WebQuests at the **WebQuest Page** (http://edweb.sdsu.edu/webquest/webquest.html).

Critical Literacy on the Internet

While the Internet makes more information available to more classrooms, it also presents new challenges to both students and teachers. One of the important challenges we face is that we are never certain about the accuracy of the information we find on the web. Traditional forces, guaranteeing some

E-MAIL FOR YOU

To: Colleagues
From: Beverley Powell (bpowell@ican.net), Ottawa, Canada
Subject: "GrassRoots"—tomorrow's socialization instrument

GrassRoots is a blossoming feature of Canada's world-class **SchoolNet** (http://www/schoolnet.ca/grassroots). It carries exciting messages behind the computer screen.

More than 3,000 GrassRoots projects have been jointly funded in Canada's schools by the federal government, provincial/territorial governments and the private sector. A fund-raising drive for $15 million aims at 20,000 projects by March 2001. Records of these Internet projects linking pupils in several schools are available through the website. They can therefore be imitated (and improved upon) by any teacher, anywhere.

GrassRoots' goals are to foster skills and employability, integrate communications technology with education and in general help prepare young people for the challenges of what Marshall McLuhan called The Electric Age.

We should be aware that collaborative projects through the Internet offer far more than improved education, in the traditional sense of that word.

As the authors of this book have noted, the Internet can build new bridges between parents and children, using a technology that affects us all. Our globally competitive economy demands high corporate and personal performance. It comes through creative workplace collaboration—not simply following the boss's orders. Our children have to learn how to surf for the best information—much more than merely for their own amusement. And they will need to know how to "mix minds" with many other people.

These learning adventures offer attractive benefits to the socialization process. Young people learn how to plan tasks, work in teams, support each other, develop mutual self-respect and improve their manners. These are nothing less than the underpinnings of civil society. Notice that they are all independent of the subject matter of the educational collaboration. In this sense, "the medium is the message." Or, to put it more colloquially, "it ain't what you do, it's the way that you do it!"

Marshall McLuhan said that we are driving into the future looking into our rear-view mirror. That was in 1964. Perhaps we are beginning to look through the windshield. One thing is quite clear. If we teachers don't do it, our students will take the wheel and show us the way!

Beverley Powell

degree of control over the accuracy of information in published books, do not exist on the Internet where anyone may publish anything. As a result, searches for information may sometimes turn up web pages created by people who have political, religious, or philosophical stances that influence the nature of the information they present to others. Or, sometimes a person simply gets the facts wrong on a web page.

As a result, we need to help our students develop critical literacies so that they can evaluate the nature of any information they find on the web and be confident about its reliability. Such skill has not always been necessary in classrooms where the textbook is assumed to be correct.

There are a number of strategies used to help students become healthy skeptics including:

> We need to help our students develop critical literacies so that they can evaluate the nature of any information they find on the web and be confident about its reliability.

- Ask students to always determine who created the information at a web site, why they might have created it, and what stance they are likely to take in relation to this information. Answers to these questions often provide insights into how the information has been shaped.

- At the main page of any site, always look for an "About" link. This will provide information to help you determine who created the site and why it was created.

- Ask students to provide at least two references for major claims they make in their written or oral reports, especially when these come from the Internet.

- Keep a bulletin board entitled "Discrepant facts: Who is right?" Encourage students to post copies of material they find containing contradictory information. These may come from the Internet or from printed material. You will be surprised how quickly students will find different spellings, different dates for events, different birth dates for famous individuals, and other information that differs between two sources.

- Discuss this issue in your Internet Workshop sessions and see if students can come up with additional strategies for evaluating the accuracy of information. Strategies might include looking to see if document references are provided, the reputation of the source (an individual you do not know versus a source with a commercial reputation to protect) or biases the author may display.

Citation Strategies for Internet References

A common question many of us have these days is how to cite information resources on the Internet. The question is so new that definitive guidelines for citation style are still evolving. The problem is compounded because so

TEACHING TIP

Sharee Mendoza received the suggestion to visit **ICYouSee Guide to Critical Thinking** (http://www.ithaca.edu/library/Training/hott.html). This is a very useful suggestion. Be certain to visit this site and explore strategies for critical literacy you can bring to your class. There are several great examples here. One shows how the quotation "Question authority!" has been attributed to at least six different sources. Be certain to use this site for Internet Workshop at the beginning of the year. Have your students visit the location and do at least one of the activities here. Ask them to also develop a list of strategies for evaluating information and share this at a workshop session.

many different types of media sources are available on the Internet: film, video, audio clips, photographs, data bases, and many others.

The best information about how to cite Internet resources may be found at the **Learning Page of the Library of Congress: Citing Electronic Sources** (http://lcweb2.loc.gov/ammem/ndlpedu/cite.html). This resource provides examples of how to cite the wide variety of media now available to our students. It also contains links to other citation style resources on the Internet. Another location containing links to many different citation guides is located at the Internet Public Library's, **Citing Electronic Resources** (http://www.ipl.org/ref/QUE/FARQ/netciteFARQ.html).

Generally, style manuals favor including the following information in a reference to Internet resources:

> Author's Last Name, Author's First Name. "Title of Document." Title of Complete Work (if applicable). Version or File Number, if applicable. Document date or date of last revision (if different from access date). Protocol and address, access path or directories (date of access).

For example:

> The U.S. Library of Congress. "Learning Page of the Library of Congress: Citing Electronic Sources." May 8, 1997. Available http://www.ipl.org/ref/QUE/FARQ/netciteFARQ.html (May 1, 2000).

Often the order of this information will change, depending upon which manual you use. And, keep in mind these conventions are changing quickly as the Internet, itself, changes. Regularly checking the citation manuals listed above will keep you current as these styles evolve.

You might also wish to have your students visit **Research** (http://nuevaschool.org/~debbie/library/research/research.html) where they will find templates for developing bibliographic references. Simply follow the example for each type of information in the appropriate boxes and the site will provide you with a copy of the complete reference.

The best information about how to cite Internet resources may be found at the Learning Page of the Library of Congress: Citing Electronic Sources (http://lcweb2.loc.gov/ammem/ndlpedu/cite.html).

Internet FAQ

How can I find out the date when a page on the Internet was last revised? Often, I like to know how recently something was created. It helps me to evaluate the accuracy of the information. Then, too, this information is usually required for a reference citation.	If you use Netscape Navigator, it is easy to find the date when a document was created or the date of its latest revision. Select "View" from the top menu bar and then select "Page info". This will open a window telling you when a page was created and when it was last revised.

Developing Independent Search Strategies While Being Sensitive to Child Safety Concerns

If we protect children by restricting their access to the Internet, they fail to develop comprehensive search strategies and do not learn how to use the full power of Internet resources.

The best policy, in the long run, is to educate children, parents, and guardians about how to use the Internet safely, develop an acceptable use policy, and always supervise student use of the Internet. This is your best insurance for all child safety issues.

One way that teachers guide Internet experiences for very young children is to bookmark safe items and limit children's Internet use to these items.

There is an inherent tension between child safety on the Internet and helping children to develop the independent search strategies necessary for effective Internet use. If we protect children by restricting their access to the Internet, they fail to develop comprehensive search strategies and do not learn how to use the full power of Internet resources. Many districts are beginning to resolve this tension by developing a graduated access policy; younger students are restricted in what they may access on the Internet while older students are provided with greater access. Some districts purchase commercial solutions with built-in graduated access to the Internet that may be set by teachers or administrators. Most districts are also developing acceptable use policies and requiring teacher supervision of Internet use.

It is impossible to completely protect children from viewing sites they should not see. The best policy, in the long run, is to educate children, parents, and guardians about how to use the Internet safely, develop an acceptable use policy, and always supervise student use of the Internet. This is your best insurance for all child safety issues.

One way that teachers guide Internet experiences for very young children is to bookmark safe items and limit children's Internet use to these items. This makes it less likely for young students to view sites that are inappropriate for their age.

A second strategy is to develop a classroom home page and provide links to each of the resources students will require on this page. You can see how to develop a classroom home page in Chapter 12.

In addition, some teachers, especially in the primary grades, limit their children to certain areas in the WWW selected with attention to child safety issues. There are a few sites on the WWW that attempt to do this. None, however, are able to guarantee that children will not be able to view inappropriate sites since links within sites change on a daily basis. Moreover, the nature of the WWW is that sites are linked to sites, which are linked to still other sites, and on and on. No area or commercial solution will guarantee the appropriateness of third level links or greater. Still, if you wish to limit the resources your students view but still allow them to develop independent search strategies, you may wish to designate certain areas as appropriate for your younger children to explore. The best sites we have found that do not charge a fee are **Yahooligans** (http://www.yahooligans.com) and **Ask Jeeves for Kids** (http://www.askjeevesforkids.com). A copy of the home page for **Ask Jeeves for Kids** can be found in Figure 4-9. These are special areas with a vast set of information resources for students and a search engine that allows them to search sites approved for children's use. You may wish to set bookmarks for these locations or designate one as your home page location (see Chapter 2). Another wonderful site is one developed by the American Library Association, **700+ Great Sites: Amazing, Spectacular, Mysterious, Colorful Web Sites for Kids and the Adults Who Care About Them** (http://www.ala.org/parentspage/greatsites/amazing.html). If you teach in the elementary grades, these are the locations to use for Internet Inquiry.

As children become older and more aware of child safety issues, you will want to allow them to view more of the Internet and to begin to use search engines for research. After all, as students grow older, we want them to de-

> The best sites we have found that do not charge a fee are Yahooligans (http://www.yahooligans.com) and Ask Jeeves for Kids (http://www.askjeevesforkids.com). These are special areas with a vast set of information resources for students and a search engine that allows them to search sites approved for children's use.

Figure 4-9.
Ask **Jeeves for Kids**
(http://www.askjeevesforkids.com),
a search engine with links screened
for children.

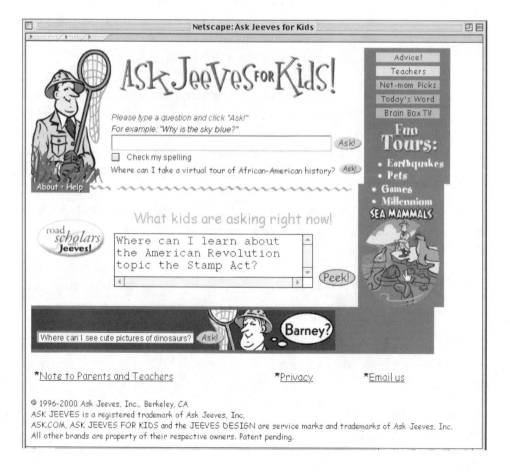

velop effective strategies for finding information efficiently. You will need to make this decision or, perhaps, it may be specified in your school's acceptable use policy.

Using The Internet to Plan Instruction: Central Sites for General Curriculum Resources

Once you consider these issues, most of your current instructional practices may be easily integrated with Internet resources as you modify Internet Workshop, Internet Project, Internet Inquiry, or WebQuests to meet your own needs. In many ways, the Internet is simply another information resource for your classroom, much like a very powerful encyclopedia. Certainly it also has special potentials, especially in the area of communicating with distant locations, collaboration with others around the world, or discussing issues with experts in the area you are studying. By and large, however, the Internet is just another information resource for your students to exploit as they engage in classroom learning activities.

Sometimes, though, it is hard to find the resources you require to develop the specific instructional resources for a unit. Of course, like Sharee, you may wish to join a mailing list (listserv) and ask others for their recommendations. Alternatively, you could explore the central sites for curriculum resources that exist on the Internet. You may wish to visit some of these general resource sites as you explore ways in which the Internet may assist you with planning. Here are some of the best general resources that exist for teachers interested in using the Internet in their classroom:

> Most of your current instructional practices may be easily integrated with Internet resources as you modify Internet Workshop, Internet Project, Internet Inquiry, or WebQuests to meet your own needs.

> Here are some of the best general resources that exist for teachers interested in using the Internet in their classroom.

- **Blue Web'n**—http://www.kn.pacbell.com/wired/bluewebn/
  This is an outstanding collection of the very best curriculum experiences for students. Each is carefully reviewed before receiving a Blue Web'n Blue Ribbon. There is also a searchable data base so you can find exactly the resource you require.

- **Education World**—http://www.education-world.com/
  A commercial site, but one rich in educational resources from curriculum, to information on state standards, to collaborative Internet projects, to teaching positions. It includes information, too, for all curriculum areas.

- **The New York Times Learning Network**—
  http://www.nytimes.com/learning/
  This location has sections for students, teachers, and parents. In addition to great lesson plans for using the free articles at the New York Times site in your classroom for current events, this location has a teacher chat area, lesson plan archives, a daily quotation, weekly news quizzes, and links to great curriculum resources in all areas.

- **SchoolNet**—http://www.schoolnet.ca/
  In English or French, this exceptional resource provides Canadian educators with an exceptional collection of instructional resources for every area of the curriculum at every grade level. Projects, links to curriculum resources, connections with other Canadian schools, and many more types of support are right at your fingertips.

- **Yahooligans Teachers' Guide**—http://www.yahooligans.com/tg/index.html
  Useful for elementary and middle school teachers, this location provides important information about teaching strategies, acceptable use policies, and citation styles. It also contains a limited collection of curriculum resources, but what is here is very good.

- **For Teachers and Parents**—http://www.gsh.org/teach/
  This location at the Global School provides links to many Internet projects and curriculum resources. It also contains useful resources to help you use the Internet effectively in your classroom.

Visiting the Classroom: Susan Silverman's Second Grade Class in New York

Susan Silverman's classroom web site tells a story about the exciting potential of Internet Project far better than we can ever hope to accomplish within the pages of this book.

If you are interested in exploring the potential of Internet Project, visit the classroom web sites of Susan Silverman. Susan Silverman shares a second grade class with Michelle Sowa at the Clinton Avenue Elementary School in the Comsewogue School District in New York. Susan's classroom web site tells a story about the exciting potential of Internet Project far better than we can ever hope to accomplish within the pages of this book.

The location we show in Figure 4-10 contains links to the many Internet projects Susan's classes have completed with other participating classes in the primary grades. These include collaborative projects developed around fall poetry, the wonderful book *Stellaluna*, research about owls around the world, and many more. If you explore some of Susan's classroom sites for various years you will see many other projects, too, including popular travel buddy projects such as Flat Stanley and Winnie the Pooh. Be certain to visit the links to some of these projects at **Internet Projects** (http://comsewogue.k12.ny.us/~ssilverman/class99/netprojects.html).

The projects Susan creates begin with her classroom curriculum and the needs of her students. Each project is aligned with the curriculum standards of her state, standards that are similar to those found in other states. Then, Susan announces her projects on a number of mailing lists (listservs) and other locations we mentioned in this chapter in order to discover teachers with similar curricular needs who are interested in collaborating with Susan's classroom. In these announcements, Susan carefully defines the purpose of

Figure 4-10.
The home page for Susan Silverman's second grade class, a great location to explore the potential of Internet Project.

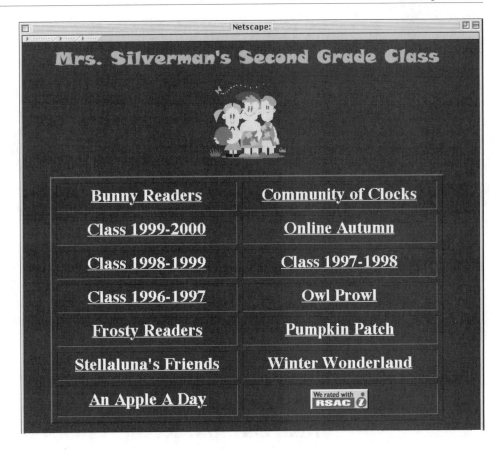

The beauty of the Susan Silverman's style of Internet Project is that each project results in rich curricular resources developed by classrooms around the world that then become available for all of us to use.

each project, the timeline for completion, and provides suggestions for how each class might contribute their special talents. You can find an example of a project description by visiting the **About this Project** link for the Online Autumn project (http://comsewogue.k12.ny.us/~ssilverman/autumn/project.html) a collaborative project exchanging fall poetry created in each of the participating classrooms.

The beauty of Susan's style of Internet Project is that each project results in rich curricular resources developed by classrooms around the world that then become available for all of us to use. Are you interested in having your class read the fall poetry of other primary grade children? Visit **Online Autumn** (http://comsewogue.k12.ny.us/~ssilverman/autumn/index.html). Is your class doing a unit on apples or pumpkins with your young students? Visit **Pumpkin Patch** (http://www.kids-learn.org/pumpkins/) or **An Apple a Day** (http://members.aol.com/Apples2nd/) to see the wonderful poems, recipes, art work, and other great resources to use immediately in your own classroom, perhaps with Internet Workshop. Susan's work with Internet Project creates new curricular resources that other teachers might also use in their classrooms. Pay a visit to this important model for instruction and be certain to let Susan know how important her work is for all of us.

A Final Word

It is not the resources available on the Internet, though these are considerable, that will make a difference for your students. Instead, your students' success at life's opportunities will be determined by what you decide to do with these resources.

Earlier we made an important point: It is not the resources available on the Internet, though these are considerable, that will make a difference for your students. Instead, your students' success at life's opportunities will be determined by what you decide to do with these resources. As you begin to incorporate the Internet into your classroom, making it an integral part of teaching and learning, you will develop new ideas and new ways of teaching. We want to encourage you to share these ideas with other teachers who are also learning about this new resource for education. Though we have no evidence, we suspect the Internet will have its greatest impact on teaching and learning through the new ideas that teachers share with one another and the new connections that are formed between teachers and students around the world. For too long, teachers have spent much of their time in school isolated from other teachers by the walls of their classrooms. The Internet allows us to transcend these walls and learn from one another about the best instructional practices. We want to encourage you to take the time to support others and to learn from others as you begin your journey to fulfill the potential the Internet provides for new ways of learning and new ways of teaching.

Instructional Resources on the Internet

AskLN—http://www.att.com/learningnetwork/askln.html
> This location, sponsored by ATT, provides an online answering service for teachers, administrators, media specialists, and anyone who is interested in using the Internet and other technologies as effective classroom tools. AskLN promises to answer any question related to Internet use in the classroom within 48 hours. Got a question? AskLN has answers!

Busy Teachers' Web Site—http://www.ceismc.gatech.edu/busyt/
> Just what it says! If you are busy, stop by. Great locations to wonderful sites organized by subject area. A wonderful resource for teaching ideas and curricular resources.

Civil War Photograph Collection—http://rs6.loc.gov/cwphome.html
> This site at the Library of Congress contains over 1,000 photographs from the Civil War, many by Mathew Brady. Viewing these images makes you feel the national conflict and struggle during this period.

Digital Dozen—http://www.enc.org/classroom/index.htm
> Each month the 13 best sites for K–12 math and science are carefully selected by the team at the Eisenhower National Clearinghouse for Math and Science and posted here. One of the finest sites for great ideas on the web! Set a bookmark! And don't forget to explore Digital Dozen sites from previous months.

Geometry Problem of the Week—http://forum.swarthmore.edu/geopow/
> Part of the exceptional math forum site, this location provides you and your students with a challenging geometry problem to solve each week.

Use it for a quick Internet Workshop and have a short workshop session at the end of the week to compare solutions.

KidsConnect—http://www.ala.org/ICONN/kidsconn.html

If your students really like to ask challenging questions about the Internet, here is the resource for you and for them. KidsConnect is a question-answering, help and referral service for K–12 students using the Internet. The goal of the service is to help students access and use the information available on the Internet effectively and efficiently. KidsConnect is a component of ICONnect, a technology initiative from the American Association of School Librarians (AASL), a division of the American Library Association (ALA). Many students are using this service to assist with homework assignments!

K–12 Statistics—http://www.mste.uiuc.edu/stat/stat.html

Organized around the NSTM standards, this location provides links and resources for helping students to understand the world of statistics. A great resource.

Reading Online—The Electronic Classroom—

http://www.readingonline.org/electronic/index.html

Devoted solely to teachers, this is a section of the International Reading Association's free electronic journal, *Reading Online*. In addition to great articles and a discussion forum, this site contains a wealth of resources for teachers including lists of Internet projects, useful WWW sites, and tips for technology use.

The Biology Project—http://www.biology.arizona.edu/

A central site for all high school biology teachers that is being developed by the University of Arizona. It includes problem sets and tutorials in biochemistry, cell biology, developmental biology, human biology, chemicals and human health, and much more. Some sections are also in Spanish.

The Constitution: A Living Document—http://www.yahooligans.com/tg/constitution.html

A complete unit with lesson plans, activities, and evaluations for students in grade 6–8 who are studying this important document.

The Exploratorium—http://www.exploratorium.edu/

A palace of hands-on science learning in San Francisco, this site makes outstanding interactive adventures in science available to the world. A great location for science, fun, and learning.

The Living Africa—http://library.thinkquest.org/16645/contents.html

A wonderful resource for studying this important continent developed as part of a ThinkQuest competition by three students: one in the US, one in The Netherlands, and one in India. The development of this resource is a story that will be increasingly repeated by our students in the future.

The Nine Planets Tour—http://seds.lpl.arizona.edu/billa/tnp/

This is the best tour through the solar system that exists. At each stop, beautiful photographs of each planetary object are displayed along with information about the object. Short sound clips and videos are also available. Many links take you to related sites. A wonderful journey!

The Particle Adventure—http://particleadventure.org/

Developed by the Lawrence Berkeley National Laboratory, here is a tour of the inner workings of the atom and tools for discovery used by scientists. The Particle Adventure is an award-winning site that introduces the theory of fundamental particles and forces, called the Standard Model. It also explores the experimental evidence and the reasons physicists want to go beyond this theory.

The United Nations Cyber Schoolbus—http://www.un.org/Pubs/CyberSchoolBus/

Is your class studying the United Nations? Visit this site developed by the UN. Take a field trip to the United Nations, explore the mission of this organization, and find teaching ideas. Many classroom activities.

VolcanoWorld—http://volcano.und.nodak.edu

Study volcanoes around the world, talk to a vulcanologist, obtain real time data on active volcanoes, and many more fun activities for kids and adults.

Listservs/Mailing Lists for Teaching With The Internet

Use standard subscribing procedures (see Chapter 3) to subscribe to the following listservs.

EDsOasis—EDsOasis@listserv.syr.edu

A mailing list for teachers assisting teachers in using the Internet. Run in conjunction with the ED's Oasis web site. Directions for subscribing are located at http://www.EDsOasis.org/Listserv.html

K12ADMIN—listserv@listserv.syr.edu

A mailing list for K–12 administrators, but the conversations focus largely on instructional issues. Over 1,000 members. The archives may be viewed at http://listserv.syr.edu/archives/k12admin.html

RTEACHER—listserv@listserv.syr.edu

A mailing list devoted to conversations related to literacy education as well as the use of Internet and other technologies for literacy and learning. The educators on this list are very supportive of teachers new to the Internet. The archives may be viewed at >http://listserv.syr.edu/archives/rteacher.html>. Directions for subscribing are located at http://web.syr.edu/~djleu/RTEACHER/directions.html

Web66—(listserv@tc.umn.edu)

The Web66 mailing list is for discussion of web use in K–12 school classrooms, primarily focused on schools that are producers of web information. Messages should be related to the web and its use in education. Directions for subscribing are located at http://web66.umn.edu/List/Default.html

English and the Language Arts: Opening New Doors to Literature and Literacy

 E-MAIL FOR YOU

To: Our readers
From: djleu@syr.edu (Don Leu), ddleu@syr.edu (Debbie Leu)
Subject: Stepping through the wardrobe

The essence of both reading and writing has always been change. Reading a book or writing a story changes us forever; we return from the worlds we inhabit during our literacy journeys with new insights about our surroundings and ourselves. Moreover, teaching students to read and write is also a transforming experience; it opens up new windows to the world, creating a lifetime of opportunities. Change has always defined our work as literacy educators. By teaching students to read and write, we change the world.

Today, reading and writing are being defined by change in even more profound ways. Internet technologies create new literacies required to effectively exploit their potentials. These technologies also make possible new instructional practices to help children acquire the literacies of their future. Traditional definitions of reading and writing will be insufficient if we seek to provide children with the futures they deserve.

The Internet opens new doors to literature and response, creating exciting new opportunities for the English/language arts curriculum. Your students can participate in an electronic discussion about Shakespeare, view a video of a favorite author explaining her writing process, read reviews of books posted by students from around the world, join a global discussion group via e-mail, quickly search on-line versions of Barlett's Quotations and Roget's Thesaurus, or engage in other wonderful experiences as you open new doors to literature and literacy.

C. S. Lewis understood what happens when you open new doors to new worlds. In *The Chronicles of Narnia*, Lewis leads us through the secret door of a wardrobe, opening a magical world full of exciting, new opportunities. We believe the Internet is another door, opening new worlds for you and your students with many new opportunities for literature and composition.

Don and Debbie

Teaching With the Internet: Tricia Abernathy's Class

It was Friday afternoon in Tricia Abernathy's class. Her class was in the middle of a workshop session. This was not an Internet Workshop session, just a regular workshop session; one she had learned from reading *In the Middle* by Nancie Atwell.

Tricia had developed a cross-curricular thematic unit around the advantages diversity creates. Her goal was to increase students' appreciation for diversity as they studied math, science, social studies, reading, writing, speaking, and listening. In math, she had experiences for students to explore number systems from several ancient civilizations, including a study of systems using bases other than 10. These included several great activities she had found at **The Math Forum** site (http://forum.swarthmore.edu/). In science, she was using the unit on biodiversity she had developed in a summer workshop at the university last year. In social studies, she developed experiences for students to better understand the cultures of both Native Americans and immigrants. In language arts, Tricia had planned experiences around "pourquoi tales", creation myths that exist in every traditional culture. Pourquoi tales explain sources of natural phenomena such as how people obtained fire, why mosquitoes buzz in people's ears, where the moon came from, or why rivers run into the ocean.

Tricia was just beginning to use the Internet in her classroom. She and her students only used it for research or for printing out materials. Others at her school were using the Internet for instruction, but Tricia was the cautious sort. She was moving gradually into the new worlds that the Internet opened, being careful not to misuse this powerful new tool.

Tricia had introduced the concept of a pourquoi tale at the beginning of the unit by engaging the class in read aloud response journal activities (Leu & Kinzer, 1999) with several examples of this genre: *The Fire Bringer* by Margaret Hodges and *Star Boy* by Paul Goble. Then she had students work in one of three literature discussion groups. Each group had a large set of pourquoi tales to read. One group read and discussed tales from the Americas, another read tales from Asia and Australia, and a third read tales from Africa, Europe, and the Middle East. She used book club activities suggested by McMahon, Raphael, Goatley, & Pardo (1997), text set activities suggested by Short (1993), and response journal activities suggested by Hynds (1997).

Tricia gave each group this assignment:

Make a class presentation about one culture using only the information in the pourquoi tales for your region. Infer aspects of that culture from the stories you read, indicating what you inferred and the evidence supporting your inferences. Also explain why the cultural patterns you found are useful. You may use the search engine, **Ask Jeeves for Kids,** as well as any books in the library.

Margin notes:

Tricia had developed a cross-curricular thematic unit around the advantages diversity creates.

Pourquoi tales explain sources of natural phenomena.

Tricia was moving gradually into the new worlds that the Internet opened, being careful not to misuse this powerful new tool.

Individuals chose different books to read from the classroom and library collections. Students also discovered and shared stories they found on the Internet during their scheduled time on the classroom computer. They liked to print out copies of each story and exchange them with others in their group.

Members of each group got together twice a week to share their literary experiences in a student-led discussion organized around a "grand conversation" (McGee & Richgels, 1990). During their grand conversations, each group discussed the pourquoi tales they were reading and what each suggested about the cultures they were studying. They also made plans for their class presentation. Once a week, the entire class came together to share the work they were doing in groups and to plan new work.

Marcus had waited a long time to make his contribution during the whole-class, workshop session. "I was using Ask Jeeves for Kids and I did a search for pourquoi stories like we're reading and I found a cool site!"

Marcus was one of those students who thrived within an organized class that also provided opportunities for individual exploration. He liked to find out things on his own.

Marcus continued with his contribution to the workshop session, "You know our group has Africa and I found this place called **AfroAmeric@** (http://www.afroam.org). And it had a place called **Myths and Fables** (http://www.afroam.org/children/myths/myths.html). It has a lot of cool legends. Ms. Abernathy, could we do an Internet Project like Ms. Bolin's class? You know, make a place like that with all kinds of creation stories from different countries and have other kids e-mail us from where they were in the world . . . like from Japan, and Indonesia, and Amsterdam. Ms. Abernathy, could we . . . you know . . . ask kids to e-mail us pourquoi tales from their countries? Then we could . . . we could put them on our class home page so other kids could read them. It would be cool to put all the stories on our home page."

"Yeah. Cool!" A chorus of thoughts emerged from the class.

"Did you set a bookmark, Marcus? Can you show us?"

Knowing she would ask this question, Marcus had done precisely that. He showed the class **Myths and Fables** (http://www.afroam.org/children/myths/myths.html) at **AfroAmeric@** (see Figure 5-1). It had many great pourquoi tales with wonderfully illustrated pages.

Then, with a telling gleam in his eyes, Marcus also showed Ms. Abernathy the home page for **Ms. Hos-McGrane's 5th-6th grade class at The International School of Amsterdam** (http://www.xs4all.nl/~swanson/origins/intro.html). Marcus knew Ms. Abernathy's ancestors came from the Netherlands and he had saved this Internet location for last. He took her to the wonderful project this class had completed: **Creation Stories and Myths** (http://www.xs4all.nl/~swanson/origins/cstorymenu.html). It was a collection of pourqoui tales from around the world they had written and collected from others. It was this site that gave Marcus the idea for the Internet Project he had suggested. As Marcus showed Ms. Abernathy and the class this great resource, he knew she would give them the green light for Internet Project.

Figure 5-1.
Myths and Fables from
AfroAmeric@ (http://
www.afroam.org/children/myths/
myths.html).

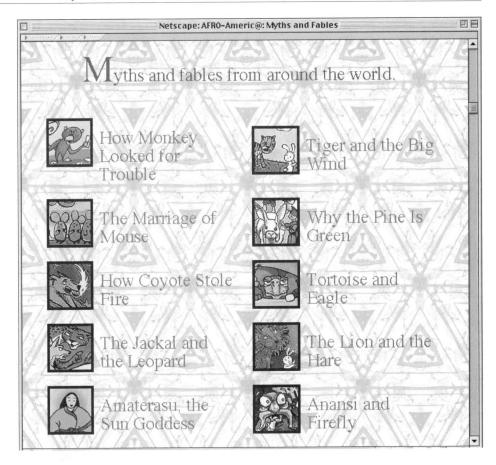

"Marcus," she said. "You certainly know how to convince me. This is wonderful! We'll see what we can do."

In this class, a "We'll see" from Ms. Abernathy was almost as good as gold.

"Yes!" several students said simultaneously, pumping their arms.

Tricia Abernathy smiled. Everyone was excited about the possibility of doing Internet Project and using their new classroom home page to publish stories from around the world.

After school that day, Tricia started thinking. She had to do some quick planning as she went over to the classroom computer. She had heard about the projects a few of the teachers were doing at her school so she talked briefly with Patty Bolin who gave some ideas and useful locations on the Internet. Returning to her classroom, Tricia visited a wonderful tutorial at the Global Schoolhouse called **Introduction to NetPBL: Collaborative Project-Based Learning** (http://www.globalschoolhouse.com/web/pbl/index.htm). Here, she studied how to develop collaborative projects on the Internet. She quickly linked to a number of useful resources that told her exactly how to set up a project, announce it to others, and post her announcement.

In just a few minutes, she had posted an announcement at a number of different locations asking teachers and students from around the world to

> Returning to her classroom, Tricia visited a wonderful tutorial at the Global Schoolhouse called Introduction to NetPBL: Collaborative Project-Based Learning (http://www.globalschoolhouse.com/web/pbl/index.htm).

contribute pourquoi tales from their cultures. By exchanging stories, they would each develop a deeper appreciation for differences and for important aspects of other cultures. She posted her project description at these locations, explaining the project and asking for other classes to join her class:

- **The Internet Projects Registry** of the Global Schoolhouse—http://www.gsn.org/pr/index.cfm

- **Global Classroom**—http://www.sofweb.vic.edu.au/gc/projects.htm
  A location in Australia

- The **Projects** location at the Australian National site, **EdNa**—http://www.edna.edu.au/EdNA

- **Intercultural E-mail Classroom Connections**—http://www.iecc.org/

Tricia also went to the web pages for several mailing lists, joined each list, and posted her project announcement. She went to the web page for **RTEACHER** (http://web.syr.edu/~djleu/RTEACHER/directions.html); the **Conversations** site (http://www.ncte.org/chat/) for English educators organized by the National Council of Teachers of English (NCTE) where she joined the **NCTE-middle** mailing list; and the home page for the **CHILD_LIT** mailing list (http://www.rci.rutgers.edu/~mjoseph/childlit/about.html), a list for educators interested in children's literature. She posted a description of her project on each of these mailing lists, inviting other classrooms to join in her collaborative classroom project.

By the end of the week, Tricia had received messages from eight different schools from around the world: Darwin, Australia; Bristol, England; Haifa, Israel; Kyoto, Japan; Newberg, New York; Dublin, California; Rapid City, South Dakota; Beaumont, Texas; and Clearwater, Florida. Each had promised to collect traditional myths from cultures in or near their location and share these in two weeks via e-mail with all of the collaborating classrooms. It was a simple project, but one Tricia felt certain would open new doors for her classroom.

Tricia had also heard from a high school English teacher in her district who was teaching a special course in storytelling. Tricia had mentioned their project to him. He wanted to know if his students could also participate, working with her students to research each story and its cultural traditions and helping her students develop storytelling performances for several of the stories. Tricia thought this would be a great way to introduce her class to this wonderful craft. It would also provide important support for the students in her class who experienced important challenges with reading and writing.

As Tricia announced the results of her work to the class the next day, everyone was full of new ideas. Each group, they decided, would work with schools from their part of the world: the Asia and Australia group would coordinate work with the schools in Darwin and Kyoto; the Americas group would work with schools in the U.S.; and the Europe, Middle East, and Africa group would work with schools in Bristol and Haifa.

Also, each group now had a new assignment, to uncover explanatory myths from cultures in their own community so that they could share these with their partner schools on this project. This would take some work interviewing parents and relatives to see what they could find. Then they would draft versions of these stories and work to revise them. Afterwards, they would polish off the final version using an editing conference with peers in class before sending it to their partner schools. And throughout this process, they would work with the high school class to develop performances for some of the stories.

Their unit would be celebrated at the end with a storytelling concert for the entire school with performances put on by her class and students from the high school. Tricia's class was humming with excitement as each group set to work.

Lessons From the Classroom

There are several important lessons we can learn from this experience in Tricia Abernathy's class. First, this story illustrates how important it is to learn from one another about the Internet. Marcus showed Tricia new ideas for Internet use, ideas that Tricia discussed with a colleague. Tricia also visited several classroom home pages, discovering wonderful models for Internet use from other teachers. In addition, Tricia relied on colleagues from the RTEACHER, NCTE-middle, and CHILD_LIT mailing lists to help develop her project. And, the collaborative relationships her class formed with other classrooms, including the storytelling class from the high school, also led to many new learning experiences. Clearly, we all learn from one another as we discover the many possibilities the Internet provides.

This story also demonstrates how exciting new curriculum resources, tested in the reality of classrooms around the world, are being developed by teachers and children and posted on classroom web pages. As Tricia discovered these resources she was amazed at how many teachers were creating these instructional resources that other classrooms were using.

In other work, we refer to this exciting potential as "The Miss Rumphius Effect," (http://www.readingonline.org/electronic/RT/rumphius.html) after the title character in *Miss Rumphius*, a book by Barbara Cooney. At a young age Miss Rumphius is told by her grandfather, "You must do something to make the world more beautiful." When she grows up, Miss Rumphius travels the world, accumulating many adventures. Eventually, however, she returns to her home by the sea and discovers a way to make the world a better place by planting lupines, beautiful wildflowers, wherever she goes. The story illustrates how a committed individual can envision a better world and then act on that envisionment, transforming all of our lives.

Margin notes:

Their unit would be celebrated at the end with a storytelling concert for the entire school with performances put on by her class and students from the high school.

This story illustrates how important it is to learn from one another about the Internet.

This story also demonstrates how exciting new curriculum resources, tested in the reality of classrooms around the world, are being developed by teachers and children and posted on classroom web pages.

Just as Miss Rumphius made the world a better place by planting lupines wherever she went, teachers and children are enriching our instructional worlds by planting new visions for literacy and learning on the Internet, transforming the nature of this new technology. These instructional resources are then used by other classrooms, making our students' worlds richer and more meaningful.

In fact, shortly after Tricia Abernathy's class completed their project and published it at the classroom home page, they received the Miss Rumphius Award for their work. This award is presented by members of the **RTEACHER** (http://web.syr.edu/~djleu/RTEACHER/directions.html) mailing list, a mailing list of literacy educators run in conjunction with *The Reading Teacher*, a journal of the International Reading Association. The Miss Rumphius Award goes to teachers who have developed exceptional curricular resources on the Internet and share these with others, making all of our instructional worlds better. If you are interested in visiting exceptional curriculum resources developed by teachers, visit the site for **The Miss Rumphius Award** (http://web.syr.edu/~djleu/RTEACHER/rumphius.html).

The story of Tricia's classroom also illustrates how Internet Project may be used to integrate cross cultural perspectives into your classroom curriculum. By creating this project and connecting with other classrooms, her students also discovered many new cultural experiences. These cross-cultural insights connected immediately with her activities in social studies and science. Internet Project provides exceptional possibilities for cross curricular integration and multicultural understanding.

This story also illustrates another lesson: The Internet provides wonderfully authentic opportunities for supporting literacy learning by connecting reading, writing, speaking, and listening. The Internet provides natural opportunities for your students to communicate about their work. This has important benefits for your students.

Reading, writing, speaking, and listening are similar processes. Supporting students in one area leads to gains in the others. In busy classrooms, we need to seek ways in which to combine subject areas which have traditionally been viewed as separate and which benefit from being combined. This is possible when we connect all four of the language modalities in learning experiences with the Internet.

After she announced the project, Tricia's class read, wrote, spoke, and listened as they had never done before. Students worked hard in the ensuing weeks to gather explanatory myths from the Vietnamese, Cambodian, African-American, Italian, Iroquois, and Chinese cultures in their own community. They wanted very much to have good stories to share with these classes in distant places. Not only did students communicate more because of this experience, but also they communicated better because their interest was so high and they were supported by members of their literature discussion group. In addition, important new writing opportunities opened up as students collected stories from their community and carefully drafted, revised, and edited

The story of Tricia's classroom illustrates how Internet projects may be used to integrate the language arts and other subject areas into your classroom curriculum.

The Internet provides wonderfully authentic opportunities for supporting literacy learning by connecting reading and writing.

these before sending them to other schools. And, as students shared the stories they found, one often saw students helping other students read them together.

Her students were especially fortunate to connect with the high school storytelling class since this added nicely to the speaking and listening experiences in this project. Listening and speaking experiences evolved naturally out of this project, as students exchanged information and planned their presentations.

This story also illustrates another important lesson: Teachers consistently report to us that publishing their students' work on a classroom home page provides many important benefits for classroom instruction. One of the greatest benefits is that students learn very quickly how important it is to revise and revise and revise their work until it is presentable to the world. When a student receives an e-mail message pointing out a spelling mistake or other evidence of writing that was quickly completed, it has a galvanizing effect. Students want to be certain their work is the best they can make it before it gets published. As one teacher wrote to us:

> Never before have I seen my students so concerned about the revision process. This used to be completed in a mechanical fashion with little apparent concern. Now, my students have 4–5 others read their work looking for parts that could be written more clearly. Going public with their work helps everyone to see the importance of clear writing for clear communication.

Finally, this story also illustrates another lesson: While the Internet contains many original works of literature for students to read, it is especially useful to enrich the literary experiences of students as they read books away from the computer. Using the Internet almost always means your students will read more books, not fewer. Immediately after Tricia announced the project, each group read much more than they had read before. While some of these stories were gathered from the Internet, many more were discovered in the school library. Virginia Hamilton's *In the Beginning: Creation Stories from Around the World* was a favorite. As one student said, "We want to be ready when we start to get our stories from Japan and Australia."

As students brought their stories back to each group, many discussions took place as they shared ideas about each culture. These experiences enriched the literary potential of the initial assignment by taking students beyond their set of books and into their local community, their library, and even the rest of the world through the Internet. Many opportunities to enrich children's literary experiences may be developed by integrating the Internet into classroom instruction.

Teachers consistently report to us that publishing their students' work on a classroom home page provides many important benefits for classroom instruction.

Using the Internet almost always means your students will read more books, not fewer.

Many opportunities to enrich children's literary experiences may be developed by integrating the Internet into classroom instruction.

E-MAIL FOR YOU

To: Colleagues

From: Tammy Payton <tpayton@dmrtc.net>

Subject: Internet Project

Hi,

I have been in elementary education for 17 years and was invited by our school corporation to create our school web site four years ago. I've been teaching in our small, bedroom community of 3,000 people for 13 years. We are really isolated! The largest town within our area is 20 miles away and it only has around 20,000 people.

For the last 3 years I have been hosting a tele-collaborative project called **E-Mail from Around the World** (http://www.buddyproject.org/less/collab/mail/default.htm). So far I have over 400 participants from 20 countries registered. This is a simple project, but one that visually demonstrates to the students, staff, and parents how the Internet brings the world to our schools.

There are so many new web based activities that are being published by teachers world-wide, that one of my favorite ways to find lessons and/or sites that integrate the Internet with the classroom curriculum is to use online databases which include lessons that have been submitted by educators. Often what you want to develop has already been created by someone else, or at least you can get an idea of what you want to do after looking at another lesson. One of my favorite sites for finding these resources is **Blue Web'n** (http://www.kn.pacbell.com/wired/bluewebn/index.html).

I believe the Internet is best used as a collaborative tool, and not just a means for retrieving information. I believe that educators' role in years to come will be how well we can get our students to collaborate with others in developing lesson content. We are living in a global community and need to teach our students how to communicate globally.

This year I have taken a sabbatical from my first grade classroom and I am redesigning and webmastering a technology project that is supported in part by the Indiana General Assembly and the Indiana Department of Education. This project is called the **Buddy System Project**. I hope you stop by and pay a visit to my web site: http://wwwbuddyproject.org.

Good luck on your journey!

Tammy
<*><*><*><*><*><*><*><*><*><*><*><*>

Tammy Payton
Franklin Institute Science Online Fellow 1998-2000
Milken National Educator Award 1998
Webmaster for Indiana Milken http://ideanet.doe.state.in.us/milken/
Webmaster for Project Buddy http://www.buddyproject.org/
mailto:tpayton@dmrtc.net

Internet FAQ	
Sometimes I try to reach a location on the WWW and I get an error message. It says that the server is not accepting connections or that the server may be busy. What should I do?	This usually is caused by one of two conditions. First, the computer where this site is located may be down for servicing. Second, too many people may be trying to get into the server at the same time, something that occasionally happens with popular educational sites during the school day. A strategy we use is to try to contact the same location three times before we give up on a busy server. Sometimes we can sneak in, even if many people are trying to reach this location at the same time. Move your cursor to the end of the address in the location bar, click, and then press your return key. Your browser will try again to connect to this location. If, after three tries, we still can not get in, we usually give up and try again later.

Central Sites for Literature

The best single location we know for young adult and children's literature is The Children's Literature Web Guide (http://www.ucalgary.ca/~dkbrown/index.html).

Central sites are well organized collections of links to important resources in a particular area. There are a number of great central sites for literature:

- **The Complete Works of Shakespeare**— http://the-tech.mit.edu/Shakespeare/works.html

- **The Children's Literature Web Guide**— http://www.ucalgary.ca/~dkbrown/index.html

- **Cyberguides**— http://www.sdcoe.k12.ca.us/score/cyberguide.html

- **Center for the Study of Books in Spanish for Children and Adolescents**—http://public.csusm.edu/campus_centers/csb/

- **The Reading Zone of the Internet Public Library**— http://www.ipl.org/cgi-bin/youth/youth.out.pl?sub=rzn0000

- **Carol Hurst's Children's Literature Site**— http://www.carolhurst.com/index.html

- **ALA's Language and Literature**— http://www.ala.org/parentspage/greatsites/lit.html

If you have an interest in Shakespeare, students at MIT have developed a marvelous central site for your classroom needs (see Figure 5-2), **The Complete Works of Shakespeare** (http://the-tech.mit.edu/Shakespeare/works.html). This amazing resource contains all of the works of Shakespeare, an electronic glossary for locating the meanings of archaic terms, discussion groups where your students can ask questions and share ideas, and much, much more. Be certain to pay a visit and explore this location. There are many opportunities for classroom activities to bring Shakespeare alive for your students.

The best central site we know for young adult and children's literature is **The Children's Literature Web Guide** (http://www.ucalgary.ca/~dkbrown/index.html) a site maintained by David Brown, a librarian at the University of Calgary (see Figure 5-3). This amazing location contains a comprehensive and organized array of links to literature resources. The types of resources

Figure 5-2.
The home page for **The Complete Works of Shakespeare** (http://the-tech.mit.edu/Shakespeare/works.html), a central site for Shakespeare study.

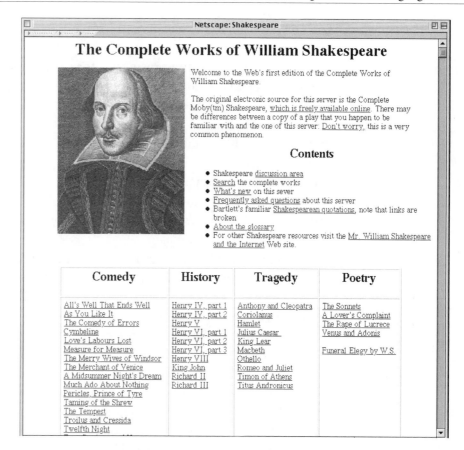

Figure 5-3.
The homepage for **The Children's Literature Web Guide**, a central site for literature (http://www.ucalgary.ca/~dkbrown/index.html).

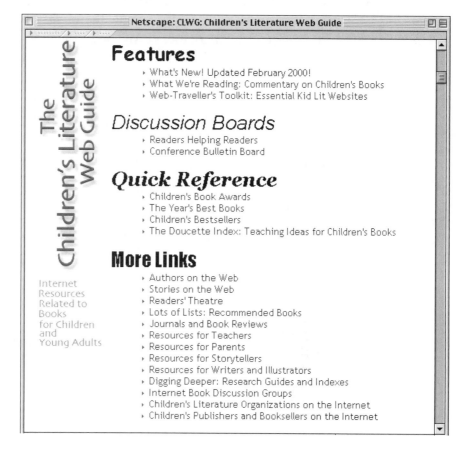

on this page are too exhaustive to list but they include everything from on-line works of literature, resources for teachers, locations about movies developed from literature, resources for parents, resources for storytellers, resources for writers and illustrators, discussion groups about literature, lists of award winners, and information about authors.

Resources at this location are designed to enrich your students' literary experiences without taking them away from books. As the developer of this site indicates, "If my cunning plan works, you will find yourself tempted away from the Internet, and back to the books themselves!" If you are serious about literature in your classroom, you should explore this site, set a bookmark, and incorporate its many resources into classroom learning projects.

Is your class reading specific works of literature and you need some quick ideas for Internet integration, perhaps even some ready-to-go Internet activities? Be certain to visit another central site for K–12 literature: **Cyberguides: Teacher Guides and Student Activities** (http://www.sdcoe.k12.ca.us/score/ cyberguide.html). This wonderful location (see Figure 5-4), being developed by Don Mayfield and Linda Taggart-Fregoso in San Diego, is the best location we have found for the immediate integration of exceptional works of literature into your K–12 classroom program. The site contains an extensive list of literary works, each containing classroom-tested lessons, activities, and evaluation strategies developed by teachers. Literature selections at Cyberguides are nicely organized by grade level appropriateness. This is one resource every K–12 teacher should thoroughly explore and use in the classroom. Set a bookmark today! And don't forget to drop an e-mail message to Don Mayfield and Linda Taggart-Fregoso, telling them what wonderful work they are accomplishing for all of us.

Be certain to visit another central site for K–12 literature: Cyberguides: Teacher Guides and Student Activities (http:// www.sdcoe.k12.ca.us/ score/cyberguide.html).

Figure 5-4.
An example of one of the many complete lessons with wonderful Internet activities available for your students at **Cyberguides: Teacher Guides and Student Activities** (http://www.sdcoe.k12.ca.us/score/ cyberguide.html).

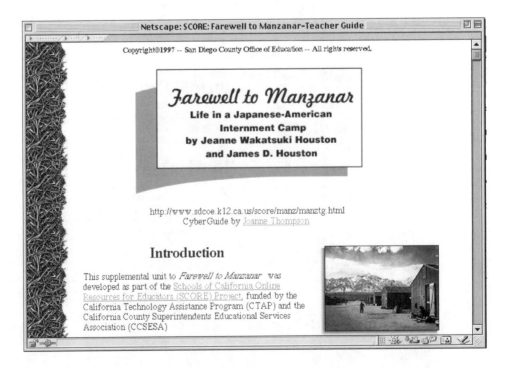

E-MAIL FOR YOU

To: Colleagues
From: "Linda Taggart-Fregoso" <ltaggart@sandi.net>
Subject: Cyberguides

Hi,

   I direct the SCORE Language Arts Site which includes Cyberguides (http://www.sdcoe.k12.ca.us/score/cyberguide.html), classroom experiences around works of literature (K—12) designed by teachers for immediate use in your classroom. These are not just written lesson plans. Each includes objectives, activities and Internet links related to the work of literature students have read, and an evaluation rubric. Most importantly, each lesson is organized around the Reading and Language Arts Standards in California. Since these are so similar to the standards in other states and countries, you will be able to use them no matter where you live.

   The voyage as director of the SCORE Language Arts Site these past 6 years has been a rewarding venture. When we set sail on this exotic trip we did not know the best course to take. Some of the most important lessons I learn come from teachers at varying levels on the technology spectrum. The real joy of creating a CyberGuide comes from working together with others to design and implement powerful lessons that work for students.

   The best CyberGuides are practitioner oriented and serve to empower students as they set sail on their reading journeys. They can be adopted and adapted by teachers from all over the globe. These CyberGuides also work with a wide range of students with significantly different backgrounds, knowledge, and skills. The more rooted in the best practices, the better the CyberGuide supports student learning.

   Standards have helped keep us on an even keel and assisted us in staying the course. When we began this project, standards were not implemented as widely as they are now. With standards, we can clearly define assessment that is communicated to the student. We provide a rubric that gives the students an opportunity to self-assess and take responsibility for their own learning.

   We hope you take a few moments to visit us and, perhaps, to contribute your own CyberGuide for others to use.

   Best wishes,
   Linda Taggart-Fregoso, Director

SCORE Language Arts Site
E-mail: ltaggart@sandi.net>

While we tend to prefer real books for most literary experiences in a classroom, it is often useful to read other works on the Internet related to ones you use in class.

In addition to these central sites, there are many central sites containing on-line works of literature for your classroom. While we tend to prefer real books for most literary experiences, it is often useful to read other works on the Internet, especially if they are related to others you use in class. It is especially nice to know that any work you find on-line may be printed out so that students may read it in the class or take it home to share with their family and friends. There are several types of on-line literature collections: older classics with expired copyrights, traditional tales, works of literature written by children, and original works published on the Internet.

You will find many older classics with expired copyrights on the Internet. Because their copyright has expired, these works may now be published on the web without violating copyright law. Older classics often are used by teachers to provide additional literary experiences for students who have read one work by an author and are interested in reading more, especially when your library's holdings are a bit thin. The problem with these classics is that they usually appear in a text-only form without illustrations. This sometimes takes away from the literary experience. Some of the best locations for classic works of literature include:

- **Project Gutenberg**—http://promo.net/pg/
  This voluntary project has a goal of providing one trillion works of literature to users by the December 31, 2001. Here you will find the complete texts of many classic works by authors such as Louisa May Alcott, Jane Austen, Aesop, O Henry, Victor Hugo, Charles Dickens, and many others. Set a bookmark!

- **Classics for Young Children**—http://www.ucalgary.ca/~dkbrown/storclas.html
  A comprehensive set of links to classic works, some of which are illustrated. These include *Little Women, The Call of the Wild, The Wonderful Wizard of Oz, The Wind in the Willows, Rip Van Winkle, The Gift of the Magi, Anne of Green Gables,* and many, many others.

Traditional tales are another form of on-line literature. These include folktales, fairytales, myths, and legends. Because so many were published some time ago and their original copyrights are out of date, many are now in the public domain and available on-line. Usually these exist in text-only versions. Occasionally, you will find illustrated versions.

Because traditional tales come from an oral tradition, there are many different versions for most stories. The richness of the web allows us to share multiple versions of the same story with students. This leads to wonderful opportunities for critical analysis as students evaluate how the versions differ, consider the types of response each provokes in readers, or determine what characterizes a "typical" traditional tale. Some of the best central sites for traditional tales include:

- **The Encyclopedia Mythica**—http://www.pantheon.org/mythica/
  This is an encyclopedia devoted to myths, folklore, and legends. An outstanding place to begin research in this area.

- **Tales of Wonder**—
  http://members.xoom.com/darsie/tales/index.html
  This is an extensive archive of folk and fairy tales from around the world—a must for any cross-cultural unit or for a unit on this genre. Set a bookmark!

- **Folklore, Myth and Legend**—http://www.ucalgary.ca/~dkbrown/storfolk.html
  A comprehensive site with many useful links to sources of information and copies of traditional tales.

Other central sites for literature contain children's voices, literature written by children. These sites are great to motivate the writers in your class and show them what is possible. Some of these locations include:

- **KidPub**—http://www.kidpub.org/kidpub
  A wonderful collection of more than 36,000 stories written by children and maintained by a father in Massachusetts who initially just wanted a place for his daughter to publish her work. Many great stories are located here and great writing activities, too.

- **Cyberkids**—http://www.cyberkids.com/
  This is a quarterly on-line magazine written by kids for kids ages 7–11. It includes articles and stories by young writers.

- **Parents and Children Together On-line**—
  http://www.indiana.edu/~eric_rec/fl/pcto/menu.html
  Sponsored by ERIC, this regular magazine contains materials written by children and is intended to support family reading at home. Great to share at open house evening.

Internet FAQ	
I have heard that some locations have authors reading their works aloud over the Internet? How does this work? How can I get my computer to do this?	New technologies for multimedia continue to appear on the Internet. Sound and video technologies are ones that are changing especially rapidly. We are beginning to find locations with stories that are read aloud for younger students. These include: Story Hour—http://www.ipl.org/youth/StoryHour/ Children's Stories—http://www.childrenstory.com/ Read Along Stories—http://www.indiana.edu/~eric_rec/fl/pcto/read.html

Reading a great story is one of the better experiences we can provide students. Often, though, our students' experience with a story is limited by knowing little about the author. Learning about an author helps students to better understand the work they are reading. This helps to contextualize the

E-MAIL FOR YOU

To: Colleagues
From: Jeanette Kenyon <jkenyon@pen.k12.va.us>
Subject: Using the WWW for Literature Units

Dear Colleagues,

My class uses the Internet frequently to enhance various literature units. During our studies of *Stuart Little* by E.B. White, and *From the Mixed Up Files of Mrs. Basil E. Frankweiler* by Elaine Konigsburg, we located several valuable resources. We also used excellent links about Central Park to locate and research places mentioned in both books. For example, the class was able to view the lake where Stuart entered a boat race as well as tour the Metropolitan Museum of Art, where Claudia and Jamie's adventures took place. Using an enlarged map from the Central Park site, we created a bulletin board highlighting pertinent landmarks from each story. At the suggestion of several students, we even posted a quiz question on our Home Page where visitors can try to locate Claudia and Jamie using map skills with the Central Park map.
Useful links include:

Maps of New York City—http://www.panix.com/clay/nyc/maps.shtml

The Metropolitan Museum of Arts—http://www.metmuseum.org/

Central Park—http://www.centralpark.org/

From the Mixed Up Files of Mrs. Basil E. Frankweiler—http://www.ctnba.org/ctn/k8/mixedup.html

The Narnia Series by C. S. Lewis led us to many interesting sites. Several students concluded the unit by creating a newspaper from Narnia (The Narnia Times) which is also posted on our Home Page. We received encouraging e-mail from a fellow C. S. Lewis fan, who hosts one of our favorite Narnia sites (see below for link).
Useful links include:

The Worlds of Aslan and C. S. Lewis—http://www.iserv.net/~dorcasb/narnia.htm

Into the Wardrobe: The C. S. Lewis Page—http://cslewis.drzeus.net

Don't overlook the wealth of original literature available to you on the Internet. I have downloaded all of *Aesop's Fables, Jabberwocky, The Gift of the Magi,* Dr. Martin Luther King's, "I Have a Dream" speech, various Greek and Roman myths, and numerous poetry selections. I can import these files into a word processing program and incorporate pictures, appropriate questions, highlighted text, and background information. Each child then has his own working copy which has been tailored specifically for our assignment. A useful link where all of these, and many more, works of literature is **Project Gutenberg**—http://promo.net/pg/
Our school Home Page can be found at:
        http://www.pen.k12.va.us/Anthology/Div/Stafford/mes/home.html
Please stop by for a visit!

Sincerely,
Jeanette Kenyon   Moncure Elementary School, Stafford, Virginia
Third Grade Teacher   jkenyon@pen.k12.va.us

Learning about an author helps students to better understand the work they are reading.

literary work and provides important information to students about why an author wrote a story, what experience in their life prompted the story, how they write, other books the author has written, and issues the author often writes about. Knowing this information enriches children's literary experiences. They are many sites on the web that will provide your students with this information. You may, of course, use one of the search engines to locate information about authors. Keep in mind, though, that most author locations (not all) have been developed with commercial interests in mind. Some of the best central sites for author locations include:

- **Authors and Illustrators on the Web—**
  http://www.acs.ucalgary.ca/~dkbrown/authors.html
  Probably the most extensive set of links to popular authors for K–12.

- **The BBC Web Guide—**http://www.bbc.co.uk/plsql/education/webguide/pkg_main.p_home
  A great resource from the BBC in the UK. Go to this site and select "English." Then search for the name of a specific author or search using the more general term "authors."

- **Ask the Author—**http://www.ipl.org/youth/AskAuthor/
  This location of the Internet Public Library, a non-commercial site, contains information about a number of popular authors including Lois Lowry, Avi, Matt Christopher, Natalie Babbitt, Daniel Pinkwater, Jane Yolen, Gary Paulson, Charlotte Zolotow, and others. Photos of the authors, a biography, and answers to questions submitted by kids are available.

Some of these locations are quite impressive, containing extensive information about the author and his/her life. Some even have listservs or bulletin boards to discuss the author's works. Some contain curriculum materials for using the author's works in your classrooms. A few of our favorites include:

- **Charles Dickens—**http://www.helsinki.fi/kasv/nokol/dickens.html
  This location contains all of the works by this important author, as well as extensive information about his life and about London during the time when he was writing. The perfect site for your study of this author.

- **Into the Wardrobe: The C. S. Lewis WWW Site—**
  http://cslewis.cache.net/
  This is the one of the best author sites around. Many rich resources including a biography, an album of photographs, recordings of the author's voice, many links to other Lewis sites, a listserv address, a usenet address, and even a live chat location.

- **The L. M. Montgomery Institute—**
  http://www.upei.ca/~lmmi/core.html

The official institute's site for Lucy Maud Montgomery, the author of *Anne of Green Gables* and other works. The location includes information about her life, additional links to related sites, information for subscribing to a listserv about her books, and sites on Prince Edward Island, her home.

- **Mark Twain**—http://marktwain.miningco.com/arts/marktwain/ A site with commercial messages, but probably the most extensive set of resources for this important author.

- **The JRR Tolkien Information Page**— http://www.csclub.uwaterloo.ca/u/relipper/tolkien/rootpage.html If you are a Tolkien fan, this is the place for you! Mailing lists, web rings, and much more. A site loaded with information.

- **My Little House on the Prairie Home Page**— http://www.pinc.com/~jenslegg/ This site contains much useful information about the author of the "Little House" series. Historical information about the characters and the locations where they lived is provided. It also features bulletin boards for those doing research on Laura Ingalls Wilder and her literary works. The site has a useful link for teachers which will take you to plans for instructional units about this author and her work.

E-MAIL FOR YOU

To: Colleagues
From: "Karen Auffhammer" <kauffhammer@msn.com>
Subject: *Maniac Magee*

```
Hello!
    I have recently read the story Maniac Magee by Jerry Spinelli and it is
by far one of my favorites. I was so excited to see a site on the WWW on
this story. Here's the URL: http://www.carolhurst.com/titles/
maniacmagee.html
    Check it out!! It provides a brief summary of the story, character
descriptions, things to discuss with your class, activities and related
books. From here you can click to see other popular books that have been
reviewed.

    Karen Auffhammer
    Curriculum Consultant
    Central Square Intermediate School
    Central Square, NY
```

Central Sites for Writing

The Internet also opens new doors to authentic writing experiences as students communicate with other writers from around the world. Students may correspond with experts about their writing, publish their work and invite comments from others, read responses to their writing, and write messages back to others. These opportunities make the Internet a wonderful resource to support student writing at all levels. There are two types of central sites in writing: those that provide a wide range of support for student writers and those that provide opportunities for students to publish their work.

Locations on The Internet That Support Young Writers

There are a number of central sites on the Internet for young writers. These locations are often important sources of support for students who are serious about their writing. Explore these locations, set a bookmark, and invite your students to take advantage of the many resources at each location.

- **Inkspot: For Young Writers**—http://www.inkspot.com/young/
  Arguably the best location to support aspiring writers under age 18, with many types of help including words of advice from authors and editors, interviews with young writers, and a Young Writers Forum. At the Young Writers' Forum, students can network with other writers and exchange ideas.

- **The Quill Society**—http://www.quill.net/
  Looking for a central site for your secondary English class? Here it is. The Quill Society consists of young writers from around the world, ages 12–24, who enjoy creative expression and wish to learn from one another. This site includes a message board for discussions between young writers, a place to publish work, a board of critics who will respond to your work with helpful suggestions, and a fun activities area. A great location for your writers!

Publishing Student Work on the Internet

The Internet provides new and exciting opportunities to publish your students' work. You may publish student work on a classroom homepage (see Chapter 12). You may also publish student work at many locations on the Internet devoted especially to this purpose. You can take advantage of these locations to engage students in comprehensive writing process activities which include prewriting, drafting, revision, editing, and publishing. When a student's work is prepared, think about submitting it to one of these locations:

- **International Kids' Space**—http://www.kids-space.org
  A great location for children to share their works of art, short stories, and music with others.

- **Cyberkids**—http://www.cyberkids.com/
  This is a magazine for kids. Each year, the magazine invites submissions for writing, art, and musical compositions from students, ages 7–11, for a contest. After a preliminary screening, readers then vote for the winners which are published. A great location for free reading time. Set a bookmark!

- **KidPub**—http://www.kidpub.org/kidpub/
  All work is published at KidPub, a publishing location for kids maintained by a parent in Massachusetts. Directions for submissions are provided. Students can even see how many people have read their work. Over 36,000 stories have been published to date. Set a bookmark!

TEACHING TIP	There are many bookstores on the Internet now such as **Amazon.com** (http://amazon.com/) and **Barnes and Noble** (http://www.barnesandnoble.com/). These locations provide opportunities to publish a review of any book your students have read and quickly see it posted. As students complete independent reading projects, invite them to write a review. Have them read the initial draft of their review during Internet Workshop and seek suggestions for revision. After the review has been revised, help students to use the search engine at a bookstore to locate their book. Then, have them post their review at this location.

Grammar on the Internet

Grammar on the Internet, you ask? Yes, indeed. There are many, interactive and creative, resources for grammar experiences on the Internet. If you take just a few minutes, you can discover the informative and engaging manner in which some locations present this information. Though the content is the same, grammar sites on the Internet present this information in a manner that certainly is different from the way we learned.

The best central site for grammar we have found has been developed by Professor Charles Darling at Capital Community College in Connecticut: **Guide to Grammar and Writing** (http://webster.commnet.edu/HP/pages/darling/grammar.htm). Pay a visit. You will be surprised and entranced by many of the resources at this very extensive resource. Just a few of the many great resources here include:

- **Interactive Quizzes**—http://webster.commnet.edu/HP/pages/darling/original.htm#contents
  Here is the place for students to test themselves on most of the important grammar principles. Great fun! There are even grammar crossword puzzles, too.

- **Principles of Composition**—http://webster.commnet.edu/HP/pages/darling/original.htm#contents
  This provides your students with all the important information to get them writing with style while they communicate their ideas clearly.

- **Ask Grammar**—http://webster.commnet.edu/HP/pages/darling/original.htm#contents
  Got a grammar question? Ask grammar has the answer. Just send your question to this web site and you will get an answer to that burning question: What are split infinitives?

Using Internet Workshop

There are as many good ideas for enriching literary experiences with the Internet as there are creative teachers with a few moments to plan a new Internet Workshop experiences. We can not be exhaustive here. We can, however, provide some examples that might serve to inspire you to think of your own creative ideas for developing Internet activities.

- **Julius Caesar Unit**—Take advantage of the activities developed at **Cyberguides** (http://www.lausd.k12.ca.us/lausd/resources/shakespeare/caesarwebguide.html) to add to your unit on Shakespeare's *Julius Caesar*. This site contains resources and directions to help students complete four compositions about this classic work: an opinion/comparison-contrast essay, an expository essay, a statement of opinion, and an argumentative essay. Use Internet Workshop to share works in progress as well as completed works. This will prompt conversations about the play and about students' different interpretations of character, plot, and theme.

- **Cinderella Studies**—Engage your class in a study of Cinderella tales from around the world. Nearly every culture has their own version of this classic tale. Compare and contrast different versions to infer what these differences might suggest about the culture associated with each story. Begin with beautifully illustrated versions from your library such as *Mufaro's Beautiful Daughters* by John Steptoe. Then have students explore the web for other versions. They may wish to start at the **Cinderella Project** (http://www-dept.usm.edu/~engdept/cinderella/cinderella.html) and **Cinderella Stories** (http://www.ucalgary.ca/~dkbrown/cinderella.html). Then have students begin exploring the web using various search engines for even more versions. A great activity for combining web use and literature in very effective ways.

- **Studying Indigenous Peoples' Literature**—If you engage students in a project studying Native Americans or other indigenous peoples, be certain to set a bookmark for **Indigenous Peoples Literature** (http://www.indians.org/welker/framenat.htm), an outstanding site developed by Glenn Welker, or **Native Ameri-**

There are as many good ideas for enriching literary experiences with the Internet as there are creative teachers with a few moments to plan a new Internet Workshop experiences.

can Indian Resources (http://indy4.fdl.cc.mn.us/~isk/mainmenu.html), another site rich in informational resources. Have students explore these sites to find out information about the culture behind each of the books they read. Have them share the information they find during Internet Workshop.

- **This Door Leads to the Internet**—Cover the outside of your classroom door with butcher paper, or another type of large paper. Have a group of students design a book cover on this paper entitled "This Door Leads to the Internet." At the same time, set bookmarks to locations with collections of stories on the Internet such as **Contemporary Writing for Children and Young Adults** (http://www.ucalgary.ca/~dkbrown/storcont.html). Have students read a story that is interesting to them during their time on the computer and then print it out. Then have students sit in a "reader's chair" at the front of the room and share their favorite selection with the class. As they finish, post the printed version of their story on the bookcover door students have designed.

- **Jan Brett's Stories**—If you and your class are reading one of many excellent stories by Jan Brett, invite students to visit the **Jan Brett Home Page** (http://www.janbrett.com/) and then share what they have discovered during Internet workshop. A similar activity could be done with any author page. This is especially useful to build background knowledge about the author and his/her works.

 ## E-MAIL FOR YOU

To: Colleagues
From: Maureen Salmon-Salvemini <msalmons@MAILBOX.SYR.EDU>
Subject: Literature sites to share

The Internet is addictive! I have found a new website: It is Eric Carle's **The Official Eric Carle Web Site** with many great ideas on how to use his books in your classroom. It's located at: (http://www.eric-carle.com/).

Additional sites include **The Magic School Bus Fun Place** (http://place.scholastic.com/magicschoolbus/index.htm), and a location where games and books can be downloaded free for Windows machines (http://www.microsoft.com/kids/freestuff.htm).

Hope these locations help you!

Maureen

Using Internet Project

Using Internet Project can be a very powerful way to develop learning experiences for your students.

Traditionally, classrooms organize learning around separate subject areas. Recently, many teachers have explored an alternative, taking a thematic approach to organize learning. Some teachers are now beginning to take a third approach as they seek to capitalize on the learning opportunities available on the Internet. These teachers organize learning experiences around collaborative, Internet projects with other classrooms around the world. Using Internet Project can be a very powerful way to develop learning experiences for your students. Project-based learning experiences are especially useful to integrate the language arts; students naturally engage in reading, writing, speaking, listening, and viewing experiences during the course of a project. One sees in these classrooms a rich interplay between content learning and English/ language arts activities, often combining Internet experiences with more familiar method frameworks including: cooperative group learning, response journals, readers' theater, process writing, inquiry projects, and other highly effective techniques.

Examples of Internet projects that emphasize the language arts include:

- **The Toni Morrison Book Club.** Students from several schools read works by this exceptional author and share their responses and web resources to discover more information about her work and her life. Works are read in a certain order and weekly responses are exchanged by e-mail and posted at one English classroom's home page. Internet Workshop is used to share responses and plan new responses with collaborating classrooms.

- **Presidential Election.** In this election research and balloting project, students research the presidential candidates in the United States, write and publish editorials at a central location to convince voters, and then conduct a mock election at school sites around the country. The results are displayed by school and state so that students can analyze voting patterns. Internet Workshop is used to coordinate much of the planning for this work as well as to discuss the results and their meanings. Math, social studies, and language arts are integrated within this learning unit.

- **Paddington Bear Travels the World.** This project sends a stuffed Paddington Bear to primary grade classrooms around the world. When Paddington arrives, he has to keep a journal describing his adventures, the cultures he visits, the sites he sees, and the students he meets. His travel journal is published at the home page of the school that first sent him on his journey and continuously updated by the classroom he is currently visiting. Other students write to him and ask him questions which are answered by the class where he is at any point in time. Other activities such as calculating mileage and locating Paddington on the map are also used. Classrooms use Internet Workshop to coordinate the work and to share correspondence. This project integrates social studies, science, math, and language arts.

- **K–1 Students Request Postcards.** This project requests that postcards from classes around the world be sent to a K–1 class in Georgia to help them develop a better understanding of locations around the world. The postcards are read in class during Internet Workshop to initiate discussion about geographical locations and then they are fastened to a map of the world next to the country they came from. Students answer each postcard with another postcard from their area as well as with an e-mail message. This project is used to initiate contact with other classrooms for future projects.

Done correctly, collaborative Internet projects can be the cornerstone of your English/language arts program.

The special advantage of Internet Project is its potential to create very powerful learning opportunities, especially in English and language arts. Communicating with students in other locations motivates your students in ways you probably have not seen in your classroom and opens the door to important cross-cultural understandings. Done correctly, Internet Project can be the cornerstone of your English/language arts program.

How do you get started? You may wish to visit several locations where teachers register collaborative projects for other teachers to find. Reading about other projects will give you ideas for your own Internet project. These sites were listed in Chapter 4.

Initially, you may wish to join someone else's project. After several experiences, though, you could develop your own project, post it, and see if you can get other classrooms to join you. For example, you may wish to adapt literature discussion groups to the Internet. Post the works of literature your students will be reading to see if other classes would be interested in reading the same work(s) and exchanging responses. Comparing responses to literature on the Internet will provide many opportunities to integrate the language arts.

TEACHING TIP	If you are interested in using Internet Project in your classroom but anxious about how to get started, simply join one of the mailing lists listed at the end of this chapter devoted to English and the language arts. Then, post a message asking others to share their experiences with this approach. Ask for suggestions that would be helpful to a person who is first attempting Internet Project. You will receive many great ideas from your colleagues. Others, too, will benefit from the suggestions colleagues share on the mailing list in response to your question.

A wonderful example of an Internet project using literature appeared two years ago on several mailing lists, inviting classrooms to participate: "Looney Lobsters Love Regional Literature." This outstanding Internet project was developed by Marjorie Duby, a 5th grade teacher at the Joseph Lee Elementary School in Boston, Massachusetts. Her project description is one of the best we have seen so we wanted to be certain to share it with you. It was

E-MAIL FOR YOU

To: Colleagues
From: Rina Hallock <rhallock@micron.net>
Subject: E-mail and projects

E-mail has opened many new vistas for teachers! What a wonderful opportunity e-mail provides for communication with teachers all around the world! For the past year and a half I have been communicating with a preschool teacher in South Africa. It has been so enriching to compare ideas and take a peek into her world. We have shared family and work anecdotes and authors that we enjoy. I was delighted to discover that she enjoys the current information coming out on brain research and that we both enjoy the same author in this area, Eric Jensen! It's been interesting to compare the problems she encounters in her school and to share what our school is like. We have discussed the current trends in education, problems we experience, and family challenges. It's been a pleasant experience interacting with her.

E-mail also provides other excellent opportunities to collaborate with teachers wherever they are. Currently I am working on my National Board Teacher Certification. There is no one in my immediate locale who is also certifying in my area. It has been valuable for me to create a "group" mailing of all the teachers in my state who are working on certification in my area of specialty. We share ideas and resources. Now I don't feel so isolated!

I also use e-mail to develop collaborative Internet projects, especially with literature. It's not hard to find teachers who are interested in the same projects in which you are interested. One way is to go to **Classroom Connect's Connected Teacher** (http://www.connectedteacher.com/home.asp) and click on Teacher Search. From that page, you can register for Connected Teacher (for free!—just the right price for most of us). Registered members are the only people who can contact other educators through Teacher Search. Once registered, you choose a search based on Name, School, Curriculum, Grade, Interest, Geography or even choose an All Fields Search.

Technology has certainly granted us a boon in education. The onus is upon us to utilize it and find new and enriching ways in which we can benefit from this opportunity. When we reach out to other teachers and share ideas, we multiply our effectiveness and enrich a multitude of students' lives.

Best wishes for continued success!
Rina Hallock
rhallock@micron.net

> "Our task is to provide an education for the kinds of kids
> we have, not the kinds of kids we used to have, or want
> to have, or the kids that exist in our dreams."
>   —K.P. Gerlack

posted on the **KIDLIT-L** mailing list, among other locations, inviting other teachers to collaborate with her classroom. Visit the home page for this project (http://bps.boston.k12.ma.us/rc328sb/looney.html) to see how other classrooms shared their regional works of literature through the travels of Larry and Lester, the "Looney Lobsters." If you are interested in the latest projects with the Looney Lobsters, be certain to visit the root page for the Looneys (http://lee.boston.k12.ma.us/d4/trav/lroot.html). We hear the Looneys are now doing writing projects.

 ## E-MAIL FOR YOU

To: Colleagues
From: Marjorie Duby <mduby@boston.k12.ma.us>
Subject: Looney Lobster Loves Regional Literature

Hello to all!
My 5th grade class in Boston, Massachusetts, and I do a variety of travel projects on the Internet with our stuffed animals Looney Larry and Looney Lester Lobster. Recently we completed a project called "Looney Lobsters Love Regional Literature." This project was designed to help all of the participating classrooms appreciate the many wonderful works of literature from different regions of the world. Here is the project description I posted on mailing lists to describe the project and invite participants. If you wish to view this project, now completed, please visit: http://bps.boston.k12.ma.us/rc328sb/looney.html If you wish or see the new projects we are doing this year, visit http://lee.boston.k12.ma.us/d4/trav/lroot.html

Project Background

Last year our traveling stuffed crustaceans, Looney Larry and Looney Lester of Boston, Massachusetts, accepted the gracious hospitality of elementary school classrooms across the United States for one school week and then were mailed to another classroom eventually returning to Boston.
They received cuddles, pets, and tours of local sites. They learned of local customs and culture. As we kept in touch with them and others through the Internet via electronic mail and our "Looney Lobster on the Loose" website at http://bps.boston.k12.ma.us/rc328sb/looney.html, we learned much virtually.
Our Looneys enjoyed traveling and learning so much that they would like to again travel the USA learning about local regional literature.

Our Project Announcement

Would you be willing to show hospitality in your elementary school classroom for one school week to our traveling Looney? During Looney's visit, would you be willing to read aloud picture books based on local lore—a folktale, a custom, a happening, a regionally identifiable daily life story?

What we will send

A small box which will include:

1. A small pouch with Looney Lobster, a small, cuddly, stuffed crustacean
2. A photo-album showing our class members—on our travels around Boston and in our classroom
3. Looney Lobster's itinerary
4. A single-use camera
5. A pouch of SASE envelopes

What we will ask that you do

1. In your message of interest, identify the title and author of a picture book/s based on your local lore—a folk tale, a custom, a happening, a regionally identifiable daily life story—which your class will read aloud to Looney during his visit to your school.
2. Immediately after being notified of your acceptance into the project, arrange to send a photo of your class (digitized, photocopy of a photo, or original photo) possibly holding a copy of the regional book they will read aloud during your school week.
3. Once accepted into the project and the "Looney Lobsters Love Regional Literature" booklist is created, begin to locate the booklist entries at your local library for read-aloud use during the scheduled school weeks.
4. Subscribe to our Looney Lobster Listserv (mailing list) which will network participants allowing students to converse about the literature and the daily experiences of Looney.
5. Send electronic mail messages related to Looney's visit to the Looney mailing list.
6. If possible, create a school-based webpage of Looney's travels and experiences linked to our "Looney Lobsters Love Regional Literature" webpage.
7. With the single-use camera, take a close-up picture of your state's license plate and two other pictures of your choice.
8. Remove one of the SASE from the box. Inside the envelope, place the front page of your local newspaper.
9. Following Looney Lobster's scheduled visit to your school, immediately send him to his next scheduled site allowing a minimum of 4 days for Priority Mail travel.

What we will be doing

1. Calculating the accumulated mileage for our Looney Lobsters.
2. Locating the latitude and longitude of each city that our Looneys visit.
3. Becoming aware of the daily time zones for each school that Looney Lobster visits.
4. Observing the daily weather of Looney's host school and comparing it to our weather.
5. Obtaining from our local library the regional literature suggested by participants for each scheduled Looney visit.
6. Reading aloud the weekly booklist suggestion to our lower grade Reading Buddies.

7. Reacting to the read aloud selections with other participant students through the mailing list.
8. Receiving the SASE information that is sent to us as our Looneys move to the next school site.

How we will let you know about Looney's travels

1. We will have a webpage which will include Looney's itinerary, the regional literature booklist, and the daily adventures of Looney.
2. Our group will telecommunicate using our Looney Lobsters mailing list and individual electronic mail messages.
3. We will gather and distribute prior to the beginning of the project, a "Looney Loves Regional Literature Participant Handbook" featuring the itinerary, the booklist resources, and the pictures of participant school classes.

   If you are interested in hosting Looney Lobster and participating in this project, please respond to:
   mduby@boston.k12.ma.us

Our project announcement resides at:
   http://bps.boston.k12.ma.us/rc328sb/rlit.shtml

= = = = = = = = = = = = = = = = = = = =

Marjorie Duby, Grade 5
Joseph Lee School, Boston, Massachusetts

"The Home of Looney Lobster"
   http://lee.boston.k12.ma.us/d4/trav/lroot.html
Visit our homepage at
   http://lee.boston.k12.ma.us/d4/d4.htm

= = = = = = = = = = = = = = = = = = = =

Using Internet Inquiry

> The intensive reading and writing experiences required in inquiry projects provides students with authentic literacy experiences where they learn much about comprehension and composition.

Inquiry approaches to the Internet are also valuable to support learning in language arts and literature. Inquiry approaches require students to engage in self-directed reading and writing projects as they explore issues of personal interest. The personal nature of these inquiry projects motivates students in exciting ways, helping them to accomplish tasks they might have thought impossible to accomplish. The intensive reading and writing experiences required in inquiry projects provides students with authentic literacy experiences where they learn much about critical thinking, comprehension, and composition.

Often teachers combine Internet Workshop with Internet Inquiry to provide special opportunities to learn from one another. Combining these methods will help you to capitalize on these special opportunities. Here are several ideas and examples for using Internet Inquiry with Internet Workshop as you engage students in Language Arts and Literature:

- **Literature Inquiry Projects**. As students encounter an interesting historical period, develop a favorite author, or encounter an fascinating location during their literary experiences encourage them to complete an Internet Inquiry. Have them use the library and Internet resources to discover all they can about their topic and question. Encourage them to share the challenges they encounter and the final results during Internet Workshop.

- **Literature Fair**. Set aside one period each month for all of your students to share their Internet Inquiry projects in literature. Use Internet Workshop to share progress and respond to questions as you build up to this special day. Have students display the results of their research on poster board or on your classroom home page. Invite students from other classes to visit during a literature fair where students can share the results of their work. After the fair, set up the poster board presentations in the school library for the entire school to see or invite other classrooms to view your students' work at your classroom home page.

- **Living Museum of Literary Authors.** Invite students to complete Internet Inquiry on the author of a work they are reading. Have them conduct research to discover everything they can about their author. Then, invite them to dress up as the author and prepare a display, sharing information they discovered about this person. Have students pose in their costumes, without movement, as other classes visit your living classroom museum of literary authors reading the displays and viewing the authors.

- **Dress Up As A Character Day.** Have students complete Internet Inquiry on a favorite character. Then, have everyone come to school on the same day, dressed as their character. During Internet Workshop, have students ask questions of one another, trying to discover the name of their character or author, using the format from the game "Twenty Questions."

TEACHING TIP	Do you use literature discussion groups in your class? Here is a way to do the same thing on the Internet between classes reading the same work of literature (K–12). Visit **Book Raps** (http://rite.ed.qut.edu.au/oz-teachernet/projects/book-rap/index.html) the wonderful location managed by Cherrol McGhee, a teacher at the Hillview State Primary School in Queensland, Australia. Here children from around the world engage in literature discussion groups about common works of literature they have read, exchanging insights about the world from a variety of cultural perspectives.

Visiting the Classroom: David Leahy's Fourth Grade Class in Oregon

David Leahy and his class in Beaverton, Oregon, explore the world of the Internet and then share their work with the rest of us.

David Leahy and his class in Beaverton, Oregon, explore the world of the Internet and then share their work with the rest of us through the results of their wonderful classroom projects. David has a real knack for knowing what will excite his students and what kinds of experiences will prepare them for our diverse world.

Take a few moments to explore the latest work of this highly productive classroom (http://www.beavton.k12.or.us/Greenway/leahy/leahy.htm). When we last looked, we counted five projects completed in just a single month. As students complete their work, David posts it to their classroom web page so they and others might see it. We especially liked the project page (http://www.beavton.k12.or.us/Greenway/leahy/99-00/rumphius.htm) where David and his students invite you to share your best ideas about how to make the world a more beautiful place.

Other work, too, might be useful to your class. Pay a visit to the book they wrote in Swahili (http://www.beavton.k12.or.us/Greenway/leahy/99-00/swahili/arusi.au). After an author visited their school, David's class worked to develop this book. You can even hear his students pronounce these Swahili words at this location.

One of the nicest projects was completed by his class in 1999, a **Virtual Underground Railway Quilt** (http://www.beavton.k12.or.us/Greenway/leahy/ugrr/index.htm). At this page, you can click on any of the quilt segments to reveal important information about each aspect of the Underground Railroad (see Figure 5-5). It is a wonderful resource for any class studying this important part of our history.

We also liked how David organized his classroom page to keep work from classes in previous years immediately available. Of course, this provides useful models for students in his current class. Just as importantly, though, it provides you with the ability to view his progression at using the Internet in his classroom. It tells an important story about the development of an outstanding site.

A Final Thought

The Internet permits rapid, written communication between people around the world, quickly fulfilling the dream many have of a global village. As a result, you have a very special tool to support literacy learning in your classroom.

Probably one of the most powerful uses of the Internet for the classroom is the potential that exists to support English and language arts. The Internet permits rapid, written communication between people around the world, quickly fulfilling the dream many have of a global village. It brings new meaning to the traditional saying, "It takes an entire village to raise a child." As a result, you have a very special tool to support literacy learning in your classroom. As you work with the Internet in your classroom, you and your students will discover many new ways to exploit this potential. Be certain to

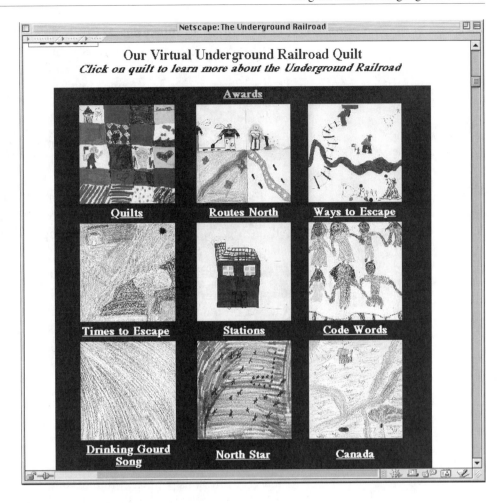

Figure 5-5.
The page for Virtual Underground Railroad Quilt from David Leahy's fourth grade class in Beaverton, Oregon (http://www.beavton.k12.or.us/Greenway/leahy/ugrr/index.htm)

share your successes with others by posting Internet Project ideas for others to join, or describe your successful experiences on a mailing list, inviting others to learn from your successful experiences.

Additional Language Arts and Literature Resources on The WWW

A+ Research & Writing for High School and College Students—
http://www.ipl.org/teen/aplus/
This page of the Internet Public Library will show your students how to write the perfect research paper.

A Time for Rhyme—http://www.grandpatucker.com/rhyme-time1.html-ssi
Having a hard time with rhyming poetry? This site will show you and your students all the tricks to write great rhyming poetry.

Bartleby Great Books Online—http://www.bartleby.com/index.html
All the great ones are here for free from Agatha Christie to Emily Dickinson, from W. E. B. Du Bois to T. S. Eliot, from F. Scott Fitzgerald to Robert Frost. Read away!

Bartlett's Familiar Quotations—http://www.bartleby.com/99/index.html
Who first coined the phrase "Snug as a bug in a rug?" Using this classic work of famous quotations will quickly tell you it was Benjamin Franklin. This on-line resource is a tremendous source for great quotations. It contains a wonderful search engine with cross links to famous authors. Set a bookmark!

The Bulwer-Lytton Fiction Contest Home Page—http://www.bulwer-lytton.com/
"It was a dark and stormy night…" Here is the home page for the whimsical literary competition that challenges entrants to compose the opening sentence to the worst of all possible novels each year. It's great fun and an energizing assignment to any writing class tired of the same old, same old.

Carol Hurst's Children's Literature Site—http://www.carolhurst.com/index.html
A useful central site for children's literature but more commercial than others mentioned in this chapter. Still a useful resource with book reviews, instructional ideas, and links to literature sites.

English: BBC Education Web Guide—
http://www.bbc.co.uk/plsql/education/webguide/pkg_main.p_results?in_cat=548
The URL may look intimidating but this is a set of links for the English curriculum in the UK, right from the BBC. Learn English from the English. What a novel idea!

Eric Carle Web Site—http://www.eric-carle.com/index.html
The web site for this popular children's author contains a bulletin board for exchanging ideas with other teachers about how best to use Carle's books in the classroom. It also contains his snail mail address in case your children wish to write him.

Help Your Child Learn to Write Well—http://www.ed.gov/pubs/parents/Writing/
A brochure for parents from the U.S. Department of Education that may be printed out and distributed at "Back-to-School Night." This provides useful information for parents about ways to assist their child with writing.

Helping Your Child Learn to Read—http://www.ed.gov/pubs/parents/Reading/index.html
An on-line book for parents written by recognized experts in the field of reading for the U.S. Department of Education. This book contains useful information on how parents may help their child to read. Print out copies of one of the chapters for "Back-to-School Night" and provide this address to parents so that they may read the entire book. A great resource.

How The Leopard Got Its Spots—http://www.sff.net/people/karawynn/justso/leopard.htp
The classic pourquoi tale by Rudyard Kipling from the *Just So Stories*. Illustrated with photographs.

Magazines—http://www.yahooligans.com/Entertainment/Magazines/
This is a central site with links to many outstanding on-line magazines for kids. A treasure trove of resources.

Multicultural Resources—http://falcon.jmu.edu/~ramseyil/multipub.htm.
Here you will find articles about multicultural children's literature as well as reviews and a host of literature selections organized by cultural groups. It is a real treasure for teachers serious about multicultural literature.

Only a Matter of Opinion?—http://library.thinkquest.org/50084/index.shtml
This award-winning site will provide you and your students will all the experiences you need to develop powerful skills at writing a variety of persuasive writing forms. The goal is to encourage everyone to write and to draw their own opinion pieces after instruction and research.

Paradigm Online Writing Assistant—http://www.powa.org/
Here is a great resource to help your high school writers polish their writing skills with a variety of formats including: informal essays, thesis/support essays, argumentative essays, and exploratory essays. It also helps students to document their sources appropriately.

Readers Theater—http://www.acs.ucalgary.ca/~dkbrown/readers.html
This location contains links to locations on the WWW devoted to readers theater. Several locations contain readers theater scripts you can print out and use in your classroom. If you use this instructional method in your class, this is the location for you!

Reading Online—http://www.readingonline.org/
This is the free electronic journal of the International Reading Association, the best on-line journal currently found on the Internet. It contains a wealth of resources including sections on the electronic classroom, new literacies, and an international forum. Special features include the use of many multimedia resources and discussion forums where you may comment on articles you read. Set a bookmark!

Resources for Writers—http://owl.english.purdue.edu/writers/by-topic-alternate.html
Here you can find all the handouts for spelling and grammatical work developed by the Writing Lab at Purdue University.

Stone Soup—http://www.stonesoup.com/
Stone Soup is a hard copy magazine with stories, poetry, and art created by young children. This location takes you to a number of stories and poems written by young children and provides directions for how students may submit work.

The Doucette Index—http://www.educ.ucalgary.ca/litindex/
Are you looking for web sites that have teaching ideas for a particular work of literature or a particular author? Here's the site for you. This index is a search engine limited strictly to children's and young adult literature. It will find instructional resources on the web related to your literature needs.

The Internet Classics Archive—http://classics.mit.edu/

This wonderful resource contains a searchable collection of almost 400 classical Greek and Latin texts (in English translation) with user-provided commentary and trivia sections. The Classics Archives features, among others, such notable pieces as Homer's *Iliad and Odyssey*, Virgil's *Aeneid, The Histories of Tacitus and Thucydides*, and Plato's *Apology*. Set a bookmark!

The Reading Zone of the Internet Public Library—(http://www.ipl.org/ youth/lapage.html)

This is a good central site for literature with many opportunities for your students. Developed at the University of Michigan, your students can read answers to questions from authors such as Virginia Hamilton, Timothy Gaffney, Shonto Gegay and others, read biographies and view photos of many more authors, discover links to many authors' home pages, read original stories or listen to them being read aloud, enter a writing context, see the book recommendations of other students, and much more. Set a bookmark!

Learning Resources—http://www.literacynet.org/cnnsf/

This site by CNN and the Western/Pacific Literacy Network offers news stories for reading or listening with accompanying exercises.

Listservs/Mailing Lists for Language Arts

Use standard subscribing procedures (see Chapter 3) to join the following listservs.

CHILDLIT

A list devoted to discussion and critical analysis of children's literature.
Subscription address: listserv@rutvm1.rutgers.edu
Home page: http://www.rci.rutgers.edu/~mjoseph/childlit/about.html

Childrens-Writing

A discussion list for children's writers and illustrators, and anyone interested in writing or drawing for kids.
Subscription address: majordomo@lists.mindspring.com

Conversations

This is the home page for many different lists run by the national Council for Teachers of English (NCTE). At the NCTE web site you can subscribe to a number of different listservs/mailing lists devoted to English education, K–12. Descriptions of each list may also be found here. Find the mailing list that is just right for you!
Home page: http://www.ncte.org/chat/

Folklore

A folklore discussion list
Subscription address: listserv@tamvm1.tamu.edu

KIDLIT-L

A listserv on children's literature.
Subscription address: listserv@bingvmb.cc.binghamton.edu

NCTE-talk—(majordomo@serv1.ncte.org)

This is the main listserv for the National Council of English Teachers, an important professional association for English Education. It is a high traffic list.

Home page: http://www.ncte.org/lists/ncte-talk/

RTEACHER

A forum for conversations about literacy in both traditional and electronic contexts. The archive for these conversations may be found at http://listserv.syr.edu/archives/rteacher.html This is a very supportive and diverse group of educators interested in literacy education. They also discuss both Internet and non-Internet aspects of literacy education.

Subscription address: listserv@listserv.syr.edu

Home page: http://web.syr.edu/~djleu/RTEACHER/directions.html

STORYTELL

A discussion list for those interested in storytelling.

Subscription address: STORYTELL-REQUEST@venus.twu.edu

TAWL—(listserv@listserv.arizona.edu)

A listserv discussion group on teaching from a whole language perspective.

Usenet Newsgroups for Language Arts

K-12 Teacher Chat Area—k12.chat.teacher

Discusses issues of K-12 instruction, including language arts.

Language Arts Curriculum in K-12 Education—k12.lang.art

A newsgroup on the language arts curriculum in schools.

Writing Instruction in Computer-based Classrooms—
comp.edu.composition

Discusses issues of writing in electronic environments.

References

Hynds, S. (1997). *On the brink: Negotiating literature and life with adolescents.* New York: Teachers College Press.

Leu, D. J., Jr. & Kinzer, C. K. (1999). *Effective literacy instruction, 4th edition.* Englewood Cliffs, NJ: Prentice Hall.

McGee, L. M., & Richgels, D. J. (1990). *Literacy's beginnings: Supporting young readers and writers.* Boston: Allyn & Bacon.

McMahon, S. I., Raphael, T. E., Goatley, V. J., & Pardo, L. S. (Eds.). (1997). *The book club connection.* New York: Teachers College Press.

Short, K. (1993). Intertextuality: Searching for patterns that connect. In D. J. Leu & C. K. Kinzer (Eds.), *Literacy research, theory, and practice: Views from many perspectives.* Forty-first Yearbook of the National Reading Conference. Chicago: National Reading Conference.

Social Studies: A World of Possibilities

E-MAIL FOR YOU

To: Our readers
From: djleu@syr.edu (Don Leu), ddleu@syr.edu (Debbie Leu)
Subject: Social Studies: A world of possibilities

We believe the Internet provides more new possibilities for social studies education than any other content area. Why? There are several reasons. First, the Internet permits our students access to extensive collections of primary source documents. By helping our students to analyze primary source documents, instead of only reading summaries of events from a text book, we develop the critical thinking and interpretive skills so central to their future. Second, having the Internet in our classroom enables students to experience different cultures through the communication experiences they have with students in other parts of the world. This is a special and very powerful potential for social studies education. Finally, there are simply more information resources for social studies education than any other subject area on the Internet.

These new opportunities, though, also present an important challenge to teachers and students: How do you quickly find useful primary source documents and how do you support the critical analysis so important with these new resources? How do you develop exciting cross-cultural projects possible with Internet technologies? How do you locate required information when so much is available? In this chapter, we will share solutions to each of these challenges.

Most importantly, we will describe effective strategies throughout the chapter, enabling you to immediately integrate the Internet into your social studies curriculum. Using the Internet opens up a world of possibilities for you and your students in social studies education.

Don and Debbie

Teaching With the Internet: Miguel Robledo's Class

It was the beginning of a new year for Miguel Robledo, his second using the Internet in his American History classes at Del Rio High School. He sat at his desk in the morning light, enjoying his coffee and thinking back to his early experiences with this new tool for teaching. He smiled a bit.

He remembered how intimidated he felt by all of the information on the Internet for social studies. He recalled wondering how he was going to remember everything without getting lost. He chuckled with the memory. He hadn't known about bookmarks or making a web page with links of favorite sites.

Miguel had started simply that first year. He was a cautious person when it came to change. Initially, he developed a scavenger hunt to develop navigational skills for his students. These scavenger hunts had students find information about the unit they were studying but not do any critical analysis of the information. He quickly discovered, though, his students already knew many of these skills required for navigating the Internet so he developed other types of learning experiences. Each week, he set up a single Internet Workshop for students to complete based on the many resources available at **History/Social Studies Web Site for K–12 Teachers** (http://www.execpc.com/~dboals/boals.html). He set a bookmark to the best location for each week's topic and developed several critical thinking questions for his students.

Each workshop activity required students to think critically and evaluate the information at a site related to their current unit. During one week of the colonial period, for example, he set a bookmark to a wonderful site, **Benjamin Franklin** (http://sln.fi.edu/franklin/rotten.html). He then directed students to explore this site and write a short essay about what they thought was the most important accomplishment in Franklin's life, explaining why they had selected this accomplishment. At the end of the week, during a short Internet Workshop session, students had a chance to compare their ideas and discuss their conclusions. The discussion really made the totality of Franklin's life come alive as students described his many accomplishments and debated about which accomplishment was most important. It was a great discussion.

In the middle of the year, as he felt more confident and knowledgeable about Internet resources, Miguel decided to use Internet Project, connecting with other classrooms around the world. He wanted his students to see how people in different cultural contexts interpreted the same historical event. He posted a project to compare perceptions of World War II (WW II) by students from several different countries at **The Global SchoolNet Projects Registry** (http://www.gsn.org/gsn/proj/index.html) and **The Global School House** (http://www.gsh.org/class/default.htm).

Each week, he set up a single Internet Workshop for students to complete based on the many resources available at History/Social Studies Web Site for K–12 Teachers (http://www.execpc.com/~dboals/boals.html).

During the middle of the year, as he felt more confident and knowledgeable about Internet resources, Miguel decided to develop an Internet project, connecting with other classrooms around the world.

Classrooms from Japan, Russia, Germany, England, Italy, and Canada agreed to participate in the project. After studying this event in their individual classrooms, students in each class wrote an essay describing the meaning of WW II to their country. These essays were exchanged by e-mail between each of the participating classes so that students could see how history is often interpreted differently by different societies. Each student then wrote a second essay describing what they had learned from reading the essays of students in the different countries.

As part of the project, participating classrooms read stories from people who lived during the 1940's. They found all of this wonderful information at the home page for **Memories** (http://atschool.eduweb.co.uk/chatback/english/memories/memories.html). They also subscribed to the mailing list (listserv) located there, also called **MEMORIES** (listserv@maelstrom.stjohns.edu). This was a mailing list where participating classrooms could exchange e-mail messages with survivors of WW II. This was an especially important experience for everyone involved as students asked questions about different events and received information from people who had actually lived through the experience. For Miguel and his students, studying about history had fundamentally changed. History was not just something they read about; it was the people they were talking with over the Internet and the experiences they shared. History had come alive.

Miguel's Internet Project was a tremendous success. It provided a powerful experience for each of the classrooms, humanizing history for everyone as classrooms learned how to communicate effectively across cultural divides, learning from one another about each other's cultural context. Some classes in the project continued exchanging information throughout the year with his class. Each teacher promised to get together again next year so they could repeat the project.

One of the extra benefits that came out of this project was the discovery of a wonderful site to contribute to ending world hunger. The class in England shared the location for **The Hunger Site** (http://www.hungersite.com/) with all of the other classes (see Figure 6-1). Once a day you may visit this site and click on a button to donate food, paid for by sponsoring companies. For each click at this site, sponsoring companies agree to contribute a small amount of money to humanitarian organizations that feed the world's needy. Corporate sponsors provide the food in return for being able to display a link and for being associated with a good cause. You pay nothing. What is most striking is the map, regularly blinking on a country where, according to statistics from the United Nations, a person dies from hunger somewhere in the world every 3.6 seconds. Three out of four deaths are of children under the age of five.

Miguel's class clicked on the site each day and encouraged others to also donate food by clicking at the site. They put a small sign about the site around the school to make certain someone clicked at the site each day from each computer in their school. They kept track and calculated that their work con-

For Miguel and his students, studying about history had fundamentally changed. History had become human.

The class in England shared the location for The Hunger Site (http://www.hungersite.com/) with all of the other classes.

Figure 6-1.
The Hunger Site (http://
www.hungersite.com/), a location
Miguel's students learned about from
a class in England. For each click
(one per day), sponsoring companies
agree to contribute to humanitarian
organizations that feed the world's
needy.

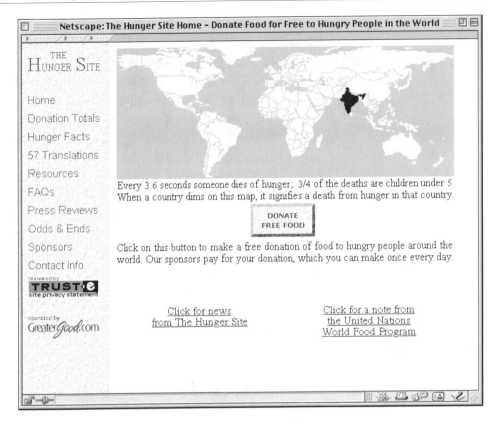

tributed nearly 1000 pounds of food each year from their high school alone—
all with just a single click on each computer each day. Miguel was proud of
his students for their actions to make the world a better place.

As the end of the year approached, Miguel decided to try Internet Inquiry. Students identified a question in American History they wanted to
explore on their own using resources on the Internet and resources in the
school library. Before they started their project, Miguel set up individual
bookmark folders for each student on his classroom computers so that students could keep track of good locations and not get these mixed up with
those of other students. He also conducted several Internet Workshops on
how to critically analyze and evaluate information at web sites.

Miguel had students complete the planning form in Figure 6-2. This helped
to focus their efforts and provide a road map for their initial work during
Internet Inquiry. After one week, he had individual conferences with students to check their progress and to make revisions in their project if these
had become necessary.

At the end of their Internet Inquiry, Miguel had each student develop a
Student-to-Student Activity. This had each student develop a learning activity related to the Internet Inquiry they had just completed and then create a
poster advertising this learning experience. Students provided the Internet
address, explained the learning activity they had developed for this site, and
advertised the virtues of completing their activity. Miguel required each student in his class to participate in at least four of these activities during the

last two weeks of school. At the end of each week, he conducted a workshop session where students shared their results of their Student-to-Student activities. It was a nice way to wrap up their study of history during the year.

Figure 6-2.
The Internet Inquiry Planning Form
Used in Miguel Robledo's Class.

Planning for Internet Inquiry

Directions: This form will help you to plan for Internet Inquiry, help to keep you on track as you complete your work, and help you to evaluate your work when you finish. Please fill in each item as completely as possible and then schedule a conference with me to discuss your planning.

Name(s): _____ Date: _____

Title of my (our) Internet Inquiry: _____

The project will be completed on: _____

The purpose of my (our) project is: _____
_____
_____

As I (we) planned my (our) project, I (we) used the following resources:
_____
_____
_____

I (we) will do the following during this project: _____
_____
_____
_____

I (we) will evaluate the project in the following manner: _____
_____
_____
_____

I (we) will begin by using the following Internet sites or by using the following words/phrases with a search engine: _____
_____
_____
_____

I (we) had a conference with Mr. Robledo about this project on the following dates:_____
_____
_____
_____

Now, however, it was the beginning of another year. Over the summer, Miguel had attended a workshop on using primary source documents with the Internet in the social studies classroom. He picked up some great strategies to try out in his class this year. He was using one of them today.

Miguel's class was just beginning their study of American history and he had designed an early activity with primary source documents to orient them to the Internet and to the critical thinking he would be expecting from them. His class was working in small groups today. Each group had a set of historical documents, books, and artifacts with information from one time period in American history. The activity called for them to use their materials to frame historical questions they would explore in upcoming weeks. Miguel had designed this activity to whet his students' interest in history and introduce them to the historical analysis of primary source documents. The activity would also develop important background knowledge, knowledge that would help his students throughout the year.

Each group had a single day to explore one of four sets of materials and develop their questions about the time period of their materials. The next day the groups would rotate to the next set of historical materials. On Friday, they would share their questions and their discoveries in a whole-class discussion during Internet Workshop. Miguel planned to organize their questions around the different time periods covered during the year, introducing themes and issues they would explore in upcoming units.

Three groups were working at their desks. A fourth group was working in pairs at the three Internet computers in his classroom, locating and analyzing original documents from the 1900s they found in cyberspace. Each day a different group would complete an activity at the computer cluster, trying to develop important questions from the primary source documents they found on the Internet during this time.

Miguel looked up to observe the group at the Internet computers. One of the first lessons he learned during his first year with the Internet was that students often spend their limited time at the computer just "surfing" for information, moving quickly from site to site trying to find something interesting. Often his students' time at the computer would run out before they had an opportunity to really read and learn anything. Or, they would sometimes end up at sites that were inappropriate for their work.

> One of the first lessons he learned during his first year with the Internet was that students often spend their limited time at the computer just "surfing" for information, moving quickly from site to site trying to find something interesting.

As a result, Miguel had set the home page location on all three computers to open to **American Memory** (http://lcweb2.loc.gov/ammem/ammemhome.html) as soon as his students connected to the Internet (see Figure 6-3). This outstanding resource from the Library of Congress contains a wonderful collection of original documents, photos, motion pictures, maps, and sound recordings for social studies education. Here, students can find all kinds of great resources including: original documents from the Continental Congress, a collection of 350 pamphlets providing insight into the African American experience from 1818–1907, movies, audio recordings of famous speeches, a collection of over 1,000 photographs from the Civil War,

Figure 6-3.

American Memory (http:// memory.loc.gov/), developed by the Library of Congress, contains an extensive collection of primary source documents including documents, photos, motion pictures, maps, and sound recordings.

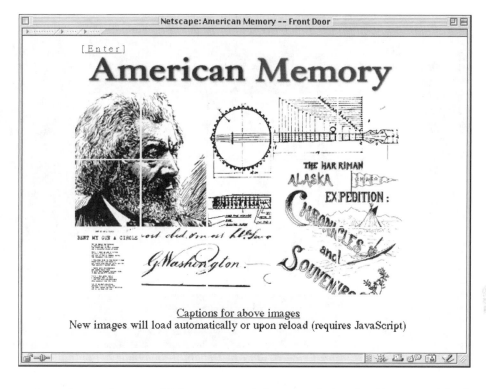

Miguel knew that students often taught one another about the Internet faster than he could teach them. Among other strategies, he set aside a portion of the bulletin board next to the computers for students to post information about the Internet.

and much, much more. This was one of the central sites he discovered during his summer workshop. Setting the home page to a central site like this saved valuable time in a 40-minute period.

Miguel knew that students often taught one another about the Internet faster than he could teach them. Among other strategies, he set aside a portion of the bulletin board next to the computers for students to post information about the Internet. Students listed useful sites and shared other information about their current work. Some students used the word processor on the computer to type these notes, so word processing skills were supported, too.

"Cool," said Sarah. She and her partner Vanita had just found a site at American Memory someone had described on the bulletin board. The site was called **"Votes for Women" 1850–1920** (http://lcweb2.loc.gov/ammem/ vfwhtml/vfwhome.html), a collection of photographs and documents about the suffrage movement in the U.S.

"Hey . . . sisters marching," Vanita said as the image in Figure 6-4 opened. They both chuckled. Then they started reading **One Hundred Years toward Suffrage: An Overview** (http://lcweb2.loc.gov/ammem/vfwhtml/ vfwtl.html), developing a greater appreciation for the struggles women have faced.

"Look, Seneca Falls. That's where they had the first women's rights convention. Cool! I went there last year."

At the computer next to Sarah and Vanita, Jonathon and his Internet partner, Josh, were working. "Hey, look! Jackie Robinson. We can study the history of baseball? That's phat!" Jonathon, had found a great source: **Jackie Robinson and other Baseball Highlights, 1980's–1960's** (http:// lcweb2.loc.gov/ammem/jrhtml/jrhome.html). They started reading about

Figure 6-4.
One of many images at American Memory in the exhibit **"Votes for Women" Suffrage Pictures, 1850–1920** (http://lcweb2.loc.gov/ammem/vfwhtml/vfwhome.html), a collection of photographs and documents about the suffrage movement.

Jackie Robinson and viewing the extensive set of documents about this famous American.

"They got Larry Doby?" asked Jonathon. Clearly, Jonathon knew his baseball history.

At the third computer, Mircalla and Jessica had found the movie section. "Look at this movie. It's San Francisco and the real earthquake. Cool!" said Mircalla. "I was born there but I never saw something like this before."

"Don't forget to write down questions you want to explore in class this year," Tanisha reminded everyone. "We're going to have an Internet Workshop session on Friday."

The group at the Internet computers got together quickly to list their questions:

1. Why didn't people want women to vote?
2. Who were some of the important women? What did they do?
3. What were the Negro Leagues like and who were some of the best players?
4. What was racism like for Jackie Robinson?
5. What was San Francisco like before the earthquake?
6. How did they put the fire out in San Francisco?

Jonathon typed their questions at the computer as the others in his group dictated them. Then they printed their questions out for Mr. Robledo on the classroom printer.

Before they went back to their desks, Mircalla and Jessica typed and posted a short note on the bulletin board next to the computer. It said:

See the FANTASTIK movie about the San Francisco earthquake on the Internet. It's at: http://memory.loc.gov/ammem/papr/sfhome.html Click where it says list the film titles.

—Mircalla and Jessica

Lessons From the Classroom

Miguel Robledo's experience illustrates a number of important lessons about integrating the Internet into your social studies program. First, it illustrates how beginning with Internet Workshop is often the easiest way to use the Internet in your classroom. Workshop experiences provide many opportunities for you to begin integrating the Internet into your classroom. Reading about the history of the Negro Leagues and then viewing a short movie about Jackie Robinson made this information come alive for Jonathon and Josh. They talked about it all day with other students and even shared this information at home. And, of course, they talked about this during Internet Workshop on Friday. The same was true for Sarah and Vanita and the documents about the suffrage movement as well as Mircalla and Jessica and the San Francisco Earthquake. Internet Workshop provides a powerful strategy for you and your students to gather information and then communicate with others about what you have learned.

Second, we again see the power of Internet Project for bringing classroom learning alive. Collaborative experiences with students at other locations around the world motivate classes as they learn important lessons. Internet Project can be an especially powerful way of organizing classroom learning experiences in social studies; it enables your students to understand how students in different parts of the world view historical, political, and social events. It enables them to better appreciate the power of different cultural experiences. Participating in the MEMORIES mailing list and sharing thoughts about WW II with other students around the world fundamentally changed the nature of historical study in Miguel's classroom.

Third, Miguel's experiences show how the Internet provides many experiences for students to work with primary source documents in their social studies curriculum. These original documents provide teachers with important instructional opportunities to help students develop critical thinking, evaluation, and synthesis skills. All of these skills will become increasingly important as our students enter the workforce in an age of information.

Miguel's experiences also show how strategies like Student-to-Student may be used to support the social learning experiences especially important with the Internet. This activity is also a nice way to wrap up a unit in your classroom, allowing students to teach one another about what they have learned.

In addition, these episodes show how Miguel's planning encouraged his students to help one another as they searched for information. The bulletin board told others where useful information was located on the WWW. Miguel

---

Beginning with Internet Workshop is often the easiest way to use the Internet in your classroom.

Internet Project can be an especially powerful way of organizing classroom learning experiences in social studies; it enables your students to understand how students in different parts of the world view historical, political, and social events.

Miguel's experiences show how the Internet provides many experiences for students to work with primary source documents in their social studies curriculum.

had encouraged all of the students to do this when they came across something they thought others might be able to use. And, he often used workshop sessions on Friday, where students could both share their discoveries and seek assistance. Social learning opportunities abound with Internet resources, and Miguel developed several ways for students to support one another as they worked. Needless to say, his encouragement to assist one another on the Internet also helped to develop a very supportive classroom community. We will show you other ways in which you can assist your students to help one another with Internet resources, an excellent lesson for life.

Finally, Miguel's experiences demonstrate how extensive the resources on the Internet are for social studies. This often requires you to help students sort through the many resources to find ones that are most useful. Often it is helpful to provide special assistance with using the various search engines to locate information. It is also helpful to develop individual bookmark folders so that students may keep track of their own bookmarks.

> Social learning opportunities abound with Internet resources.

Central Sites for Social Studies Education

Because there are so many Internet resources for social studies education, a central site strategy is often necessary for quickly locating Internet resources directly related to your learning goals. Fortunately, there are several exceptional central sites on the Internet available for social studies education. We divide them into two basic categories: central sites for social studies resources and central sites for teaching social studies.

Central sites for social studies resources contain extensive collections of links to great social studies resources for your classroom. These are systematically organized in various topics to make it easier for you to find the information you require. While these sites may have links to actual teaching units, they are often best for finding primary source documents and secondary sources that explore various aspects of the social studies curriculum.

> Because there are so many Internet resources for social studies education, a central site strategy is often necessary for quickly locating Internet resources directly related to your learning goals.

General Social Studies Resources

The best central sites for general social studies resources that we know include these locations:

- **The Library of Congress Home Page**—http://www.loc.gov/. There is probably no better location for multimedia access to primary source documents about the United States. Your students can view items ranging from the original draft of Declaration of Independence in Thomas Jefferson's handwriting to the Vietnam War POW/MIA database. It is a most impressive resource for your social studies program. Included in separate sections are: **Thomas** (http://thomas.loc.gov/), the official source of legislative information for the U.S. Congress; **Exhibitions** (http://lcweb.loc.gov/exhibits/), a collection of recent exhibitions at the

E-MAIL FOR YOU

To: Colleagues
From: Richard Strauss <ras100@netheaven.com>
Subject: Using the Internet at our school

Hi,

We've had internet access in our school for about 4 years and I've learned a lot from the experience. Here are some lessons that we have learned:

1. Start small. For your first Internet experience keep things very simple. One of our best first activities at the 5/6 level was on the constellations. We found one good site and bookmarked it on each computer in the classroom. Each student was given a constellation to research. They drew a picture of it in art class, answered five questions about the constellation using the web site, and combined both into a PowerPoint presentation. Parents loved watching the slide shows at the end of the year.

2. Keep kids busy with organized experiences. Most students, if left to their own devises, will stay on non-educational web sites. Though we haven't gone to it, Internet Explorer has an easy to check "history" section so you can track what sites your students have been to.

3. Plan carefully for e-mail buddy projects. E-Pal projects seem like great ideas but are very hard to pull off. To be successful, have the whole project organized thoroughly. The more structure you provide, the better the results. Keep the duration of the project limited and only work with another teacher that is as dedicated as you are. Kids get very upset when they don't get a letter back in certain time period.

4. Kids love to make up web pages. Our kids will stay after school any day of the year to work on creating their own web page. I've been able to reach some of our toughest students through a web page creation class. There is a real feeling of accomplishment for them and everyone can see their final results.

5. Use web pages for Internet Workshop. Children don't have to search for any of the information. I go one step further by including a blank answer sheet that is linked to the page and printable. Start small with one or two questions. We're starting to build whole units using the web-based workshops.

6. Get your feet wet. My most technologically challenged teachers have made a 180-degree turn around once they experienced success with a simple Internet activity. I showed one reluctant teacher a few good teacher resource sites like Yahooligans and she found some great activities for her classes. She was hooked!

7. If you don't succeed at first, don't give up. We've had many flops but we've learned as much from the flops as we did from the success stories.

Best wishes,

Rich
Lake George Elementary School, Lake George, NY
http://www.lkgeorge.org/elementaryweb/

Library of Congress; **Using the Library** (http://www.loc.gov/library/), providing you with access to the extensive catalogs of the Library of Congress and many others, and **The Library Today** (http://www.loc.gov/today/), containing information about the most recent information and events at our nation's library. It is a most impressive resource for your social studies program.

- **Learning Resources**—http://www.schoolnet.ca/home/e/resources/index.asp

  A central site for Canadian resources that is part of SchoolNet. See, especially, the link to social studies. A wonderful collection of all things Canadian!

- The **History/Social Studies Web Site for K–12 Teachers**—http://www.execpc.com/~dboals/boals.html

  This is one of the best single locations we know for social studies resources (see Figure 6-5). The home page for this location only hints at the many resources it contains. Pay a visit to this site and explore some of the many topics. You will find an amazingly exhaustive set of resources organized in an easy to understand hierarchical structure.

Figure 6-5.
A wonderful central site for social studies education: the **History/Social Studies Web Site for K–12 Teachers** (http://www.execpc.com/~dboals/boals.html).

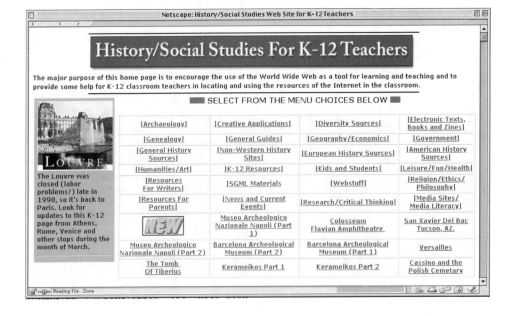

- **Nebraska Department of Education Social Science Resources HomePage**—http://www.nde.state.ne.us/SS/ss.html

  This location, developed by the state of Nebraska, contains an extensive set of resources for social studies education organized by area (history, civics/government, economics, and geography) and themes. The server tends to run a bit slowly sometimes. Be patient. Your wait will be rewarded.

- **The Cornell Theory Center Arts and Social Science Gateway**—http://www.tc.cornell.edu/Edu/ArtSocGateway/
  A nice collection of excellent resources may be found at the Social Studies section of this location developed at Cornell.

Central Sites for Teaching Social Studies

Central sites for the teaching of social studies provide specific tools for instruction including Internet units, Internet Projects, lesson plans, WebQuests, and other resources.

Central sites for the teaching of social studies provide specific tools for instruction including Internet units, Internet Projects, lesson plans, WebQuests, and other resources. Some of the best we have found include:

- **Blue Web'n Applications: Social Studies**—http://www.kn.pacbell.com/wired/bluewebn/fr_History.html
- **S.C.O.R.E. History/Social Science**—http://score.rims.k12.ca.us/
- **The Learning Page: American Memory**—http://memory.loc.gov/ammem/ndlpedu/index.html
- **Thinkquest Winners**—http://www.thinkquest.org/library/entries.shtml
- **Lesson Plans and Resources for Social Studies Teachers**—http://www.csun.edu/~hcedu013/index.html

Using Internet Workshop

Sometimes, it is easiest to begin using the Internet in your classroom with Internet Workshop. This may be especially useful as you begin to explore the extensive resources available on the Internet in social studies. Simply locate a site on the Internet with content related to the learning objectives in your classroom and develop an activity that encourages students to explore that site, bringing what they learned to the workshop session for sharing and discussion. The easiest way to find a good location is to visit one of the central sites for social studies education identified earlier. Then develop an activity related to that site and assign this activity to your students. They can complete it during their weekly time at the computer. Afterwards, discuss their experiences during a short Internet Workshop session.

Nearly any set of good resources from the central sites above might be used in this fashion. If you are studying the Civil War, for example, you may wish to set a bookmark for **The Civil War Letters of Galutia York** (http://www.snymor.edu/pages/library/local_history/civil_war/) and invite students to read the letters of this Union soldier, taking notes in a journal about this soldier's view of himself and his country. For the same workshop session, you might also set a bookmark for **The Timeline of the Civil War** (http://rs6.loc.gov/ammem/tl1861.html) in the **Selected Civil War Photograph Collection** (http://rs6.loc.gov/cwphome.html). Have your students read and view the pictures, printing out one picture and doing research about the battle to

E-MAIL FOR YOU

To: Teachers
From: Linda Shearin <lshearin@bellsouth.net>
Subject: Canada Comes Alive

Dear Teachers,

The Internet is a great tool for making Social Studies come alive for students. In North Carolina 5th grade students engage in a comparative study of peoples and regions of the Western Hemisphere. I located **Canadiana** (http://www.cs.cmu.edu/Unofficial/Canadiana/README.html), a treasure trove of information on Canada.

From **Canadiana** I located Canadian school homepages for each province in Canada. I then e-mailed the schools to see if there was a class who would be interested in engaging in a short term research project with our students. Fifth grade classes brainstormed questions they would like answered about homes (types of building materials, size, cost) and schools (schedules, subjects, homework) in the Canadian communities. It is difficult to find current and detailed information on these particular topics in print materials.

The first year we did this it was evident our students were still stuck in the "Age of Exploration," assuming Canadians still lived in log cabins and cooked over open fires. What a wonderful opportunity this presented to correct some misconceptions about lifestyle. This worked both ways since our students were amazed at the Canadian students asking if all our students were "wanded" for weapons before entering our school. A great discussion ensued about how the Canadians might have developed this impression.

When the responses arrived from the Canadian students our 5th graders were surprised to find out that there were many similarities between themselves and their Canadian counterparts. They also enjoyed comparing the various school descriptions to our school.

The 5th graders used the correspondence and information gathered from other Canadian sources on the Web and in print to write a research paper in the form of a narrative based on a trip to their chosen province. In addition to being able to include information from the Internet they learned how to properly cite Internet sources.

In order to plan for a future literature connection we also solicited a list of "best books," fiction and non-fiction, about Canadian authors to add to our school Media Center.

Simple but effective communication made our neighbors to the north more real to us, and us to them.

Linda Shearin
Fred J. Carnage Gifted & Talented Magnet School for Accelerated Studies in Math, Science, and Technology
Raleigh, NC

determine its significance. Post these photos and descriptions on a bulletin board in your classroom for everyone to see.

During Internet Workshop, students could share their observations after reading this diary and viewing these photos. Use your students' observations to draw conclusions about the Union soldiers of that era and the manner in which they thought about their country. These activities would serve as a powerful introduction to the human side of the Civil War.

For younger students studying Abraham Lincoln, set a bookmark for the wonderful resource developed by Tammy Payton, a first grade teacher in Loogootee, Indiana: **Abraham Lincoln Classroom Activities** (http://www.siec.k12.in.us/~west/proj/lincoln/class.htm). Have them complete as many of the activities as they can and then share their work during an Internet Workshop session.

For students in grade 5 or 6 studying Benjamin Franklin, invite them to visit a series of activities located at http://www.sdcoe.k12.ca.us/score/ben/bentg.html. Have them complete any one of the activities and bring their work to a workshop session to share as you read together the book *Ben and Me* by Robert Lawson.

Setting up Internet Workshop experiences such as these in your classroom is a good way to ease yourself and your students into simple activities before attempting the richer, but more complex, experiences that are also possible with Internet Project, Internet Inquiry, or a WebQuest.

Using Internet Project

Previous chapters have described the important role Internet Project may play in your classroom. The chapters also identified locations such as **Global SchoolNet's Internet Project Registry** (http://www.gsn.org/pr/index.cfm), **SchoolNet's Grassroots Project Gallery** (http://www.schoolnet.ca/grassroots/e/project.centre/search-projects.html) where you may search for Internet projects others have developed. Previous chapters have also identified mailing lists such as those found at **Intercultural E-mail Classroom Connections** (http://www.stolaf.edu/network/iecc/), **WEB66** (http://web66.coled.umn.edu/List/Default.html), or **WWWEDU** (http://edweb.gsn.org/wwwedu.html) where you can receive announcements about projects others are planning or post your own project description to invite participants. Internet projects are especially useful in social studies since they allow you to compare your students' experiences with those of students in other cultures. Often, communicating with a class in another part of the world will make your study of that culture come alive as you exchange information about experiences. This is what happened in Miguel Robledo's and Linda Shearin's classes.

If you are just beginning to use Internet Project, it is often easiest to find a project posted by another teacher and seek to join a learning experience

---

For younger students studying Abraham Lincoln, set a bookmark for http://siec.k12.in.us/~west/proj/lincoln/class.htm

Setting up Internet Workshop experiences such as these in your classroom is a good way to ease yourself and your students into simple projects before attempting the richer, but more complex, experiences that are also possible with Internet Project and Internet Inquiry.

Internet projects are especially useful in social studies since they allow you to compare your students' experiences with those of students in other cultures. Often, communicating with a class in another part of the world will make your study of that culture come alive for your students as you exchange information about experiences.

If you are just beginning to use Internet Project, it is often easiest to find a project posted by another teacher and seek to join a learning experience that seems appropriate for your class.

that seems appropriate for your class. Then, as you develop more experience with Internet Project, you will have a better sense of where to advertise for cooperating classes and how to develop a project that others will be interested in joining. We encourage you to visit the sites listed above and explore the many opportunities available for your class through an Internet project. Examples of projects posted in the past at these sites include:

- **Menus of the World.** Posted by a middle school teacher in Washington, this project sought collaborating classrooms around the world to learn more about each other's culture through their food. Each week, classes exchanged e-mail messages containing a typical daily menu from their part of the world for four people, plus the estimated cost for each item in the meal using the local currency. The menu was used as a springboard for classrooms to ask questions about the cultural meanings for different food items: what unusual items were, how food was obtained, who prepared the food, how the meal was served and how the meal was eaten. Each meal's cost was also converted into the currency used in each classroom to compare costs of common foods, as well as the average cost for each meal.

- **Geo Game** (http://www.gsn.org/project/gg/index.html) This Internet Project is actually a contest. Each participating class completes a questionnaire about their own location including information about latitude, typical weather, land formations, nearest river, time zone, points of interest, direction from the capital, population, and other items. These are then mailed to the project coordinator who removes the name of the location and then returns the questionnaire items to participants. Participants try to locate the city for each set of items using maps, atlases, and reference materials on the Internet.

- **A Cultural Macbeth**. To foster the cultural exchange of ideas and interpretations of Shakespeare, three schools in Germany invited other classes to exchange their views about the characters in this play. Each week a different character was discussed via e-mail with students. Classrooms from six different countries shared different interpretations of each character. The students quickly discovered how character interpretation is powerfully influenced by one's cultural context. At the same time, students learned much about one another's culture as they discussed the reasons behind their interpretations of each character.

Using Internet Inquiry

Internet Inquiry helps students develop independent research skills and explore questions that are personally important. Internet Inquiry projects may

E-MAIL FOR YOU

To: Colleagues
From: Gary Cressman (cressman@inspire.ospi.wednet.edu)
Subject: An Internet Project in Social Studies

Hi! When studying our Civil War, students always come up to me and say how they are related to such and such or that their ancestors fought in such and such a battle. I decided to find out if I could link my students to other students and they could discuss their ancestors and relate their stories to our unit on the Civil War. I listed an Internet project with **I*EARN** which stands for International Education and Resource Network (http://www.iearn.org/iearn/). They have many different project areas, and I chose to put it in the Social Studies area (http://www.iearn.org/iearn/projects.html). I did this project with my six 8th grade U.S. History classes, with about 175 students total.

There is a monthly fee to join I*EARN. I was in contact with them from home and school using text-only e-mail. Usually I had my students compose their work during class and I would send them off at night when the I*EARN connection charges were lower. I also would collect messages during the evening at home and post them the next day on the wall. But often my students wanted to know if there was any mail that day, so I said OK and we checked our mail. It was wonderfulllllllll when a message would come in and the student it was addressed to was there to receive it. All mail came to me; my students did not have their own accounts or addresses.

One of the I*EARN moderators in Spain picked up my message and passed it on to a Belgium UN relief worker. The next day I received a message from a 16 year old Bosnian boy with a cry for help from his refugee camp in northern Bosnia. The message was actually sent in Serbo-Croatian, and an English translation came a day later; I do not know who did the translating. I had no thoughts of including our study of the US Civil War with civil wars in our society today. But things changed quickly. So I shared this message with my students and they started writing letters of support to this boy. This got my students following current events in a way that would not have been possible otherwise.

A few days later, a message came from some high school students in New York who were writing a newspaper about human rights abuses, which a civil war is. They asked if my students could join in their discussion. Of course we did. And 27 of my students were included in the paper, Liberty Bound, published by the Cold Spring Harbor High School. The age difference between the students did not make a difference as it turned out. In fact, it made my students become more concerned that they did not sound too young.

We were also contacted by a High School in northern Israel and asked if my students could help teach their students about our civil war. This connection was again made for us by one of the I*EARN moderators. In return, their students sent us stories about their experiences during the Gulf War.

Internet projects have had a powerful impact on my students' learning. I have found that the best projects are those where you have a tight bond/connection/commitment from the people on the other end to stick to the project. Often these happen in unexpected ways.

Gary Cressman
Chair, History Department and Computer Resource Teacher
Enumclaw Junior High School
Enumclaw, Washington

cressman@inspire.ospi.wednet.edu

Internet Inquiry helps students develop independent research skills and explore questions that are personally important.

be developed by small groups or by individuals. You will recall from Chapter 4 that Internet Inquiry often includes these phases: question, search, analyze, compose, and share. Sometimes Internet Inquiry will also include an evaluation phase, when the project is evaluated, often by the students themselves. Involving students in self-evaluation experiences is helpful in getting them to become more aware of how to develop successful research and learning experiences.

Internet Inquiry is often effectively combined with Internet Workshop sessions. During this time, students and groups may share what they have learned in their research as well as the roadblocks they have encountered. These conversations enrich the study of your unit at the same time they provide students with useful new ideas to explore as they seek answers to their questions.

Internet Inquiry is often effectively combined with workshop sessions. During this time, students and groups may share what they have learned in their research as well as the roadblocks they have encountered. These conversations enrich the study of your unit at the same time they provide students with useful new ideas to explore as they seek answers to their questions.

Student-to-Student

One of the best ways to learn something is to teach it to someone else. This is the idea behind Student-to-Student activities.

One of the best ways to learn something is to teach it to someone else. This is the idea behind student-to-student activities. As your students use the Internet during a unit, consider using this type of experience at the end of the unit as you summarize and review the learning that has taken place.

During a student-to-student activity, students first identify a useful web location related to their studies. Then they develop a learning experience using the web site for other students to complete. Here are several examples:

- After her class completed a unit on the Civil War, a student discovered a multimedia experience on the Underground Railroad developed by **National Geographic**. This student set a bookmark for **Underground Railroad** (http://www.nationalgeographic.com/features/99/railroad/) and asked other students to take this journey. At the end, each student had to write one message describing their feelings in a journal for others who follow them to read before beginning their own journey. The entire journal is displayed at Back to School Night for parents to read.

- Another student, completing a unit on stories from around the world, invited others to visit the **Creation Stories and Myths** page (http://www.best.com/~swanson/creation/cstorymenu.html). He asked each student to list the two stories they liked the best from the many wonderful stories at this site. These choices were added to a continuously updated graph using a spreadsheet program on the computer.

- Another student, completing a unit on ancient civilizations, invited classmates to explore **The Ancient Olympic Games Virtual Museum** (http://devlab.dartmouth.edu/olympic/), a wonderful site, and then write an imaginary letter home to their parents in Athens describing what they saw.

After students develop their learning activity in a Student-to-Student lesson, they design a poster, advertising the web site and describing what students will be required to do. These poster advertisements are then displayed around the room so that everyone can read them to select the site they wish to visit and the activity they will complete. Often, teachers will distribute a list of the sites and ask students to obtain the signature of the person who developed the activity they complete. This indicates that they have successfully completed their activity.

Student-to-Student lessons can be useful for organizing Internet activities during the final weeks of a unit in your classroom. It may be used, of course, in all subject areas but, because there are so many resources on the Internet for social studies, it is especially useful in this area.

TEACHING TIP	Student-to-Student is a great way to culminate Internet Inquiry. If your students have been exploring individual inquiry projects, set aside at least one day for them to share their work by having each develop a short activity on the Internet. Create a page with a list of all the Internet activities and invite your students to complete as many as possible. When they complete an activity designed by another student, have them obtain the signature of the student who developed the activity along with a brief evaluation. This is an especially nice experience if you have access to an entire lab of Internet computers. Each student can set up their own station. Have half of the class visit the student stations and the other half share their Internet activity at a computer. Then rotate groups.

 E-MAIL FOR YOU

To: Colleagues
From: Linda Swanson <swanson@best.com>
Subject: Amsterdam Social Studies Web

Dear Teachers,

   Students and teachers at the International School of Amsterdam have been engaged in a number of Internet-based projects. ESL students in the secondary school sent a request via Kidlink/Kidsphere for information on endangered species from other schools/countries. The response was overwhelming and led to a six week intensive correspondence with schools in Canada, Russia, USA, and Finland. We exchanged letters, reports, questionnaires and even circulated a petition amongst the participants supporting the movement to save the endangered mountain gorillas of Rwanda. Students were exposed to a much wider range of issues than was available in their course book. The students also noticed the experience significantly improved their writing skills.

Middle school students who were studying the writings of Jack London began an e-mail correspondence with students in Fairbanks, Alaska, who were reading "The Diary of Anne Frank". Our students had visited the Anne Frank house in Amsterdam on numerous occasions and were able to provide the Alaskan students with additional information about The Netherlands, Amsterdam and even Anne Frank herself. The Alaskan students responded with information on the Klondike, the gold rush, native peoples of Alaska and frequent updates of the Iditarod Sled Dog Race. The correspondence lasted for several months and culminated in the visit of the Alaskan students to Amsterdam in May of that year. Our students took them on a guided visit of the Anne Frank house and in return the Alaskan students put on a series of plays illustrating the life and times of Jack London. In addition to new friendships, both groups benefited from the shared exchange of information about the places they live.

Following the success and enthusiasm generated by these two projects, a group of grade six students and their teacher began to experiment with electronic publishing on the Internet. The class selected some of their best social studies projects, designed a small web page and provided links to related Internet resources. Thus began the Grades 5/6 Social Studies Web which to date comprises some fifteen different projects and can be found at the following address: http://www.xs4all.nl/~swanson/origins/

Their web site has evolved in years since its inception to becoming an integral part of the teaching / learning program. Internet publishing has sparked the students' interest in presentation skills and good writing and design issues. Most importantly, they have discovered the benefits of publishing to a real world. To date they have corresponded with professional storytellers (in response to their project on "Creation Stories"), historians ("Ancient Civilizations"), university students ("Human Origins") and students and teachers from numerous countries.

In addition to their normal library research they have learned how to deal with the variety of registers and (often contradictory) information available on the Internet. They have corresponded with copyright holders asking permission to adapt or reproduce materials for their projects while learning how to properly acknowledge a variety of published information sources. In return, their work has been acknowledged by others in the online community—most notably, the extensive list of annotated resources which they produced for their study of ancient civilizations.

Publishing and exchanging information via the Internet has enhanced the educational experience of our students and invigorated our social studies curriculum. Most notably, we discovered first-hand what others have stressed—that many of the Net's best resources are human beings.

Linda Swanson
Internet Resource Manager
International School of Amsterdam
Amsterdam, The Netherlands
(now living in the San Francisco Bay Area, California)

Using WebQuests

WebQuests provide an immediate solution to your need to integrate the Internet into your classroom. We encourage you, however, to carefully evaluate any WebQuest before deciding to use it in your classroom, just as you would any other curricular material.

WebQuests are a popular instructional strategy within social studies and increasing numbers of WebQuests are appearing on the Internet. As you will recall from Chapter 4, a WebQuest usually contains each of these elements: an introduction, a task definition, a description of the process, a list of information resources, guidance in organizing the information, and a concluding activity. WebQuests provide an immediate solution to your need to integrate the Internet into your classroom. As such, they are often used in classrooms. We encourage you, however, to carefully evaluate any WebQuest before deciding to use it in your classroom, just as you would any other curricular material. We believe each of the following questions should be asked before using any WebQuest:

1. *Does this WebQuest meet my curriculum goals and learning objectives?* How? What do my students learn from this experience? What does it teach? Is this important?

2. *How much time will this take my students?* Is this time well spent or could we accomplish more in less time with another learning experience?

3. *Does the WebQuest require my students to think critically about information and evaluate the information they encounter?* Does higher order thinking take place during the WebQuest or are students only required to develop literal, factual knowledge?

4. *Is this WebQuest developed so as to accommodate individual learning needs and interests?* Will all of my students be able to benefit from this activity? If not, what must I do to meet individual differences?

5. *Is there an opportunity for students to share the results of their WebQuest with the rest of the class for discussion and additional learning?* How do students share their learning with the rest of the class, enriching everyone's insights about what took place?

6. *Do students know, in advance, how their work on the WebQuest will be evaluated?* Will students know what is important to accomplish in the activity based on how it will be evaluated?

7. *Are all of the links on the WebQuest active and appropriate for my students?* Have I completed the WebQuest myself, and checked each of the links to resources that appear?

Of course, not all WebQuests will be able to pass answers to these questions. As with any curriculum you use in your classroom, you should carefully evaluate the experience before using it. Do not simply assume that since it is a WebQuest on the Internet it must be a good experience for your students. Some will be; some will not. Good teaching always requires that careful judgements be made about the learning experiences you select for your students, whether they appear on the Internet or in more traditional formats.

One of our greatest concerns about WebQuests is that they often have students working alone, in pairs, or in small groups without ever getting back together with the entire class to share, exchange, and discuss their experiences.

One of our greatest concerns about WebQuests is that they often have students working alone, in pairs, or in small groups without ever getting back together with the entire class to share, exchange, and discuss their experiences. We encourage the use of a short workshop session following each WebQuest so that you have a better understanding of what children learned in order to plan upcoming experiences and so you can shape and support the learning that takes place as students describe the meanings they developed from their experiences. You have an important role to play in WebQuests. This should not be left entirely to the person who designed the WebQuest. You know your particular students' needs better than anyone else.

Having raised these concerns, here are some examples of the better WebQuests we have discovered for use in social studies. Others may be found at most of the central sites for teaching social studies that we listed earlier in this chapter. You may wish to evaluate these examples to see if you believe they are appropriate for your social studies classroom:

- **Battle of the Battlefields**—http://score.rims.k12.ca.us/activity/battle/ Which of many revolutionary battlefields should receive money for a museum to commemorate its historical significance? Your team must decide which of several battles was most important in the revolutionary war and receive this museum.

- **Searching for China**—http://www.kn.pacbell.com/wired/China/ChinaQuest.html What actions should the U.S. take in its policy towards China? Your team develops a Group Report that contains a Three Point Action Plan. Each person of the team takes the part of an expert in one of these areas, contributing their special perspective to the question: business, cultural, religious, human rights, environmental, and political.

- **The Little Rock Nine**—http://www.kn.pacbell.com/wired/BHM/little_rock/ Using historical resources, information about previous solutions, and an exploration of the situation in their own community (see Figure 6-6), students work in a group in order to answer the question, "What, if anything, should be done to racially desegregate U.S. schools?"

Search Strategies in Social Studies

There are so many wonderful resources on the Internet for teachers and students it is sometimes hard to find what you want. It is easy to get lost as you explore first one site and then another and then still another. There are several strategies you and your students might find useful as you explore the many resources in social studies.

E-MAIL FOR YOU

To: Lifelong learners, risk-takers, experimenters, and pioneers of new technologies

From: Marjorie Duby <mduby@boston.k12.ma.us>

Subject: Simulations and other experiences on the Internet

I have been developing collaborative internet simulations with other classrooms. Though it's a social studies activity, it incorporates writing, reading, mathematics, geography, and science. It deals with students assuming the roles of 1700s colonial characters.

In collaboration with an educator from Washington whose class represents colonial characters living in a middle colony, my students represent a northeast colony, specifically Boston. Each class describes their charter and populates their colony with "characters" appropriate to the time and place. Our students "become" those characters as they face challenges or problems created by the other colony, leading through the Revolutionary War period and the creation of our original Declaration of Independence.

Simulations need obstacles so, representing Parliament, the two collaborating teachers send e-mail challenge messages to the colonies. At colonial town meetings, our "characters" make decisions about their daily lives based on the political events of the day. Our colony sends e-mail challenges to specific members of the other colony which they must resolve.

Living in Boston with access to the Freedom Trail sites and a National Park Service site, we make use of many resources for our simulations. Students begin their study by reading "If You Lived in Colonial Times" and complete an interview challenge. (http://lee.boston.k12.ma.us/d4/curr/stand/wr/ifcoltimes.asp) After that introduction, I use many children's literature and primary source document resources (http://lee.boston.k12.ma.us/d4/curr/rev/colsim/resources.asp) available in my classroom. Students write a biographical sketch of Paul Revere (http://lee.boston.k12.ma.us/D4/curr/rev/biosketch.asp), read "Ben and Me," "The Fighting Ground," or "My Brother Sam Is Dead," as well as a book taking place during the Revolutionary War period for presentation as a booksharing project. In class, we focus on "the invisibles" of the time who include women, servants, Africans, apprentices, and Native Americans around the theme of condoned mob actions.

I have an overall site for the Revolutionary Period at http://lee.boston.k12.ma.us/x1/revper.asp with an overview of activities. I have broken that down to English Language Arts activities at (http://lee.boston.k12.ma.us/d4/curr/stand/amrevstandELA.asp) and Mathematics activities at (http://lee.boston.k12.ma.us/d4/curr/stand/amrevstandMATH.asp).

This Revolutionary Period activity is but one project I chose to share with all of you. I, like most of you, am constantly attempting to broaden what I do in my classroom by using whatever connections I can make to the work we do. Exploits I have attempted through the years are available for sharing at our homepage located at http://lee.boston.k12.ma.us/d4/d4.html or linked to that page. I have targeted curriculum resources on a webpage at http://lee.boston.k12.ma.us/d4/curr/stand/cls.asp

Stop by, pay us a visit, and keep us in mind as collaborators for one of your memorable projects.

Marjorie Duby, Joseph Lee School, Boston, MA

= =

Marjorie Duby, Grade 5, Joseph Lee School, Boston, Massachusetts
Class webpage: http://lee.boston.k12.ma.us/d4/d4.html

= =

Figure 6-6.
The Little Rock 9 WebQuest (http://www.kn.pacbell.com/wired/BHM/little_rock/), an excellent classroom experience for social studies.

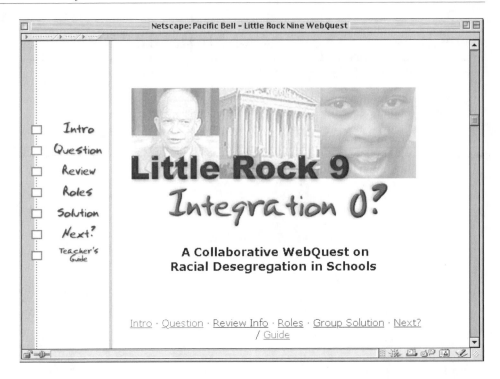

The easiest strategy is to visit one of the comprehensive social studies sites listed earlier in the chapter and begin to explore the many resources located there. Usually these are organized by topics and sometimes they have an internal search engine, that will only search within its site. The best of these are probably **Blue Web'n Applications: Social Studies** (http://www.kn.pacbell.com/wired/bluewebn/fr_History.html) and the **History/Social Studies Web Site for K–12 Teachers** (http://www.execpc.com/~dboals/boals.html), an extensive listing of hundreds of locations on the WWW useful for supporting social studies education. It is likely that you will find many useful resources simply by visiting either location.

If you are seeking something very specific on the WWW, you may wish to use one of the search engines by clicking on the "Search" button with Netscape Navigator or Internet Explorer. This will connect you to a page with several search engines such as Excite, Yahoo, Infoseek, Lycos, or Hot Bot. Here you can type in the words that best describe what you are looking for and click on the button that says "Search" or "Find". This will search the Internet for related web sites.

These search engines usually try to match the words you provide to words that appear on various pages in the WWW. Thus, it is best if you only use key descriptive words likely to be on the pages you are seeking. For example, the best way to search for something about the pyramids of Giza in Egypt is to simply type in "pyramids Giza Egypt". Avoid the use of words like "the" "of" or "a" since the search engine will look for these in addition to the other words you enter, listing every page it finds containing the word "the" "of" or "a". Some search engines will allow you to do a more advanced search by clicking on a button. At this location you can usually ask

E-MAIL FOR YOU

To: Colleagues
From: Jeanette Kenyon <jkenyon@pen.k12.va.us>
Subject: Using the Internet for Social Studies

Dear Colleagues,

Every March my 3rd grade class follows the Iditarod Sled Dog Race using the Internet as our main source of information. Cooperative learning teams decide on a particular musher to follow throughout the race. A large Alaskan map is posted along with pictures, daily race information, weather reports, and interesting race news. The students move their "musher" pin along the trail daily as the race progresses. There are wonderful sites on the World Wide Web which post daily race updates as well as a wealth of background information about the race, the mushers, history of the Iditarod, and life in Alaska. This year, the sites that I found most useful included:

http://www.newsminer.com/iditarod/

http://www.starfishsoftware.com/idog/index.html

http://www.iditarod.com/iditarod/

The links change nearly every year and you might wish to conduct your own search using one of the many search engines. Coverage improves greatly every year but many sites do not become functional until shortly before the race begins. This year coverage included live video and audio clips of race highlights.

It is very easy to incorporate map skills, math practice, including reading charts and graphs, weather studies, cultural lessons, geographical land forms, and even animal rights issues into the unit. There is always a high level of excitement as the students scan the latest race standings and move their musher along the trail. I use a variety of additional materials but my favorites include works by Gary Paulsen and Shelly Gill, who has compiled a very comprehensive curriculum guide for the Iditarod. These books are all available online from Amazon Books at: http://www.amazon.com

Sincerely,
Jeanette Kenyon
Third grade teacher
Anne E. Moncure Elementary School
Stafford, Virginia
jkenyon@pen.k12.va.us

the search engine to search by the exact phrase or sentence. This will permit an even more precise search for the type of information you are looking for.

Another very useful strategy is to join a mailing list and ask other members for their recommendations of useful web sites. This often leads to great locations since these teachers will have already used them in their classrooms. You may, for example, wish to subscribe to **NCSS-L**, a listserv for teachers of social studies run by the National Council for the Social Studies. Information on how to subscribe to this list is available at: http://www.ncss.org/links/listserv.html

Other listservs or mailing lists are described at the end of this chapter. If necessary, see Chapter 3 to review the procedures for subscribing to mailing lists.

Developing Critical Thinking about Web Resources

Internet technologies raise new issues about our relationship to content area information, especially within social studies. In a world where anyone may publish anything, how does one evaluate the accuracy of information one finds? In a world where new juxtapositions of multiple media forms may be created, how do we help children critically evaluate the variety of meanings inherent in the multiple media forms in which messages appear? Clearly, what has traditionally been referred to as critical reading or critical thinking assumes greater importance and new meaning with the introduction of Internet technologies into the content area classroom.

Open networks, such as the Internet, permit anyone to publish anything; this is one of the opportunities this technology presents. It is also one of its limitations; information is much more widely available from people who have strong political, economic, religious, or ideological stances that profoundly influence the nature of the information they present to others. As a result, we must assist students to become more critical consumers of the information they encounter. Such skills have not always been seen as important in classrooms where textbooks and other traditional information resources are often assumed to be correct.

How do we do this? What skills become important when evaluating information on the Internet? We find that helping students to think about five questions provides new, and more critical, insights into the meaning of information at a web page: Who? What? When? Where? and How?

- *Who created the information at this site?*
  - Can you determine the person or the unit that created this site?
  - What is the background of the creator?
  - Is this a commercial (.com), organizational (.org), or an educational (.edu) location?

> Internet technologies raise new issues about our relationship to content area information, especially within social studies. In a world where anyone may publish anything, how does one evaluate the accuracy of information one finds?

> We must assist students to become more critical consumers of the information they encounter.

> We find that helping students to think about five questions provides new, and more critical, insights into the meaning of information at a web page: Who? What? When? Where? and How?

- *What is the purpose of this site?*
    — Can you locate a link that tells you what this site is about? What does it say the purpose of the site is? How confident can you be that this is a fair statement?
    — Knowing who created the site, can you infer why they created it?

- *When was the information at this site created?*
    — How recently was the information at this site updated?
    — Is it likely this information has changed since it appeared? How? Why?

- *Where can I go to check the accuracy of this information?*
    — Are the sources for factual information clearly listed so I can check them with another source?
    — If not, how confident can you be in the information at this location?

- *How will the information at this site be shaped by the stance taken by the creator of the site?*
    — Knowing who created this site and what the stated or implicit purpose is, how does this probably shape the information or the activities here?
    — What biases are likely to appear at this location?

Helping students to regularly think about answers to these questions, perhaps by posting them next to your Internet computers and discussing them during workshop sessions, will go far toward supporting their critical evaluation of the information they discover.

There are also a growing number of locations on the Internet to assist you and your students in developing your critical analysis skills about information at web sites. For a general online set of references you should visit **Bibliography on Evaluating Web Resources** (http://www.lib.vt.edu/research/libinst/evalbiblio.html) at the library of Virginia Tech or **Critical Evaluation Information** (http://school.discovery.com/schrockguide/eval.html). You might also wish to develop an Internet Workshop for your students around the location we mentioned earlier in this book **ICYouSee:T is for Thinking** (http://www.ithaca.edu/library/Training/hott.html). Additionally, you might have students in grades 6 and above complete one, or both, of these WebQuests:

Evaluating Web Pages: A WebQuest—
http://mciunix.mciu.k12.pa.us/~spjvweb/evalwebteach.html

The Quality Information Checklist—
http://www.quick.org.uk/menu.htm

Figure 6-7.
Setting individual "favorites" folders
in Internet Explorer.

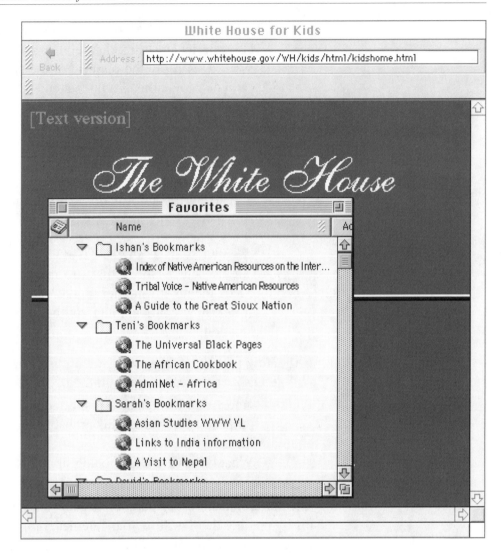

Using Individual Bookmark (Favorites) Folders

You may face a challenge when you have an entire class doing Internet Inquiry with many individuals setting "bookmarks" (the term used with Netscape Navigator) or "favorites" (the term used with Internet Explorer). In a single-computer classroom, your list of bookmarks/favorites will become lengthy and confusing. Versions 3.0 and later of both Netscape Navigator and Internet Explorer allow you to solve this problem by making a separate bookmark/favorite folder for each student in your class.

To make individual bookmark folders with Internet Explorer, go to the menu item "Favorites" and select "Open Favorites." Once your "Favorites" window is open, go to the menu item "Favorites" again and select New Folder for each new folder you wish to create. Type in the name of a student next to one of the folders. Repeat this for each student in your class and you will have a bookmark window that looks similar to Figure 6-7.

Now that you have a location for each student to place their favorites with Internet Explorer, you will need to show students how to keep their favorite locations organized. Each time a new favorite location is added, it will be added to the end of the folder list. Remind students to open the "favorites" window and drag and drop their favorites into their own bookmark folder. This will help to keep the list of favorites organized for your students.

With Netscape, the process is somewhat similar. To make individual bookmark folders you must first open the bookmark window by clicking on the "Bookmarks" menu item at the top of your Netscape Navigator screen. Select the item called "Edit Bookmarks". This will open a separate window for editing and adding new bookmark folders, one for each student. To add a folder for each student, click on the menu item called "File" at the top of your screen and select "New Folder". A window will then open asking you to name this new folder. Simply type in the name of a student here and then select OK to close the window.

With Netscape, you may designate one folder at a time to receive new bookmarks. You will need to show students how to make certain they designate their folder to receive new bookmarks. That way, when they add a new bookmark, it will be placed within their folder and not within a folder belonging to someone else.

Designating a student's folder to receive new bookmarks is not difficult. Show students how to open the bookmark window in Netscape Navigator by clicking on the Bookmarks menu item at the top of your screen and selecting "Edit Bookmark." As you did before, this will open the window for editing bookmark folders. Now, highlight the folder of the student who is working at the computer by clicking on it once. Then, click on the menu item at the top of your screen called "View" and select "Set as New Bookmarks Folder." Whenever this student adds a new bookmark, it will be placed in his or her folder, since this is now the active bookmarks folder.

Next, go back up to the menu item at the top of your screen called "Item" and select "Set to Bookmark Menu Folder." This will make only the bookmarks in this student's folder appear when the Bookmark menu item is selected at the top of the Netscape Navigator screen. Close the bookmark window and this student is ready to begin.

Before students begin their session, have them open the bookmark window, designate their folder by clicking on it, and then select the "Set as New Bookmarks Folder" and "Set as Bookmark Menu Folder." This will make their folder the active bookmark folder. You may wish to cover this strategy during an Internet Workshop session.

Visiting the Classroom: Mr. Sangiuliano and Mrs. Reinalda's Multiage Class in Rhode Island

We do not only study social studies; we also live it in our daily lives. Social studies education is learning how to make our world a better place. That is

We do not only study social studies; we also live it in our daily lives. Social studies education is learning how to make our world a better place.

Internet FAQ	
I'd like to use the same bookmark file at home and at school. Can I do this?	Sure! You can copy your bookmark file from one computer onto a floppy disk and then place it on another computer. This will then become the new bookmark file. Be careful, though, because it will replace the previous bookmark file, unless you move this to a safe location when you save it. In Netscape, your bookmark file can be found in your Preferences folder in your System file. It will be in a folder called Netscape *f*. Simply copy this file and place it in the same location on another computer. With Internet Explorer, your favorites (bookmarks) can be found in the preferences folder of your system file, too. It will be in a folder called Explorer. Follow the same directions to move it from one computer to another.

the lesson we draw from visiting the multiage classroom (grades 1–3) of Mr. Sangiuliano and Mrs. Reinalda in Barrington, Rhode Island (http://booksontapeforkids.org/class/).

These two teachers have developed a wonderful model for preparing students to understand the importance of community service and care about others who may be suffering. Their class project, Books on Tape, is one that all of us should follow in our classrooms. The goal of this wonderful project is to send at least two packages with books on tape to two hospitals in each state. Each package contains a children's book, an audio tape of a student reading it aloud, illustrations, and letters from their students.

Visit the link from their classroom web page (see Figure 6-8) to **Books on Tape** (http://booksontapeforkids.org/) to see how this project is organized. It really is quite simple and easy for other classes, at all levels, to emulate. In their own words from this page, here is what they do:

1. First, we choose children's books and practice reading them.

2. Then, we record ourselves reading the books onto cassette tapes.

3. Finally, the cassette tapes, pieces of artwork, the books, photographs of the readers, and letters, are packaged and sent to children in hospitals across the country.

The class has attracted several sponsors to support their important work.

You can discover more about this project by following the links at their project site. You will find a map indicating which states have received their contributions as well as a list of story books they have sent and photos of students working on the project. It is a highly innovative way to make reading come alive for the young children in this class. The smiles on their faces tell a story that is much more powerful than we can describe here. We hope you consider a community service project such as this for your own classroom. Learning how important it is to make our world a better place is perhaps the most important lesson any of us can learn from social studies.

Figure 6-8.
The classroom web page of Mr. Sangiuliano and Mrs. Reinalda's multiage class in Rhode Island (http://booksontapeforkids.org/class/). Be certain to visit their "Books on Tape" community service project.

Instructional Resources on the Internet

Adbusters: Culturejammers Headquarters—http://www.adbusters.org/home/
A location to help your middle school and high school students develop critical media literacy insights about the commercial world around them.

America Dreams through the Decades—http://www.internet-catalyst.org/projects/amproject/toc.html
This is an extensive interdisciplinary project for upper elementary, middle school, and high school classes that takes them through an extended WebQuest using primary source documents available at the Library of Congress American memory site.

Black History: Exploring African-American Issues on the Web—http://www.kn.pacbell.com/wired/BHM/AfroAm.html
This exceptional site contains six separate resources for the study of African-American issues: a hotlist of links to important resources on the Internet, an interactive treasure hunt, a subject sampler, a WebQuest on the Little Rock 9, a WebQuest on the Tuskegee Tragedy, and a videoconference.

Contacting the Congress—http://www.visi.com/juan/congress/
Use this location to quickly send any of the members of the US Congress an e-mail message about your concerns. It may also be used to request information for units you are planning.

Cybrary of the Holocaust—http://remember.org/
This is an incredibly extensive cyber library of resources for individu-

als wishing to study the Holocaust. Audio interviews from survivors, written recollections by survivors, works of literature, images, and a wide array of resources depict this dark period in our history to ensure that we do not forget.

Exploring Ancient World Cultures—http://eawc.evansville.edu/index.htm
This location consists of "an introductory, on-line, college-level 'textbook' of ancient world cultures, constructed around a series of cultural pages consisting of: The Ancient Near East, Ancient India, Ancient Egypt, Ancient China, Ancient Greece, Ancient Rome, Early Islam, and Medieval Europe." The site contains an anthology, chronology, essays, maps, and an interactive quiz for each of the cultures. This site links to a search engine that brings you Internet resources.

Harriet Tubman and the Underground Railroad—http://www2.lhric.org/pocantico/tubman/tubman.html
Designed by students in Mrs. Taverna's second grade class, this site includes a timeline, a quiz, character sketches, and crossword puzzles about Harriet Tubman. Also included are activity ideas for incorporating the content into the classroom as part of an interactive lesson plan.

Journey Back in Time to Ancient Rome—http://www.richmond.edu/~ed344/webquests/rome/frames.html
A WebQuest intended for upper elementary and middle school students using a jigsaw approach. Students use teamwork and the Internet to explore Ancient Rome and learn about daily life, myths, and government. Each person on the team learns one piece of the puzzle and then comes together to get a better understanding of the topic.

Letters Home From an Iowa Soldier in the Civil War—http://www.civilwarletters.com/home.html
These letters home bring to life the struggles of a country and the experiences of an individual. Nice primary source documents for the study of US History. Lesson ideas are included.

MapQuest—http://www.mapquest.com/
This is one of the better interactive map services on the WWW. Your students can explore maps of nearly any region, right down to locating their own home on a map of your city. This is a wonderful location to develop map reading skills with your students as you study different regions. Set a bookmark!

My Hero—http://myhero.com/home.asp
This site for elementary and middle school students allows you to read about heroes, many of whom come from history, as well as submit their own stories. Those heroes can be famous individuals or parents. Step-by-step instructions are listed at the site.

National Council for the Social Studies—http://www.ncss.org/
This home page for the major professional organization devoted to social studies education contains a nice set of links organized around the ten themes for the Curriculum Standards for Social Studies.

National Geographic Society Home Page—

http://www.nationalgeographic.com/main.html

The home page of the National Geographic Society provides a wealth of information for students related to the programming and books of this organization. Within the site is a great location (http://magma.nationalgeographic.com/education/index.cfm) for lesson ideas on geography, an area of the curriculum that is often neglected. Also located at this site are maps which may be printed out by students for reports.

Nova Online/Pyramids: The Inside Story—http://www.pbs.org/wgbh/nova/pyramid/

Take a guided tour inside the great pyramids of Giza, read about the history of these magnificent wonders, share the recent discoveries of archeologists, and come away with a new appreciation for the accomplishments of this ancient civilization. A great site for any class studying ancient Egypt.

The Early American Review—http://earlyamerica.com/review/

An on-line journal on the people, issues, and events of 18th century America. A wonderful scholarly resource for high school students in an American history course.

The Role of American Women in World War II—

http://www.muscanet.com/~mather/

This is an Internet WebQuest where students, working in groups, examine the various roles of women during the war, research the Internet, interview a World War II survivor, then create and publish an oral history.

The Smithsonian Home Page—http://www.si.edu/newstart.htm

The Smithsonian Institution calls itself "The nation's treasure house for learning." This site certainly does it justice. Many outstanding links to the wonderful resources of this fine institution.

The White House for Kids—http://www.whitehouse.gov/WH/kids/html/kidshome.html

Have your students take a tour of the White House and visit the president and his family. Students may also leave a message for the President, read a newsletter for students, and experience several important historical moments that have recently taken place. A great location for Internet Activity in the elementary grades.

Do You Know Your State Capitals?—http://www.cris.com/~kraft/capitals/

Set a bookmark for this interactive game for younger students studying geography.

Listservs/Mailing Lists for Social Studies

Use standard subscribing procedures (see Chapter 3) to join the following listservs.

H-HIGH-S—LISTSERV@H-NET.MSU.EDU
> A mailing list for high school teachers of social studies.

H-Net Discussion Networks—http://www2.h-net.msu.edu/lists/
> This web page contains links to the home pages for many mailing lists in social studies.

MEMORIES—listserv@maelstrom.stjohns.edu
> This listserv allows students to talk with survivors of World War II.

NCSS-L—http://www.ncss.org/links/listserv.html
> The Instructional Technology Committee of National Council for the Social Studies has established this listserv for interested Internet users to share information and ideas about social studies education in grades K–12 and in teacher education.

TAMHA—LISTSERV@LISTS.WAYNE.EDU
> Conversations about teaching American history.

Science: Using the Internet to Support Scientific Thinking

E-MAIL FOR YOU

To: Our readers
From: djleu@syr.edu (Don Leu), ddleu@syr.edu (Debbie Leu)
Subject: Using the Internet for science education

It is essential that we prepare each of our students to think scientifically if we hope to prepare them for the futures they deserve. Each of us needs to help our students in this area, even if our primary teaching responsibility is not in science education.

Science education is not just about learning facts. At its core, science education helps students to think scientifically. This simply means helping them to ask questions and seek logical answers through observation, reading, writing, and critical analysis. As noted in the National Science Education Standards, science education needs to provide both a "hands on" and a "minds on" experience. Some teachers lack confidence in this area. Approached with the proper perspective, however, science education can become the center of every classroom as you use it to integrate language arts, math, social studies, and other subject areas.

The Internet can be a valuable tool in this process. Learning to use the Internet, itself, is a scientific process as you and your students make hypotheses about how the Internet works and then test these with your browser. Internet Workshop may be especially useful in these efforts.

In addition, the Internet provides extensive resources to help your students as you cultivate their ability to look at the world scientifically. These include an extensive set of science museums where your students can interact with exciting demonstrations of scientific principles, experts available to answer students' questions about any aspect of science, on-going scientific studies where your students may contribute their observations and help to interpret the results, listservs on teaching science where you may obtain valuable ideas to bring to your classroom, and lesson plans to help you with your science teaching.

Don and Debbie

Teaching With the Internet: Anne Miller's Class

As her fourth grade class completed the beginning activities of their first day of school, Anne wrote this word in big, bold, capital letters: SETI. Next to it she wrote: http://setiaathome.ssl.berkeley.edu

"Here's a new word for us this year," she said. "Has anyone ever heard of this?"

She heard murmurs: "It's a web site."

"The Internet."

"The Internet? Cool!"

"That's right," she said. "It's on the Internet and 'SETI' stands for these words."

Next to SETI, Anne wrote: Search for Extraterrestrial Intelligence.

"You know what 'Search' means and you know what 'Intelligence' means. Now how about this word, 'Extraterrestrial?'"

"Outer space," announces Narita. "It means outer space. It was in the movie 'Contact' with Jodie Foster. She looked for radio signals coming from people in outer space…"

Over the summer, Anne had discovered an exciting science project on the Internet, called **SETI@Home** (http://setiathome.ssl.berkeley.edu). The project allows anyone with an Internet computer to become a participating member of the research team searching our galaxy for radio signals from intelligent life (see Figure 7-1). This federally funded project, located at the University of California, Berkeley, uses the enormous radio telescope in Arecibo, Puerto Rico, to collect radio signals from outer space. These are sent to Berkeley for analysis. Anyone with a computer can download a program that regularly analyzes a small portion of these radio signals for patterns indicating intelligent life.

> Over the summer, Anne had discovered an exciting science project on the Internet, called SETI@Home (http://setiathome.ssl.berkeley.edu)

Figure 7-1.
SETI@Home (http://setiathome.ssl.berkeley.edu) provides a screen saver that allows you to search for radio signals from intelligent life outside our solar system. The project is run from the University of California, Berkeley, and is available to anyone with an Internet computer.

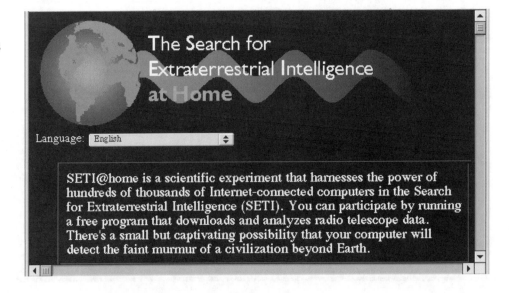

More than one million computers around the world automatically receive packets with radio data, process these radio signals, and send the results back to Berkeley over the Internet. Much of this work takes place at night while people leave their computers on but do not use them.

The program uses a screen saver, a program with an image that regularly changes. Screen savers are used to keep a computer screen from "burning" a fixed image onto the monitor when it is left on for long periods of inactivity. This screen saver automatically picks up new data from Berkeley and conducts the analysis. It shows the results of each computer's SETI analysis in a continuously changing graph and results page. When it has completed the analysis, the results are sent to Berkeley over the Internet and new data is acquired for additional analysis.

By harnessing over a million desktop computers, this project can analyze far more data than it could ever hope to analyze with a single, large computer at Berkeley; there simply isn't a computer large enough to keep up with the data. This creative project *distributes* the workload to all of the participating computers around the world. It follows the traditional adage, "Many hands, make light work." Distributing work like this ends up being a far more efficient way to accomplish complex tasks.

> By harnessing over a million desktop computers, this project can analyze far more data than it could ever hope to analyze with a single, large computer at Berkeley; there simply isn't a computer large enough to keep up with the data.

You may download the screensaver software from the SETI@home site. If your computer finds a signal from outer space, you receive recognition for your achievement along with the other members of the scientific team. It is an exciting new way in which to conduct research.

Anne had been careful to check with her districts' computer manager to be certain it was all right to join this project. By e-mail, she had heard from teachers in Tennessee that some computer networks were not powerful enough to participate. The computer person in her district indicated that there wouldn't be any problems with their new network; it was powerful enough to handle the traffic, even if every computer in their district participated in the study.

"Just think of it," Anne said to her class. "If our computer discovers a signal from outer space, we will be on TV and in all of the newspapers. Everyone will recognize you as the kids who discovered another civilization in outer space."

Her class sat for a moment thinking about this. Very quickly, they started firing questions right and left to Anne.

"You mean we can really see if there is a message from space?"

"How do we know if we found a signal?"

"I'm gonna tell my sister about this."

"We'll be famous!"

That brief introduction served to inspire Anne's students throughout the rest of the year. They were scientists, doing important work on their computer over the Internet. Every morning, her students wanted to check the overnight results. The local newspaper even printed a story about their work.

Of course, this was not all they accomplished with their single, classroom computer linked to the Internet. The **SETI@Home** project, however, served to continually motivate her students in the scientific process. During the year, her students discovered how scientists must carefully check and recheck their work through independent replication as they read the procedures to be followed if someone found a signal coming from outer space. They found this at the **Declaration of Principles Concerning Activities Following the Detection of Extraterrestrial Intelligence** (http://www.seti-inst.edu/post-detection.html). They also learned about many other critical vocabulary concepts related to the search for extraterrestrial life: Gausian curves, MHz, pulsing signals, radio waves, Fourier Transforms, chirp rates, spectrum, and much more. They also learned how scientists have calculated the possibility of finding life on another planet using a mathematical formula anyone could understand. They even listened to the actual radio signals received at Arecibo to hear what these sounded like. They also read news articles about **SETI@Home** and even a work of science fiction, available on the Internet, someone had written in which the SETI project played a central role. They corresponded with other students around the world who were also analyzing signals and, using their Internet computer and a small and inexpensive video camera, they arranged a videoconference with several SETI scientists who explained their work and answered questions.

> They corresponded with other students around the world who were also analyzing signals and, using their Internet computer and a small and inexpensive video camera, they arranged a videoconference with several SETI scientists who explained their work and answered questions.

Anne's year included many other important experiences with a single Internet computer in her classroom. Her class also completed a unit on the solar system and integrated language arts experiences by reading *This Planet Has No Atmosphere* by Paula Danzinger and *A Wrinkle in Time* by Madeleine L'Engle. She set bookmarks on Internet Explorer for **The Nine Planets Tour** (http://seds.lpl.arizona.edu/billa/tnp/), **The Hubble Space Telescope** (http://www.stsci.edu/), and the home page for the current **Space Shuttle** mission at NASA (http://www.ksc.nasa.gov/shuttle/countdown/). She developed several short Internet Workshop assignments for students to complete at these locations. She also subscribed to several listservs for science educators, following the conversations to see if she could get additional ideas for her class. One of the best conversations mentioned the **National Standards for Science Education** and gave the URL for this document (http://www.nap.edu/readingroom/books/nses/html/). She explored this site and its links, learning about the recently adopted standards for science and getting several useful ideas, especially the concept of science as inquiry.

Over a holiday break, Anne discovered the location for **NASA Quest's Online Interactive Projects** (http://quest.arc.nasa.gov/interactive/index.html), a wonderful site with opportunities for her students to work directly with the men and women scientists at NASA (see Figure 7-2). From here, she located a number of Internet projects for her class. These allowed her class to collect data and contribute to on-going investigations through Internet Project. They also enjoyed several on-line chat sessions with several women who were members of shuttle teams. They talked about the career opportunities that exist in science. These were wonderfully supportive mentoring experiences for her students. Most importantly, the NASA scien-

Figure 7-2.
The home page for Women of NASA, one of the online projects available at **NASA Quest's Online Interactive Projects** (http://quest.arc.nasa.gov/interactive/index.html).

tists opened the world of science to her students by sharing their excitement for the important work they do.

Toward the end of the year Anne decided to try Internet Inquiry with cooperative group science projects. Students worked in groups of twos and threes to identify an important scientific question. Then they used the Internet and their school library to try and discover the answer. Workshop sessions twice a week seemed to really help students on their inquiry projects. At the end of the unit, the class held a science fair with each group setting up a "poster session", describing their question, their work, and what they had discovered on a large poster board. Each of her students also developed a Student-to-Student activity. Every student had to visit these and complete at least five of the student-to-student activities during the week.

One of the inquiry projects was completed by Tyronne and Alex. Both of them had been interested in the ant farm Anne had brought into the classroom after the winter holidays. They were fascinated by the continuous activity of these insects. The question they wanted to answer in their Internet Inquiry was "Do ants ever sleep?" When they shared this question during a workshop session, other students had all kinds of suggestions. They could check in the library for books about animals. They could check on the Internet by doing a search with one of the search engines for "ants" and "sleep". Someone also gave them the URL for **The Mad Scientist Network**, a place on the Internet where they could ask a scientist this question (http://www.madsci.org/). And, someone else suggested they mark one ant and watch it for 24 hours to see if it ever stopped moving and actually slept. The idea of staying up all night caught their attention and they pleaded with Anne to take the class ant farm home over the weekend. She finally relented and, after they selected one ant ("Hooty") and marked him with a non-toxic marker, Anne dropped the ant farm off at Alex's house Friday after school.

Tyronne and Alex made observations every fifteen minutes in their science journal for an entire day and learned that Hooty never stopped to take a rest or stop working. They even took some pictures for their poster session at the science fair. They created a wonderful poster which presented all of their work. It included photos, a written report describing their research, and the conclusions they reached. They also included the e-mail message in Figure 7-3 from a scientist in Australia. They were pleased they had figured out a way to answer their question using a method that even the adult scientist had not considered.

> They were pleased they had figured out a way to answer their question using a method that even the adult scientist had not considered

Figure 7-3.
Tyronne's and Alex's response from an Australian scientist on **The Mad Scientist Network** (http://medinfo.wustl.edu/~ysp/MSN/posts/archives/dec96/841965056.Zo.r.html)

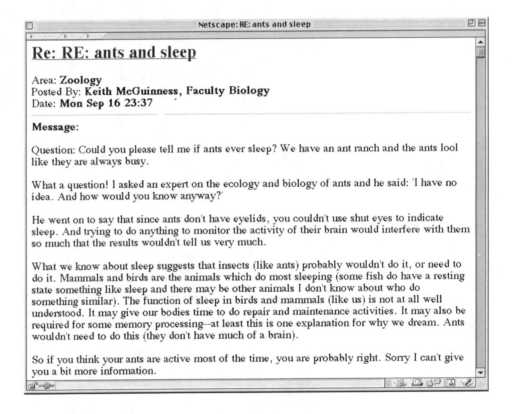

> Re: RE: ants and sleep
>
> Area: **Zoology**
> Posted By: **Keith McGuinness, Faculty Biology**
> Date: **Mon Sep 16 23:37**
>
> **Message:**
>
> Question: Could you please tell me if ants ever sleep? We have an ant ranch and the ants lool like they are always busy.
>
> What a question! I asked an expert on the ecology and biology of ants and he said: 'I have no idea. And how would you know anyway?'
>
> He went on to say that since ants don't have eyelids, you couldn't use shut eyes to indicate sleep. And trying to do anything to monitor the activity of their brain would interfere with them so much that the results wouldn't tell us very much.
>
> What we know about sleep suggests that insects (like ants) probably wouldn't do it, or need to do it. Mammals and birds are the animals which do most sleeping (some fish do have a resting state something like sleep and there may be other animals I don't know about who do something similar). The function of sleep in birds and mammals (like us) is not at all well understood. It may give our bodies time to do repair and maintenance activities. It may also be required for some memory processing--at least this is one explanation for why we dream. Ants wouldn't need to do this (they don't have much of a brain).
>
> So if you think your ants are active most of the time, you are probably right. Sorry I can't give you a bit more information.

> That year, many new worlds opened to Anne's class through the exciting experiences with science.

That year, many new worlds opened to Anne's class through the exciting experiences with science. A number of students announced they were now going to become scientists. It had been a very productive year.

Lessons From the Classroom

This story from Anne Miller's classroom has several important lessons for each of us to consider. One of the most important lessons comes from the **SETI@Home** project. This project vividly demonstrates the power of distributing processing—distributing a complex task among many people who accomplish small parts of the larger activity. Distributing work among many different people will be a central aspect of our future in a world of networked information resources. A parallel notion, distributed learning, will exist in our classrooms with the Internet. The notion of distributed learning is a powerful one for you to consider.

Teachers sometimes describe this change to us as moving from a "sage on the stage to a guide at the side." What they mean is that a teacher changes from being the only expert at the head of the class to being one of many members of a classroom community with expertise, each one knowing something very special and important to others.

Most of us first see this change when we have students in our classroom who begin assisting us when our computer freezes, when the printer isn't working, or when something else fails. Suddenly, a student's expertise becomes visible and critical to our classroom's success. As digital technologies become more important to our classrooms and as they repeatedly change, it is impossible for anyone to keep up with everything taking place. You will see each student becoming an expert in a particular area that interests him or her. One child might be an expert with knowing the best resources about Jan Brett, another with information about butterflies, and still others will become experts in other information areas or other aspects of technology.

This change, by the way, reflects the changes taking place in the world of work today. The highly structured and top-down model of business and industry has changed to a far more decentralized model in order for companies to successfully compete in a highly competitive global economy. Nimble, aggressive companies are taking advantage of individual employee's expertise to survive; inflexible and tightly structured companies that ignore their employees' special talents fail in a world of rapidly changing information and technology. Thus, it is important that we prepare children for these new worlds of literacy and life-long learning they will experience as adults.

Which teaching methods help us to achieve this goal? Internet Workshop and other workshop approaches accomplish this better than any other we know. Each serves to support children as they develop individual areas of expertise and then learn how to share their knowledge and seek the knowledge they require from others. Knowing whom, when, and how to ask for information becomes more important than even having information in these new worlds. That is what Internet Workshop accomplishes.

A second important lesson we learn from Anne's class is that the Internet provides many helpful resources to assist you in developing an exciting and dynamic science program in your classroom, a program consistent with the National Science Education Standard's emphasis on thinking scientifically through inquiry.

A third lesson is also clear—Internet projects are a powerful way of helping your students to think scientifically as they work collaboratively with others to gather data and interpret the results. Working with the scientists at NASA and other classrooms around the world provided Anne's students with an exciting and authentic science experience. They learned much about this spe-

---

Teachers sometimes describe this change to us as moving from a "sage on the stage to a guide at the side."

Which teaching methods help us to achieve this goal? Internet Workshop and other workshop approaches accomplish this better than any other we know.

The Internet provides many helpful resources that can assist you in developing an exciting and dynamic science program in your classroom, a program consistent with the National Science Education Standard's emphasis on thinking scientifically through inquiry.

Working with the scientists at NASA and other classrooms around the world provided Anne's students with an exciting and authentic science experience.

cial way of looking at the world. Several locations on the WWW provide opportunities for your class to engage in Internet projects, or to develop your own projects and invite others to join.

Finally, Anne's class demonstrates how Internet Inquiry is an excellent vehicle to help your students think scientifically as you develop a science-as-inquiry program in your classroom. Science is as much a verb as it is a noun. Having students identify questions they wish to answer and then helping them to develop techniques for answering their questions is important in preparing students who not only *know* science but also *do* science.

E-MAIL FOR YOU

To: Colleagues
From: Linda Hubbard (lhubbard@mail.tempe3.k12.az.us)
Subject: Classroom Activities on the World Wide Web

In my fifth grade classroom we combine the use of NASA web sites and NASA satellite TV. During each shuttle mission, while school is in session, we watch the shuttle launch, live, if possible. Then we access the various WWW sites which provide us with background and real-time information about the particular mission. We have the chance to "log in" as visitors to the shuttle, learn about the crew, monitor the progress of any science experiments, and watch the tracking map for the orbits. The **NASA Human Space Flight** (http://spaceflight.nasa.gov/index-n.html) gives great information about current shuttle missions. For information on the shuttle crew currently in space we use **Crew Status** (http://spaceflight.nasa.gov/shuttle/crew/index.html). One of the class favorites is the web site which displays the global tracking map of the shuttle flight, **NASA Realtime Data** (http://spaceflight.nasa.gov/realdata/index.html).

All of these activities give us opportunities to relate our curriculum in all areas to real-world space exploration. We also use the flight schedule information from the web sites to find out when the astronauts will be working in the open payload bay or making a space walk. We tune in to NASA TV to watch those live when we can. The web sites also give us a chance to see photos taken during the mission. Finally, our interest in current missions has led us to explore NASA web sites with historical information from the start of the space program. **NASA Space History** (http://spaceflight.nasa.gov/history/index.html) is very interesting.

With each shuttle mission we monitor, we discover more web sites to explore. All of which makes our science unit on exploring space much more meaningful for all of us.

Linda Hubbard
5th grade teacher
Tempe School District No. 3

Central Sites for Science Education

Science is as much a verb as it is a noun. Having students identify questions they wish to answer and then helping them to develop techniques for answering their questions is important in preparing students who not only know science but also do science.

There are a number of central sites on the Internet for science education. One type provides you with a wide array of links to useful curricular and other resources for science education. Others will provide you with ready-to-go instructional activities in science including science units, ideas for science demonstrations, or lesson plans. Finally, some locations will be useful if you wish to subscribe to mailing lists (listservs) related to science education. Each will be useful to you as you consider the broader issues of your science education program.

If you only have time to visit one central site, pay a visit to the Eisenhower National Center for Mathematics and Science Education (http://www.enc.org:80/index.htm).

If you only have time to visit one central site, pay a visit to the **Eisenhower National Center for Mathematics and Science Education** (http://www.enc.org:80/index.htm). This federally-funded project provides K–12 teachers with a central source of information on mathematics and science education. The home page image hardly gives a hint of the tremendously useful resources available here (see Figure 7-4). We have found the best resources linked to the image labeled "Action" or "Reform in Action." Click on this image. One section contains links to a monthly "Digital Dozen," 13 great sites on the Internet for math and science education that change each month. This location, alone, is worth the visit.

Another section in the "Action" section contains an excellent collection of lessons and activities for your students. In addition, there is a location

Figure 7-4.
The home page for the **Eisenhower National Clearinghouse for Mathematics and Science Education** (http://www.enc.org:80/index.htm), an outstanding central site for science education.

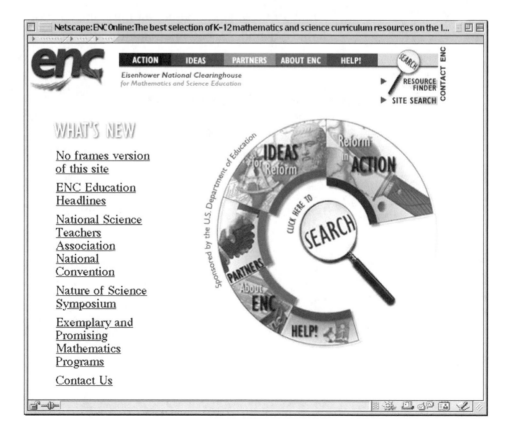

where you may ask experts in the field of science education any question that will improve your classroom program. These experts will provide you with answers to help you meet your students' needs. The web site also has a resource finder, allowing you to search an extensive set of instructional resources by topic or key word. Finally, this site contains a section where you may read various publications related to science education. Clearly, this WWW location is of tremendous utility as you seek to use the Internet to improve your classroom science program. Set a bookmark!

A second useful central site in science is the location of the **National Science Teachers Association Recommended Websites** (http://library.advanced.org/20117/). Here, members and non-members may recommend a useful website in science education. Recommendations are organized by area.

Another site to use as a jumping off point is **Frank Potter's Science Gems** (http://www.sciencegems.com/) Though it now has become a commercial site, it contains over 11,000 links to outstanding science resources on the WWW. What is especially nice about this location is that resources are organized by science area (e.g., Physical Science, Earth Science, Life Science, etc.) and by topic within each area (e.g., within Earth Science there are locations for measurement, earth, solar system, astronomy, atmosphere, land/oceans, and natural resources). Each topic is also organized by grade level. The organizational scheme used at this site allows you to quickly find resources for units you are planning to teach in your class.

Another type of central site provides teaching plans for busy teachers. Many of these are good beginning points as you consider ways in which to help your students become scientifically literate and think scientifically. One of the most comprehensive sites is **Lessons and Activities for Science** (Select http://www.enc.org:80/classroom/index.htm and then find the link at the bottom of the page). This is a location within the Eisenhower National Center for Mathematics and Science Education site mentioned earlier. It contains many links to outstanding locations containing lesson plans and activities. Exploring these locations will give you many good ideas for your science program.

Teachers often use demonstrations to catch students' interest and get them to think scientifically. There are a number of useful locations on the WWW with demonstrations you can provide to your class to illustrate scientific principles or to initiate conversations about causes and effects. One of the best collection of demonstrations is **The Exploratorium Science Snackbook** (http://www.exploratorium.edu/publications/Snackbook/Snackbook.html). This allows you to quickly replicate many of the exciting exhibits at one of the world's premier science museums. A third location with exciting demonstrations is **Whelmers** (http://www.mcrel.org/whelmers/). Developed by Steven Jacobs, these demonstrations catch students by surprise and get them to really think about physical principles. Each is aligned with the National Science Education Standards.

One of the best collection of demonstrations is The Exploratorium Science Snackbook (http://www.exploratorium.edu/publications/Snackbook/Snackbook.html).

TEACHING
TIP

> If you wish to keep up with the most recent developments in earth science, take a look at **Web Earth Science for Teachers** (http://www.usatoday.com/weather/wteach.htm), a location within *USA Today*. This has an extensive list of science links closely related to current event items in the news. There are also links to lesson plans and activities you can use in your classroom. This is an especially good resource for integrating weather resources into instruction.

Using Internet Workshop

Internet Workshop is a good way to begin using the Internet in your classroom for science education. Internet Workshop assignments are easy to set up and require minimum navigation knowledge by either you or your students. Locate a site on the Internet with content related to your science unit, perhaps by using one of the central sites described above, and set a bookmark for this location. Next, develop a thoughtful activity that requires students to use the information at the site. Then, assign the activity to your students to complete during the week. Finally, share your experiences during Internet Workshop.

Excellent Internet Workshop assignments may be developed from the many resources located at science museums around the world. These often provide exciting simulations, demonstrations, or science puzzles for students. By developing appropriate Internet Workshop assignments, you can engage your students in scientific thinking.

A good place to begin is the **Science Learning Network** (http://www.sln.org/), a central site for museums and science educators around the world. Their **Inquiry Resources Page** (http://www.sln.org/resources/index.html) contains links to outstanding, interactive science activities designed by the finest science museums that exist. Activities range from a virtual cow's eye dissection for a unit on optics to a visit to Leonardo da Vinci's workshop. It also contains links to many great science activities at different museums and a searchable data base that allows you to quickly find science activities by topic and grade level. In addition, this location contains wonderful resources for collaborating with other science teachers around the world including: an on-line chat area, a projects area, and a bulletin board. Stop by and explore this important location supported by the National Science Foundation.

The best science museum we know for students is San Francisco's Exploratorium. It used to be that only Bay Area students were fortunate enough to access the many exciting and informative science exhibits there. Now, anyone with an Internet connection can participate. Be certain to pay a visit to the **Exploratorium Home Page** (http://www.exploratorium.edu/). You won't regret it. You may also wish to visit an excellent collection of links to interactive science museums around the world at **Hands-on Science Centers Worldwide** (http://www.cs.cmu.edu/~mwm/sci.html).

Excellent Internet Workshop assignments may be developed from the many resources located at science museums around the world. These often provide exciting simulations, demonstrations, or science puzzles for students.

The best science museum we know for students is San Francisco's Exploratorium.

Here are several examples of Internet Workshop assignments that might be developed for science units:

- **The Science of Cycling.** Invite your students to visit this Exploratorium location (http://www.exploratorium.edu/cycling/index.html) to gain a scientific view of a common activity—cycling. Use a jigsaw grouping technique and assign small groups to different aspects of the science of cycling: the wheel, braking and steering, frames and materials, aerodynamics, and human power. Have each group explore their section, completing the interactive simulations of items such as braking distance under different conditions, and then prepare a short presentation during Internet Workshop to explain the science of their area.

- **A Virtual Dissection of a Cow's Eye**. If you are doing a unit on optics or physiology, you may wish to set a bookmark for The Cow's Eye Dissection (http://www.exploratorium.edu/learning_studio/cow_eye/). Here students are taken step-by-step through the dissection with supporting glossary terms for the parts of the eye; RealAudio sound clips from the Exploratorium staff explain what is taking place. This location also contains a program students can download to your computer that will help them to learn the physiology of a cow's eye. Have students explore the entire WWW location in order to draw an accurate illustration of a cow's eye with each of the important parts labeled. On a separate page, have them explain how this important body part works. Post these next to your computer as they are completed. Afterwards, have them ask an expert from the Exploratorium via e-mail a really great question about how a cow's eye works. Post questions and answers.

- **Storm Science.** During a unit on weather for third or fourth graders, set a book mark to **Hurricane: Storm Science** (http://www.miamisci.org/hurricane/), a location at the Miami Science Museum. Have students track several hurricanes on an interactive map, make a storm hunter plane, read narratives from the members of a family that survived a hurricane, make several weather instruments, and contribute a story of a personal disaster or a work of art to the healing quilt. After the experience, have students send a really good question about the weather to a scientist at **The Mad Scientist Network** (http://www.madsci.org/). Post questions and answers as they arrive.

> Internet Workshop assignments such as these will enable you to support science units with Internet experiences that require little preparation time, yet provide important experiences for your students.

Internet Workshop assignments such as these will enable you to support science units with Internet experiences that require little preparation time, yet provide important experiences for your students.

E-MAIL FOR YOU

To: Colleagues
From: Beverley Powell (bpowell@ican.net)
Subject: My Romance with SchoolNet

Based on my experience in elementary teaching and information consulting, I think that all the teachers reading the new edition of this book should be aware of the educational potential of Canada's **SchoolNet** (http://www.schoolnet.ca).

SchoolNet is a collaboration between federal, provincial, and territorial governments, the education profession and industry. It ties in Canada's elementary and secondary schools, libraries and museums. It is a world-class educational resource offering a vast range of informational opportunities. For example:

The GrassRoots Program—http://www.schoolnet.ca/grassroots/
Motivates teachers and students to design, create and implement pedagogically sound interactive classroom projects for the Internet.

SchoolNet Digital Collections (SDC)—http://www.schoolnet.ca/collections/
Exhibits more than 100 collections from Canadian archives, libraries, museums, etc. A federal Industry Canada program contracts with young students to produce this multimedia portrait of Canada.

Special Needs Education Network—http://www.schoolnet.ca/sne/
Provides access to Internet resources for parents, teachers, schools and others in the education of students with special needs.

International Program—http://www.schoolnet.ca
Increases understanding among peoples of the world. Students and teachers around the world, with the help of sponsors, collaborate on projects using cultural themes. Expertise and exemplary practices are exchanged. Global entrepreneurship is encouraged. The World Bank has been involved.

SchoolNet RINGS Projects—http://stemnet.nf.ca/Projects/RINGS
Allows students to work together in groups or RINGS to contribute and discover new information using the Internet as a medium.

Other SchoolNet services: First Nations home page, provincial educational networks, resources by subject, newsletter, gopher, MOO, CHAT, mailing lists, newsgroups, and FTP. A new Teaching Ideas Exchange is planned for a near-future launch.

In short, **SchoolNet** is the crown jewel of the Canadian educational establishment. It is being used by a growing number of other countries. I believe that it carries implicit values of "caring"—a pedagogy nurturing manners and civility—and a platform we are going to hear a lot about in the future. Teachers and students all over the world are invited to enrich the international dimension of their learning, through collaborative projects, contributing to our future peace and prosperity.

Beverley Powell
Ottawa, Canada

Using Internet Project

Internet Project is useful in science for several reasons. First, it creates situations where students help one another to discover important concepts. Internet Project takes natural advantage of opportunities for socially mediated learning, opportunities that are so powerful within the Internet for science education.

Second, Internet Project provides natural opportunities for curricular integration with science and other subject areas. Internet Project requires students to engage in language arts experiences as they communicate with others via e-mail. These experiences also lend themselves to social studies, as students learn about different parts of the world and the social and cultural characteristics that define those locations. In addition, Internet Project often requires students to engage in math experiences. A project comparing weather patterns in different parts of the world, for example, will require students to record rain amounts, wind speed, and temperature and calculate the means for these over an extended period of time. Students may also have to compare and perhaps graph meteorological data reported from other locations. Thus, Internet projects in science contain inherent possibilities for curricular integration, an important concern for busy teachers who have to continually squeeze new additions to the curriculum within school days that do not expand.

Finally, when Internet Project is designed appropriately, it can foster scientific thinking. Thinking scientifically involves developing and evaluating best guesses about why things are the way there are. This can be an important part of any Internet project in science. Classes in different parts of the world often see the same issue in different ways because of different cultural traditions. Internet projects in science allows students to question one another, decide upon appropriate ways of evaluating competing hypotheses, gather information, and evaluate that information to reach conclusions that are agreed to by all parties.

> Internet projects in science allows students to question one another, decide upon appropriate ways of evaluating competing hypotheses, gather information, and evaluate that information to reach conclusions that are agreed to by all parties.

As you begin to consider Internet projects around science topics, be certain to visit the central locations for this approach described earlier to find examples of Internet Project: **NASA Quest's Online Interactive Projects** (http://quest.arc.nasa.gov/interactive/), **Global SchoolNet's Internet Project Registry** (http://www.gsn.org/pr/index.cfm), the **CIESE Online Classroom Projects** (http://k12science.stevens-tech.edu/currichome.html), **Kidlink** (http://www.kidlink.org/), or the **ATT Virtual Classroom** (http://www.att.virtualclassroom.org/index.html). Examples of projects posted previously (many continue to run each year) include:

- **International Boiling Point Project—**
  http://k12science.stevens-tech.edu/curriculum/boilproj
  This Internet project site has your students gather data, contribute your results to a common forum, and then analyze related data from around the world. A great Internet project for any class.

- **Earth Day Groceries Project**—http://www.earthdaybags.org/
Each year participating classes obtain grocery bags from local supermarkets, decorate them with environmental messages, and then return them to be used at the grocery store by customers (see Figure 7-5). Students share photos and reports of their accomplishments at a central site. A teacher at the Arbor Heights Elementary School in Seattle, Washington, has developed this wonderful environmental awareness project. Over 1,200 schools around the world participated last year, distributing nearly 400,000 grocery bags decorated with messages about the environment.

Figure 7-5.
The Earth Day Groceries Project (http://www.earthdaybags.org/), a great environmental awareness project site, developed by a teacher at Arbor Heights Elementary School in Seattle, Washington.

- **The Global Water Sampling Project**—
http://k12science.stevens-tech.edu/curriculum/waterproj/index.html
Interested in having your class study the water in your community? Here is an Internet Project for middle school and high school students to gather and share data about the water quality of a local river, stream, lake or pond with other fresh water sources around the world. Projects run in the fall and spring. This project is coordinated by the Center for Improved Engineering and Science Education (CIESE) located at Stevens Institute of Technology in Hoboken, New Jersey.

- **Monarch Watch**—http://www.MonarchWatch.org/
Here is a wonderful opportunity to participate in science studies

of the Monarch butterfly, sponsored by the Department of Entomology at the University of Kansas. The site contains an extremely comprehensive set of resources for studying Monarchs and sharing your observations, especially of their migration through your area. Find out about migration patterns, join one of several science projects, learn how to raise and release Monarchs in your classroom, learn how to start a butterfly garden near your classroom, and communicate with scientists who study these beautiful creatures. Set a bookmark!

- **The Journey North**—http://www.learner.org/jnorth/
  Over 250,000 students from all states in the US and provinces in Canada participate in this annual tracking of migrations and changes in daylight, temperatures, and all living things. Students share their own field observations with classrooms across the hemisphere. In addition, students are linked with scientists who provide their expertise directly to the classroom. Several migrations are tracked by satellite telemetry, providing live coverage of individual animals as they migrate

- **Where in the World is Cynthia San Francisco**—http://k12science.stevens-tech.edu/curriculum/weather/c3whome.html
  This project took students on a real world scientific investigation in which they used Internet resources to solve "the crime of the century." For a two week period, students received clues which took them to the location of the United States' leading nuclear physicist, Cynthia San Francisco, who had been kidnapped by a hostile organization. Clues came from real-time weather data, such as satellite images, weather stations and current weather maps. Students used interactive weather web sites in conjunction with the clues to determine the location of Dr. San Francisco. Along with each clue, classes received a hands-on experiment/ activity which students explored to better understand the weather concept to which the clue related. With each new clue students also received the answer to the previous one, thus allowing teachers and students to confirm that they were on the right track. During the project, students collaborated with other participating schools as well as with an expert meteorologist who would answer all of their weather related questions.

- **Night Of The Comet**—
  http://quest.arc.nasa.gov/comet/index.html
  Sponsored by NASA at their page for **Online Interactive Projects** (http://quest.arc.nasa.gov/interactive/index.html#archives), this project provided a forum for observing and discussing the passing of Comet Hyakutake. Students at over 100 locations around the world contributed their observations, questions, and answers

to this "First Virtual Star Party". Students could ask experts at NASA questions, send in their photos of the comet for viewing by others, read about comet facts, and participate in a series of experiments. Be certain to visit the location describing current projects (http://quest.arc.nasa.gov/interactive/) to discover new opportunities in space science. Set a bookmark!

- **Worldwide Weather Watch**
  A first grade teacher from Macedon, New York, and second grade teachers from Mound, Minnesota, posted this science project and attracted classrooms from the US; Canberra, Australia; and Tasmania. Primary school students around the world compared global weather conditions by sharing monthly e-mail reports about their weather, what they wore and what they were did outside. Students learned about different temperature scales, seasonal change in different hemispheres, measurement, math, cultural variation, and language arts.

Internet FAQ	
I am using Netscape 4.5 in my fourth grade class. Why do I always get an "Out of Memory" message after several students use the Internet in the morning?	There are a number of reasons for an "Out of Memory" message. This message is telling you that your RAM (Random Access Memory) or the memory allocated to Netscape has reached its limit. There are three possible solutions. First, see if you can obtain additional RAM. This requires inserting one or several new chips. You will need to talk to the technical support person at your school about this. Second, try having each student quit Netscape when they finish their session. Netscape keeps track of each site you visit and this list often gets lengthy, taking up much of Netscape's memory allocation. Quitting Netscape deletes this list and frees up memory. Third, you may choose to use an earlier version of Netscape. These require less RAM and will give you more memory to use as you navigate the WWW.

Using Internet Inquiry

Children have so many questions about the world around them and there are so many resources on the Internet to engage them in careful study of natural phenomena that Internet Inquiry should be an important part of your science program.

Internet Inquiry is a perfect vehicle for helping your students to think scientifically, critically, and carefully about the natural world. Students have so many questions about the world around them and there are so many resources on the Internet to engage them in careful study of natural phenomena that Internet Inquiry should be an important part of your science program.

You will recall that Internet Inquiry usually contains five phases: question, search, analyze, compose, and share. In the first phase, students identify an important question they wish to answer; usually this is related to the unit you are studying. You can support this phase by participating in group brainstorming sessions or by conducting an Internet Workshop around the topic of important questions that might be explored. In addition, you may wish to brainstorm individually with students who are having difficulty identifying an intriguing question. Another very nice strategy during this phase is to set a bookmark for science museums or other science sites and encourage students to explore these locations for an interesting question to address.

E-MAIL FOR YOU

To: Colleagues
From: Jan Barth <wex018@mail.connect.more.net>
Subject: A great science idea for the Internet

Hello!

   I would like to share an idea for classroom Internet use with you. You can use this idea if you have one or many terminals available. If only one terminal is available, a team of students can take turns searching and presenting information. If several terminals are available, then students can work either individually or in teams to get information. Sites should be bookmarked ahead of time to make the best use of the student's time in the classroom.

   In my 8th grade unit on conservation of resources, classes used the net to research an environmental disaster, the Exxon Valdez oil spill in Alaska on March 24, 1989. Each student prepared a report about how the spill occurred, the impact it had on plant and animal life and the food chain, and the methods of clean up after the spill. They used all their accumulated information about the spill and clean up efforts to devise a way to clean up a simulated oil spill in the classroom. Teams of 3 students worked cooperatively to determine the best way to clean up the spill. They were to consider cost of the materials and time for the clean up. If you desire, a competition can be held between teams to determine winners. Be sure to have a scoring guide in place before the teams begin their planning and the actual competition takes place. That way, students know what they are working toward.

   The students loved researching about the oil spill on the net. They found pictures, great information about how the spill occurred and information about the clean up and the effect of the spill on the living organisms. The great thing about researching this particular spill is that there are follow-up research projects that are collecting data about the long term affects to the ecosystem. Science and technology issues can be combined in a reflective essay where students think about the future of this ecosystem and the demand for oil which ultimately was responsible for the ecosystem's destruction.

   I hope I have given you some useful ideas about how to use the Internet. I would be glad to share more about the unit, just e-mail me!
   Good luck!

Jan Barth
Brookfield Middle School
Brookfield, Missouri 64628
wex018@mail.connect.more.net

During the second phase, search, students look for information and/or perform experiments to address the question they have posed. They may search on the Internet for useful resources, experiments, and demonstrations. Students should also be encouraged to use more traditional resources that may be found in their classroom or school library.

During the third phase, analyze, students analyze all of the information they have in order to respond to the question they initially posed. Sometimes this phase leads to a straightforward answer derived from several supporting lines of evidence: the results of an experiment, a graph of data, an e-mail response from a scientist, documentation from several books or Internet locations, or an e-mail message from another student studying the same question. Often, the analysis phase may be supported by peer conferences where students share their results and think about their meanings. Or, you may wish to use Internet Workshop to support students' analytic skills.

TEACHING TIP	Internet Inquiry often leads students to other interesting questions and ideas about the issues they study. When students develop an especially intriguing question during their work, invite them to discuss it with an expert via e-mail. Communicating with experts via e-mail can be very helpful to students and brings them into the real world of scientists who are also exploring interesting questions. Be certain, however, students only use these resources when they are unable to discover an answer on their own. People at ask-an-expert sites do not like to do homework for students who should really do it on their own. You can help by conducting an Internet Workshop session on how to ask the best question possible. A list of e-mail addresses and WWW locations where students may contact experts in science is provided in Figure 7-6.

The fourth phase, compose, requires students to compose a presentation of their work. This may be a written report, a poster board display, or an oral report with displays of evidence. You may wish to follow process writing procedures to support this phase by engaging students in drafting, revision, and editing conferences.

The final phase, share, is an opportunity for students to share their work with others and respond to questions about their investigation. Some teachers set aside a regular time one day a week for sharing Inquiry Projects as they are completed. You may wish to use a variation of an Author's Chair in your classroom by designating a Scientist's Chair for use during presentations of Inquiry projects. Alternatively, you may wish to have a science fair in your classroom at the end of each unit where students may display their work and answer questions as students circulate around, visiting each of the presentations. Or you may wish to conduct a Student-to-Student activity as described in Chapter six.

Internet Inquiry can be an exciting aspect of your classroom and your science program. It provides independent explorations of the scientific world, opportunities to contact real scientists about important issues, and opportunities to support the development of scientific thinking.

Figure 7-6.
WWW locations and e-mail addresses for contacting experts in various fields

General Locations for Contacting Experts in Science

Ask an Expert—http://www.askanexpert.com/askanexpert/
This is a general site with links to a wide range of experts.

Ask a Mad Scientist—http://www.madsci.org/
This wonderful resource will put you in touch wide a wide range of scientists around the world.

Ask a Science Expert—http://www.sciam.com/askexpert/
Obtain answers from experts in many scientific fields from the experts at the journal *Scientific American*.

Ask a Science Expert—http://sln.fi.edu:80/tfi/publications/askexprt.html
Obtain answers to questions about science from the Franklin Museum in Philadelphia.

Locations for Contacting Specific Types of Experts in Science

Ask an Astronaut—http://www.nss.org/askastro/home.html
Obtain answers to questions about space, science, and being an astronaut.

Ask an Astronomer—http://image.gsfc.nasa.gov/poetry//ask/askmag.html
Obtain answers to questions about stars, planets, comets, and other aspects of astronomy.

Ask Dr. Science—http://www.ducksbreath.com/index.html
Obtain answers to all kinds of questions about science.

Ask an Earth Scientist—http://www.soest.hawaii.edu/GG/ASK/askanerd.html
Obtain answers to questions about the natural workings and natural history of the Hawaiian Islands and the world.

Ask a Geologist—http://walrus.wr.usgs.gov/docs/ask-a-ge.html
e-mail: Ask a Geologist@usgs.gov
Obtain answers to questions about rocks, geology, and earth forms.

Ask a Gravity Expert—http://www.physics.umd.edu/rgroups/gen_rel_the/question.html
Obtain answers to questions about gravity.

Ask an Ocean Animal Expert—http://www.whaletimes.org/whaques.htm
e-mail: whaletimes@whaletimes.org
Obtain answers to questions about all types of marine animals.

Ask a Paleontology Expert—http://www.ucmp.berkeley.edu/museum/pals.html
Obtain answers to questions about dinosaurs and paleontology.

Ask a Vulcanologist—http://volcano.und.nodak.edu/vwdocs/ask_a.html
Obtain answers to questions about volcanoes from experts in this field.

E-MAIL FOR YOU

To: Colleagues
From: Ruth Musgrave <seamail@whaletimes.org>
Subject: Using Ask-an-Expert Sites Effectively

"Dear Jake, the SeaDog, I'm doing a report and need to know . . . "
One of the most popular portions of our website **WhaleTimes SeaBed**
(http://www.whaletimes.org/) is "Ask, Jake, the SeaDog." Kids and adults
from all over the world have written Jake to ask about whales, dolphins,
sharks, penguins and other ocean animals. Other experts have also opened
the door to their world and knowledge via their website or an "ask an
expert" site. This, of course, is one of the extraordinary capabilities of
the Internet—allowing students to ask questions direct to the expert.
Such interaction is the essence of the World Wide Web.
Here are some tips to help your students work with "ask an expert"
sites:
Be specific. "How long is a whale shark?" is easy to answer because it
is specific. Some questions, though, are a little vague, like, ". . . I
need to know everything about whales. . . ." Some seem dangerously
close to asking us to write their report, ". . . list three shark adaptations and describe how they're used . . ." WhaleTimes responds to all
requests. We can provide specific facts, general information, even help
with the vocabulary words which may be slowing a student down from
discovering the answer on their own. Not all "expert" sites respond to
questions in the same way or same time frame. Some reply with a list of
links or books, others may post answers on the website rather than a
personal reply. You may want to try a few to see the kinds of responses
you receive.
Plan ahead. When the e-mail says, ". . . and I need it in an hour . . ."
somebody may be disappointed. Although we try to answer within 48
hours, we may take as long as a week. Other sites may take longer to
respond. If part of your assignment requires students to ask an expert
questions, you'll need to allow them time to receive a response.
Be realistic. Getting an answer about fish should be easy, right? Maybe
not. There are 25,000 different kinds of fish. So asking for a list of
all of them isn't realistic. Sometimes finding information on some
topics is a challenge, even for the expert Experts are happy to supply
basic information, but generally are unable to spend hours researching
a student's project.
Be polite. Student's need to remember, experts are taking time out of
their day to help them. "Please" and "thank you" are always appreciated.

Whether asking "Jake, the SeaDog" about whales or a race car driver
about cars, interacting with an expert is an excellent way for students to
learn about careers, motivate them to learn more, make homework more personal, and hopefully, make a lasting impression on the satisfaction of
discovering something new.

Best wishes on your journey!
Ruth Musgrave, Director <seamail@whaletimes.org>
WhaleTimes SeaBed (http://www.whaletimes.org)

Using WebQuests

As you consider the use of WebQuests in your classroom, it is important to keep in mind that each should be evaluated in terms of these questions before deciding to use it in your classroom:

1. Does this WebQuest meet my curriculum goals and learning objectives?

2. How much time will this take my students?

3. Does the WebQuest require my students to think critically about information and evaluate the information they encounter?

4. Is this WebQuest developed so as to accommodate individual learning needs and interests?

5. Is there an opportunity for students to share the results of their WebQuest with the rest of the class for discussion and additional learning?

6. Do students know, in advance, how their work on the WebQuest will be evaluated?

7. Are all of the links on the WebQuest active and appropriate for my students?

When a WebQuest is able to meet each of these concerns, you have discovered a powerful tool to support the critical thinking, evaluation, and careful reasoning that is at the heart of any effective program in science education. These types of WebQuests can provide students with exciting opportunities to develop scientific thinking about the world around them.

If you teach biology, you might, for example, wish to have your students complete the WebQuest called **DNA for Dinner?** (http://www.gis.net/~peacewp/webquest.htm). This experience will challenge your students to evaluate the appropriateness of eating genetically engineered foods (see Figure 7-7). At the beginning, students gather and evaluate current information about the genetic engineering of food crops, discovering how genes in plants can be changed, why they are changed, and what the possible side effects might be, if any. Then they draft a law to guide what should be done to label genetically engineered products. This law is presented to the class and debated. Finally, your class e-mails government officials to tell them what type of legislation should be enacted. This is a wonderful teaching resource to get your students thinking critically about the scientific and the legal questions surrounding this issue.

If you teach physics, you might have your students complete the WebQuest called **How Far Does Light Go? Debate** (http://www.kie.berkeley.edu/KIE/web/hf.html). In this debate project, prepared at the University of California at Berkeley, your students are challenged to examine the scientific properties of light using evidence from the Internet and then take a position about one

When a WebQuest is able to meet each of these concerns, you have discovered a powerful tool to support the critical thinking, evaluation, and careful reasoning that is at the heart of any effective program in science education.

Figure 7-7.
DNA for Dinner (http://www.gis.net/~peacewp/webquest.htm) an example of a WebQuest for science education that challenges students to gather information, think critically, and then act on that information in a socially responsible manner.

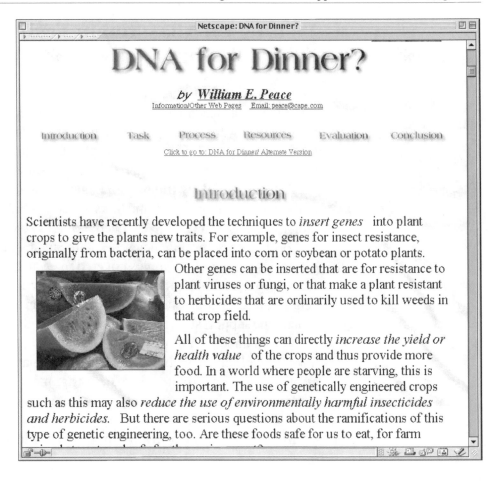

of two competing theories. After gathering information and taking positions, groups present their arguments and respond to questions from other students.

If your class is exploring ecology, you might wish to explore the many great resources in a unit called **Planet Earth** (http://powayusd.sdcoe.k12.ca.us/mtr/). Here, your students may participate in a series of activities that lead up to the WebQuest called **Conflict Yellowstone Wolves** (http://powayusd.sdcoe.k12.ca.us/mtr/ConflictYellowstoneWolf.htm). This requires students to investigate both sides of the issue surrounding the reintroduction of wolves into the Yellowstone ecosystem. After they decide upon their position, they use the information resources they have gathered to write an group letter to important public policy individuals asking them to support or reject the reintroduction of wolves to Yellowstone.

If you are interested in additional WebQuests for your science classroom, be certain to stop at the science section of Blue Web'n (http://www.kn.pacbell.com/wired/bluewebn/).

These and many more WebQuests may be used to bring important energy and enthusiasm to your science program as you engage your students in critical thinking about scientific information and application to real world issues and action. If you are interested in additional WebQuests for your science classroom, be certain to stop at the science section of **Blue Web'n** (http://www.kn.pacbell.com/wired/bluewebn/).

Visiting the Classroom: Leslie Bridge's High School Biology Classes in New Jersey

The biology class web site of Leslie Bridge is an outstanding example of how to effectively integrate Internet resources into a high school curriculum, regardless of subject area.

Exploring the high school biology website of Leslie Bridge, a teacher at Point Pleasant Beach High School in New Jersey, one immediately notices the work of a very organized, dedicated, and caring teacher. You also notice an outstanding example of how to effectively integrate Internet resources into a high school curriculum, regardless of subject area.

At Leslie's **Biology Index Web Pages** (http://www.ptpleasantbch.k12.nj.us/bridge/index.html) you will find links to her general biology class and her AP biology class (see Figure 7-8). Each provides students with a clear description of the course proficiencies, assignments, lecture notes, and a carefully organized outline of the topics covered in each class. Within these outlines Leslie provides links to web resources that will assist her students in understanding each topic she covers. These links are carefully chosen to provide exactly the support students might require, whether it is a virtual cell simulation for an understanding of cell biology, practice problems in genetics, or links to the Mendel Web for additional information on the life and experiments of this important biologist. Assignments are neatly organized by marking period and thoughtfully constructed.

Leslie uses Internet resources to expand upon her class lectures; they are not used to take students away from essential learning with flashy anima-

Figure 7-8.
Leslie **Bridge's Biology Index Web Pages** (http://www.ptpleasantbch.k12.nj.us/bridge/index.html) are an outstanding example of how to incorporate Internet resources into the high school science program.

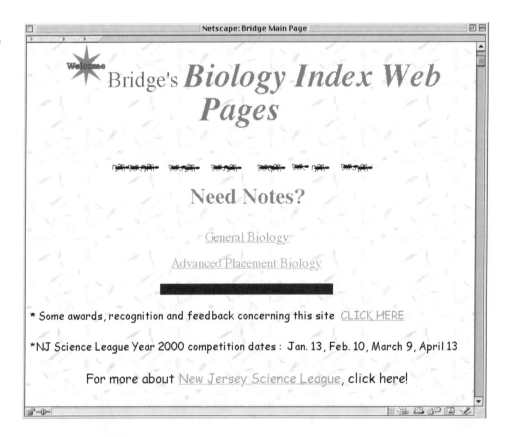

tions or sound. Each site has been carefully selected to closely fit the learning goals for that session. One imagines students exploring these great resources, drawing a better understanding of the information she presents in class. It is a wonderful example for all of us to consider for our own classes.

Instructional Resources on the Internet

AeroNet—http://library.thinkquest.org/25486/
> Interested in the physics of flight, as well as the history of aviation? Here is the site for you. A ThinkQuest award winner. Amazing visuals and demonstrations.

Air Travelers—http://www.omsi.edu/sln/air/
> For the upper elementary grade levels, this great resource provides an introduction to the basic principles of buoyancy, the properties of gases, temperature, and the technology involved in hot air ballooning. It includes activities, teacher background information, and a gallery of photos.

Bill Nye The Science Guy—http://nyelabs.kcts.org/
> A great resource related to the popular series on your local Public Broadcasting System television station. There is, of course, information on programming including home science demonstrations and lessons for upcoming topics. There is also a location to send the science guy e-mail. More importantly, there is a search engine that will connect you to outstanding science sites on the WWW. Science rules, indeed!

Critical Issues Forum—http://set.lanl.gov/programs/cif/
> The Los Alamos Nuclear Labs invite you and your students to participate in the study and articulation of public policy about how best to address issues and circumstances involved in safeguarding nuclear weapons. You will find challenging curricula in five areas focusing on the nuclear world. High school teams prepare and present a final position paper of their conclusions and recommendations to a panel of scientists at Los Alamos National Laboratory, thus giving them a say in decisions regarding our nuclear future.

El Niño or El No No—http://powayusd.sdcoe.k12.ca.us/elnino/El_Nino.htm
> Students in this WebQuest initially gather background information in order to become more familiar with the phenomenon know as El Niño. Then they analyze both historical and real time data from a buoy at the equator, as well as one in San Diego, to construct a model to determine if we are currently in an El Niño cycle. They write a speculation paper on the possible effects of El Niño and submit their work to a local community leader in San Diego.

Ewe 2—http://powayusd.sdcoe.k12.ca.us/ewe2/
> This is an inquiry-oriented activity that explores the science and ethics of cloning. It "…places students in the position to ask great questions, seek out the answers, develop new relationships, and take a stand on a current hot issue: cloning." This case study approach to WebQuests in-

cludes warm-up activities, instructions for teachers, forums, and grading rubrics.

General Chemistry Online—http://antoine.frostburg.edu/chem/senese/101/
Looking for a central site for your chemistry class. Here it is with everything you and your students need to supplement your classroom work. A great resource!

Help Your Child Explore Science—http://www.nsta.org/parents/
Developed by the National Science Teachers Association, this informative brochure may be printed out and distributed at your school's Back to School Night to help parents and guardians understand what they can do to support their child in science.

Jumbo—http://www.jumbo.com/
Looking for shareware and freeware to download and use in your classroom for science units? Here is the location with the largest set of programs to download on the WWW. Check out the science and the education sections for many useful resources.

Kit and Kaboodle—http://www.kitkaboodle.org/
A creative science curriculum with many exciting science learning experiences for grades 3–5. Registration is required but the resources are free. Funded by the National Science Foundation.

Live from Antarctica—http://quest.arc.nasa.gov/antarctica/index.html
Here are enough resources for an entire year's project on science taking place in Antarctica. Dates and times for a series of related television programs are listed, as well as a teacher's guide and classroom lessons, questions and answers between students and scientists, a bibliography of related resources, links to other sites with information on the Antarctic, weekly newspapers published in the Antarctic, and contact with scientists studying the plant life and the ozone hole.

Mars Missions—http://marsweb.jpl.nasa.gov/
During a five-day period this past year, more than 260,000,000 visited the WWW location of the Mars Pathfinder Project to learn about the most recent developments and view the latest photos from the Martian surface. Here is the main site for all of NASA's scientific explorations of Mars, including upcoming visits. Stop by to see some remarkable images and learn about some remarkable scientists!

Mr. Biology's High School Website—http://www.hiline.net/~siremba/
Looking for resources for your high school biology course. Here it is. Links to sample quizzes, interactive simulations, virtual dissections, and much more. Set a bookmark!

Physics 2000—http://www.Colorado.EDU/physics/2000/index.pl
From the University of Colorado, this site introduces principles of physics in an interactive and friendly manner with interactive simulations. Subjects range from electromagnetic waves and particles to microwave ovens to classic experiments in atomic physics.

Rainforest Action Network—http://www.ran.org/ran/
If you are engaged in an ecology or rainforest unit, here is a great location to find out about the latest efforts to preserve these important parts of our ecosystem. Many links for those who are serious about preserving our planet and its systems.

Science Resource Center—http://lapeer.org/Search/Search.html
A great collection of demonstrations, simulations, labs and other resources contributed by science teachers around the world.

Skateboard Science—http://www.exploratorium.edu/skateboarding/
Want to get your skateboarding students interested in science? Here is the place. Wonderful resources to explain how skateboarders perform all their tricks. From the talented folks at the Exploratorium Museum in San Francisco.

The Franklin Museum Science Institute—http://www.fi.edu/
This is one of the finest science museums around, devoted to helping children think scientifically and explore the fantastic world around them. There are so many great experiences for students it is hard to know where to start. Perhaps with the science of thrill rides? Maybe an interactive exhibit on the workings of the heart? Or maybe explore the adaptations of animals to urban environments? You may even follow the life of a high school biology classroom. Wonderful. Set a bookmark!

The Great Plant Escape—http://www.urbanext.uiuc.edu/gpe/index.html
This series of mystery adventures from the Illinois Cooperative Extension Service is designed for 4th and 5th grade students who are asked to "help Detective Le Plant and his partners Bud and Sprout unlock the amazing mysteries of plant life." The site combines web-based activities with hands-on experiments. It includes six cases, a glossary, links, and a guide for teachers.

The Hubble Space Telescope's Public Page—
http://oposite.stsci.edu/pubinfo/
Here is the location for the Hubble Space Telescope and all of the wonderful science taking place with this instrument. Many incredible photos of deep space illustrating a number of new insights discovered with this technology. Many links for teachers and students interested in space study are also found here.

The Jason Project—http://www.jasonproject.org/
Each year, the JASON Foundation for Education sponsors an amazing scientific expedition with curriculum developed for grades 4 through 8. Students participate in the expedition through "… live, interactive programs."

The Nine Planets: A Multimedia Tour of the Solar System—http://seds.lpl.arizona.edu/billa/tnp/
Want to get your upper elementary grade and middle school students interested in space science? Have them take this tour of the solar system, visiting each of the planets and their major moons. Many stunning photographs and the latest science resulting from recent probes to these unusual worlds. Set a bookmark!

The Science of Hockey—http://www.exploratorium.edu/hockey/
Why is ice slippery? How can you make a puck fly 100 mph? Are you fast enough to stop a puck? Developed with the assistance of the NHL's San Jose Sharks, this site explains the science behind hockey. It includes RealVideo and Audio interviews with top scientists and NHL players and coaches.

The Why Files—http://whyfiles.news.wisc.edu/index.html
Funded by the National Science Foundation and located at the University of Wisconsin, this location provides you and your students with science information behind recent news stories. What evidence is there of life on Mars? A climatologist studies changes in the Earth's climate. What causes Mad Cow disease and how do humans catch it? How does amber preserve DNA? These and many more questions are answered here along with related links to other sites on the WWW.

Virtual Labs and Simulations—
http://home.stlnet.com/~grichert/applets.html
If you are looking for a way to demonstrate different scientific phenomenon with virtual modeling and simulations, here is the place for you. A wonderful set of simulations including things such as Galileo's Law of Falling Bodies, Newton's First Law—Inertia, Hooke's Law, Kinematic Friction and Kinetic Energy, and much more. If you recognize any of these, be certain to pay a visit. Great examples for your classes to see.

Webcytology: An Exploration of Unicellular Life—
http://library.thinkquest.org/27819/
Designed for students in grades 5–12 interested in exploring unicellular biology. The site contains an amazing interactive simulation where "...users create their own species of life and then put it to the test in a virtual petri dish where it will both respond to varying environmental conditions and interact with other people's organisms." Create your cell and see how it survives.

Virtual Frog Dissection Kit—http://www-itg.lbl.gov/vfrog/
An outstanding demonstration of the potential of the Internet for science education. Think of all the poor frogs that will be saved! This site, developed by the Lawrence Berkeley National Laboratory contains a great dissection experience where students learn about a frog's internal organs and systems. Videos are also available. At the end, students may also play the Virtual Frog Builder Game, where they try to put a frog back together. Set a book mark!

VirtualEarthquake—http://vflylab.calstatela.edu/edesktop/VirtApps/
VirtualEarthQuake/VQuakeIntro.html
VirtualEarthquake is an interactive computer program designed to introduce you to the concepts of how an earthquake epicenter is located and how the Richter Magnitude of an earthquake is determined. Concepts such as seismometer, seismograph, and epicenter are explained and students see how scientists study earthquakes.

VolcanoWorld—http://volcano.und.nodak.edu/
Here is a wonderfully interactive location to explore volcano science.

View maps of active volcanos, talk to vulcanologists, view videos of the most recent eruptions, explore a host of educational links. This is a tremendous resource for a somewhat unusual, but very exciting, topic.

You Can With Beakman and Jax—http://www.beakman.com/
Based on the television program *Beakman's World,* this location is great for curious young scientists who want to figure out how the world works. It has a location where students can ask questions about the natural world and also an interactive set of demonstrations illustrating answers to questions such as: What does smoking do to your lungs? How does a thermometer work? Why does the moon look bigger on the horizon? How does a sundial work? How does the moon power the tides? A good question is a powerful thing!

Bulletin Boards for Science Education

The National Science Teachers Bulletin Board—http://www.nsta.org/messages/
A nicely organized and active bulletin board run by the NSTA. All science topics covered.

Teacher Talk Bulletin Board—http://earthsky.worldofscience.com/BBS/Teacher-Talk/index.html
A bulletin board for science educators run by the people who organize the Earth and Sky Series on NPR. All science topics are covered.

Connect with Schools and Educators—http://www.sln.org/schools/index.html
The location for the bulletin board run by the Science Learning Network. All science topics covered.

Usenet Newsgroups for Science Education

k12.ed.science—Discussion about the science curriculum in K–12 education.

misc.education.science—Discussion of issues related to science education.

k12.chat.elementary—Informal discussion among elementary students, grades K–5.

k12.chat.junior—Informal discussion among students in grades 6–8.

k12.chat.teacher—Informal discussion among teachers in grades K–12.

Math: Thinking Mathematically on the Internet

 E-MAIL FOR YOU

To: Our readers
From: djleu@syr.edu (Don Leu), ddleu@syr.edu (Debbie Leu)
Subject: Using the Internet for Math Education

Since 1989, when the National Council of Teachers of Mathematics (NCTM) published *Curriculum and Evaluation Standards for School Mathematics*, a change in the way we view mathematics education has taken place. We see it in school classrooms where teachers increasingly engage students in critical thinking and communication through math experiences. These require basic skill knowledge but also emphasize mathematical insight, reasoning, and problem solving. Increasingly, children realize math is a sense-making experience as they become active participants in creating knowledge and communicating that knowledge to others. These changes continue today as the NCTM has just published even newer standards for mathematics (See http://www.nctm.org).

The Internet can help you to realize the potential all children have for thinking mathematically. There are many useful sites to engage your students in important math experiences and to help them communicate with others about what they are learning. We were certainly surprised to find such an active and exciting math community on the Internet. The National Science Foundation has supported the development of several outstanding central sites. In addition, there are sites with intriguing puzzles, software to download, weekly math challenges, biographies of famous women in math, mathematicians who answer your students' questions, lesson plans, a homework center for students, and even ol' Blue Dog who will answer any four-function math problem your students throw his way . . . by barking out the answer! We hope you enjoy all of these locations.

Don and Debbie

Teaching With the Internet: Elissa Morgan's Class

"I want to show you our Web Math". Clarissa pulled her mom over to the Internet computer in the Math classroom. They sat down to see what Clarissa had been talking about every night during dinner. It was Open House evening and Clarissa had her mom come early so they would have the Internet all to themselves. "See, here is what we do each day at the beginning. We read about the numbers for today."

Since today was the first of the month, they read a portion of the page for the number one at **About Today's Date** (http://www.nottingham.ac.uk/education/number/), a site located at Nottingham University in England:

> An ace is number one in playing cards. French playing cards are marked "1" instead of "A". A cyclops is a creature with one eye and a dromedary is a camel with only one hump. There is only one of lots of things. There is only one President of the United States, there is only one Atlantic Ocean and there is only one you. All of these are unique. (http://www.nottingham.ac.uk/education/number/Num1.htm)

"Ms. Morgan has a quiz to see if somebody knows the new vocabulary words when we go home. I print it out for my group so we all know it," Clarissa said.

"Today she asked us what a dromedary was and we knew the answer in my group," Clarissa said proudly.

"See, now here we got the Problem of the Week (see Figure 8-1). These are to tease our brains and make us smarter and we got to work together 'cause that's the best way to learn,' Ms. Morgan says. Julie and me, we always figure it out, but sometimes we ask our mentors to help. See, all we need to do is send them an e-mail message and they give us good clues. It was easy this week. See?"

Clarissa had selected the bookmark for **Math Problem of the Week** (http://forum.swarthmore.edu/elempow/) a site with a new math problem each week that really challenged students to think. This was a regular, weekly assignment in Elissa Morgan's room. Often there would be a group of students at the computer talking about the problem and trying to figure out the best strategy to solve the answer. Usually she didn't mind since she wanted her students to learn how to learn together. Sometimes, though, she had to tell them to be a bit quieter when they got too excited and noisy. This was a good noise, though. She could usually hear them arguing about how to solve the problem as they learned from one another.

"See, and here's what I'm doin'. It's a report on famous women in Math and it's about Hypatia. She discovered parabolas but she was killed in Egypt 'cause they thought she was a witch. She was just smart. I'm putting my report on our class web page. Ms. Morgan's helping me." As she spoke, Clarissa showed her mom some of the locations she had used in her re-

Figure 8-1.
An example from the **Math Problem of the Week** site (http://forum.swarthmore.edu/elempow/)

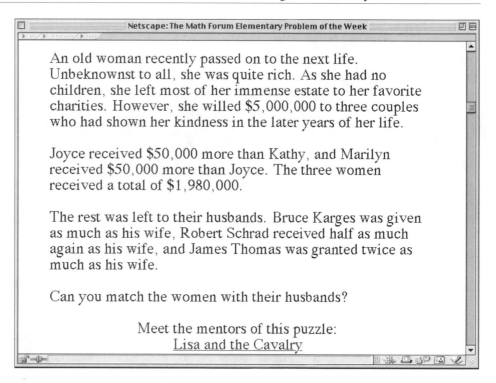

An old woman recently passed on to the next life. Unbeknownst to all, she was quite rich. As she had no children, she left most of her immense estate to her favorite charities. However, she willed $5,000,000 to three couples who had shown her kindness in the later years of her life.

Joyce received $50,000 more than Kathy, and Marilyn received $50,000 more than Joyce. The three women received a total of $1,980,000.

The rest was left to their husbands. Bruce Karges was given as much as his wife, Robert Schrad received half as much again as his wife, and James Thomas was granted twice as much as his wife.

Can you match the women with their husbands?

Meet the mentors of this puzzle:
Lisa and the Cavalry

search, **Past Notable Women of Mathematics** (http://www.cs.yale.edu/homes/tap/past-women-math.html) and **History of Mathematics** (http://www-groups.dcs.st-and.ac.uk/~history/index.html).

"And here is where we did our fractals project," Clarissa said as she showed her mom the site called **Fractals** (http://math.rice.edu/~lanius/frac/). "Fractals are cool! Here is the Sierpinski Triangle we made when we did this (see Figure 8-2). We had to measure and find all the midpoints in our triangles." Clarissa pointed to the bulletin board and the large fractal made from students' separate fractals.

Then, Clarissa took her mother over to another location in the room where there was a display called food prices around the world. It showed the results of an Internet project. Their class had posted an Internet project designed to compare the price of a Big Mac, regular fries, and soda, along with other food items around the world. Each class reported on the price for each item and then used the average hourly salary for their country to calculate how long it took to earn each food item. The participating classes shared the results with one another so they could compare the price of common food items in each of their countries. Each participating class was completing a unit on statistics. They studied common statistical concepts by working through the lessons at a site called **Statistics Every Writer Should Know** (http://www.robertniles.com/stats/) and then linked to an excellent resource containing economic statistics for each participating country, **Finding Data on the Internet** (http://www.robertniles.com/data/). "See, we need to work 11 minutes for a Big Mac," said Clarissa. "And in Russia they have to work two hours."

Figure 8-2.
The Sierpinski Triangle, a location at **Fractals** (http://math.rice.edu/~lanius/frac/).

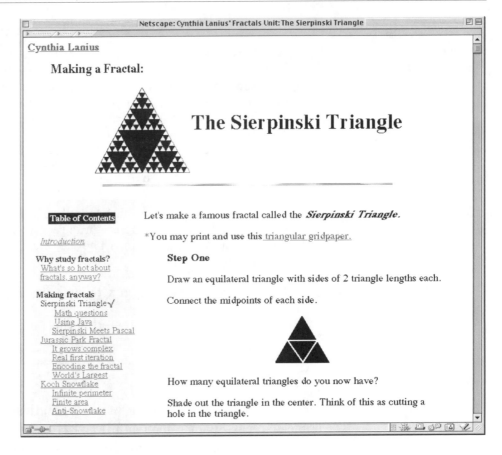

Clarissa's mom was thinking that math had certainly changed since she went to school. She had a conversation with Ms. Morgan about this because she wasn't certain how she could help Clarissa at home. Ms. Morgan gave her a copy of an article she had obtained at the US Department of Education web site and printed out, **Helping Your Child Learn Math** (http://www.ed.gov/pubs/parents/Math/index.html). It contained all kinds of useful ideas for parents to use at home to assist their children. "Yes," Clarissa's mom thought to herself on the way home, "Math certainly has changed."

Lessons From the Classroom

Clarissa's story from Elissa Morgan's classroom illustrates several useful lessons for us to consider as we look at the Internet for Math education. First, the Internet profoundly changes the possibilities for Math education in fundamental ways. The availability of extensive resources on the Internet enriches the nature of mathematics education and changes it as much as when school textbooks first appeared for elementary students during the 18th and 19th centuries. The Internet allows teachers and students to study mathematics in important, new ways consistent with the recent standards adopted by the National Council of Teachers of Mathematics and the emphasis on

First, the Internet profoundly changes the possibilities for Math education in fundamental ways. The availability of extensive resources on the Internet enrich the nature of mathematics education and change it as much as when school textbooks first appeared for elementary students during the 18th and 19th centuries.

mathematical insight, reasoning, and problem solving. As with other areas of study, we will see that Internet Workshop, Internet Project, Internet Inquiry, and WebQuests are all possible in Mathematics education. Each may be used to integrate learning with other subject areas.

In addition, the Internet provides a wealth of mathematical data which may be used to help students learn more about themselves and the rest of the world. Just as Clarissa's class developed new insights about living standards around the world, your class may use the Internet to reach new conclusions based on data available through the Internet.

Finally, the Internet provides opportunities for students to communicate their developing insights and to compare them with those of other students, in their class and around the world. Increasingly, math lessons ask students to communicate their insights about patterns they see in the world around them. The Internet provides important opportunities to accomplish this.

Central Sites for Math Education

You can use a number of sites for a jumping off point as you begin to explore the Internet for math education. Most of these have links that will take you to a wide range of locations designed to support your math program. These will include sites that may be used for Internet Workshop, Internet Project, Internet Inquiry, or WebQuests. Central sites may also contain links to lesson plans and locations where you can share ideas with other teachers about math education. A few will contain links to publications that allow you to keep up with developments in math education. Usually these central sites are more permanent and stable locations; they will be less likely to move to another location, disappear, or turn into a subscription service that will require a fee. They are often supported by a state or federal unit, or by a non-profit organization or university. We encourage you to begin your explorations at one of these central sites.

As with science, one of the better central sites is the **Eisenhower National Center for Mathematics and Science Education** (http://www.enc.org:80/classroom/index.htm). We especially like the location in the "Reform in Action" section called the "Digital Dozen", 13 great sites on the Internet for math and science education that change each month. There is also an archive for sites that have received this award in the past. In addition, there is a great selection of lesson and activity locations and a "Resource Finder" that will help you locate curriculum resources for classroom projects. Be certain to begin your exploration in math at the Eisenhower National Center for Mathematics and Science Education.

Another outstanding central site is the **Math Forum** (http://forum.swarthmore.edu/) at Swarthmore College, funded by the National Science Foundation (see Figure 8-3). The goal of this location is "... to build a community that can be a center for teachers, students, researchers, parents,

---

The Internet provides a wealth of mathematical data which may be used to help students learn more about themselves and the rest of the world.

As with science, the best single site may be the Eisenhower National Center for Mathematics and Science Education (http://www.enc.org:80/index.htm).

Another outstanding central site is the Math Forum (http://forum.swarthmore.edu/) at Swarthmore College, funded by the National Science Foundation.

E-MAIL FOR YOU

To: Fellow Educators
From: Linda Shearin
Subject: Enhancing communication between school and home

Hello fellow educators,

Much has been written about using the Internet and the WWW to communicate with others around the world in order to bring a variety of virtual experiences into our classrooms. I have found the Internet to be very useful in this way.

However, we can also use the communication opportunities available via the Internet to connect with our students and parents in new and different ways that strengthen the relationship between school and home.

I have provided my students with my e-mail address so that they [and their parents] would have another avenue for communication. My homework assignments are posted online weekly. The web site I use also has an e-mail option. I will admit that initially I did have reservations. Would I get a lot of prank e-mail? Would parents and students take advantage of the 'easy' access?

To date, my initial concerns have been unfounded. Parents and students both have readily taken to this new dimension in communication with the teacher. All of us have found e-mail communication to be invaluable. When a student is absent they can more easily be kept up to date with assignments. It is easier for me to respond to parent concerns, and provide feedback. We even use e-mail to set up appointments such as a phone conference or school conference at a mutually agreeable time thus reducing time spent on phone tag.

But what I find most exciting in expanding my communication options is the opportunity the Internet provides me for mentoring my students. Being available to my students via the Internet helps me to provide timely instruction as and when it is needed. Questions can be addressed outside of the normal school timeframe.

While not a perfect solution, realizing that all students do not yet have Internet access, enhancing communication between school and home via the Internet is a powerful tool in helping students achieve success.

Linda Shearin

Fred J. Carnage Gifted & Talented Magnet School for Accelerated Studies in Math, Science, and Technology

Raleigh, NC

educators, citizens at all levels who have an interest in mathematics education." They have done an exceptional job by providing many useful resources for teachers, students, and others. In addition to links to useful math sites on the web, the Math Forum maintains chat areas and listservs/mailing lists for students and teachers to share ideas and questions about math. **Dr. Math** (http://forum.swarthmore.edu/dr.math/) is also on call to answer questions from you or your students. Dr. Math is a great resource for homework! The Math Forum is an exceptional site on the web. Be certain to explore the many resources here.

Figure 8-3.
The home page for **The Math Forum** (http://forum.swarthmore.edu/), an important central site for math education.

A third central location you may wish to visit is **Math Archives** (http://archives.math.utk.edu/newindex.html). Located at the University of Tennessee, this site has an especially good collection of interactive math experiences and free software you may wish to download and use in your classroom. The Math Archives provide resources for mathematicians at all levels, not just K–12 educators, but there are many wonderful resources here for the K–12 educator. There is also a nice collection of links to WWW resources for math in a section called "Topics in Mathematics." You will find a visit to this location well worth your time.

The Math section at the **Resources** (http://www.schoolnet.ca/home/e/resources/) section of **Canada's SchoolNet** (http://www.schoolnet.ca/home/e/) may also be useful as you begin to explore links to math resources. This location contains a number of links to math sites you will find useful. At the present time, this list is not organized by topic or grade level but SchoolNet is quickly evolving and it looks like this will be an important resource.

The **Math** (http://www.csun.edu/~vceed009/math.html#Math) section of **Web Sites and Resources for Teachers** (http://www.csun.edu/~vceed009/) is also very useful as a jumping off point into the web for math education. These sites are located at California State Northridge and maintained by two professors in the School of Education. At the Math site, there are many links to locations with lesson plans for busy teachers. There are also links to a number of good board games. Another section contains links to ideas and activities to support your math program. All of the sites at this location contain resources that are useful to classroom teachers. It appears to have been developed by people who really understand teachers' classroom needs.

Finally, you may wish to participate in one of the mailing lists located at the end of this chapter, or view one of several discussion boards available to math educators. One of the more important conversations taking place is located in the **Teachers Lounge** (http://forum.swarthmore.edu/t2t/discuss/) of the Math Forum. Join in and share your questions, concerns, and insights or just follow the conversations taking place.

Using Internet Workshop

If you explore some of the central sites described above you will quickly find many exciting locations related to the units in your math program. These are great places to use as you develop assignments for Internet Workshop, the fastest way to bring the resources of the WWW into your classroom for math and other areas of your curriculum. Developing an assignment for Internet Workshop is easy. Locate a site on the Internet with content related to your math unit and set a bookmark for this location. Then develop an activity that requires students to use that site. Assign this activity to your students to complete during the week. Some teachers will develop a number of different activities related to the site and then ask students to complete as many as possible during their computer time. Work completed during the week may be shared during a weekly workshop session.

Many teachers will develop assignments for Internet Workshop from one of several locations on the web that provide a weekly math challenge for students, a math problem that requires careful thinking to solve. Alternatively, some teachers will just print out this math problem each week and duplicate copies for their students. One location with weekly problems for students is **Brain Teasers** (http://www.eduplace.com/math/brain/), a location sponsored by Houghton Mifflin. Each week, a new problem is presented by grade level. If students require it, they may click on a "Hint" or a "Solution" button. There is also an archive of problems used in the past.

The Little Math Puzzle Contest (http://www.microtec.net/academy/mathpuzzle/) is another site with a weekly math problem for students, especially students in Canada. This site presents a single, ungraded problem for students. There is also an archive and a winner's list. You must have a password to access the answer at this site. Teachers may obtain the password via e-mail.

Other sites, too, may be used for Internet Workshop. These may be located by exploring some of the central sites for math education described earlier and creating activities related to your units of study. Here are just a few ideas to get you started with your own Internet Workshop assignments:

- **Dr. FreeMath**—http://ois.unomaha.edu/drfreemath/
  Dr. FreeMath is an electronic mail project where one mathematics question per month will be researched and answered from each elementary class. Past examples of questions include: How much water evaporates in the ocean each year? Why is any number to the zero power equal to one? What is pi not really equal to 22/7? Have individuals bring their best questions to Internet Workshop and then work together to pick one that is sent to Dr. FreeMath.

- **Biographies of Women Mathematicians**—
  http://www.agnesscott.edu/lriddle/women/women.htm
  This site contains a developing set of biographies. The group creating this site is looking for others to research famous women mathematicians and submit additional biographies. Invite students to read about one of these favorite women and bring their story to Internet Workshop.

- **MacTutor History of Mathematics Archive**—
  http://www-groups.dcs.st-and.ac.uk/~history/
  Extensive links to sites with information about the history of math. A nice location to set up a weekly question related to math history that will help students develop a richer understanding of math concepts.

- **The Fruit Game**—http://www.2020tech.com/fruit/index.html
  A simple interactive game, originally called Nim, with a hidden trick. See if your students can explain the trick in writing. Share your best guesses during Internet Workshop.

- **Interactive Mathematics Miscellany and Puzzles**—
  http://www.cut-the-knot.com/
  Forget the title. Check this site out! It has an incredible list of links to games, activities, and puzzles that will keep your class busy all year with Internet Workshop! Set a bookmark!

Using Internet Project

While it may take more time and planning, Internet Project is an important instructional tool for several reasons. First, Internet Project supports cross-

Internet FAQ	
Sometimes when I go to a site on the WWW it tells me that I need a "Java-capable browser". How do I know if I have this? What does this mean?	You have a Java-capable browser if you are using Netscape 3.0 or later, or if you use Internet Explorer 3.0 or later. A Java-capable browser is one that will run special programs put on the web to assist with animation, sound, or video. These enhance the multimedia capabilities of web locations. You are using a Java-capable browser if you see animated objects at some web sites. These might be a message that moves along the bottom of your window or objects that spin around in place. Java-capable browsers also permit multiple windows to be open at any single web site.

curricular learning experiences. Language arts is almost always a part of any Internet project in math since projects require students to communicate with others about their thinking. In addition, social studies and science are also frequently a part of these projects. An insightful teacher will plan to take advantage of these natural opportunities for cross-curricular integration.

In math, Internet Project is important because it encourages students to work together to develop the ability to think mathematically. Part of thinking mathematically is being able to communicate problem solving strategies to others and to listen as others describe different approaches to proofs. This is supported when classrooms are communicating with one another, modeling their approaches to solutions and explaining their answers.

> Internet projects in math are also important because they encourage students to work together to develop the ability to think mathematically.

There are several examples of Internet Project in math that run continuously and have a site on the WWW. **The Noon Day Project: Measuring the Circumference of the Earth** (http://k12science.stevens-tech.edu/noonday/noon.html) is a project in which students recreate the classic experiment conducted by Eratosthenes over 2,200 years ago to determine the circumference of the Earth. Collaborating with students from other schools throughout the world at roughly the same time, classes measure the length of a shadow cast by a meter stick, share this data electronically, use scale drawings and a spreadsheet to make comparisons, and use this information to estimate the circumference of the earth.

Another project site for mathematics is **The Global Grocery List Project** (http://www.schoollife.net/schools/ggl). This project has your students enter grocery list data from their location and then conduct a variety of analyses using a worldwide data base of prices and foods contributed by other classes around the world. It is an outstanding way in which you can integrate social studies with mathematics.

There are also several stock market competitions that take place between classrooms on the Internet. **Good News Bears** (http://www.ncsa.uiuc.edu:80/edu/RSE/RSEyellow/gnb.html), a year-long stock market game for middle school students, is one such location. Here, students participate in a contest using on-line stock market data as they do research and then buy and sell stocks in an attempt to maximize their portfolio. It is an excellent experience that brings mathematical thinking to real world problems and solutions. Another is called **Stock Market Millionaires Club** (http://students.washington.edu/jwerle/stockproject.htm#top).

E-MAIL FOR YOU

To: Colleagues

From: Jodi Moore (jbmoore@pen.k12.va.us)

Subject: Using the Internet for Math

Hi! The Internet is a tool that will motivate and excite all your students, especially in math. There are countless web sites available to entice even the most reluctant learners. I print a problem for my class each week from **Brain Teasers** (http://www.eduplace.com/math/brain/) or **The Elementary Problem of the Week** (http://forum.swarthmore.edu/elempow/). The problems provide an avenue for healthy competition, as well as practice and discussion within the classroom.

My students also frequent various web sites which provide useful information for research and reference on mathematicians and related mathematical topics such as the **MacTutor History of Mathematics Archive** (http://www-groups.dcs.st-and.ac.uk/~history/). This information enhances classroom instruction and helps math takes on a new and exciting face. Enlivening the classroom environment with the real world is motivating. Students display confidence locating information readily and they are able to apply the knowledge they have collected.

Lastly, students in my class have been able to integrate history and math by joining seven other schools from the U.S., Newfoundland (Canada), Germany, Saudi Arabia, and Australia in an Internet project. During a three-month period we all agreed to write four different articles with information about our school and the history and geography of our area. After composing each short research project, students at each school wrote five math problems based on the research. This was then sent using e-mail to the other six schools. Students in the participating schools solved the problems and sent back their answers. We were able to check the solutions as well as analyze any errors. It was especially interesting to listen as students decided if it was a computational error, an error in writing the problem, or a misinterpretation of the data. My students also benefited from the submissions of the other six schools. Each of the teachers in the project often collaborated to "lead" the problems in a particular area to provide appropriate practice and subsequent mastery.

I thoroughly enjoy the opportunities the Internet allows me to provide my students. Just like any other new toy, limits must be set and specific rules must be devised. Still, this powerful tool will literally make all the difference in the world with students. I can honestly say I am glad technology has arrived!

Jodi Moore, 6th grade teacher   Battlefield Middle School
jbmoore@pen.k12.va.us   11120 Leavells Rd.
                                     Fredericksburg, VA 22407

Other projects may be joined by reviewing projects posted at the traditional locations on the Internet such as **Global SchoolNet's Internet Project Registry** (http://www.gsn.org/pr/index.cfm), **SchoolNet's Grassroots Project Gallery** (http://www.schoolnet.ca/grassroots/e/project.centre/search-projects.html), and **Intercultural E-mail Classroom Connections** (http://www.stolaf.edu/network/iecc/). If you see a project that matches your instructional needs for an upcoming unit, be certain to join.

Alternatively, you may wish to work with your class during Internet Workshop to develop an Internet project in math that you post and invite others to join. Be certain to plan this far enough in advance that you can attract enough participants and develop communication links. Examples of projects that you may wish to post for others to join include:

- **Problems for Problem Solvers** Invite other classrooms to join you in exchanging interesting math problems to solve together. Appoint one class each week to be the lead class on a rotating basis. The lead class is responsible for developing five problems or puzzles that are sent to participating classes who then have a week to return the answers. The lead class is also responsible for responding to each class and the solutions they suggested. Each week, another class becomes the lead class and circulates five new problems or puzzles for everyone to solve.

- **Heads or Tails?** Here is a simple probability project for younger students. Invite other classes to flip a coin from their country ten times and record the number of times that heads turn up. Repeat this ten times. Then have them send the results to your class. Record the data, write up the results, and send back a report with the percentage of times heads turns up during a coin toss. You may wish to invite participating schools to exchange the coins they flipped so that young children become familiar with different currency systems.

- **Graph Your Favorite** (http://www1.minn.net:80/~schubert/Graph.html) This activity was completed by students in grade 2, 4, and 6 classrooms in Michigan, Minnesota, Canada, Australia, and California. Students in eight participating classes voted each week on their favorite item in one category: pets, holidays, sports, school subjects, food. The data was calculated separately for boys and for girls. Participating classes sent their data to the project coordinator who compiled the results each week and e-mailed it to everyone for further analysis. Students used the data in raw form to make their own spreadsheets, both manually and by computer. They also made computer bar graphs and pie graphs, as well as manually drawn bar graphs. Then they analyzed the graphs and drew conclusions.

TEACHING
TIP

Developing an Internet Project in Statistics

Here is a project for middle school or high school students who are exploring statistics. Invite a group of participating classes to join you in working through the experiences at **Statistics Every Writer Should Know** (http://www.robertniles.com/stats/). After completing these experiences, have each class develop group projects to analyze and report comparative statistics from their country, state, or nation on some category where numerical data is kept. Use the site **Finding Data on the Internet** (http://www.robertniles.com/data/) to obtain these data. Then share the reports that were developed and provide responses to each report.

Using Internet Inquiry

Part of thinking mathematically involves identifying questions that are important to you and then seeking answers to those questions. Internet Inquiry allows you to support these more independent experiences among your students.

Part of thinking mathematically involves identifying questions that are important to you and then seeking answers to those questions. Internet Inquiry allows you to support these more independent experiences among your students.

You will recall from the previous chapters that Internet Inquiry usually contains five phases: question, search, analyze, compose, and share. Students identify an important question they wish to explore, search for resources to help them understand the information related to this question, analyze the data they have obtained, compose a presentation of their work, and then share their work with others. These steps may also be used to structure Internet Inquiry in mathematics.

Sometimes, it is possible to organize Internet Inquiry around interesting sites that already exist on the Internet. Examples include the very rich sites that exist for the following:

- **Pi Mathematics**—http://www.ncsa.uiuc.edu:80/edu/RSE/RSEorange/buttons.html
  Have students read about the history of pi, view a video, complete several different activities, calculate the best deal on several pizzas, and share their favorite pizza topping with students around the world. Have them write up a report on their experiences and share them with others. Soon, you will have to have a sign up list for this site during Internet Inquiry.

- **A Fractals Lesson**—http://math.rice.edu/~lanius/frac/
  Have students explore this site during Internet Inquiry, making a fractal, learning how fractals are related to chopping broccoli, and viewing fractals on the WWW. Then have them prepare a poster session on fractals for the class including examples they printed out from sites on the WWW.

- **Mega Mathematics**—http://www.c3.lanl.gov/mega-math/
  There are so many wonderful Internet Inquiry possibilities at this site it is hard to know where to begin (see Figure 8-4). From a seemingly simple coloring problem that has perplexed cartogra-

Figure 8-4.
The home page for **Mega Mathematics** (http://www.c3.lanl.gov/mega-math/)

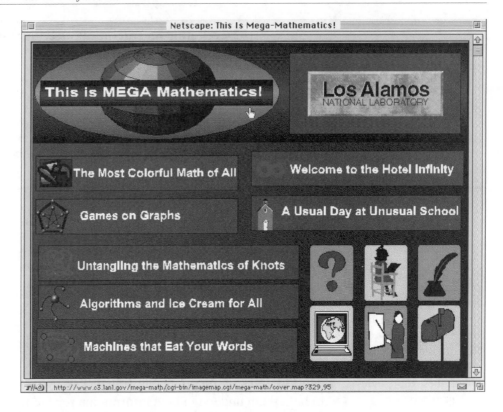

phers for centuries, to the mathematics of knots, to issues of infinity, to graphs and games, this site has enough intriguing issues to keep any student thinking mathematically for a year. Point students to this site and stand back. Set a bookmark!

Another approach to Internet Inquiry is to encourage students to explore sites containing links to many different topics in mathematics. As students explore these sites, encourage them to explore and define a project they wish to complete. You could direct them to any of the central sites described earlier in the chapter or you could direct them to some of these locations:

- **Knot a Braid**—
  http://camel.math.ca/Recreation/kabol/knotlinks.html
  Here is a great math location for students searching for an Inquiry project. Each week a new site is selected in math. Previous links are available so that you can go down the list until you find something really interesting. It won't be hard at this location.

- **Interactive Mathematics Miscellany and Puzzles**—
  http://www.cut-the-knot.com/
  Have students do Internet Inquiry on one of the puzzles or problems at this site. Be certain to encourage them to report on the history behind the problem as well as the problem itself. They may wish to visit some of the history sites mentioned earlier to gather information.

As you do more Internet Inquiry with your students consider having a Math Fair where students present their projects in a "poster session." If you can, schedule this at a time when parents can attend so that they can witness all the wonderful things you are doing with your students.

TEACHING TIP	**Teacher2Teacher** Often each of us has a specific question about teaching math or the need for new resources to enliven our math class. When you have a question, be certain to visit the important resources at Teacher2Teacher in **The Math Forum** (http://forum.swarthmore.edu/t2t/). This resource provides you with access to some of the best math educators in the country who are ready to answer any question you might have. Be certain, though, to review their archive of answers first, to see if someone has already addressed your question.

Using WebQuests

For some reason, WebQuests are not as frequently found on the Internet for math compared to other subjects. Nevertheless, a little searching will uncover a number of WebQuests that might be appropriate for your classrooms.

If you teach at the high school level and are looking for a WebQuest on statistics, you might find **Baseball Prediction** (http://www.wfu.edu/~mccoy/NCTM99/baseball.html) useful. In this experience, students must analyze statistical correlations between a team's winning percentage and several performance indicators in order to make a recommendation to management about which type of player to acquire: a home run hitter, a high-average hitter, a hitter who bats in more runs, a base stealer, or a pitcher with a low earned-run-average. If you have any baseball fans, this would be a big hit.

If you teach math in grades 4-8, you might be interested in using **Best Weather** (http://www.wfu.edu/~mccoy/NCTM99/weather.html), a WebQuest where you must develop a definition of good weather and then evaluate the weather statistics in several cities, making graphs for each, as you present the case for which city has the best weather. Student presentations are then displayed for Open House Night.

If you teach grades 6–12, you might wish students to complete **World Shopping Spree** (http://www.wfu.edu/~mccoy/NCTM99/shopping.html). In this WebQuest, you find four common objects for sale in four different countries. Then, converting each cost into dollars, you determine which country has the best buy for each item.

A final example of a math WebQuest is **Titanic: What Can Numbers Tell Us About Her Fatal Voyage** (http://asterix.ednet.lsu.edu/~edtech/webquest/titanic.html). In this activity students evaluate several data bases containing statistical information on survivors and deaths from this tragedy. Students use these data in the construction of spreadsheet tables, with appropriate graphics, to illustrate specific statistical conclusions.

Visiting the Classroom: The Home Page of Loogootee Elementary West in Indiana

Classroom home pages are usually part of the home page for their school and the best example of a school home page is one at Loogootee Elementary West in Loogootee, Indiana, developed by Tammy Payton (http://mercury.siec.k12.in.us/west/). Tammy is on leave from her position as a first grade teacher, but she has developed a wonderful model for what a school web site should accomplish.

Of course, this school site has the important information for parents and students including links to the school calendar, a page describing the curriculum at the school, descriptions of recent projects by classes at the school, and e-mail links to contact the teachers at the school (see Figure 8-5). More than these typical components, however, this school site is widely recognized for the well-organized collection of useful instructional resources on the Internet for teachers, students, and parents.

The focus of this school site is really on teaching and learning with the Internet. It is a wonderful resource to support teachers, children, and parents.

Figure 8-5.
The home page of Loogootee Elementary West in Indiana is a wonderful example of a school home page (http://mercury.siec.k12.in.us/west/).

Many teachers visit this site from other schools to discover new and exciting resources for their own classroom. You will find an extensive set of links to Internet projects, a page devoted to teaching links organized by content area, articles about teaching and learning, directions for developing web pages, and links to screened search engines for children. The front page at this school site also has links to great resources for holiday and seasonal study. It is a masterful work by a teacher who really knows the Internet. If your school is beginning to develop its own web page, you should be certain to visit this location to see what is possible.

Instructional Resources on the Internet

100th Day of School Celebration—

http://www.siec.k12.in.us/~west/proj/100th/

As you approach the 100th day of school each year in your primary grade classrooms, here is a series of great activities to celebrate the magic behind the number 100. Send and receive a hundred e-mails, see how hundreds of jelly beans can make hundreds of thousands, and many more great, quick projects for your class.

About Today's Date—

http://acorn.educ.nottingham.ac.uk/cgi-bin/daynum

Have students visit this page each day to find out interesting information about each of the numbers from 1 to 31. Your kids will learn a lot by just reading the information at these pages. Post the information in class, too, in your math center. Make a bookmark!

Additional Resources—http://score.kings.k12.ca.us/additional.html

This is a teacher friendly collection of great math resources for your classroom. Many useful links for teaching and learning. Set a bookmark!

ArithmAttack—http://www.dep.anl.gov/aattack.htm

How many basic math problems can you solve in one minute. This non-commercial site challenges you and your students. Set a bookmark and see how much each student can improve their scores for addition, subtraction, multiplication, and division during the year. A great location for the elementary grades. You may even download this software for free.

Arithmetic Software—

http://forum.swarthmore.edu/arithmetic/arith.software.html

Do your students need new and fun ways to master basic arithmetic? Here is a central site for great freeware and shareware you can download right to your classroom computer. Set a bookmark!

Blue Dog Can Count!!—http://kao.ini.cmu.edu/bdf.html

Blue dog answers all your basic math problems by barking out the answers. A fun site and especially useful in the primary grades for developing basic math skills.

Classroom Links–Math—
http://www.enc.org/classroom/claslinx/nf_resmath.htm
Here is a set of great links to wonderful sites for mathematics education. From a fractal microscope, to a location for Googolplex, to Virtual Polyhedra, this site has outstanding sites for students and teachers. Set a bookmark!

Explorer: Mathematics—http://unite.ukans.edu/explorer-db/browse/static/Mathematics/index.html
The Explorer is a collection of educational resources including instructional software, lab activities, and lesson plans for K–12 mathematics and science education. A nice collection for busy teachers to obtain very useful resources. Set a bookmark!

Finding Data on the Internet—http://www.robertniles.com/data/
Here is the place to get nearly every piece of statistical data on states, countries, cities, and other geographical and political units. A treasure trove for data snoopers and a great place for older students to explore during Internet Inquiry. If you work with high school students, set a bookmark!

Flashcards for Kids—http://www.edu4kids.com/math/
This location lets you set up flashcard experiences for your students for addition, subtraction, multiplication, and division at several different levels of difficulty. It also lets you run flashcards in a timed or untimed mode and keeps your score for you. A great resource for students learning their basic facts.

Geometry Classroom Materials—http://forum.swarthmore.edu/geometry/geom.lessons.html
Are you looking for a range of Internet resources for your course in geometry? Here is your answer, a great collection of teaching tools from The Math Forum.

Geometry Problem of the Week—http://forum.swarthmore.edu/geopow/
Part of the Math Forum at Swarthmore College, this location provides you and your students with a challenging geometry problem to solve each week, as well as an archive of past problems.

Interactive Algebra Tutorials—http://www.accessone.com/~bbunge/Algebra/Algebra.html
Do your students need additional practice on various types of algebra problems? Just set a link to this location to provide them with practice, immediate feedback, and support.

Jumpin' Jehosaphat the Counting Sheep—http://www.dodds1.com/Java/Jj.html
Here is a sheep that will solve addition, subtraction, multiplication, and division problems for your younger students. It jumps and counts out the answer, in Sheepese. Much fun! It runs better with Internet Explorer 3.0 or later than with Netscape.

KidsConnect—http://www.ala.org/ICONN/kidsconn.html
Sponsored by the American Library Association, KidsConnect is a ques-

tion-answering, homework help and referral service for K–12 students on the Internet. If your students have questions about math and you are not available, this is a great resource. The goal of the service is to help students access and use the information available on the Internet effectively and efficiently. Useful for math, but other subject areas, too.

Knot a Braid of Links—

http://camel.math.ca/Recreation/kabol/knotlinks.html

Here is a great resource from Canada that announces a best site of the week via e-mail. It also includes a great collection of best sites from the past. Many links to very useful resources may be found here.

Macalester College Problem of the Week—

http://forum.swarthmore.edu/wagon/

If you are looking for math challenges for your high school classes, here is a wonderful site. Use each weeks problem to run a brief Internet Workshop on Fridays to see if anyone has come up with the solution.

MacTutor History of Mathematics Archive—

http://www-groups.dcs.st-and.ac.uk/~history/index.html

Interested in the history of mathematics? Here is the URL 4 U. Find out who the mathematician of the day is, or read the biographies of famous mathematicians and learn about their accomplishments. It contains many unique links to sites about the history of mathematics.

Middle School Problem of the Week—

http://forum.swarthmore.edu/midpow/

Great challenges for your middle school math classes, these problems are brought to you by The Math Forum. Conduct a brief Internet Workshop each week to solve each puzzle.

NCTM Standards—

http://standards-e.nctm.org/1.0/89ces/Table_of_Contents.html

This is the document that has had a powerful effect on the way many people think about mathematics instruction. Reading it can provide you with useful insights about this area of the curriculum. New standards for math education will appear in 2000. Be certain to visit the NCTM site to get links to the new standards when they appear (http://nctm.org/).

Numbers in Search of a Problem—

http://score.kings.k12.ca.us/junkdrawer.html

Looking for real world statistics for problems in your class? Here is a great site with statistics on everything from sports to population to the stock market.

Statistics—http://www.learner.org/exhibits/statistics/

Learn about central statistical concepts as you follow a fictional race between two candidates by reading news bulletins. Discover what a random sample is, what "margin of error" means, and why polls aren't always right.

Statistics Every Writer Should Know—http://www.robertniles.com/stats/

This is an excellent tutorial for students learning about simple statistics including means, medians, per cent, per capita, and more. A great interactive tutorial to help middle school students understand these concepts.

Listservs/Mailing Lists for Math Education

Follow the usual subscription procedures outlined in Chapter 3 to join this list.

NCTM-L—listproc@sci-ed.fit.edu

A discussion group on math education sponsored by the National Council of Teachers of Mathematics. Archives are available at: http://forum.swarthmore.edu/epigone/nctm-l/

Special Ideas for Younger Children: Using the Internet in the Primary Grades

 E-MAIL FOR YOU

To: Our readers

From: djleu@syr.edu (Don Leu), ddleu@syr.edu (Debbie Leu)

Subject: Using the Internet in the Primary Grades

The primary grades are aptly named. In these grades (K–3), children receive their primary learning experiences, experiences that will last a lifetime. If you are a primary grade teacher, you are already aware of this issue. You are concerned about the start you provide for your students and you have shouldered this additional responsibility because you believe you have something special to contribute to their young lives. Thoughtful Internet use becomes especially important at these grade levels. The decisions you make about Internet use in your classroom are critical to children's success in later grades. Especially important will be how you respond to child safety issues and the growing commercialization of the Internet.

You will find in this chapter a number of ideas to assist you with these responsibilities and a number of web sites that are especially useful when working with young children. New technologies such as Shockwave are providing us with many exciting resources for young children. Talking storybooks, electronic coloring books, dogs that bark out the answers to math problems, a guided tour of the White House, and a number of other resources are all available to assist you. We expect you and your students will enjoy these experiences as you make new discoveries about the world around us.

Don and Debbie

Teaching With the Internet: Sarah Shanahan's Class

Dominique, Juan, and Mika were working together at the Internet computer in their kindergarten classroom.

"Let's listen to *The Ant and the Grasshopper*. Ms. Shanahan said we could listen to that story. She said it was a good one," Mika said.

They clicked on the link to this story (see Figure 9-1) and waited a moment for the Shockwave plug-in to load. Earlier, Sarah had downloaded the Shockwave and Flash plug-ins (http://www.macromedia.com/shockwave/download/) onto her classroom computer. These new plug-ins opened an entire world to her kindergarten class. They enabled her children to listen to storybooks that were read aloud and many more engaging experiences with multimedia. Wonderful animations, video, and speech enabled her young children to engage in important learning experiences on the Internet. Today, her students were listening to an outstanding read-aloud, *The Ant and the Grasshopper* (http://www.hiyah.com/library/ant_hopper.html).

Dominigue said, "We got to write down a word from the story and draw a picture. That's what she said. Where's that word 'ant?'"

"Listen," Juan said, pointing to the word "Ant." "That's it right there. See, the person just read it. It starts with A."

"And we got to draw a picture of that ant, too," said Mika. "Stop the reading. I want to draw that picture just like the book."

Figure 9-1. The read-aloud storybook *The Ant and the Grasshopper* (http://www.hiyah.com/library/ant_hopper.html) that Sarah Shanahan's kindergarten class listened to with their Internet computer.

Juan and Mika wrote down the word "Ant" and drew a picture to share during Internet Workshop. Being the individual she was, Dominique wrote down the word "Grasshopper" and drew a picture of this character instead. They started listening again to the story as soon as they finished. As they listened, they also added to their drawings.

At the end of this beautiful story, Mika said "Look, the message says we gotta read the Swahili book today, too. Go to the Swahili book. Click there. Go to the Swahili book."

They clicked on the link to an alphabet book in Swahili a class in Oregon had developed (http://www.beavton.k12.or.us/Greenway/leahy/99-00/swahili/index.htm). The children in David Leahy's class had recorded their pronunciations for each word, many of which came from the book *Jambo Means Hello* by Muriel Feelings. Mika and his friends listened to the class in Oregon reading words in Swahili. They talked about the words and the pictures as they listened to the words being pronounced.

"We gonna write them an e-mail," said Mika. "Ms. Shanahan said we can write them an e-mail in Workshop today."

Each morning, Sarah read a morning message to the children. Each morning message mentioned an Internet Workshop activity for her children to complete. She knew their interest in this new classroom resource would mean that many would try to read this part of the message on their own. Today the message was:

> Wednesday, May 10
>
> It is a rainy day.
>
> Today we will have music.
>
> Please listen to the story on the computer, "The Ant and the Grasshopper."
>
> Listen to the Swahili Alphabet Book, too.
>
> Shall we send them an e-mail message?
>
> Ms. Shanahan

"My turn," announced Kevin as he walked over to the computer corner. He pointed to the clock. "The big hand is on 12 and Ms. Shanahan said it's my turn when the big hand's on 12. You gotta stop now. My turn."

Dominque, Juan, and Mika moved over for Kevin and watched as he clicked on **What is it?** (http://www.uq.oz.au/nanoworld/whatisit.html) of **Nanoworld** (http://www.uq.oz.au/nanoworld/nanohome.html), a site in Australia with many strange-looking photographs taken with an electron microscope (see Figure 9-2). Each week, Sarah selected a picture from the files at this location or from **Scanning Electron Microscope** (http://www.mos.org/sln/sem/index.html) and had students draw a picture of the object and then write a description of what they thought it was. It was always great fun to have students share their pictures and read their invented spelling for this activity during a brief Internet Workshop.

Each morning, Sarah read a morning message to the children. Each morning message mentioned an Internet Workshop activity for her children to complete.

"Cool. It's a monster."

"No, it's a dinosaur."

"It's a monster bug."

Ignoring all of these suggestions, Kevin carefully drew his picture of the strange shape and wrote below his picture:

KEVIN

I THK S A KRB

"What you say?" asked Justin.

Proudly, Kevin read his work, "I think it's a crab."

Figure 9-2.
An image from the "What is it?" quiz (http://www.uq.oz.au/nanoworld/whatisit.html) at the **Nanoworld Image Gallery**. These images can be used in writing activities for young children.

Lessons From the Classroom

This episode from Sarah Shanahan's classroom demonstrates how the Internet contains many fine resources for the very youngest learners at school.

This episode from Sarah Shanahan's classroom demonstrates how the Internet contains many fine resources for the very youngest learners at school. In a short period of time, her students had many important experiences with stories, letters, writing, and listening skills. There are many locations on the Internet for supporting young children as they learn important lessons about the world around them.

The episode also illustrates how thoughtful teachers can integrate Internet Workshop into their instructional practices. In this class, Sarah always began each morning with a "Message of the Day". She read this with her children as a Language Experience Activity, exposing her children to print and show-

Sarah began to include Internet Workshop in her "Message of the Day" for the class. She found that students paid particular attention to the Internet activities she wrote in the message and would refer to it often throughout the school day.

ing them how to use print to obtain information. After taking a course on teaching with the Internet, Sarah began to include Internet Workshop in her "Message of the Day" for the class. She found that students paid particular attention to the activities she wrote in the morning message and would refer to them often throughout the school day. Children would come up to the message and point to each word as they tried to read it. Others would point to it from the computer as they reminded others of what they were supposed to do.

The episode in Sarah's class also illustrates a third lesson: It is important for lower grade classrooms to receive the very best technology possible. Sarah had one of the few color printers in her school and a powerful multimedia computer, capable of playing speech, animation, and sound very quickly. The color printer helped her children to quickly acquire color names when they printed out their color drawing with KidPix software. The multimedia computer allowed her children to listen to many things on the Internet with Shockwave and RealAudio technologies. A favorite right now was listening to classic folk and fairy tales read aloud over the Internet.

It is important for lower grade classrooms to receive the best technology possible.

Last year Sarah wrote a memo to her principal. She pointed out that her kindergarten always had the oldest computer in the school and this limited her children's learning opportunities. She suggested that younger children really deserved the very best technologies so they could benefit from having stories read aloud to them on the Internet, learn color names faster, and view the memory-rich, multimedia resources available on the Internet. She pointed out that older students could read text but that her students needed the new speech technologies to assist with learning to read and write. She also noted that a color printer would ensure her children learned color names. Apparently, her arguments were compelling; at the beginning of the year she found a multimedia computer and color printer in her classroom. Sarah took full advantage of their potential to support her young children.

There is also a final lesson in this short episode. Sarah, made judicious choices in her selection of sites to use in the classroom, avoiding the most blatant of commercialism that pervades web sites for young children. She had a rule in her class never to use a site with banner ads. She thought long and hard about whether to use the story **The Ant and the Grasshopper** (http://www.hiyah.com/library/ant_hopper.html) because it has a commercial logo for Hiyah.com. Eventually, she decided that the quality of this resource outweighed the appearance of a commercial logo and there was no overt attempt to sell a product. It was a tough decision, however. Sarah had learned it was hard to make simplistic decisions in this area such as never using a ".com" site in her class. Some ".com" locations didn't overtly sell products or services while some ".org" and ".edu" locations did. Sarah had learned these decisions needed to be made carefully and each location needed to be explored thoroughly. She did this with each site she used in her classroom.

Sarah, made judicious choices in her selection of sites to use in the classroom, avoiding the most blatant of commercialism that pervades web sites for young children.

E-MAIL FOR YOU

To: Colleagues
From: Doug Crosby <kiwi@digisys.net>
Subject: First Grade Projects In Our Class

Hi all!

In a previous year I was involved with two new major projects that you may want to take a look at. The first is an exciting, ongoing collaboration project that my first-graders did with our local nursing home. We visited the residents throughout the year, reading to them and enjoying their company. Our final project was for each of my students to interview a resident, find out their family backgrounds, likes etc., and then write a book about their partner either in fiction or non-fiction form. The culminating activity was to present these books to the residents at the end of our school year. This was a tremendously rewarding activity, both for my kids and the residents. Some great friendships formed. We reported our activities on our class home page where you can see photos and a write-up of the project. Take a look at: http://www.digisys.net/cherry/nurshome.html

The other interesting project was a collaboration between our school and Lockheed Martin, the company that puts together the space shuttles. They selected our school as one of five from each state to be part of their Student Signatures in Space Program. On Space Day we celebrated space by having the whole school sign a poster which was then sent back to Lockheed where the signatures are scanned onto disk and flown aboard a space shuttle flight. We reported on the event at: http://www.digisys.net/cherry/spaceday.html This is a great ongoing project and the kids are really excited about the fact that their signatures are space bound.

We have also continued to e-mail on a regular basis a class in New Zealand. There are so many possibilities for using the Internet. We have a lot of fun thinking up new ones!

~~~~~~~~~~~~~~~~~~~~~~~~~~~~~
Doug :-)} - The Kiwi at Cherry.
~~~~~~~~~~~~~~~~~~~~~~~~~~~~~

Doug Crosby,
Cherry Valley School,
Polson MT
www.digisys.net/cherry
kiwi@digisys.net

General Issues for the Primary Grades

There are several issues that require special attention if you are fortunate enough to work with children in the primary grades: ensuring child safety, supporting emergent navigation skills, and seeking supportive technologies for your children. Each is essential to keep in mind as you work with young children on the Internet.

Child safety is a critical concern for young children unfamiliar with the Internet. As a teacher, you are responsible for your students' physical safety in the classroom. You are also responsible for new safety issues that now arise because of the Internet. Chapter 2 described the nature of software filters and acceptable use policies. These help to establish rules for the appropriate use of the Internet and prevent young children from viewing objectionable locations. Chapter 4 described several locations on the Internet where all links are screened for child safety, another important strategy if you work with young children.

Primary grade teachers will need to pay particular attention to child safety on the Internet. We have always discussed fire safety and traffic safety in primary classrooms. Now we must begin to discuss Internet safety. You may wish to discuss issues of Internet safety as they arise in your class within an Internet Workshop framework as described in Chapter 4.

Teachers in the very youngest grades (K–1) will often limit children's use of the Internet to sites they have bookmarked or locations with links on their classroom home page. This limits the viewing of inappropriate locations. Others impose a rule similar to the "Four Click Rule" developed by Isabelle Hoag for her young students in Amsterdam (having students count each click as they link to new sites and telling them not to click more than four times). This, too, limits exposure to inappropriate locations.

Internet safety also applies to e-mail. Increasingly, school districts require all incoming and outgoing e-mail messages for primary grade students go through the teacher's e-mail account. This way, you may monitor the e-mail communication of your students and help to ensure their safety. Should you find any inappropriate messages from strangers, you should immediately report the incident to your principal or another designated person in your district. You should also respond to the message, indicating that you have reported it to a supervisor.

Another important aspect of Internet use in the primary grades is to help children learn basic navigation strategies. Learning about hyperlinks, bookmarks, mouse skills, and other emergent navigation strategies are important for the very youngest learners. You should not assume these skills in your students, but rather, plan systematically to support their development. Working with partners during computer time, using Internet Workshop, and developing very simple scavenger hunts for your young students are all ways to support this aspect of Internet use. Simple scavenger hunts that students complete in pairs or small groups are especially useful. Scavenge hunts have

---

Child safety is a critical concern for young children unfamiliar with the Internet.

We have always discussed fire safety and traffic safety in primary classrooms. Now we must begin to discuss Internet safety.

Should you find any inappropriate messages from strangers, you should immediately report the incident to your principal or another designated person in your district. You should also respond to the message, indicating that you have reported it to a supervisor.

E-MAIL FOR YOU

To: Colleagues
From: Isabelle Hoag <hoag@eruronet.nl>
Subject: Child safety

Hi!
I was both nervous and excited when my class got hooked up to the Internet! I asked several people for their ideas about having the kids surf around and about making my own page. They sure helped me. I hope my ideas help you, too.
First, I was worried my third-graders might find a site I would not want them to see for some reason. To guard against this, I made up the "Four Click Rule." My students must first ask to use Netscape. Then, they must start with a site I have saved on our list of "favorites" or "bookmarks." They can follow four links from that starting point, but then they must return or start with another bookmark. They can also show me sites they would like to add to our bookmarks.
Next, I was worried that they would buy something or download a virus or sign up for something. There are many attractive blinking icons that scream "click here!" and children are being taught to follow instructions! So my class has strict instructions to never, ever write their name or give out any information when they are surfing. They must come and get me if they are asked for information.
Finally, when setting up my own pages, I wrote a permission slip similar to the ones I use for field trips. Only photos, work, and first names of children for whom I have permission slips are used. I only use first names and never identify children in photos.
This is a new technology and, if treated with respect and caution, it is a valuable resource in the class! Have fun!

Isabelle Hoag, Primary School Teacher
The International School of Amsterdam

---

students search for information at various locations on the Internet and then share their results with the rest of the class during a workshop session. These develop navigation strategies as students also practice functional reading and writing tasks.

Here is another suggestion for the very youngest children: When you ask students to write down an answer during a scavenger hunt, look for words that are displayed on the screen so that they may copy them onto their worksheet. This will make it easier for children to successfully complete this experience as you help to develop early literacy skills.

Finally, we want to speak up in support of primary grade teachers seeking and receiving supportive technologies to assist the youngest learners. Often, school districts follow a "hand-me-down" policy with computers. In these districts, primary grade classrooms receive the oldest computers that are passed down from the high school, to the middle school, and finally to the elementary school. This is unfortunate since the youngest learners benefit the most from the latest technologies and the most powerful computers. Children who struggle with decoding may play audio clips to support their reading experiences. Newer, multimedia computers also provide animations and other supportive technologies to explain challenging concepts. In order to take full advantage of these types of Internet resources you will require a computer with at least 64 MB of RAM (a type of memory). This much memory is required to run the latest versions of Netscape and Internet Explorer with multimedia plug-ins while you also run word processing and other software. If you find yourself teaching in the primary grades without a computer capable of using the multimedia technologies at web sites, consider Sarah Shanahan's approach—take your concerns to your principal, explaining the greater need young children have for the latest technologies.

> If you find yourself teaching in the primary grades without a computer capable of using the multimedia technologies at web sites, consider Sarah Dye's approach—take your concerns to your principal, explaining the greater need young children have for the latest technologies.

Central Sites for the Primary Grades

As you look for central sites for young children it is important to keep in mind child safety concerns. One place to begin your search is at **Yahooligans** (http://www.yahooligans.com/). This is one of the largest collections of useful sites for children with links that are screened for child safety before being accepted. As with all lists, though, one can never guarantee the contents of links that move away from these sites. Thus, you must still monitor student use. You may wish to set a bookmark for Yahooligans and allow students in the older primary grades access to this information. For younger students, you may wish to preview locations, set bookmarks, and only allow children to use the bookmarks you have set.

> Probably the best central site screened for child safety is **Great Sites** (http://www.ala.org/parentspage/greatsites/amazing.html). This resource has been developed by the American Library Association and includes over 700 outstanding locations for children.

Probably the best central site screened for child safety is **Great Sites** (http://www.ala.org/parentspage/greatsites/amazing.html). This resource has been developed by the American Library Association and includes over 700 outstanding locations for children. Be certain to explore the wonderful resources here.

There is also an excellent central site for young children located at **Berit's Best Sites for Children** (http://db.cochran.com/li_toc:theoPage.db). These have been screened and rated. Each also contains a short review describing the contents. Many will indicate the approximate grade level for the activities at the location.

Keeping it Simple: Using Internet Workshop

As you visit central sites for the primary grades you will quickly find many locations that fit into Internet Workshop. These may include coloring books, alphabet books, and stories, some of which are read aloud. They will also

Internet FAQ

Should I be concerned about using commercial sites in my classroom? How can I tell if a location on the WWW has commercial intentions if there aren't any advertisements?	As you consider which central sites for young children to use, you should pay attention to why a site was developed. Many central sites for young children are located at commercial locations. These can be identified by the ".com" at the end of their URL. Commercial sites sometimes seek to exploit the marketing potential available when many young children visit their location. Of the central sites identified in this chapter, only the one developed by the American Library Association is not a commercial site.

E-MAIL FOR YOU

To: Colleagues
From: clewis01@mail.orion.org (Cathy Lewis)
Subject: Being Careful with Young Children on the Internet

When children are little we tell them to stay away from hot stoves. "HOT" should convey danger. On the other hand, little ones also see GOOD things coming from the stove and hunger surpasses the urge to touch. It is just like this with the Internet for grade school students. It's "HOT", but they are also hungry for information.

At the beginning, I believe students should be guided to web sites that answer their questions. Goals and objectives should be determined before they begin and the students should have some type of assessment to be sure they learned what they needed.

Picking up the Internet is like thumbing a regular book. There are times you just want to thumb through and enjoy the pictures and at other times you NEED TO KNOW SOMETHING. Students will need time for both, but in schools our time is so limited that goals and objectives should be determined that enhance the curriculum and not leave young minds bewildered with "thumbing through the pages."

The Internet has HOT items, so let's be sure we are cooking with fire and not explosives. Both will do the job, but the latter will end in disaster.

Cathy Irene Lewis
Reading Specialist
St. Mary's School Grades 3-4
Pierce City, MO

The Internet provides many opportunities to support your younger children in the classroom, especially with the use of Internet Workshop.

include activities in all of your content areas: language arts, math, science, and social studies. The Internet provides many opportunities to support your younger children in the classroom, especially with the use of Internet Workshop.

As you have already discovered, Internet Workshop is easy to develop. Simply find a location related to your classroom curriculum, set a bookmark for it, develop a brief activity, and then have your students complete this activity during the week. You may want to develop several activities for your students to explore during the week instead of just one. Often, it is useful to include a writing activity with the assignment to support young children's developing literacy ability. These writing experiences may then be shared during a workshop session at the end of each week.

Here are some examples of Internet Workshop that might be used with students in the primary grades:

- **The Prince and I**—http://www.nfb.ca/kids/main2.html
  Have your students explore this magical kingdom as they go on a mission to find the Prince and deliver a secret message. Share discoveries during a workshop session. You can also play Magic Squares, Scrambled Words, and Rhyme Time, send the Prince some of your own art and stories to display, or search for hidden treasure. This is a wonderful site, developed with child safety strategies in mind, run by Canada's National Film Board. It is intended for elementary school children in grades K to 6 (see Figure 9-3). Uses Shockwave or Java plugins.

Figure 9-3.
A page from the National Film Board of Canada's **The Prince and I** (http://www.nfb.ca/kids/main2.html)

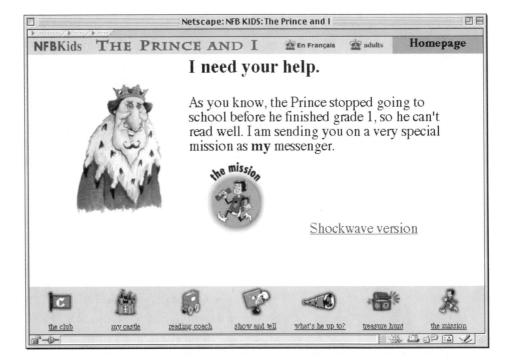

- **Poem Pack**—http://www.bbc.co.uk/education/wordsandpictures/longvow/poems/fpoem.shtml
  A wonderful location for working on long vowel patterns in phonics containing ten cute poems with animations and audio. Have students listen to the funny poems and complete other exciting activities located at **Long Vowels** (http://www.bbc.co.uk/education/wordsandpictures/longvow/index.shtml). Then, have students bring to your workshop session at least two words containing long vowel sounds. As they read their words, make a list for the entire class to see. Part of the many exciting resources at the BBC site in the UK. Uses Shockwave plug-ins.

- **Alex's Scribbles - Koala Trouble**—http://www.scribbles.com.au/max/bookmain.html
  This site from Australia features an extensive collection of wonderful stories about Max, the koala bear, by Alex Balsom (5 years old) and his dad. It is quickly becoming a classic on the Internet for young children. The stories contain hyperlinks within the illustrations; these require children to click on the correct location in the illustration in order to move forward in the story, thus supporting reading comprehension. Have children draw a picture of Max and write their own story after reading one of these delightful adventures. Then have them read their stories during Internet Workshop.

- **Boowa and Kwala**—http://www.boowakwala.com/
  This location is for our very youngest students, ages 3–6. There are so many different possibilities here for Internet Workshop. Visit different countries, learn new songs and play interactive games. This site uses Flash and has lots of music, sounds and animations. Available in both English and French.

- **Internet Coloring Books**—There are a number of coloring books on the Internet for very young children to enjoy. Have children print out their work and then write about their picture. They can read and share their work during Internet Workshop. Be careful, however, about screening sites for commercial messages. Interactive coloring books provide opportunities to color illustrations right on the screen. A nice, non-commercial example is **Draw Your Own Picture** (http://www.coloringpage.org/drawing.htm). Shockwave is required for this site. Non-interactive coloring books contain black and white illustrations to be printed out and then colored. They include **The Happy Earth Day Coloring Book** from the EPA (http://www.epa.gov/docs/Region5/happy.htm), **Smokey's Coloring Book** (http://flame.doacs.state.fl.us/Fp/color.html), and **FEMA's Coloring Book** (http://www.fema.gov/kids/games/colorbk/color1.htm).

- **Hangman at Kids Corner**—http://kids.ot.com/cgi/kids/hangman
  Here is a fun site for this traditional game. Children select letters as they try to guess the spelling of a word. This is a great place for kids to develop their decoding and spelling talents as they complete an Internet activity. Invite students to print out their successful work and share it during Internet Workshop. Set a bookmark!

- **Blue Dog Can Count**—http://kao.ini.cmu.edu/bdf.html
  At this location, children can write an addition, subtraction, division, or multiplication problem and listen as Blue Dog barks out the answer. This is a great place to check one's work. Better yet, have one student write the problem while the other predicts the answer. Then see if they agree with old Blue Dog. Great fun. Set a bookmark!

- **Jumpin' Jehosaphat the Counting Sheep**—
  http://www.dodds1.com/Java/Jj.html
  Here is another site like Blue Dog only Jumpin' Jehosaphat jumps and bleets out the answer. It doesn't seem to work as smoothly as Blue Dog unless you have a very fast Internet connection.

In addition to these traditional uses of sites for Internet Workshop, it is also possible to use your computer without requiring any navigation at all by your students. This is a very safe experience for your children since they only view an image you have bookmarked on the computer. For example, find an unusual image each day to display on the screen and encourage your students to draw a picture of this image and then write down what they think it is. A great source of these images is the **Nanoworld Image Gallery** (http://www.uq.oz.au:80/nanoworld/images_1.html) where you will find images taken by an electron microscope. Sometimes images will contain the label for the item. This is also useful for students who may wish to copy the word down as they write a sentence describing the picture they see. This can easily be set up as an Internet Workshop for kindergarten classrooms with children's pictures and writing shared during a brief workshop session at the end of the day.

Internet FAQ	
I how seen hundreds of locations on the WWW but I never know if I am looking at something "good." How can I tell if I am looking at an "outstanding" web site?	The definition of an outstanding web site is, of course, subjective. You may, however, wish to review the criteria the American Library Association uses to define outstanding web sites. They organize an extensive criteria list around these elements: authorship/sponsorship, purpose, design and stability, and content. Take a look and see if you agree. Their **Selection** page is located at: http://www.ala.org/parentspage/greatsites/criteria.html.

Using Internet Project

Permanent sites for Internet Project in the primary grades are beginning to appear on the Internet. Given the power of this type of experience we suspect more will soon follow. One of the more comprehensive locations is **The Mind's Eye Monster Exchange Project** (http://www.win4edu.com/minds-eye/monster). This site puts classes together that wish to participate in a collaborative language arts project (see Figure 9-4). Then, students draw a picture of a monster and write a description of their monster picture. Paired classes exchange their descriptions and attempt to draw a picture of what they think the other students' monsters look like. Finally, the images of all monsters are posted at the Monster Exchange Project so that classes may see the originals and compare them with the descriptions that were written. Many lesson plans and extension ideas are also listed at this location for teachers. This is wonderful Internet Project idea for any primary grade classroom. The opportunities for language arts experiences, as students communicate about their monster images, are exceptional.

Another permanent project location on the Internet is **Monarch Watch** (http://www.MonarchWatch.org/). If you wish to plan a project around this beautiful species of butterfly, this is the place for you (see Figure 9-5). The location contains an amazingly extensive set of resources designed for chil-

Figure 9-4.
The home page for the **Mind's Eye Monster Exchange**, an outstanding Internet project location for primary grade children (http://www.win4edu.com/minds-eye/monster).

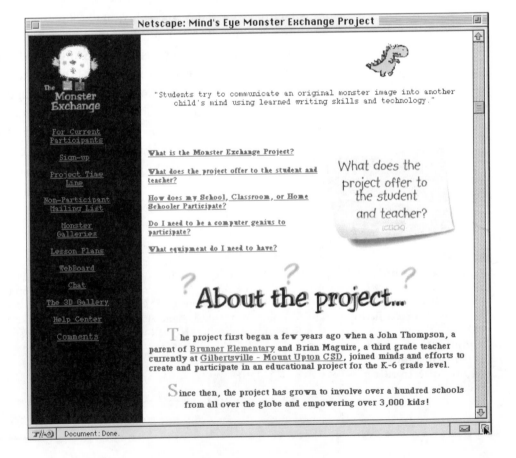

Figure 9-5.
To develop an Internet project about Monarch butterflies, be certain to visit **Monarch Watch** (http://www.MonarchWatch.org/).

dren and teachers to learn more about butterflies. Your students can raise butterflies, band them, release them into the wild, and track their progress as reports come in from observers around North America. Pay a visit to this excellent resource.

In addition to permanent sites such as these, you should also visit locations on the Internet where less permanent Internet Projects are described, inviting you and other teachers to join in classroom interchanges. Or, you may come up with your own idea for a great project and invite other teachers to join you by posting it at one of these locations. Locations where teachers post projects and invite others to join them have been described in other chapters. They include:

- **The Global SchoolNet Projects Registry**— http://www.gsn.org/pr/index.cfm

- **SchoolNet's Grassroots Project Gallery**— http://www.schoolnet.ca/grassroots/e/project.centre/search-projects.html

- **KIDPROJ**—http://www.kidlink.org:80/KIDPROJ/

- **Classroom Connect's Connected Teacher Database**— http://www.connectedteacher.com/teacherContact/search.asp

TEACHING TIP	**Visit Susan Silverman's Model for Internet Project** Susan Silverman is a technology integration teacher in the Comsewogue School District in Port Jefferson Station, New York. She has developed a wonderful model for Internet Project that all of us could use in our classrooms. Take a look at some of her exceptional projects developed with other classrooms around the world. These are located at **Mrs. Silverman's Second Grade Class** (http://kids-learn.org/). Susan posts a project description on many mailing lists, inviting other classes to join in as they explore a particular topic using the Internet to develop reading and writing experiences. Each participating class creates a web site containing their finished work and Susan develops a web site with links to everyone's pages. Susan and her collaborators have developed projects on Stellaluna, **Fall Poetry**, Clocks and Time, Owls, Pumpkins, Winter, Apples, and much more. Take a look at this exceptional model of collaborative teaching and learning over the Internet. Try it in your own classroom

Examples of projects you may wish to consider joining or developing for primary grade students include:

- **The Eric Carle Book Club.** Invite other classes to read works by Eric Carle (or another popular author). Then, using writing process activities, share children's written responses to these works with each classroom. Also, consider polling each class about their favorite books by this author and sharing the results with other classes. When all of the results are in, have each class develop a graph to display the results. Send the results of your work to the author and see if he responds. The Eric Carle homepage is located at: http://www.eric-carle.com/ You may find a link to his e-mail address at this site.

- **Amazing Insects.** A third grade class in Minnesota studied insects during the year and shared the results of their studies with classes around the world. They exchanged information about these amazing creatures. Writing, math, literature, and science are woven into this project.

- **Playground Chants Around the World.** Playground chants are part of every child's culture no matter where they go to school. Have your students write these down carefully and exchange them with classes at other locations around the world. Communicate with classes to find out the meanings of chants that are unfamiliar to your students. This is a wonderful way to support reading and writing in your primary grade classroom and to discover important aspects of other cultures.

- **Teddy Bears Travel the World.** Have each participating class purchase a small teddy bear and send it to one of the other classrooms. In each class, the teddy must go home with a different child each night. Each child must then write a description of what they did, where they went, and what it was like at their location. These should be developed with the parent/guardian and returned

Playground chants are part of every child's culture no matter where they go to school. Have your students write these down carefully and exchange them with classes at other locations around the world.

to school. Each day, these messages go out to each participating class to be read by the students. A map can be marked to show where each teddy is in the world. At the end, teddy bears can be mailed back to the home classroom with souvenirs from its host classrooms.

 E-MAIL FOR YOU

To: Colleague
From: Jeanette Kenyon <jkenyon@pen.k12.va.us>
Subject: Using The WWW To Help Students Who Must Relocate

Dear Colleague,

Living in a transient community often necessitates mid-year relocation of many of our government and military families. To ease the trauma of moving to a new community and school, I make use of the many resources available on the World Wide Web. The children are then able to locate their new community and familiarize themselves with the area before the move is actually made. Frequently, we find information and are able to connect with their new school. Gathering pictures, maps, and information about local businesses, activities, and schools, can make the transition much easier for an elementary child. The entire class becomes involved in calculating distances, comparing local geography, and even contacting individuals or interest groups in the area. Two excellent resources to use are:

    http://web66.coled.umn.edu/
    http://city.net/

Sincerely,
Jeanette Kenyon
Third Grade Teacher
Anne E. Moncure Elementary School
Stafford, VA
jkenyon@pen.k12.va.us

Using Internet Inquiry

Internet Inquiry occurs less frequently in the primary grades than it does at other grade levels.

Internet Inquiry occurs less frequently in the primary grades than it does at other grade levels. Part of the reason for this is child safety. Parents are often reluctant to have their young children independently exploring resources on the Internet. As a result, school boards often will place limits on children's independent Internet use at these younger levels. A more common reason, however, is that children at this age are still developing navigation skills. Because these skills have yet to be completely developed, it simply takes too long for many students to acquire useful information about a topic or project that interests them. Finally, the speed of obtaining information on the Internet is also impeded by young children's emerging literacy ability. Even when children do find resources that are related to their inquiry project, they are not always able to understand the information. Thus, independent inquiry projects are less common in the primary grades.

It is useful, though, to spend time supporting children as they develop navigation skills. Indeed, some teachers will focus on navigation as a subject for Internet Inquiry. Usually this is developed during Internet Workshop time when teachers encourage children to share some new strategy they have discovered and to seek advice about something they do not understand. Teachers, too, will develop navigation skills through the use of regular scavenger hunts on the Internet, usually in groups or pairs. These results will be shared during Internet Workshop as a way of discussing navigation strategies.

TEACHING TIP	**Join the Read in Project** The Read In Foundation organizes an event each year to support the reading of outstanding literature. Develop an Internet project around this event and encourage the reading of exceptional works of literature as you communicate with popular children's authors and with other classrooms. In 1998, participating authors included: Lloyd Alexander, Avi, Bruce Balan, Judy Blume, David Boyd, Karleen Bradford, Eve Bunting, Bruce Coville, Paula Danziger, Ed Emberley, Virginia Hamilton, Daniel Hayes, Joan Irvine, Jackie French Koller, James Moloney, Ann M. Martin, Evelyn Clarke Mott, Connie Porter, Aaron Shepard, R. L. Stine, Rob Thomas, David Wisniewski, and Jane Yolen. Visit the site for **Read In** (http://www.readin.org/main1.htm) and participate!

Using WebQuests

WebQuests are especially important to evaluate in the primary grades since some of your students will be less independent at reading directions and less familiar with navigating the Internet effectively. Thus, it is essential to provide opportunities for students to work together on these experiences so they may benefit from the natural support that comes from working together. Given the concerns about WebQuests mentioned earlier and these special concerns for the primary grades, you may wish to consider using WebQuests in your classroom.

The largest source for primary grade WebQuests may be found at the **Schools of California Online Resources (SCORE)** (http://score.k12.ca.us/). Others may be located by using a search engine. Here are examples of some of the fine activities available for you to use in your classroom:

- **Cinco de Mayo—**
  http://www.zianet.com/hatchelementary/Cinco.html
  This wonderful celebration of Hispanic culture was developed by Cheryl Cox, a second grade teacher at Hatch Valley Elemen-

tary School in New Mexico. On their adventure, students work in groups of four to learn about the history of Cinco de Mayo and Hispanic culture by reading great works of children's literature, conducting research, making a piñata, and fixing a Mexican meal to celebrate the holiday. A wonderful learning experience. Set a bookmark!

- **Konnichiwa: Welcome to My World**—
  http://score.rims.k12.ca.us/activity/konnichiwa/index.html
  This WebQuest was designed for first grade, but is probably more appropriate for second or third grade. Students work together to write a book to help a new student from Japan feel welcome at your school. They read and research comparisons between life in the US and in Japan, and then each student creates one page to be included in a class book for the new student.

- **Frog and Toad are Friends**—
  http://www.sdcoe.k12.ca.us/score/frog/frogtg.html
  After reading this great book by Arnold Lobel, students color a frog from the Internet, make an origami frog, and write a letter to a new keypal friend. A nice set of experiences for second-graders doing a unit on frogs or reading the Frog and Toad series by Arnold Lobel.

- **Grandfather's Journey**—
  http://www.sdcoe.k12.ca.us/score/grand/grandtg.html#1
  After students read and enjoy this touching book by Allen Say they print out a map, plot the journey in the story, use a distance calculator on the Internet to determine the distance, explore the world of watercolor, and visit many locations in Japan over the Internet in order to write a letter to a friend describing their journey.

- **I Like Books**—
  http://www.sdcoe.k12.ca.us/score/books/bookssg2.html
  In this WebQuest, students read this work by Mark Browne and then complete several activities, helping them to identify their favorite genre, contributing one page to a class book about their favorite reading selections, and then write a story themselves.

Commercials in the Classroom: The Commercialization of Educational Sites on the Internet

In the past two years, we have observed the rapid commercialization of educational resources on the Internet. We see this as new e-companies appear, developing educational resources to attract teachers and children, and then selling banner ads to generate income. We see this as children's authors and

E-MAIL FOR YOU

To: Colleagues
From: Doug Crosby <kiwi@digisys.net>
Subject: Early literacy and the Internet

Dear friends,

How things change, just three years ago we had just one dial-up account to the Internet, now with lots of hard work we have high speed connections in all our classrooms and our teachers are finding new projects every day.

I would like to tell you about two ways in which we have integrated our schools strong emphasis on early literacy development with technology through our school web site. Quite a number of years ago we moved away from using a basal reading program because we realized that all our students were at different places on that literacy continuum. In its place we have developed a centralized reading resource for all students, kindergarten through fourth grade.

In order to do this we have leveled over 1000 books for instructional reading and entered them onto a database which we have made available to other schools through our school web site. Teachers can request a copy and we send it out via e-mail attachment. You can see photos of our reading resource at (http://www.digisys.net/cherry/CentRR.htm).

Another way we have shared our celebration of literacy is through the use of a digital camera during our annual literacy week. During this week each classroom decorates their door like a book cover and on one day we all dress up as our favorite story book characters. Last year we used the digital camera to record these events for the making of class books and for posting at our web site. This proved to be very popular, particularly with out of town relatives who could see what their grandkids, nieces and nephews were up to at school. The book covers and teacher characters can be viewed at http://www.digisys.net/cherry/literacyweek.html

The Internet is a wonderful resource and we are have just as much fun creating for the Internet as we do visiting other sites.

~~~~~~~~~~~~~~~~~~~~~~~~~~~
Doug :-)} - The Kiwi at Cherry.
~~~~~~~~~~~~~~~~~~~~~~~~~~

Kindergarten Teacher/Computer Guy,

Cherry Valley School,

Polson, Montana.

www.digisys.net/cherry

kiwi@digisys.net

Since writing the previous edition, the most significant change we notice on the Internet is the growing commercialization of educational resources. We worry greatly about this trend.

their publishers develop web sites containing instructional materials to promote their work and sell more books. We see this as teachers themselves begin to develop their own ".com" sites, directing others to these commercial locations with links from their classroom homepage. Since writing the previous edition, the most significant change we notice on the Internet is the growing commercialization of educational resources.

We worry greatly about this trend. Never before has there been such a direct pipeline into the classroom from companies interested in developing brand recognition and loyalty among future consumers. The Internet permits this and the commercial world is keenly aware of the potential for profit in having this direct access to an important and relatively uninformed consumer group, the young children in our classrooms.

Should teachers play a part in this new effort to have commercials in the classroom? We think not. Our role should be to avoid exposing our students to as many of these commercials as possible as we educate them about how to critically understand the nature of this information.

Some organizations such as **The Center for Commercial-Free Public Education** (http://www.commercialfree.org/index.html) have been concerned about commercials in the classroom but, to date, their efforts have only been directed at television systems such as Channel One, lucrative cola contracts, and other traditional forms of advertising that are becoming more common in schools.

As educators, we need to seriously consider the new challenges we face with commercials in the classroom that enter over the Internet.

As educators, we need to seriously consider the new challenges we face with commercials in the classroom that enter over the Internet. In the next few years, districts will be developing their own policies about the use of commercials in the classroom with Internet technologies. We suspect it will become an increasingly important issue for all of us. As we all think carefully about these new developments, here are several thoughts that we have about this issue:

- Wherever possible we should select Internet resources that do not have banner ads or pop up windows selling products. These locations should only be used if they are central to learning an important aspect of the curriculum that may not be acquired in another, commercial-free manner.

- We should develop lessons and teach students to critically analyze the commercial aspects of the Internet so that they may make informed decisions about overt commercial messages and covert data gathering procedures as they visit various web sites.

- We should make every effort to avoid hosting our classroom home pages on commercial sites that provide free space for web pages in return for banner ads and pop up commercials. We should encourage our districts to place our classroom pages on their servers so that we do not need to resort to these commercial alternatives.

- We should tell students in primary grade classrooms not to click on a banner ad or pop up window, should these appear.

- We should teach all students to never provide their names or e-mail addresses to anyone without first seeking permission from their parents.

- We should avoid making links on our classroom web pages to commercial sites including award images that, when clicked, actually take the viewer to a commercial location. Many of the awards given to teachers for their good work are actually links to commercial sites.

- All that we do should ensure that our students are thoughtfully protected from commercial interests at the same time we educate them in understanding both the overt and the hidden aspects of commercialism that appear on the Internet.

Visiting the Classroom: Jack Fontanella's Kindergarten Class in Alaska

Some believe that kindergarten classes do not need a classroom web page. They say that children at this age are just too young for the Internet. Jack Fontanella proves how wrong this view is.

Some believe that kindergarten classes do not need a classroom web page. They say that children at this age are just too young for the Internet. Jack Fontanella proves how wrong this view is. Take a look at his wonderful classroom home page (http://www.jsd.k12.ak.us/hbv/classrooms/Fontanella/fontanejhbvHome.html) in the Juneau School District (see Figure 9-6).

Looking through his classroom pages one sees a teacher who cares deeply about the children in his classroom and a teacher who understands the needs of parents with children who are just beginning their school journey. If you spend a few minutes exploring his classroom web page, you will also see the outstanding work he does to display his students' accomplishments, communicate important information to parents, and explore the many professional resources on the Internet for early childhood educators. You will also see the connections he has made to many other kindergarten teachers around the world.

Jack is clearly an outstanding educator. You see it in the photos of students at work on projects in the classroom, you see it in the important information he provides to parents, you see it in the artwork his students complete, and you see it in the links to professional resources he has discovered on the Internet. If you are a teacher in the primary grades, this section alone is worth a visit.

Take a close look at the extensive information he provides to parents at the "Welcome to Kindergarten" page and at the "Parent's page." All of the important information about classroom policies and procedures are here, as well as links to many other resources that parents of kindergarten children might wish to explore.

Don't neglect a visit to the many art projects students complete in Jack's class. Take a careful look at the KidPix artwork his students constructed in

Figure 9-6.
The home page of Jack Fontanella's kindergarten class in Juneau, Alaska (http://www.jsd.k12.ak.us/hbv/classrooms/Fontanella/fontanejhbvHome.html).

making an Internet alphabet book. And look at their holiday cards as well. There are some very talented children in this class exploring their special views of the world around them.

Finally, notice how Jack has developed a web page with links to many other kindergarten classrooms on the Internet. Visit as many as you can and develop an understanding of the new communities of educators coming together through the work of outstanding educators such as Jack Fontanella.

Kindergarten teachers will come away from a visit to this location thinking of the many new possibilities the Internet provides for constructing connections with parents and guardians, children, and other kindergarten teachers. Classroom home pages not necessary for kindergarten classes? Not a chance!

Instructional Resources on the Internet

Animal Tracks—http://www.nwf.org/nwf/kids/
> The National Wildlife Federation has developed this site for kids interested in animals and the environment. It contains interactive games for the youngest users, riddles and jokes for older students, and even articles from past issues of *Ranger Rick*. Many articles also appear in Spanish. A nice location during units on animals and the environment. Set a bookmark!

CIERA—http://www.ciera.org./

The Center for the Improvement of Early Reading Achievement is a federally funded effort to study and improve early reading. This location has many important resources for any primary grade educator interested in early literacy.

Chucky's Concentration—http://www.pappyland.com/games/chuck.htm

A memory game for young children based on the classic Concentration game. Uses Shockwave. Rich in sound and animations.

Early Childhood Teacher Pages—http://www.nauticom.net/www/cokids/teacher.html

A collection of links to important resources useful to every early childhood educator.

Early Literacy Activities—http://curry.edschool.virginia.edu/curry/centers/pals/pals-activities.html

A great collection of activities for supporting early literacy instruction in your classroom. Also a number of nice ideas for assessment of emergent literacy.

Games for Children Ages 1 to 5—http://www.kidspsych.org/oochy2.html

Don't let the name fool you. You simply must visit this site to see the wonderful thinking activities for young children. The use of a Shockwave plug-in provides new levels of sound and animation in these very creative thinking activities for young children. Set a bookmark!

Games for Children Ages 6 to 9—http://www.kidspsych.org/oochina.html

More great thinking activities and games for your students using a Shockwave plug-in. Set a bookmark!

Little Fingers Shockwave Parlor Index—http://www.littlefingers.com/shockwave/loading.html

Here is a set of great activities to practice important early learning skills including alphabet name knowledge, telling time, counting numbers, counting change, and much more. Uses Shockwave.

Minutes from ME—http://sln.fi.edu/qa96/meindex.html

A series of columns from a primary grade teacher, Margaret Ennis, who is a fellow at the Franklin Museum. Her articles contain many great ideas for working with very young children on the computer. Each one contains very practical ideas and lesson ideas to use immediately in your classroom.

Online Autumn—

http://comsewogue.k12.ny.us/~ssilverman/autumn/index.html
Susan Silverman, a second grade teacher on Long Island, is a master of Internet projects. She has acquired an international reputation for her outstanding work. If you are doing work on seasonal change in the fall with your primary grade classroom you simply must visit this location. It contains links from around the world to projects by other classrooms where children wrote poetry, stories, and art about autumn. Set a bookmark!

Preschool Activities—http://www.eecs.umich.edu/mathscience/
funexperiments/quickndirty/preschool.html
A wonderful collection of lesson ideas for hands on science experiments for young children.

Resource Center: Hall of Early Childhood Education—
http://www.tenet.edu/academia/earlychild.html
A great collection of resources for early childhood education brought to you by the University of Texas. Includes sections for parents, teachers, and children.

Shockwave Games for Younger Children—
http://www.kidsdomain.com/games/shock.html
A great collection of activities for young children using Shockwave. You should screen these to select ones that actually lead to supporting your classroom program, but many are quite useful.

Smokey Bear's Official Home Page—
http://www.smokeybear.com/index.html
Here is a great location for an Internet activity during Fire Safety Week. Kids can play several games about fire safety, take a quiz and see how they do, and even e-mail Smokey. Set a bookmark! Sponsored by the USDA Forest service.

Stage Hands Puppets Activity Page—
http://www3.ns.sympatico.ca/onstage/puppets/activity/index.html
If you are interested in using puppets in your classroom here is a site for you! Puppet activities are a wonderful way to support language development in the primary grades.

The White House for Kids—
http://www.whitehouse.gov/WH/kids/html/home.html
Have your children take a tour of the White House. A fun activity for your students to complete as an Internet Activity. Your students can even write a letter to the president. Set a bookmark!

Listservs/Mailing Lists for the Primary Grades

Use standard procedures for subscribing to these lists. See Chapter 3.

Early Childhood Mailing List
Subscription procedures appear at: http://users.sgi.net/~cokids/
Mailing_Lists.html

Archives are located at: http://www.listbot.com/cgi-bin/
subscriber?Act=view_archive&list_id=COKIDS

ECENET-L—listserv@postoffice.cso.uiuc.edu
A discussion group on early childhood education (0–8 years). Subscription procedures are described at: http://ericps.crc.uiuc.edu/eece/listserv/
ecenet-l.html

Message archives are located at: http://askeric.org/Virtual/
Listserv_Archives/ECENET-L.html

PROJECTS-L—listserv@postoffice.cso.uiuc.edu

A group interested in using a project approach in early childhood education.

Subscription procedures are described at: http://ericps.crc.uiuc.edu/eece/
listserv/projec-l.html

Message archives are located at: http://www.askeric.org/Virtual/
Listserv_Archives/PROJECTS-L.html

RTEACHER—listserv@listserv.syr.edu

A discussion group to support literacy learning in the elementary classroom sponsored by *The Reading Teacher*, a journal of the International Reading Association.

Subscription procedures are described at http://web.syr.edu/~djleu/
RTEACHER/directions.html

Message archives are located at: http://listserv.syr.edu/archives/
rteacher.html

Usenet Newsgroups for the Primary Grades

k12.chat.elementary—Informal discussion among elementary students, grades K–5.

k12.chat.teacher—Informal discussion among teachers in grades K–12.

pnet.school.k-5—Discussion about K–5 education.

Using the Internet to Increase Multicultural Understanding

 E-MAIL FOR YOU

To: Our readers

From: djleu@syr.edu (Don Leu), ddleu@syr.edu (Debbie Leu)

Subject: Increasing our understanding of
diverse cultural traditions

We are excited by the opportunities the Internet provides to increase multicultural understanding and celebrate the diversity that defines our lives. As we observe conflicts around the world, based largely on the inability of different cultural and religious groups to respect and understand one another, it helps us to better appreciate the few stable societies with diverse cultural traditions. The United States and Canada for example, are home to over 100 different linguistic groups, over 700 religions, and countless ethnic and cultural groups. The U.S. has the greatest variety of multi-ethnic households in the history of the world. In the Los Angeles School District, more than 80 different languages are taught. Societies like the U.S. and Canada only survive if each member develops a common commitment to respecting the rights of others and the cultural context from which they come. This is not something that should be left to chance. Instead, we need to actively support multicultural understanding at every opportunity. The Internet is a new and very special tool in these efforts. Clearly, though, we need to do more.

This chapter will demonstrate how this new technology can draw each of us closer to others who come from different cultural contexts. Understanding others and the cultural context from which they come is an increasingly important goal as we build a global village with this new technology.

Don and Debbie

Teaching with the Internet: Cheryl Chan's Class

"I don't understand why it hurts their feelings when we say we are studying their culture."

"But I don't understand why we can't write to Native American students," said Desmon. "I don't understand why it hurts their feelings when we say we are studying their culture."

Desmon was reporting during an Internet Workshop session in Cheryl Chan's social studies class. The students in her class were doing Internet Inquiry in a unit designed to increase multicultural understanding and build a classroom community. Celebrating different cultural traditions helped to accomplish these goals. Students had been working in groups on Internet Inquiry projects.

Each group had selected a different culture to explore. One group had selected a Hispanic theme and was reading literature and studying about the many different Hispanic cultures. They had found many useful locations on the WWW by beginning their study at the **Latin American Network Information Center LANIC** (http://www.lanic.utexas.edu/), especially the site for **Primary and Secondary Education** (http://www.lanic.utexas.edu/la/region/k-12/). They were now exploring (see Figure 10-1) **México para Niños** (http://explora.presidencia.gob.mx/) and the English version **Mexico for Kids** (http://explora.presidencia.gob.mx/index_kids.html). They were trying to determine who developed these sites, why they developed them, and what this suggested about the information located here. Cheryl had introduced the unit with an activity on critical literacies and this group was putting the information they learned to good use.

Figure 10-1.
The home page for the Spanish version of **México para Niños** (http://explora.presidencia.gob.mx/) that students in Cheryl Chan's class evaluated.

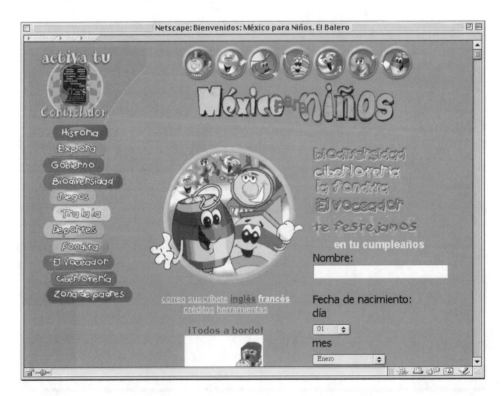

Others had picked an African-American theme and had decided to focus on the connections they saw between the poetry of Langston Hughes, the actions of Rosa Parks and Martin Luther King, Jr., and the civil rights struggle. They had located a wonderful model of a web page they were going to follow as they put their report together, **Timeline of the American Civil Rights Movement** (http://www.wmich.edu/politics/mlk/). Two members of the group knew how to make web pages so they were all hard at work gathering information and exploring the connections they found.

Another group had picked a Japanese theme and were studying the literature and cultural traditions of this culture. Through **Web66: International School Web Site Registry** (http://web66.coled.umn.edu/schools.html), this group had linked up with another class in Kyoto and were exchanging e-mail messages, discovering many important insights about each other's cultural traditions.

Desmon's group was studying Native American literature and cultures, especially the common respect they all expressed for Mother Earth. Desmon's group had read many of the prayers, poems, and stories on the Internet at locations such as **Indigenous Peoples' Literature** (http://www.indians.org/welker/framenat.htm) and **Index of Native American Resources on the Internet** (http://www.hanksville.org/NAresources/) as they developed a growing respect for the traditions, struggles, and views of Native Americans. **A Line in the Sand** (http://www.hanksville.org/sand/) had been especially useful in understanding why many Native Americans did not want their sacred traditions widely distributed over the Internet. In addition, they read a number of books from the library including: *Thirteen Moons on Turtle's Back*, by Bruchac and London, *Giving Thanks: A Native American Good Morning Message* by Chief Jake Swamp, *Ceremony—In the Circle of Life* by White Deer of Autumn, *Buffalo Woman*, by Gobel, and *Chief Sarah: Sarah Winnemucca's Fight for Indian Rights* by Morrison. They had also been exploring some of the many Native American sites on the web.

They were excited when they found a great location, **Native American Indian** (http://indy4.fdl.cc.mn.us/~isk/mainmenu.html), and discovered a place to post a message (http://indy4.fdl.cc.mn.us/~isk/schools/schlbook.html) in hopes of linking up with Native American students who might be interested in becoming KeyPals. But then they came across a message from the author of this site saying:

> Non-Indians: teachers, kids, please do not say "studying Native Americans and want to correspond with some." This is offensive, racist. This service is primarily a way for Indian kids to get in contact with each other, not a method of providing specimens for study by your class or students.

Desmon was sharing his question with the rest of the class during their regular workshop session. "I didn't know that I was being racist," he said. "And I don't want to hurt anyone's feelings. I just want to understand more about their culture."

Desmon's group was studying Native American literature and cultures, especially the common respect they all expressed for Mother Earth.

"It makes you feel like a thing, not a person," she noted. "And, there are many different Native American cultures, not just one."

The discussion in Cheryl's class was useful in developing greater respect and sensitivity for others, issues at the heart of effective cross-cultural communication and understanding.

This event prompted a lively discussion in Cheryl's class. Some couldn't understand the reason behind the message until Michelle asked how they would feel if someone wrote: "We are studying girls, or Hispanics, or African-Americans, or boys, and we want to correspond with some."

"It makes you feel like a thing, not a person," she noted. "And, there are many different Native American cultures, not just one." This made many students think again about how the person who developed this web site must have felt when reading messages like this.

The discussion in Cheryl's class was useful in developing greater respect and sensitivity for others, issues at the heart of effective cross-cultural communication and understanding. It increased children's awareness of the power of words and how the words one uses in a message may unintentionally hurt people. It also helped students develop greater sensitivity to different cultural traditions and how one must be respectful of cultural differences on the WWW.

Toward the end of their conversation, Cheryl pointed out how important it was for Native American students to have a space on the WWW to communicate with other students from Native American cultures and that one needed to respect this right. She also noted that some Native American students were interested in communicating with students from non-Native cultural traditions. She said that she had found a location on the web at the **Grassroots** section of SchoolNet (http://www.schoolnet.ca/grassroots/), where Native American and non-Native American classes who wanted to exchange e-mail could do so. She wasn't certain if this was open to their class, but she said she would send a message and see if this would be possible.

Lessons From the Classroom

It is clear the Internet provides special opportunities to help everyone better understand the unique qualities in each of our cultural traditions. No other instructional resource available in your classroom is as rich in its potential for developing an understanding of the diverse nature of our global society and for helping each of your students to walk in someone else's footprints.

This episode from Cheryl Chan's classroom has several important lessons for us to consider as we think about using the Internet to increase multicultural understanding. First, it is clear the Internet provides special opportunities to help everyone better understand the unique qualities in each of our cultural traditions. No other instructional resource available in your classroom is as rich in its potential for developing an understanding of the diverse nature of our global society and for helping each of your students to walk in someone else's footprints.

Cheryl sought to take advantage of this potential. Each group in her class defined and completed an Inquiry project celebrating a special cultural group. Cheryl gave each group several guidelines to follow: each project had to treat the culture with respect, it had to include literature and Internet experiences as part of the project; and, each group had to develop a learning experience for the rest of the class based on something they had learned from that culture. One group was building a display and learning center in their classroom with many cultural artifacts. Another group was planning on a poetry reading, a readers theater presentation, and an Internet Activity. A third group was developing a reading corner and a bulletin board. The fourth group was planning a read aloud activity and an Internet scavenger hunt for everyone to complete.

Using the Internet to celebrate the diversity that exists in our world is important for a variety of reasons. Bringing this information into your classroom sends an important message to your students about the respect and dignity each of us needs to accord every human experience. Integrating Internet resources from different cultures into your curriculum is central to accomplishing this important goal. Children feel pride in themselves and their culture when all cultural experiences are valued for the contributions they make to a rich and vibrant society. In addition, students develop a richer appreciation of the historical forces that have shaped our societies and the contributions made by different cultural groups. Finally, the Internet allows all students to explore issues of social justice. Exploring issues of social justice is essential to preparing children for citizenship in a diverse society where these issues are fundamental to our collective well being.

The episode from Cheryl's class also teaches us a second lesson: e-mail experiences with others may be very useful as you consider using the Internet to increase multicultural understanding. E-mail allows your students to immediately communicate with others around the world from different cultural traditions in order to learn more about their unique heritage. This opportunity has never before existed in school classrooms; it enables your students to engage in powerful cross-cultural experiences that may be used to develop understanding and respect for others.

E-mail, however, is a two-edged sword in developing multicultural understanding. On the positive side, e-mail removes many of the visual trappings that normally impede conversations between members of different cultural groups; we tend to ignore physical differences and focus, instead, on considering the ideas and experiences of the person with whom we communicate. This is what the students who studied Japanese cultural traditions experienced in Cheryl's class. On the other hand, when we bring stereotypes about a cultural group to e-mail conversations, these stereotypes often appear unintentionally between the lines of our messages and may be hurtful to the recipient. This is what happened with students leaving messages at the location called Native American Indian. E-mail communication between different cultural groups requires sensitivity to the recipient and an ability to anticipate how any message might be interpreted as you compose it. Often, it forces us to confront stereotypes we may have but may not realize. These are good lessons for all of us to learn.

Central Sites to Increase Multicultural Understanding

Many locations on the Internet provide a comprehensive set of resources to help your students appreciate and understand different cultural traditions.

Children feel pride in themselves and their culture when all cultural experiences are valued for the contributions they make to a rich and vibrant society.

E-mail allows your students to immediately communicate with others around the world from different cultural traditions in order to learn more about their unique heritage. This opportunity has never before existed in school classrooms.

E-mail communication between different cultural groups requires sensitivity to the recipient and an ability to anticipate how any message might be interpreted as you compose it. Often, it forces us to confront stereotypes we may have but may not realize. These are good lessons for all of us to learn.

E-MAIL FOR YOU

To: Colleagues

From: Angeles Maitland Heriot <maitl_sh@sminter.com.ar>

Subject: Developing Cross-cultural Relationships

Hello!

St. Hilda's School, Argentina, is a prestigious bi-lingual institution located in the Province of Buenos Aires. I teach Language, Literature, and Religious Knowledge in English as a second language to 17 boys and girls of 11–12 years old.

The Internet Project for this age group, called "To Be or not to Be" is one of the few interdepartmental projects linking the Spanish and English sections, (and the work of their teachers). The departments are separate in that they have their own authorities and time tables, as well as staff and curricula. Therefore, the project stands as an experimental joint venture.

The computer teacher renders his lessons in Spanish, and he has a basic comprehension of English. He is responsible for our Internet Project, and I, the teacher of English to the same group of students, provide him with translations whenever necessary. The purpose of the project is to give children a meaningful task in their computing lessons to connect our children with the outer world, since our school is located in a small suburb in the Province of Buenos Aires, and the exchange with other schools or children is scarce.

From a broader perspective, the Internet allows our young users to become aware of the geography, history, and culture of the world. It is hoped that our pupils will enlarge their knowledge, and increase their curiosity about other places and races, while learning to respect different values and ways of living, and to use English to communicate effectively. The incentive to "talk" with other children all around the world is extremely powerful. The Internet is an ideal medium, since it requires an informal writing style, thus allowing the writers certain "literary licenses" (spelling, misprints, punctuation misuse). Pupils may feel more at ease when they are not required to rewrite their messages. The Internet encourages children to write and to practice their typing to enjoy the thrill of receiving a message!!!

On the other hand, teachers need to guide their pupils' work, so that the context and content of the letters are not misleading and/or inaccurate. A little time is required before children realize that no matter how instantaneous the whole process may be, there is still the need to think to be able to express their aims clearly.

I'll be very glad to answer any question you would like to ask with reference to the Internet at school. We are only experimenting with this service in our Argentine context. More connections and more servers are just beginning to appear in the market, offering lower costs and better services.

Angeles Maitland Heriot
Junior 7 Teacher St. Hilda's School Buenos Aires, Argentina
e-mail: maitl_sh@sminter.com.ar

Many locations on the Internet provide a comprehensive set of resources to help your students appreciate and understand different cultural traditions.

You may wish to review the resources at these sites as you develop Internet Workshop, Internet Project, and Internet Inquiry with your students. A few locations also contain WebQuests.

It is possible that some of the central sites we identify in this section may contain links that eventually link to locations where issues of sexual orientation are considered. While we believe these issues are important for older students to consider, we recognize that a number of communities may feel uncomfortable allowing younger students to access these sites. We mention this so that you may make informed judgments about locations you make available to your students.

The best central sites to support instruction in multicultural understanding include:

- **Yahooligans: Around the World**—http://www.yahooligans.com/Around_the_World/
  This may be one of the better central sites for classrooms in the elementary grades exploring cultural diversity. Especially useful is the section on cultures, but all areas will have links to resources that may be immediately used in the classroom. Set a bookmark!

- **Diversity**—http://www.historyserver.org/hssweb/asia-afr.html
  This is an enormous collection of links to sites on the WWW related to diversity and multicultural education. It is part of the larger History/Social Studies Web Site for K–12 Teachers. Sections include: general sources, disabilities, migration and immigrant resources, Jewish resources, Asian-American resources, African-American resources, Women's Studies resources, Native American resources, and Hispanic resources.

- **Cultures of the World**—http://www.ala.org/parentspage/greatsites/people.html#b
  Here is a central site with many extensive resources selected by the American Library Association as appropriate for children from preschool to age 14. Many great resources.

- **Walk A Mile in My Shoes: Multicultural Curriculum Resources**—http://www.wmht.org/trail/explor02.htm
  Developed by schools in the Albany, New York, region, this location is designed specifically for teachers new to the Internet and includes many links in areas such as multicultural literature, multicultural sites for kids, locations for multicultural e-mail exchanges, sites with links on specific cultural groups, and sites with links to schools all over the world.

- **Multicultural Pavilion**—
  http://curry.edschool.Virginia.EDU/go/multicultural/
  Located at the School of Education at the University of Virginia, this location is very well organized and growing very rapidly. The most useful area is a "Teachers' Corner" where you will find a set

of links to important locations on the WWW for multicultural education, links to on-line resources for teachers and students, several historic archives, and links to on-line literature for students.

- **Latin American Network Information Center**—
http://www.lanic.utexas.edu/
A great location with many sites and resources devoted to the study of Latin America. The education area is especially useful. Some of the locations are in Spanish. Set a bookmark!

 E-MAIL FOR YOU

To: Colleagues
From: Bill Farrell <farrellb@ride.ri.net> <xyz101@uriacc.uri.edu>
Subject: Multicultural Understanding

Dear Colleague,

A topic that appeals to me is multi-cultural understanding and one of my favorite sites is **Web66** (http://web66.coled.umn.edu/schools.html), the International Registry of schools on the web. This site has links to many, many schools around the world. These links will tell you about a school and many times have e-mail links to the schools. You may be able to begin a collaboration with another school by sending them a short e-mail message about your school and students while requesting information about their school and students. This is a great way for students to begin pen pal correspondences. If they are willing, you might be able to continue this e-mail relationship while continuing to share information about your individual communities and customs. Students can exchange recipes from their countries and culminate an activity with a world's fair type of event in which the children assume the roles of their foreign partners. I truly feel that if more and more children are exposed to other children around the world via e-mail and the Internet, we will ultimately have a safer world and better place for all of us. This kind of relationship was not possible two years ago. If you don't succeed with one school, try another and I'm quite sure you'll find a school that is more than willing to collaborate on a project with you. I wish you good luck on your Internet odyssey and hope to run across your school someday on the information superhighway.

```
    Bill Farrell
    Computer Literacy Teacher
    Chariho Middle School
    ****************************************
    William L. Farrell
    Computer Specialist, Grades 5-8
    Chariho Regional Middle School
    e-mail: farrelb@ride.ri.net
    http://www.chariho.k12.ri.us/cms/index.html
    ****************************************
```

Keeping it Simple: Using Internet Workshop

Some teachers like to devote a weekly Internet Workshop activity to increasing multicultural understanding as a regular part of their curriculum, each week exploring a different cultural experience on the Internet and discussing this experience during a workshop session.

Exploring links at these central sites will immediately give you ideas for an Internet Workshop activity designed to increase multicultural understanding. Some teachers like to devote a weekly Internet Workshop activity to increasing multicultural understanding as a regular part of their curriculum, each week exploring a different cultural experience on the Internet and discussing this experience during a workshop session.

TEACHING TIP	**Ideas for Internet Workshop**
	When you are trying to increase multicultural understanding with Internet Workshop, it is important to keep two ideas in mind. First, try to provide opportunities for students to work together on these assignments. When two students work on Internet Workshop together, opportunities develop for important exchanges to take place about these issues. This almost always leads to conversations that are important to developing greater respect and sensitivity about other cultures, especially if you establish this value in your classroom. Second, provide an opportunity to share students' thoughts and responses after they complete their activity, perhaps during the workshop session. This allows you to support the respect and sensitivity about other cultures that you are trying to develop.

Here are some examples of Internet Workshop that might be used to support greater multicultural understanding:

- **On the Line**—http://www.ontheline.org.uk/
  See how people in eight different countries on the meridian line from Europe through Africa share the same time of day but lead very different lives. Have students select one country and come to the workshop session with a presentation on the culture of their country.

- **Mancala**—http://imagiware.com/mancala/
  This strategy game from Africa is often found in classrooms. Here it is in a virtual form. A great site for your students to play this game against the computer as you study African or African-American cultural traditions. It contains clear directions and the program will even give you hints if your game is not going very well. Share strategies during your workshop session. Make a bookmark!

- **MultiCulturalPedia**—http://www.netlaputa.ne.jp/~tokyo3/e/
  This site has been compiled from information about culture and customs sent by individuals from around the world. The site is also in Japanese.

- Afro-Americ@'s **Black History Museum**—
http://www.afroam.org/history/history.html
For older students, this is one of the finest collection of resources on several important aspects of African-American history. It includes important sections on resistance during slavery, The Tuskegee Airman, Jackie Robinson, The Black Panther Party, Black or White, The Million Man March, The Scottsboro Boys, and World War II. Be certain to devote a number of workshop sessions to explore each of these areas in your social studies program.

- **Kid's Window**—
http://sequoia.nttam.com:80/KIDS/kids_home.html
Developed in a joint project between Stanford University and NTT from Japan, there are enough great resources here to design Internet Workshop sessions for an entire unit on Japan. Audio is included throughout the site. This location is probably most appropriate for the elementary grades, but everyone can enjoy the wonderfully rich insights into Japanese cultural traditions. Invite students to read one of several classic Japanese folk tales such as *Momotaro* or listen to it read aloud in Japanese and English. Have students order lunch and then write what they ordered in both English and Japanese. Have students attend language class in Hiragana, Kanji, or Katakana, and then share what they learned during Internet Workshop. Have students finish up by following the directions to make an origami crane. Older students may also wish to visit a companion site, **Japan Window** (http://www.jwindow.net/). Set a bookmark for both locations!

- **Martin Luther King Jr.**—
http://www.seattletimes.com/mlk/index.html
An outstanding site designed for teachers and students to reflect on the legacy of this famous American (see Figure 10-2). Developed by a newspaper in Seattle, this location includes an interactive timeline of his life and contributions, audio clips of important speeches, reflections on his life from many individuals, a photo tour of the civil rights movement, information about the national holiday in the U.S., classroom ideas, and opportunities to communicate with others about the significance of Dr. King's accomplishments. A must for celebrating his life with many resources for Internet Activity. Set a bookmark!

- **Kwanzaa Information Center**—
http://www.melanet.com/kwanzaa/
Kwanzaa is the African-American spiritual holiday initiated by Dr. Maulana Ron Karenga in 1966. Today it is celebrated in an increasing number of homes. This location at Melanet provides a

Figure 10-2.
The home page for **Martin Luther King Jr.** at the Seattle Times (http://www.seattletimes.com/mlk/index.html).

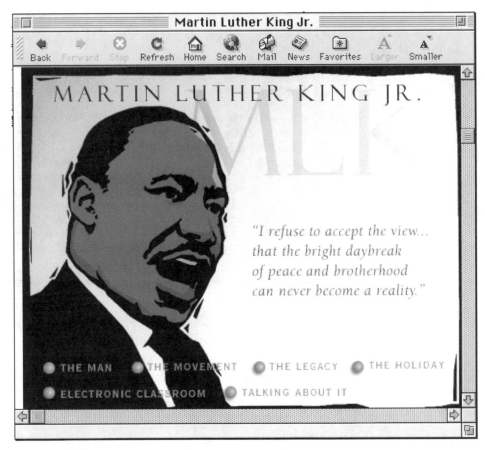

rich set of information resources about this holiday. It explains how it is celebrated and the meaning of the important symbols. Have your students read the information at this site and come to Internet Workshop prepared to share what they have learned.

- **Maya/Aztec/Inca Center of the Lords of the Earth—**
  http://www.realtime.net/maya/
  A rich site with many resources designed to help students recognize the many accomplishments in history, geography, geology, astronomy, archaeology, anthropology, and art that existed in the Americas before Christopher Columbus's arrival. Have your students explore these pages and bring one important cultural achievement to share and explain during Internet Workshop. Use this time to discuss the rich heritage that existed in the Americas before its discovery by Europe.

Using Internet Project

Internet Project is, perhaps, the best method to develop multicultural understanding among your students. When your students communicate with students from another cultural context, many important insights are shared about how we are all alike and how we are different. Children have a special

Internet Project is, perhaps, the best method to develop multicultural understanding among your students. When your students communicate with students from another cultural context, many important insights are shared about how we are all alike and how we are different.

TEACHING TIP

Going Beyond Study and Communication to Action

It is important to study different cultural experiences in order to better understand the diversity that defines our world. It is also important, though, to go beyond understanding to social action, seeking to make our world a better place. Seek ways with your students to engage in community action projects, either right in your community or over the Internet. Students have used the Internet to support relief efforts in devastated parts of the world, to support efforts of famine relief at locations such at **The Hunger Site** (http://www.hungersite.com/), or to support the purchase of rain forest habitat at locations such as **Rain Forest Care** (http://rainforest.care2.com/). If you are working at the high school or middle school level you might wish to seek other social action or volunteer projects in you community by visiting **Project America** (http://www.project.org/index.html). This resource, originally developed by two high school students, puts you in touch with organizations in your immediate area who seek volunteer assistance with a number of projects, many of which permit your students to act in positive ways on their developing knowledge of diversity. It is a wonderful resource, enabling all of us to make our world a better place.

way of cutting right through social trappings to share essential information with one another. Their queries, which sometimes might be perceived as offensive to an adult, are often appreciated for what they are by other children—an honest attempt to understand the world around them. Guiding children into these new types of cultural interchanges on the Internet can do much to increase your students' appreciation for cultural differences. It is a wonderful way to celebrate diversity in your classroom.

The traditional sites for Internet Project described in previous chapters may be useful as you seek out projects with classes from different cultural contexts. Sometimes, though, it takes a special effort to contact classrooms from other cultural contexts. You may have to initiate contact directly with teachers and schools. We encourage you to do so because the rewards are so great. Not every teacher or school will respond to your requests, but enough will respond to make this a valuable strategy. Locations to help you to make these contacts include:

- **KIDLINK**—http://www.kidlink.org/
  You must visit this site if you are interested in participating in an international project with your class. The goal of KIDLINK is to create a global dialog among the youth of the world. It is open to all students through secondary school and is run by KIDLINK Society, a grass roots and volunteer organization. Here you will find many wonderful forums for your students to communicate with children around the world. Language translation services are available as well as IRC chat sessions. There are locations for student-to-student as well as classroom-to-classroom contact. Both Internet projects and e-mail keypal exchanges are available at this outstanding location. Set a bookmark!

- **Intercultural E-mail Classroom Connections—**
  http://www.stolaf.edu/network/iecc/

This exceptional service is provided by St. Olaf College in Minnesota to bring together schools from all over the world. When you join one of the mailing lists at this location, you will have e-mail access to teachers and schools around the world. Your school can take part in a variety of e-mail exchanges and classroom collaborations as invitations appear on the list. Or, develop your own and invite others to join. Be certain to thank the organizers at St. Olaf College for their wonderful contributions, bringing many different classrooms together from all over the globe. Set a bookmark!

- **International WWW Schools Registry—**
  http://web66.coled.umn.edu/schools.html
  Visit this site and travel around the world to visit the home pages of schools in Australia, Japan, Canada, the U.S., Europe, and many other locations. Contact some of the schools to see if they are interested in an Internet Project with your class.

Internet FAQ	
I am trying to locate a person and their e-mail address on the Internet. How do I do this?	There are several search engines devoted to locating people on the Internet. You may wish to try **Bigfoot** (http://www.bigfoot.com/) or **WhoWhere?** (http://www.whowhere.com/). Each searches large data bases of people such as phone books and e-mail directories. You may also use a regular search engine by typing in the complete name of the person you are looking for, in case they are listed on a web page somewhere on the Internet. Use the complete name and use a search engine such as **HotBot** that enables you to search for "The Person".

Examples of projects you may wish to consider joining or developing to increase multicultural understanding include:

- **Breaking Bread Together.** Breaking bread together is a traditional way to begin a cultural exchange about important matters. Invite several classes from around the world to participate in an e-mail collaborative project as you exchange foods from your countries and eat a common meal on the same day. Each class sends a small package of culturally significant foods to participating classes along with directions for their preparation. Before the common meal and on the day of the celebration, classrooms exchange information via e-mail about each type of food and its significance within their culture. Differences in time zones may prevent immediate back and forth of e-mail messages, but some classrooms schedule their event on a weekend day or in the evening so they can communicate in real time. Other classrooms have their e-mail exchange take place during the following days. Great fun and very important insights always result from this activity.

- **Who are our Heroes?** Invite classes from several different cultural contexts to participate in a heroes project. Each student in participating classes can write a description of their greatest hero, explaining what it is about this person that makes them admirable. Classes then exchange these essays in order to understand who students in different cultural contexts admire. Then, provide an opportunity for students to ask questions of one another about their essays, especially information that may relate to their culture. Use Internet Workshop to share essays and discuss the qualities each hero shares. These essays and conversations provide an ideal opportunity to discover important aspects of different cultures. This project could be extended to include heroes in different categories: parent/guardian heroes, teacher heroes, sports heroes, politicians, etc.

- **Weekly News From Around the World.** Invite classes from around the world to contribute two or three news articles each week from their classroom about local events. Have one class collect these articles via e-mail and distribute a weekly world newspaper to each of the participating classes. Writing about local events for students in another cultural context forces students to develop greater sensitivity to the needs of their readers from different cultural contexts. Use Internet Workshop to plan new articles and read those contributed by others. Discussing these events develops a better understanding of the cultural context in different parts of the world.

- **Explanatory Myths From Around the World.** Every culture contains a set of explanatory myths that explains the creation of natural elements—why the sun comes up each day, where fire came from, how a mountain or lake was created, or where the face in the moon comes from. Invite schools from different cultural contexts to research, write, and share these stories with students from different cultural contexts. Read these stories during Internet Workshop and discuss what each may say about the culture from which it came.

- **KeyPals.** During the course of the year, help your students develop KeyPals with several classes around the world. Share these individual messages during Internet Workshop and discuss what each suggests about its cultural context. You may wish to also visit **Intercultural E-mail Classroom Connections** (http://www.stolaf.edu/network/iecc/), **KIDLINK** (http://www.kidlink.org/), or **International WWW Schools Registry** (http://web66.coled.umn.edu/schools.html) to make contact with classes who wish to participate (see Figure 10-3).

Figure 10-3.
KIDPROJ (http://www.kidlink.org/ KIDPROJ/index.html), one of many project pages located at **KIDLINK** (http://www.kidlink.org/).
KIDLINK is an outstanding volunteer organization that puts your classroom in touch with other classrooms around the world, helping everyone discover the advantages of diversity.

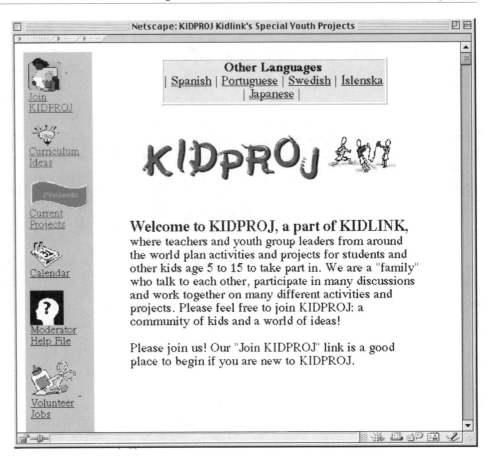

Using Internet Inquiry

Using Internet Inquiry along with workshop sessions to share and exchange learning experiences can be especially powerful in developing multicultural understanding.

Using Internet Inquiry along with workshop sessions to share and exchange learning experiences can be especially powerful in developing multicultural understanding. Individual students often have an interest in a particular cultural context, either their own or one with which they have a special connection. Exploring these interests with Internet Inquiry can be an effective approach since learning focuses on questions that are personally significant. Be certain to invite your students to develop inquiry projects in this area.

When students work in groups, they often share new insights, interpretations, and resources. This leads to important new directions as students pursue related questions.

There are several ideas to keep in mind as you pursue Internet Inquiry for multicultural understanding. First, where appropriate, encourage your students to form group inquiry projects. When students work in groups, they often share new insights, interpretations, and resources. This leads to important new directions as students pursue related questions. With support, these groups may also be able to conduct their own, regular Internet Workshop sessions focusing on the topic of their inquiry projects. If you can accomplish this, you and your students will have established an important vehicle for learning about multicultural understanding.

E-MAIL FOR YOU

To: Colleagues
From: Linda Shearin <lshearin@bellsouth.net>
Subject: Connecting with Thailand

Greetings virtual travelers,

Over the past year my students and I have been engaged in building a web page with Benchamatheputit School in Petchburi, Thailand. It has been a wonderful experience for us all!

Chumlong Buasuwan, a teacher at Benchama School, has taught me a great deal about his culture and his students. We have worked together to plan the web page reflecting the commonalties and differences between his school and mine. His students wrote a touching poem celebrating what we share in common that appears on the first page of the web site.

What has amazed me most, and my students also, is that the Thai students created all their work on the web page in English. Although English is their second language and many students don't consider themselves fluent, they have done extraordinary work.

We have faced some challenges over the course of our partnership. Our school calendars are not quite compatible so communication between the students was sometimes affected. Chumlong and I found it challenging to communicate for planning purposes via online chats because Thailand is 12 hours ahead of the US. This time difference also precluded online chats or teleconferences between the two schools.

My students experienced culture shock when they found out that Petchburi has three royal palaces. "What," they said, "do we have in Raleigh, NC, that can compare with that?" We had to look more closely at our own community to find aspects of it that the Thai students would find appealing.

Nevertheless, we have all thoroughly enjoyed our partnership. We are planning this year to collaborate on an online newspaper featuring activities at both schools, while we continue to update our original web page. Chumlong is an outstanding and innovative educator. I am looking forward to learning more from him as we continue our work together!

Good luck on your own journeys!

Linda Shearin

Fred J. Carnage Gifted & Talented Magnet School for Accelerated Studies in Math, Science, and Technology

Raleigh, NC

Ideas for Internet Inquiry

Encourage your students to develop KeyPals with other students from the cultural context they are exploring. This will be an important source of information for your students. Discussing common issues that matter with someone from another cultural context is the best way to understand that context. Encourage your students to share these exchanges with their group and the rest of the class.

Be certain to have students share their multicultural learning within the structure of Internet Workshop on a regular basis. When many students share their new insights and their questions about a variety of cultural contexts everyone gains new insights about the diversity that exists in this world.

Second, be certain to have students share their multicultural learning within the structure of Internet Workshop on a regular basis. When many students share their new insights and their questions about a variety of cultural contexts everyone gains new insights about the diversity that exists in this world. Moreover, discussing these matters openly helps to remove stereotypes and sends your students a powerful message about the respect we should accord each culture.

Using WebQuests in Your Classroom

WebQuests for developing multicultural understanding seem a natural. Collaboratively exploring issues of difference within a heterogeneous grouping can have a powerful effect in developing a greater appreciation for the diversity that defines us. Unfortunately, however, good WebQuests in this area have been somewhat slow to develop and appear on the Internet. We will make a special effort to post links at our website (http://web.syr.edu/~djleu/teaching.html) to the best new ones that will inevitably appear. Stop by and take a look!

This is not to say that we lack models for exceptional WebQuests that promote a greater understanding of cultural diversity. A few do exist, such as the following:

- **Six Paths to China**—
  http://www.kn.pacbell.com/wired/China/#webquest

  This outstanding collection of activities includes both the full WebQuest described in Chapter 6, **Searching for China** (http://www.kn.pacbell.com/wired/China/ChinaQuest.html), as well as a number of other, more focused WebQuests. As a complete package, it is the perfect place to begin your exploration of this diverse and fascinating culture. Be certain to set a bookmark!

- **Tuskegee Tragedy**—
  http://www.kn.pacbell.com/wired/BHM/tuskegee_quest.html
  An outstanding WebQuest for secondary school students, enabling them to explore the tragedy of Tuskegee, compare it to other events such as gun control, abortion, and the use of internment camps, and then determine whether Tuskegee was a unique event or one

E-MAIL FOR YOU

To: Colleagues
From: Dana Eaton <dana_eaton@nhusd.k12.ca.us>
Subject: The Internet in our Classroom

The Internet in our classroom isn't something we struggle to integrate, rather it is the foundation for many things we do.

The Internet is a vital resource to gather pictures, sounds, text, and movies for many of the projects we do. When we decided to build a MiWok Roundhouse in our fourth grade classroom, we successfully scoured the Internet looking for pictures and instructions. We also found legends, rituals, and even a movie that showed the construction of a roundhouse foundation (http://www.nhusd.k12.ca.us/Searles/Homepage_40/roundhouse.html).

We have worked hard to organize these resources so that they are more useful for our school. Michael Price, David Larson and I have spent the last few years creating a Searles Surfers section of our school homepage that allows students a safe and quick directory of useful Internet sites (http://www.nhusd.k12.ca.us/Searles/searleslinks.html).

The Internet is a communication tool between teachers and families. We took many pictures of projects and published many of those projects on our own classroom web page. Families were able to log on at home and develop a better understanding of things that were happening at school. We hosted a Family Technology Night where families who did not have home access could come and view class homepages. We had relatives across the country that were able to instantly keep up with their grandchildren, brothers, sisters, nephews, and nieces at the click of a button (http://www.nhusd.k12.ca.us/Searles/Homepage_40/40SearlesEaton.html).

The Internet is a communication tool between students and the world. Each student in my class has his or her own personal web page and e-mail address. A poem that might have been shared inside the classroom was now instantly published to the world. We have had City Councilman e-mail students about their publications because they were able to view them on the Internet. Publishing to a worldwide audience is also great motivation for a student who is attempting to do their best work (http://www.nhusd.k12.ca.us/Searles/Homepage_40/juan.html).

The Internet will be common in every classroom very soon. It will be a common classroom resource along with dictionaries, encyclopedias, and libraries. There is just too much potential for it not to be.

    Dana Eaton
    Grade 4
    Searles Elementary
    Union City, CA
    dana_eaton@nhusd.k12.ca.us

that we must continually guard against. At the end of their research, students write letters to the authors of articles they have read and researched on the Internet, sharing their opinions. This is a powerful WebQuest with equally powerful learning outcomes. Part of the many fine resources at Blue Web'n.

- **Black History: Exploring African-American Issues on the Web**—http://www.kn.pacbell.com/wired/BHM/AfroAm.html An excellent collection of resources at Blue Web'n permitting you and your students to study a number of important issues related to many African-American experiences. Included are a **Black History Hotlist** (http://www.kn.pacbell.com/wired/BHM/bh_hotlist.html) with links to many sites on the Internet, an **Interactive Treasure Hunt and Quiz** (http://www.kn.pacbell.com/wired/BHM/bh_hunt_quiz.html), a series of short explorations called **Sampling African America** (http://www.kn.pacbell.com/wired/BHM/bh_sampler.html), and a full WebQuest on racial desegregation called **Little Rock 9 Integration 0?** (http://www.kn.pacbell.com/wired/BHM/little_rock/).

Visiting the Classroom: The Harriet Tubman Page Developed by Terry Hongell and Patty Taverna in New York

A visit to **Harriet Tubman and the Underground Railroad** (http://www2.lhric.org/pocantico/tubman/tubman.html), developed by Terry Hongell and Patty Taverna, teaches each of us important lessons (see Figure 10-4). There are, of course, the many lessons we can learn about the life of this famous African American and the important work she accomplished. You will discover these as you explore the many links and resources created by these two, very talented teachers and the students with whom they work. Visit the timeline of Harriet's life with art and text from the students in Patty's class and then take an interactive quiz they developed. Read the short biographies they have developed and gain a greater appreciation for the life Harriet led. Read the poems this class wrote and print out the crossword puzzles they developed after conducting inquiry projects about Harriet's life. Finally, explore the marvelous links they have placed at their page, taking you and your students to new locations with new information resources about Harriet Tubman. Yes, there are many lessons we can learn from this remarkable woman and this location will help our students to understand them.

The collaboration between the classroom teacher, Patty, and the technology teacher, Terry, is a model that each of us might seek to follow.

There are also important lessons at this location for the Internet journeys we are all taking. The collaboration between the classroom teacher, Patty, and the technology teacher, Terry, is a model that each of us might seek to follow. By combining the instructional insights of Patty and her students with the technology insights of Terry, they are able to achieve much more

Figure 10-4.
Harriet Tubman and the Underground Railroad (http://www2.lhric.org/pocantico/tubman/tubman.html), developed by Terry Hongell and Patty Taverna.

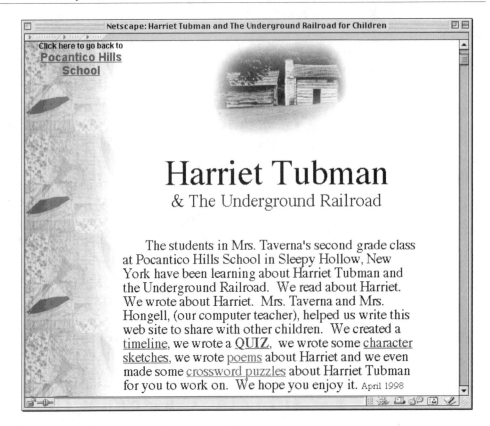

than the sum of their individual skills. Most importantly, by posting these curricular resources on the Internet, we can all benefit from their work.

As networked information resources become more extensive and complexly structured, and as the Internet continues to change, no one person can be expected to know everything there is to know about teaching with the new technologies of literacy; these technologies will simply change too quickly and be too extensive to permit any single person to be literate in them all. Each of us, however, will know something useful to others. This will distribute knowledge about how to best use the Internet in the classroom. Each of us needs to be open to new collaborative ventures with other teachers as we each seek to improve instruction in our own classrooms. Terry and Patty show us how this can be done and the exciting resources that can result. It is an important lesson for us all.

Instructional Resources on the Internet

Africa Online: Kids Only—
http://www.africaonline.com/AfricaOnline/coverkids.html
A nice location for your students to learn about Africa. They can read Rainbow Magazine—a Kenyan magazine for kids, play African games and decode messages, learn about the over 1000 languages in Africa, meet African students on line, find a keypal, or visit the home pages of schools in Africa. Set a bookmark!

Amazon Interactive—http://www.eduweb.com/amazon.html
> A wonderful site for learning about Amazonia and the people who call this beautiful place home, including the Quichua people. Many exciting learning activities appear here.

Cranes for Peace—http://www.he.net/~sparker/cranes.html
> Cranes for Peace began as a project to collect paper cranes to be sent to Hiroshima for the 50th anniversary of the bombing as a wish for peace. It was based on the book *Sadako and the 1,000 Cranes*. A Japanese legend holds that folding 1000 cranes (senbazuru) so pleases the gods the folder is granted a wish. Now, this is a location to celebrate peace each year by making origami cranes and sending them to be placed at the memorial to Sadako in Seattle, or to the peace shrine in Hiroshima. Visit this location to find out more about this wonderful book and the many Internet projects it has sparked for peace. Set a bookmark!

Jewish Culture and History—
> http://www.igc.apc.org/ddickerson/judaica.html
> One of the more extensive sites on the Internet on Jewish culture with many links to other locations including links to Virtual Jerusalem and the Tour of Israel. More appropriate for older students.

KIDPROJ'S Multi-Cultural Calendar—
> http://www.kidlink.org/KIDPROJ/MCC/
> Here is another wonderful resource for your classroom developed by KIDLINK, a non-profit organization. This location contains a great data base of celebrations taking place each day around the world, along with ideas for connecting the calendar to your curriculum. Set a bookmark and let the good folks at KIDLINK know how much you appreciate their efforts.

Latin American Children's Resources—
> http://www.zonalatina.com/Zlchild.htm
> From Zona Latina, this location contains links to a number of children's resources from Latin America, including many in Spanish.

National Civil Rights Museum—http://www.midsouth.rr.com/civilrights/
> The home page for this museum. Take the interactive tour of the exhibit to learn about this continuing struggle.

Native American Indian Resources—
> http://indy4.fdl.cc.mn.us/~isk/mainmenu.html
> One of the richest locations on the Internet for the Native American community. Information about Native history, literature, biographies, herbal knowledge, environmental concerns, schools, politics, you name it. The talented webmaster for this site recently passed away, so it is not clear yet if this resource will continue its important work. We hope someone will step forward to continue her mission. Set a bookmark!

Native Web Resources—http://www.nativeweb.org/resources/
> This is a great location for resources on Native cultures. It contains many useful links to a variety of Native American resources including information about tribal units, literature, newsletters and journals.

The First Americans—http://www.germantown.k12.il.us/html/intro.html

A great project developed by the third graders at Germantown Elementary School in Illinois, providing us all with a new resource for our study of Native Americans.

The National Women's History Project: Links—http://www.nwhp.org/links.html

A wonderful collection of resources on the Internet about women's history. Set a bookmark!

The Simon Wiesenthal Center—http://motlc.wiesenthal.com/index.html

The homepage for this organization with links to thousands of important resources covering the Holocaust and other issues of Jewish struggle.

The African American Mosaic—http://www.loc.gov/exhibits/african/intro.html

An online exhibit from the Library of Congress exploring Black history and containing many primary source documents.

Listservs/Mailing Lists for Increasing Multicultural Understanding

Use standard procedures for subscribing to these mailing lists. See Chapter 3

CULTUR-L—listserv@vm.temple.edu

A discussion group on cultural differences in the curriculum. Follow typical listserv procedures to subscribe.

MCPavilion—majordomo@virginia.edu

This is the WWW location for an active discussion group at the Multicultural Pavilion web site.

Directions for subscribing are located at: http://curry.edschool.Virginia.EDU/go/multicultural/issues.html

MULTC-ED—listserv@umdd.umd.edu

A discussion group on multicultural education, K–12. Follow typical listserv procedures to subscribe.

MULTICULTURAL-ED—listproc@lists.fsu.edu

A discussion group on multicultural education. Follow typical listserv procedures to subscribe.

NAT-EDU—listserv@indycms.iupui.edu

A discussion group on K–12 education and Indigenous Peoples. Follow typical listserv procedures to subscribe.

Including All Students on the Internet

E-MAIL FOR YOU

To: Our readers
From: djleu@syr.edu (Don Leu), ddleu@syr.edu (Debbie Leu)
Subject: Insuring Internet Equity Within Classroom Communities

Internet equity has become an important issue within the educational community. It is important to provide more equitable access and ensure that we do not leave any members of our society behind. Most of this discussion, though, has focused on how to ensure equal Internet access between schools and school districts. This is one important aspect of Internet equity. Another is to do everything we can to ensure equal Internet access *within* individual classroom communities. This aspect of equity has gone largely unnoticed.

Sometimes, for example, a few students in a classroom become so exited about electronic learning they tend to dominate the use of limited electronic resources, inadvertently excluding others in the process. At other times, students who fall behind in navigational skills at the beginning sometime fail to take full advantage of their computer time because they are uncertain about how to accomplish tasks and are too embarrassed to ask for assistance. At other times, challenged students do not always participate in Internet experiences for any of a number of reasons. This chapter recognizes each of these issues as it seeks ways to ensure equitable Internet access for each child in your class.

Don and Debbie

Teaching With the Internet: Monica Ashburn's Class

Monica Ashburn noticed the group of her students excited about what they had just discovered on the Internet. "Cool!" someone said again. Each time someone said "Cool!" a few more students were attracted to the computer to see what was taking place. She was pleased with the enthusiasm her students experienced about learning as they used the Internet. She was also concerned.

"Maya, isn't it your turn at the computer" Monica asked one of the quieter members of her class. She had noticed Maya reluctant to claim her computer time when others, because of their excitement, did not leave the computer according to the classroom schedule. Maya was so shy she missed her computer time several times last week. Monica was determined not to let this happen again. She encouraged the group at the computer to quickly finish their work and allow Maya her full turn on the Internet.

"Can I help Tora when I am done?" asked Maya. Tora was a student with limited vision. Tora and Maya often worked together.

"That would be great," said Monica, "And could you change the font size to 48 like I showed you?" Changing the font to this larger size in Netscape Navigator enabled Tora to read the information on the screen. "And then maybe ask Orlando to translate the Spanish message you two received from the class in Argentina. Have him translate your answer, and type it up, too. I would like to e-mail your message after school today." Monica had found a partner class to exchange e-mails with using **Intercultural E-mail Classroom Connections** (http://www.stolaf.edu/network/iecc/), a resource sponsored by St. Olaf's College in Minnesota (see Figure 11-1).

A little later, Monica saw Orlando concluding the translation of Maya and Tora's e-mail message to students in Argentina. The three of them were talking back and forth as Orlando was trying to complete the translation. This activity was especially nice since it accomplished several things at once. Of course, Maya and Tora were assisted in getting their message out. In addition, however, it gave Orlando a sense of pride in his ability to speak and write in Spanish. Last year, this was seen as a handicap. After the Internet entered his classroom with opportunities to correspond in Spanish, Orlando's linguistic ability was seen in a very different light. Being fluent in Spanish was now an asset that was much in demand, especially after Monica established connections with several Spanish-speaking classrooms around the world. Finally, working on a translation with Maya and Tora helped Orlando develop a better understanding of English at the same time it helped Maya and Tora develop a better understanding of Spanish. Listening to their conversation as they worked on the translation showed that each student was learning much about each other's language. It was a wonderful experience to observe.

Figure 11-1.
The home page for **Intercultural Classroom Connections** (http://www.stolaf.edu/network/iecc/), a wonderful location for connecting with classrooms in other parts of the world by participating in mailing lists.

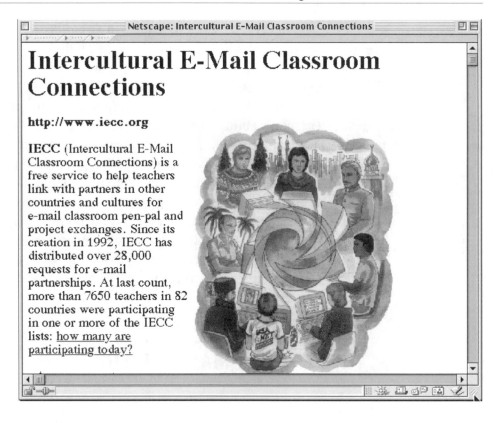

Intercultural E-Mail Classroom Connections

http://www.iecc.org

IECC (Intercultural E-Mail Classroom Connections) is a free service to help teachers link with partners in other countries and cultures for e-mail classroom pen-pal and project exchanges. Since its creation in 1992, IECC has distributed over 28,000 requests for e-mail partnerships. At last count, more than 7650 teachers in 82 countries were participating in one or more of the IECC lists: how many are participating today?

Lessons From the Classroom

This episode from Monica's classroom illustrates an important lesson for all of us to consider: the sensitive orchestration of classroom environments by an insightful classroom teacher can help to support Internet access for all students. Just having a computer connected to the Internet does not guarantee equity of access for each of your students. You must work actively to ensure equity in your classroom.

The sensitive orchestration of classroom environments by an insightful classroom teacher can ensure successful Internet access for all students.

One element of this active orchestration is being sensitive to times when students' enthusiasm for their work on the Internet impedes others' access to this important resource. Having a regular schedule for Internet use, as suggested in Chapter 4, provides a certain level of equity in your classroom. In addition, however, you will have to carefully monitor student use as Monica did, watching for those moments when students become so enthusiastic they lose track of time and prevent access by others.

Another important element in the active orchestration of equity is to be certain you are aware of ways to accommodate the unique learning needs of each child in your classroom. Adjusting the font size for Tora enabled her to access the world of text information available on the Internet. Previously, she had been limited to large-print books and the use of a special magnifier. The Internet permitted Tora to access an enormous amount of information, simply by enlarging the size of the browser font on Netscape Navigator or Internet Explorer. Text-to-speech technology is also becoming more widely available to assist her and other children who might benefit from this feature.

Orchestrating equity in your classroom will mean thinking differently about linguistic diversity. Instead of viewing a non-English first language as a handicap, linguistic diversity suddenly becomes a valuable asset when you think about ways in which to utilize this talent as you communicate with classes around the world.

Finally, orchestrating equity in your classroom will mean thinking differently about linguistic diversity. Instead of viewing a non-English speaker as handicapped, linguistic diversity suddenly becomes a valuable asset when you think about ways in which to utilize the skills of a speaker of a language other than English as you communicate with classes around the world. Orlando's ability in Spanish became a special talent that was valued by all members of his class when Monica saw the potentials it provided for Internet communication. These opportunities gave Orlando a tremendous sense of self worth as he became a central member of the classroom community. Moreover, Orlando acquired English much more rapidly as he translated messages and served as a conduit for communication with Spanish-speaking communities. While this was taking place, students in his class were also learning many new words in Spanish. Everyone gains when non-native speakers are included in classroom communities by teachers who know how to orchestrate equity.

 # E-MAIL FOR YOU

To: Colleagues

From: Anne Nguyen (amnguyen@FREESIDE.SCSD.K12.NY.US)
        cnguyen742@aol.com)

Subject: Supporting ESL students through e-mail

Hi!

   I'm sure it's obvious, but I had a wonderful experience with some of my former students recently. I have two e-mail addresses—one through my district that I had not used in four weeks because of the summer holidays. Last week I went to school and checked my district account. I had about 12 e-mail messages—all from my students from last year. I poured over each and every one of the messages and laughed in amazement. I was amazed at what they had to say. Students seemed more willing to share personal information with me in this format and asked readily for advice too.

   These are ESL students and I realized what a good method this was not only to practice their writing skills, but also reading—to read the replies they would receive—and those from teachers or American students would most likely have correct grammar and spelling—a good model! But I think the best thing is the ease with which a teacher can touch base with ALL students.

   This experience has cemented an idea I have for my students next year. I am going to make sure all my students get e-mail addresses at the beginning of the year and are able to use them to communicate with each other, as well as with me.

   Anne Nguyen (amnguyen@FREESIDE.SCSD.K12.NY.US) (cnguyen742@aol.com)
   ESL Teacher
   Syracuse City School District, Syracuse, NY

Orchestrating Equity in Your Classroom

Chapter 4 described several strategies for orchestrating equity within Internet classrooms. Posting a schedule for all students to follow, rotating assigned computer times to avoid regular schedule conflicts, and rotating partners at the computer in a one-computer classroom are all useful strategies. In addition, however, there are several important issues for you to consider. These will require you to make subtle adjustments that happen moment to moment in your classroom as you seek to individualize learning experiences for each of your students.

Monica experienced one of these issues when she noticed a group of children at the computer excited about what they had discovered for the unit on diversity the class was studying. As enthusiastic as they were, Maya was losing important time on their only Internet computer because this group had forgotten their obligation to turn the computer over to the next person on the schedule. This is a common event in most classrooms and requires you to periodically monitor the computer schedule you establish for your class, reminding students when it is time to turn the computer over to the next person. You may also wish to bring this concern up during Internet Workshop and remind students why it is important to provide everyone with an equal amount of time on the Internet.

Another issue occurs when individual students fail to develop efficient navigation strategies for Internet use. Falling behind in this area prohibits students from acquiring as much useful information as other students who have become proficient at navigating the Internet. There are several techniques to help you to minimize this problem. First, observe carefully. Pay exceptionally close attention to the navigation strategies students develop or fail to develop as they work on the computer. Second, pair students who have not picked up important strategies with others who have acquired these strategies. Provide opportunities for these students to work together on the Internet. Many useful strategies can be acquired in this manner but be certain to also provide individual time for students to practice new skills on their own; often, when you pair a proficient navigator with a less proficient one, the former dominates navigational decisions. Third, provide short tutorial sessions for students who are weak in navigation strategies. You may choose either a small group or an individual format. In either case, focus on a central strategy you have noticed that students lack. Finally, be certain to use discussions during Internet Workshop to both evaluate and teach navigation strategies. This is a perfect time to listen to students describe how they use the Internet and, at the same time, support students who have failed to acquire these skills.

Be certain to use discussions during Internet Workshop to both evaluate and teach navigation strategies. This is a perfect time to listen to students describe how they use the Internet and, at the same time, support students who have failed to acquire these skills.

It may also be the case that gender differences exist with respect to Internet use. While we have no hard data on this phenomenon, we have noticed that boys will sometimes dominate Internet use in a classroom and that some girls may express less interest in using this resource. You should watch for this in your class to see if it exists. Sometimes, communication experiences on the Internet are especially engaging for girls. You may wish to consider ways to exploit this interest by developing an Internet Project with communication opportunities between members of different classes. This may equalize any gender differences you see in your classroom.

Another issue to consider as you seek to support all students in your class is the unique potential of the Internet for supporting ESL students. Some districts are fortunate enough to have special bilingual programs or ESL programs for students. In addition, the Internet may provide you and your students with a very special opportunity. Just as Monica did, you may seek out opportunities where non-native English speakers can use their skills with their native language to support classroom learning. This reverses traditional attitudes about one's non-English linguistic background from a disadvantage into an asset. Many good things will result from this change in perspective.

A final issue to consider is how to support challenged students in your class who have been formally identified with special learning requirements. In some cases, technology may be able to adapt to these students' needs as was the situation with Tora in Monica's class. In all cases, there are resources on the Internet to provide useful information about accommodations you can make in your classroom to help each student reach his/her full potential.

> Just as Monica did, you may seek out opportunities where non-native English speakers can use their skills with their native language to support classroom learning. This reverses traditional attitudes about one's non-English linguistic background from a handicap into an advantage. Many good things will result from this change in perspective.

TEACHING TIP

Many web pages are inaccessible to students with various disabilities because of the way they are designed. Organizations such as the **Center for Applied Special Technology (CAST)** (http://www.cast.org) and the **National Center for Accessible Media** (http://www.wgbh.org/wgbh/pages/ncam/) have developed criteria that may be used to evaluate the degree to which a web site meets basic principles of universal design. If a web site meets these basic design principles it will display a visual certificate such as the one below. Look for this certificate as you make decisions about which Internet resources to use in your classroom. If you wish to evaluate the extent to which your classroom web site meets principles of universal design and access, be certain to visit **Bobby** (http://www.cast.org/bobby/). Here you can have your web site evaluated online. You will automatically receive a report indicating any accessibility and/or browser compatibility errors found on your page. If the report indicates your site meets the Bobby standards, you are entitled to display a Bobby Approved icon on your site.

Opportunities for ESL Students

The Internet provides several special opportunities for ESL students in your class. You have already seen the one adapted by Ms. Ashburn. Developing an Internet Project with schools who use the same language as an ESL student in your room is a wonderful method for supporting linguistic development. Having an ESL student assist with translations places that stu-

To find a school with students who speak the language of ESL students in your class, you may wish to pay a visit to **Web66** (http://web66.coled.umn.edu/) and explore their **International Registry of K12 Schools on the Web** (http://web66.coled.umn.edu/schools.html).

Many students will find it exciting to listen to radio stations around the world with the Internet, especially if they have a partner with whom to exchange the information.

dent in a valued role within the classroom's activities. If you have your student work with others on the translations, both native and non-native speakers will develop a better understanding of one another's language. To find a school with students who speak the language of ESL students in your class, you may wish to pay a visit to **Web66** (http://web66.coled.umn.edu/) and explore their **International Registry of K12 Schools on the Web** (http://web66.coled.umn.edu/schools.html). Locate several possible schools and drop them an e-mail message with a list of projects you would be interested in completing together.

If you have an ESL student whose English ability is insufficient for this role, you may wish to try another approach. Pair the student with a native speaker in your class. Give them a regular Internet Activity assignment related to the country or culture from which the ESL student comes. To help you find Internet resources about this country or culture visit **Excite Travel** (http://www.city.net/). Follow the links to the country you wish to visit. Especially useful will be the country's major newspapers. These contain many interesting news items in the first language of your student.

Or, you may wish to have your students listen to a radio station in the country or culture from which the ESL student comes. This can be done by visiting the **Stations Guide** (http://realguide.real.com/stations/) location at RealAudio and searching for radio stations by the student's language or geographical region. Alternatively, you could visit Yahoo's **Live Radio** site (http://dir.yahoo.com/News_and_Media/Radio/By_Region/Countries/) and search for the on-line radio stations in a target country. Many students will find it exciting to listen to radio stations around the world with the Internet, especially if they have a partner with whom to exchange the information.

Conducting an Internet activity about the ESL student's country will engage both students in conversation about something familiar to the ESL student. This will motivate both students and make conversation easier for the ESL student. Be certain to include a writing activity as part of the Internet activity to foster collaborative second language learning between the two students.

You may wish to direct the two students to develop their own Internet activity. For the first week, for example, you may ask the two students to visit the sites in the student's country of origin and create a list of Internet Activity assignments they want to complete. Then use this list to guide work during subsequent weeks. You might rotate partners every few weeks to allow the ESL student to meet and work with other members of your class. If you conduct an Internet Workshop session each week, you may wish to have the two students report the results of their assignment to the class. This provides a nice opportunity to support oral, as well as written, language development.

Other resources you may find useful on the WWW for supporting ESL students in your class include:

- **The Internet TESL Journal**—This is really one of the best central sites with links for teachers (http://www.aitech.ac.jp/~iteslj/links/TESL/) and links for students (http://www.aitech.ac.jp/~iteslj/links/ESL/). It's non-commercial and "optimized for speed", containing no frames or graphics. It's updated frequently, so there are few dead links (see Figure 11-2).

- **E. L. Easton: Materials For Teaching English**—
  http://eleaston.com
  Here is another excellent site with ESL links for a variety of levels and purposes, as well as to other relevant sites such as "flags of the world"

- **Center for Applied Linguistics**—http://www.cal.org/
  A national center for language study and application with many links to a wide variety of ESL resources.

- **Dave Sperling's ESL Cafe**—http://www.eslcafe.com
  This is one of the most popular general sites for ESL students and teachers. It seems to contain more commercial links than it used to, but it's still a good site for teachers and older students. It offers bulletin boards and chat as well as web links.

Figure 11-2.
Selected Links for ESL Students from The Internet TESL Journal (http://www.aitech.ac.jp/~iteslj/links/ESL/), a good location for ESL learning experiences.

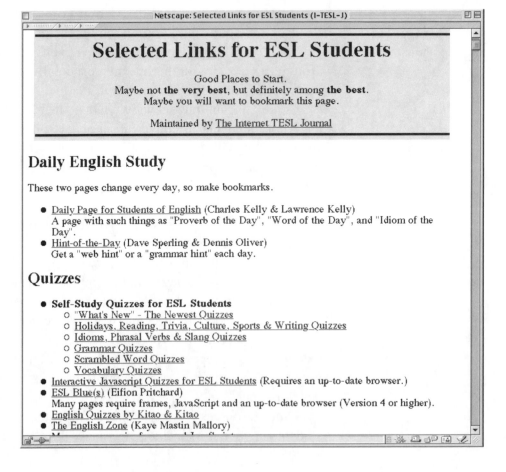

Netscape: Selected Links for ESL Students (I-TESL-J)

Selected Links for ESL Students

Good Places to Start.
Maybe not **the very best**, but definitely among **the best**.
Maybe you will want to bookmark this page.

Maintained by The Internet TESL Journal

Daily English Study

These two pages change every day, so make bookmarks.

- Daily Page for Students of English (Charles Kelly & Lawrence Kelly)
  A page with such things as "Proverb of the Day", "Word of the Day", and "Idiom of the Day".
- Hint-of-the-Day (Dave Sperling & Dennis Oliver)
  Get a "web hint" or a "grammar hint" each day.

Quizzes

- **Self-Study Quizzes for ESL Students**
  - "What's New" - The Newest Quizzes
  - Holidays, Reading, Trivia, Culture, Sports & Writing Quizzes
  - Idioms, Phrasal Verbs & Slang Quizzes
  - Grammar Quizzes
  - Scrambled Word Quizzes
  - Vocabulary Quizzes
- Interactive Javascript Quizzes for ESL Students (Requires an up-to-date browser.)
- ESL Blue(s) (Eifion Pritchard)
  Many pages require frames, JavaScript and an up-to-date browser (Version 4 or higher).
- English Quizzes by Kitao & Kitao
- The English Zone (Kaye Mastin Mallory)

TEACHING TIP

At the beginning of the year, develop an Internet Workshop session around the ThinkQuest resource **Seeing DisABILITIES from a Different Perspective** (http://tqjunior.advanced.org/5852/). A very simple way to do this is to have your class explore this wonderful resource and bring to the workshop session three ideas to share that they learned about disabilities from this important resource (see Figure 11-3). It is an important way to begin the year, bringing issues of diversity and difference to your entire class. Note that this site was developed by students in grades 4–6 at Sherwood Elementary School in Illinois as part of the ThinkQuest Junior annual competition (http://www.thinkquest.org/). Consider developing a project for this contest or the ThinkQuest contest with your students.

Figure 11-3.
Seeing DisABILITIES from a Different Perspective (http://tqjunior.advanced.org/5852/), a great resource to help your students become more sensitive and knowledgeable about differences. This is an award winner in the Junior ThinkQuest competition.

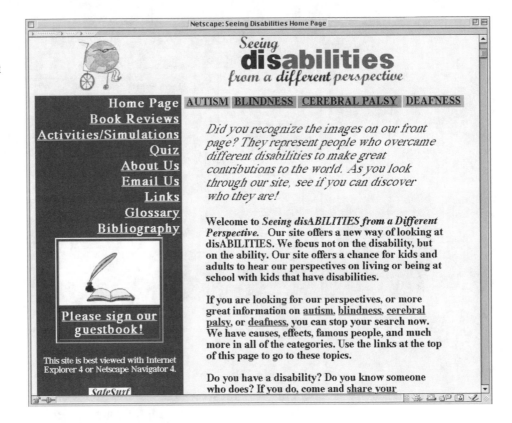

Opportunities for Children Who are Visually or Hearing Challenged

The Internet also provides special opportunities for children who are visually or hearing challenged. For children who are visually challenged, a common problem is often a dependency on large print texts, texts which do not always coincide with the materials used in the classroom. Alternatively, large and bulky readers are sometimes used. Both are less than ideal solutions for many students.

Netscape and Internet Explorer offer an opportunity to enlarge the print size appearing on the computer screen to nearly any size one wishes. This allows children who are visually challenged to access a wide range of information that might otherwise be inaccessible to them. To do this in Netscape,

Netscape and Internet Explorer offer an opportunity to enlarge the print size appearing on the computer screen to nearly any size one wishes. This allows visually impaired children to access a wide range of information that might otherwise be inaccessible to them.

select the "Edit" item from your menu bar and then select "Preferences". Within "Preferences", select the category for "Fonts". You will see a window similar to Figure 11-4. Select the size you wish to use for both variable and fixed width fonts. You may select any size you wish. Note that one choice is "Other". This allows you to type in sizes larger than 24. In Internet Explorer, you may change font size by simply clicking on the "Larger" or "Smaller" buttons in the main IE toolbar.

Figure 11-4.
The preferences folder in **Netscape**, showing how to change the size of the font used to display text information on the WWW.

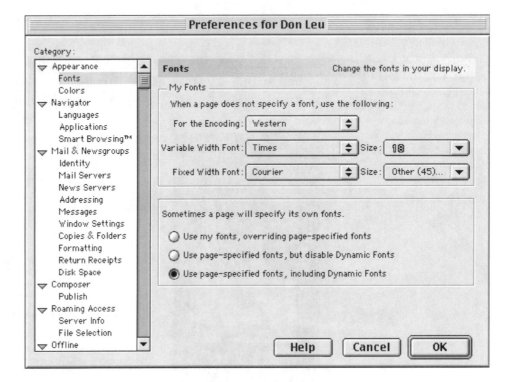

Enlarging the font size for children who are visually challenged works especially well on web pages that use a lot of text. It works less well at those sites with graphics since graphics are not enlarged with this approach. In these situations you may wish to use software that enlarges the entire screen, not just text. With the more recent Macintosh systems, this is already available to you in Easy Access. If you can't locate this feature, if you need to download this software, or if you wish to read about using this software, just visit the Apple location **Access Features** (http://www.apple.com/education/k12/disability/easyaccess.html). If you use a Windows system, visit the **Microsoft Accessibility Home Page** (http://www.microsoft.com/enable/) for similar solutions.

You may also wish to visit these central sites for visually challenged students to locate additional resources:

- **Blindness Resource Center**—http://www.nyise.org/blind.htm
  The best central site for visually challenged and blind individuals. Set a bookmark!

- **Macintosh Disability Shareware and Freeware—**
  http://www.ecnet.net/users/gnorris/place.shtml
  A wonderful set of links to adaptive technology developed by a person who is visually challenged.

- **Apple's Disability Resources—**
  http://www.apple.com/education/k12/disability/macaccess.html
  Resources for your Macintosh machines.

There are also locations on the web to support hearing challenged students. You might begin by visiting **The Deaf/Hard of Hearing** (http://www.familyvillage.wisc.edu/lib_deaf.htm) location of the Family Village site. This has links to excellent resources on the web, as well as information about chat and mailing lists for students. Another useful location is **SERI Hearing Impairment Resources** (http://www.hood.edu/seri/hearing.htm). Or, you might wish to explore **DeafWorldWeb** (http://dww.deafworldweb.org/) a central site for the deaf community.

Several other locations may be useful for all students in your classroom. **Sign Language Dictionary Online** (http://dww.deafworldweb.org/sl/) provides videos for many signs and will help your students learn more about deafness (see Figure 11-5). **A Basic Dictionary of ASL Terms** (http://www.masterstech-home.com/ASLDict.html) provides an extensive signing dictionary. You may wish to make these sites a regular part of Internet Workshop and begin to develop the ability to sign with your hearing students. Sharing new signs during Internet Workshop helps everyone become more skilled in communicating with hearing challenged children.

Figure 11-5.
A great location for all students,
Sign Language Dictionary Online
(http://dww.deafworldweb.org/sl/).

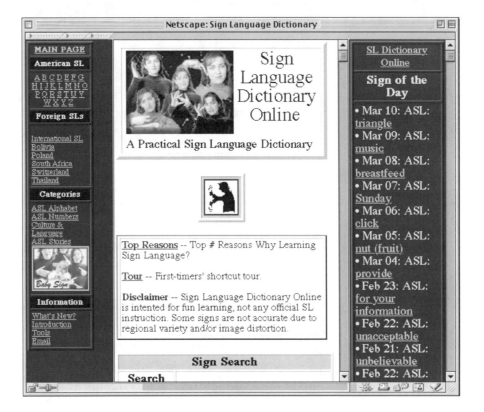

<table>
<tr>
<td>
TEACHING TIP</td>
<td>Here is a way to conduct a simple Internet Workshop with your students, developing the ability to communicate with a limited set of ASL signs. Set a bookmark or a link to **Sign Language Dictionary Online** (http://dww.deafworldweb.org/sl/). Give students a set of high frequency words that may be combined in different ways to make a variety of sentences: I, you, we, it, play, see, eat, read, baseball, funny, apple, ice cream, book, etc. Then, using this Internet site, have them learn one sentence to share during the workshop session. Encourage students to visit this location often, learning the symbol of the day and sharing it with the rest of the class. By the end of the year, your students will have developed important, initial signing skills and started a journey to better understand and communicate with the deaf community.</td>
</tr>
</table>

E-MAIL FOR YOU

To: Colleagues
From: Nicole Gamble <ddnrg@IX.NETCOM.COM>
Subject: Diversity

```
    My students learned a very valuable lesson this week about diversity
and empathy. We have been reading Princess Pooh by Kathleen Muldoon. It's
a story about two sisters, one of whom happens to be in a wheelchair.
After talking about what might be difficult about being in a wheelchair,
we invited a first grade student who uses an electric wheelchair into our
classroom to demonstrate how it works. She answered a lot of our questions
and the students were very interested in what she had to share. In our
discussion we found out that she was unable to use a drinking fountain in
school because the only wheelchair accessible drinking fountain had been
broken all year. After she left, my class asked if they could write a
letter to the principal and find out about fixing the drinking fountain.
They wrote the letter, took it to the principal, and the drinking fountain
got fixed! The principal came into the class and told everyone that she
appreciated how much they cared. It turns out that new parts for the
drinking fountain had been ordered and had arrived, but the maintenance
department hadn't made it a priority to fix it. What a great lesson.

    Nicole
    Graduate Student
```

Opportunities for Other Students Who are Challenged

Accommodating Internet experiences for other students in your class who have been formally identified as requiring special assistance does not differ substantially from the types of accommodations you make in other areas of your curriculum. Two ideas, though, may be useful as you seek to provide opportunities for each of your students to learn and grow.

Our informal observations suggest the Internet may provide special motivational opportunities for those children who have been less successful in previous academic tasks.

Share new information about navigation strategies with students who have been less successful in school learning tasks before you share it with others. Then, have these students teach others the new information. This quickly puts students who have been less successful into a privileged position, a position these students seldom experience in classroom learning tasks.

First, our informal observations suggest the Internet may provide special motivational opportunities for those children who have been less successful in previous academic tasks. We have seen this happen enough times in school classrooms to believe something important is happening. We do not know the reason for this phenomenon. It may be that multimedia resources provide multiple sources of information (graphics, animations, audio, video, etc.) so that students are not just dependent on a single, textual source for information that has always given them difficulty. It may be that the interactive nature of this environment and the new types of strategic knowledge that are necessary offer an advantage to certain types of children, children who have not been previously advantaged in non-electronic environments. Or, it may be that the Internet kindles a new spark of interest among students who have lost interest in learning. In any case, it happens often enough that we should think about taking advantage of the phenomenon.

One way to do this is to share new information about navigation strategies with students who have been less successful in school learning tasks before you share it with others. Then, have these students teach others the new information. This quickly puts students who have been less successful into a privileged position, a position these students seldom experience in classroom learning tasks. The effects of this strategy can sometimes be quite dramatic as less successful students suddenly feel empowered and become more interested in learning. We encourage you to try this strategy.

A second idea is also useful. Spend time exploring sites on the WWW that can provide you with more information about your students who have been formally identified as requiring special assistance. There are many useful ideas for instruction and many other informative resources on the web. Exploring these sites will provide you with important assistance as you seek to include all students in your classroom activities. Sites we have found helpful include:

- **Special Education Resources on the Internet (SERI)**—
  http://www.hood.edu/seri/serihome.htm
  This is one of the best central sites on the Internet for special education resources (see Figure 11-6). It contains a comprehensive and well organized set of links to locations important for special education issues.

- **Family Village**—http://www.familyvillage.wisc.edu/
  This is an excellent central site about mental retardation and other disabilities. Set a bookmark!

- **Internet Resources for Special Children**—http://www.irsc.org/
  This is another central site, very useful, with extensive resources on special education.

- **The Council for Exceptional Children**—
  http://www.cec.sped.org/
  A major professional organization in special education.

Figure 11-6.
SERI (http://www.hood.edu/seri/serihome.htm), a central site for special education resources.

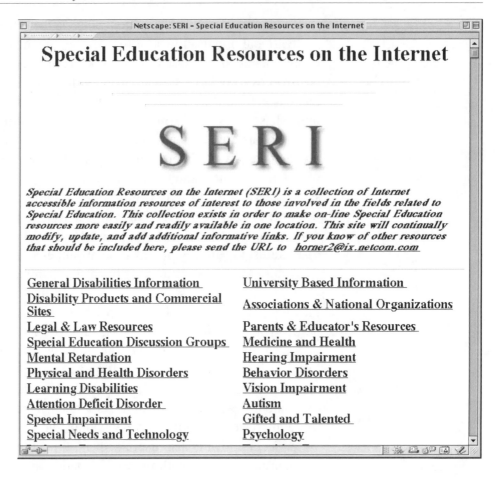

Special Thoughts About Special Students

Each and every child has unique needs that must be recognized as you make instructional decisions. You must always consider each student's background and abilities as you use the Internet in your classroom. Nothing is more important.

As you plan instructional programming for children with special needs in your classroom, we hope you keep two ideas in mind. First, each of your students is, in fact, a child with special needs. Each and every child has unique needs that must be recognized as you make instructional decisions. You must always consider each student's background and abilities as you use the Internet in your classroom. Nothing is more important.

Second, legal and categorical designations used for legal and administrative purposes must never limit your instructional decisions regarding individual children, or your expectations for their achievement. The use of labels has brought important benefits to students whose needs have too long been ignored, but we must ensure that those labels do not prevent us from recognizing the individuality each of us expresses in our daily lives.

Visiting the Classroom: Fred Roemer's Fifth Grade Class in Florida

We're exhausted. We have just finished exploring a portion, a portion mind you, of the classroom web page for Fred Roemer's fifth grade class in Pinellas

County, Florida: **Mr. Roemer's Fifth Grade Polar Bears** (http://www.pb5th.com/index.htm). How does he do it? There is so much wonderful information for his students and so many resources to support their learning. We are certain we have not seen everything—and we spent several hours at this location! There are so many practical ideas for us in the work Fred and his class are doing and so many important lessons to consider.

Read the Daily Log, for example, to discover what is taking place with the Polar Bears each day. This is written daily by one of the students in his class and illustrated with digital pictures. It is a perfect language arts project for students, each of whom will end up writing 6-8 descriptive narratives about something important and familiar over the course of the year. We are certain it generates critically important learning experiences for each classroom reporter. This is a really exciting idea all of us could use in our classrooms, especially since so many states include a descriptive essay in their state writing assessment.

Another important lesson is how Fred and his class use their web page to build community within the classroom. They begin each year by developing a class mission statement. This past year it was this: "The purpose of the polar bears is to have fun while learning, to learn to think for ourselves, to do our best, and to learn how to be more respectful and successful." From there, Fred and his class work hard to develop an esprit de corps that is very special, much of it through the many web pages showing their work, their dreams, and their many wonderful accomplishments. Having a moniker, The Polar Bears, that is used in his class and throughout the class web page also contributes to their special community, as does the fact that he "loops" with his class, having the same group for several years. But looking at their class web page, we have to believe that this is a critical piece of the puzzle.

Finally, Fred's classroom page shows all of us many new elements we could use in our own class pages. Take just a few moments and you will encounter new elements you could use with your classroom: a free and easy-to-use, online poll that immediately generates a graph of the results; an online word search; clear descriptions of assignments with examples of formatting requirements for all to see, the results of an Internet project with KidsLink, on-line grade reports available to parents and students, and much more. Take a look! You will learn a lot about the potentials of the Internet for your classroom. Fred's students are fortunate to have him as their teacher.

Instructional Resources on the Internet

Activities For ESL Students—http://www.aitech.ac.jp/~iteslj/s/
> Just what it says. A nice location with useful resources.

Apple's Disability Resources—http://www.apple.com/education/k12/disability/macaccess.html
> Here is the location for getting in touch with all kinds of information about adaptive technologies provided by Apple Computer and other com-

panies. This location also includes many free or shareware programs to use with your computer, links to disability related resources on the WWW, and opportunities to communicate with others about disabilities and teaching/learning issues. Set a bookmark!

Autism Resources—http://www.vaporia.com/autism/
A site with many links to resources related to Autism and Asperger's Syndrome including links to on-line discussions, mailing lists, news, treatment methods, research, and much more.

Blindness Resource Center—http://www.nyise.org/blind.htm
A great location with extensive information about blindness and resources to inform teachers and assist students.

ESL/LINC Learner Sites—
http://Home.InfoRamp.Net/~teslon/jims_links.shtml
Here is a useful site which links to many ESL reading, writing, and listening sites; it provides site quality ratings and lists grade levels.

ESL Multimedial Language Learning—
http://user.gru.net/richardx/index.html
This is a site with links to reading, writing, and listening sites; it also includes an academic section and cultural information section.

Inclusion Resources—http://www.hood.edu/seri/inclu.htm
A nice collection of links related to inclusive education. The information at this location can provide useful background information to teachers new to inclusion.

Inclusion—http://www.uni.edu/coe/inclusion/
An outstanding collection of resources designed for the teacher who practices, or will soon practice, an inclusion model in the classroom. Links to teaching strategies, strategies to prepare for inclusion, and many supportive Internet resources.

Intercultural E-Mail Classroom Connections—http://www.iecc.org/
This is a site to find keypals and partner classes with speakers of other languages.

Interesting Things For ESL Students—http://www.aitech.ac.jp/~itesls/
Just what it says. Pay a visit!

Learning Disabilities Association of America—http://www.ldanatl.org/
The home page for this organization with over 60,000 members. This location provides links and resources for individuals interested in learning more about learning disabilities.

Learning Disabilities—
http://www.kidsource.com/kidsource/content/learningdis.html
This website contains a booklet from the National Institutes of Mental Health. It explains learning disabilities to parents.

International Dyslexia Association—http://interdys.org/
The International Dyslexia Association (IDA) is an international, non-profit, scientific and educational organization dedicated to the study and treatment of dyslexia. This location provides access to its many resources related to this important learning disability.

Microsoft Accessibility Home Page—http://www.microsoft.com/enable/
This is the location for links to many accessibility technologies if you use a Windows operating system. Many free downloads and links to important resources appear here.

Pizazz—http://darkwing.uoregon.edu/~leslieob/pizzaz.html
This is a great site for creative writing with handouts for all ages and levels.

Randall's ESL Cyber Listening Lab—http://www.esl-lab.com/
This site contains nice listening activities. It requires Real Audio or Shockwave plugins but these are free on the Internet.

Special Needs and Technology Resources—http://www.hood.edu/seri/tech.htm
Here is an extensive collection of links to a wide variety of technology resources.

The Family Village Inclusion Resources—
http://www.familyvillage.wisc.edu/education/inclusion.html
Another nice location to provide resources for teachers interested in inclusive education. Contains links to locations to communicate with others, research, on-line newsletters, and web sites related to inclusion.

Theme-Based Pages—http://darkwing.uoregon.edu/~leslieob.themes.html
A location that is great for discussion topics and debates, as well as persuasive writing assignments at the high school level; assembled by an ESL teacher, but most sites are not specifically for ESL learners; topics are most appropriate for secondary learners.

Listservs/Mailing Lists for Including All Students on the Internet

Follow standard procedures for subscribing to the mailing lists below. See Chapter 3.

DEAFKIDS—listserv@sjuvm.stjohns.edu
A discussion group for children who are deaf.

CHATBACK—listserv@sjuvm.stjohns.edu
A discussion group on special education.

INCLUSIVE-EDUCATION—mailbase@mailbase.ac.uk
An Inclusive education discussion list.

SPECED-L—speced-l@uga.cc.uga.edu
A special education discussion list.

TESLK-12—listserv@cunyvm.cuny.edu
A discussion group on teaching English as a second language in grades K–12.

Developing a Home Page for Your Classroom

 E-MAIL FOR YOU

To: Our readers
From: djleu@syr.edu (Don Leu), ddleu@syr.edu (Debbie Leu)
Subject: Developing A Classroom Home Page Is An Important "Four-For"

We are nearing the end of our journey together. You have accomplished much in a short period of time. There is one final topic we wanted to share with you: developing a classroom home page on the WWW. This isn't that hard to do. Really! It will take you less than 30 minutes to learn how to do this.

You have already seen many outstanding examples of classroom home pages by teachers featured in this book. Now it is time for you to begin your own journey in this area.

Learning to develop a home page is what we call a "four-for", something that gives you *four* important results *for one* activity. In a life where time is always a precious commodity, any "four-for" should be treasured. What are the four important results a home page will achieve?

First, developing a home page helps your students. It provides a location for publishing student work and it allows you to organize safe links to Internet locations so students can easily access the information you want them to use. Second, developing a home page also helps other teachers. As you develop instructional materials and links to information resources, you will find other classrooms visiting your page, benefiting from your instructional ideas. Third, developing a home page enables you to forge a tighter link between home and school. As more computers enter the home, parents can use your home page to see what is taking place in your classroom and communicate with you about their children. Finally, developing a home page helps the teaching profession. As you develop a home page for your class, it projects an important image of professionalism to the public—teachers embracing new technologies and using these in powerful ways to guide students' learning. We hope you take the time to develop a home page for your class. It will be useful for your students, other students, parents, and our profession.

Don and Debbie

Teaching With the Internet: Tama Forth's Class

It was 8:35 a.m. in Room 102.

"And I wanted to tell you that I have added a new link on our classroom home page called Virtual Tours. You may wish to visit **Virtual Tours** (http://www.virtualfreesites.com/tours.html) when you are working on Internet Inquiry. There are hundreds of tours of museums, cities, and government locations related to your work. It is a commercial site, though, with banner and other ads so be careful where you are clicking." Tama Forth was in the middle of the morning announcements to her class before the morning got underway.

"I also wanted to remind you that since this is Friday, you should be certain to write a short message to your parents or guardians about your work this week. Do this with e-mail or on the word processor. Tell them something special you have done this week. If they have an e-mail address, send it with my e-mail account and remind them to visit our classroom home page on the Internet. You can also type your message on AppleWorks and print it out to take home. I would like to check these before you leave today." Tama made this assignment each Friday. She found these little notes forged a new type of home-school connection, initiating important conversations at home about what was taking place at school. This helped her students.

"We have received three new messages from other schools that visited our home page yesterday. One was very impressed with our wildlife poems we did at the beginning of the year. Also, a student in Germany wanted to know if we could provide her with more information about the Battle of Lexington and Paul Revere's ride. Could you respond to this message, Katherine. You might want to send her a copy of your report. Please use my e-mail account. There was also a message from a teacher in Prince Rupert, Canada, telling us how much he liked our home page. I posted a copy of each message on our 'E-mail Around the World' board next to the computer. Read these new messages about the great work you are all doing in this class."

At the beginning of the year, Tama had taken a workshop on developing a classroom home page on the Internet. She worked her way (see Figure 12-1) through **Writing HTML: A Tutorial for Creating WWW Pages** (http://www.mcli.dist.maricopa.edu/tut/index.html). HTML is the programming language used on the WWW. She also learned how to use Netscape Composer, an HTML editor, to quickly make her home page. This made developing pages for the WWW as easy as typing with a word processor. She wondered why no one had told her before how easy this was to do. Somehow, she had thought developing a WWW page required many years of experience and a lot of technical training. She quickly discovered that if you can use a word processor, you can use a web page editor like Netscape's Composer. You don't need any additional skills, just a curious mind.

As Tama had told her colleagues, "If I can do this, anyone can." She had concluded that all someone really needed was a few minutes to play around

Figure 12-1.
The home page of **Writing HTML**, one of the better tutorials for learning about HTML and creating classroom home pages (http://www.mcli.dist.maricopa.edu/tut/index.html).

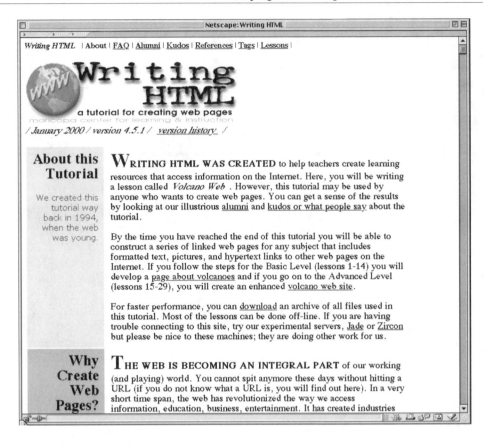

with an HTML editor like Composer and a location on the Internet to place your home page. The workshop and the tutorial were nice, but not necessary.

Tama had set up several sections on the first version of her classroom home page. One contained the wildlife poems they did earlier, another contained a set of links she used for Internet Workshop, another displayed the research they had done on the Battle of Lexington during the Revolutionary War, and another contained photos and a description of the field trip they recently took to Bunker Hill. She also put her e-mail address on the home page so parents could get in touch with her or send messages to their children when they wanted to surprise them at school. Clicking on this address immediately opened an e-mail message window with her address in the "To" box.

As Tama had told her colleagues, "If I can do this, anyone can."

Lessons From the Classroom

This episode in Tama Forth's class illustrates several important lessons about developing and using a classroom home page on the Internet. First, it shows that developing a home page is easy to do if you already are familiar with basic word processing. The HTML editors now available with Internet browsers and word processors make it simple to create a classroom home page. Anyone can do this.

Developing a home page is not all that complex if you already are familiar with basic word processing. The new HTML editors appearing with Internet browsers make it easy to create a classroom home page.

This episode also shows how a home page helps to organize Internet resources for classroom instruction. Tama used her home page to organize

E-MAIL FOR YOU

To: Colleagues
From: Janice Smith (jesmith@earthlink.net)
Subject: The home page for my English classes

Hi,

My classroom home page is located at: http://home.earthlink.net/~jesmith
   I created this enrichment/resource page for my eighth graders, but I am
thrilled to receive e-mail from teachers and students across the country
who visit my site regularly. It feature sections on literature, language,
biography, writing, technology, etc. and showcases the work of my own
student authors.
   In class, we make frequent use of the lessons on the New York Times
Learning Network and other online resources, particularly those dealing
with writing instruction, WebQuests, and other learning activities.
   The Internet has become a valuable tool in my classroom to enhance the
English/Language Arts curriculum.

   —Janice
   Ms. Smith's English Page
   http://home.earthlink.net/~jesmith

---

each thematic unit. She simply created a page for each thematic unit during the year and added useful links for each Internet Workshop, Internet Project, Internet Inquiry, and WebQuest. The nice thing about a web page was that she could reuse the units the following year without much additional effort. Setting up organized sets of links in this fashion also assisted her Internet safety program. Tama always previewed the sites she included to be certain they would not lead her students off into areas of the web they should not be exploring.

Third, the episode shows how a home page may be used to publish the work that students complete in a classroom. Tama always had a writing project for each thematic unit. These projects went through each phase of the writing process. In the final phase, students published their work on the classroom home page so that everyone in the class could read it and so that others around the world might see the wonderful writing her students did. The most avid readers of the web site, Tama discovered, were the students themselves and their parents. Several times at the local library, she found a student showing work to parents on the Internet computer located there. She also knew that some parents viewed this work from home because several parents had left her messages. And a few told her they liked to show off their child's work to others in their office.

A home page may be used to publish the work that students complete in a classroom.

One of the more powerful aspects of the Internet in school classrooms is that it allows teachers to develop curriculum that is immediately available to others throughout the world.

Home-school relationships are also strengthened when you develop a classroom home page.

Parents who see your classroom home page become more aware of the many wonderful things you do to support their children's development.

Notice also how a home page for your class assists other classrooms. Often, you will develop a thematic unit that other teachers may wish to use. Or, sometimes another teacher will send you an e-mail message, asking questions about your unit. One of the more powerful aspects of the Internet in school classrooms is that it allows teachers to develop curriculum that is immediately available to others throughout the world. This potential will be exploited with increasing regularity in the future.

Home-school relationships are also strengthened when you develop a classroom home page. While not all families have immediate access to the Internet, this is rapidly changing as increasing numbers of families are coming online or using Internet connections at your school or local library. Having a home page allows your parents to view their children's work and all the fine things you are doing in the classroom. It also provides an opportunity for parents and guardians to drop you an e-mail message when they have a question. The Internet provides many new opportunities to work with the families of children in your class.

Finally, a home page for your classroom accomplishes another important goal, it projects an important image of teachers as professionals. Parents who see your classroom home page become more aware of the many wonderful things you do to support their children's development. We are used to many members of the tax-paying public thinking that anybody can teach children. Putting up a home page, displaying your students' work, and inviting parents into your electronic classroom displays the many talents we all have as teachers. This is of central importance when school systems rely upon taxpayers to support their efforts, especially in a period when the teaching profession is sometimes criticized by individuals who are unfamiliar with what we do and what we know.

Examples of Classroom Home Pages

We have already seen many examples of classroom home pages throughout previous chapters. As we consider developing a home page for your classroom, you may wish to explore three additional examples of classroom home pages. In Carlsbad, California, **Brittany Buchel's Classroom Home Page** (http://teachers.eusd.k12.ca.us/bbuchel/) shows parents and others what takes place in her class (see Figure 12-2). She uses an extensive photo page to document the activities in her class, giving us a wonderful window into their many adventures. This also provides parents with an opportunity to see what their children experience at school. Projecting your classroom culture like this is important for your students. It tells them their work is valued as it prepares them for the world of their future. Many other elements on this page are also directed to parents: a weekly letter, a calendar, a list of sight words, fun activities to do at home, a wish list, and many other resources. Brittany also has a location for parents and others to contact her by e-mail. This en-

E-MAIL FOR YOU

To: Colleagues
From: Sharon Hall <LHall@cinci.rr.com>
Subject: Developing my classroom home page

Developing a classroom home page has been a wonderful experience. (Visit us at http://mrshall.cjb.net) As I built my web site I thought it would be a good place to share monthly activities of my class with parents and others that might be interested. I had seen other classroom sites and wanted to do something similar.

As I added pictures and information about our class, I also began adding other features to the site. I wanted a place to put some of my favorite links, mainly for my own information. I developed a brochure for making a web site to use at a technology conference, and I thought that this would be useful information for my site also. Over the period of the last couple of years I have been adding items that I felt might be useful to other teachers, to parents, and to members of our community.

I have become a more effective teacher by using the Internet. The Internet is so much more than just a bunch of web pages. I subscribe to a variety of mailrings that provide me with resources and support for other teachers. Through my involvement with a 1st Grade Mailring, I have networked with teachers all over the country to receive lesson plans and ideas in all subject areas. Other mailrings provide me with up-to-date information on classroom research and technology.

The biggest winners have been my students. They are provided the opportunity to participate in projects with students all over the country. We have shared information with others and reflected upon what we have found. Children are given the opportunity to write and read with a real purpose. This skill will stay with them for a lifetime.

Best wishes on your Internet journey!

Sharon
http://mrshall.cjb.net
E-mail:LHall@cinci.rr.com

ables Brittany to stay more closely in contact with the parents of her students.

Sue Pandiani, a teacher on Cape Cod, has spent the past several years organizing her class around the theme "The North Star Navigators," an idea based on an online book by Peter Reynolds, *The North Star* (http://www.fablevision.com/northstar/read.html). Her class has been fortunate enough to work with this author as both of them explore new worlds for students. **Sue Pandiani's classroom home page** (http://www.capecod.net/voyage/index.html) is inspired by this book (see Figure 12-3). It contains sections enabling her to publish students' work, forge links with parents,

E-MAIL FOR YOU

To: Colleagues

From: Doug Crosby (cherry@digisys.net)

Subject: Using the Internet in First Grade

Greetings!

Spring had finally arrived in Montana after a particularly long and cold winter. It was time to take our first grade field trip, this year we were off to a local biological station.

All year we had been publishing class books using a variety of media but we wanted to make our field trip report something special. Our school had recently posted a home page on the Internet so we decided to publish our field trip report for all the world to see.

It was kind of a gray day with showers threatening but we had already postponed the trip once so off we went with our digital camera in hand. It turned out to be a wonderful day with a great variety of learning activities taking place. We snapped away with our camera; there were the aquatic insects, the stream, the microscopes, and of course the big log where we all sat to eat lunch!

After returning to school we all sat around the computer to view the photos and within a short time we had come up with a whole class report which was typed directly on the screen. It looked great once we posted it on our web page. We have had a lot of fun reading e-mail from people around the world who have come across our report (http://www.digisys.net/cherry/Mr.Crosbyfield_trip.htm) and just dropped a note to say well done.

This has been a wonderful experience for my first graders in electronic publishing and a great introduction into the world of their futures.

Doug Crosby, First grade teacher   Cherry Valley School
kiwi@digisys.net Polson, Montana
http://www.digisys.net/cherry

provide resources to several Internet projects her class is completing this year, and share teaching ideas with others who visit her site.

Ms. Hos-McGrane and Linda Swanson, at the International School in Amsterdam use a home page (http://www.xs4all.nl/~swanson/origins/intro_five.html) to display the wonderful work of students in social studies classes (see Figure 12-4). The projects these classes are completing are really quite remarkable. Many other classrooms are beginning to use these social studies projects as resources and models to inspire their own work. A special aspect of this wonderful collaboration is that it helps students stay in touch with their class, even if they leave and travel to another location in the

Figure 12-2.
The classroom home page created by Brittany Buchel for her class (http://teachers.eusd.k12.ca.us/bbuchel/).

Figure 12-3.
Sue Pandiani's home page: **The North Star Navigators** (http://www.capecod.net/voyage/index.html).

world. This is important because students at this school often move with their parents to new locations around the world. The home page provides a wonderful way for them to stay in touch with the work of their classmates.

Figure 12-4.
The home page of Ms. Hos-McGrane's class (http://www.xs4all.nl/~swanson/origins/intro_five.html).

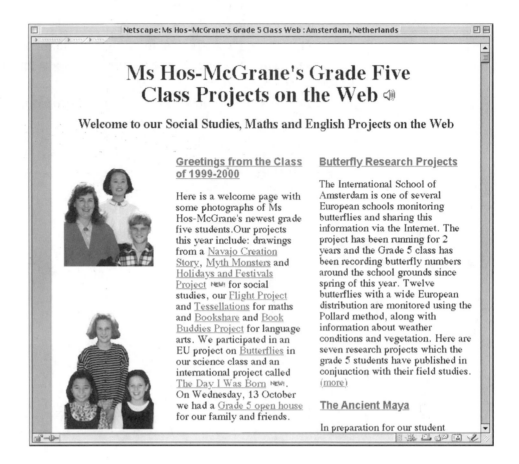

Learning How to Develop Your Own Classroom Home Page

To develop a home page, all you really need to know is how to type with a word processor.

Developing a home page may seem intimidating. After all, a programming language is used to create pages on the web. Fortunately, though, new tools are available that will automatically convert what you type into the programming language used on the web. So, even knowing this programming language is not as necessary as it once was. To develop a home page, all you really need to know is how to type with a word processor. If you also know how to copy and paste graphics, that is an added bonus.

The programming language used most often to design home pages on the WWW is called HTML, HyperText Mark-up Language. An example of HTML can be found in Figure 12-5. When a browser such as Netscape or Internet Explorer reads a file that is written in HTML, then converts it into what you see on your computer screen. So, if a browser read the HTML file in Figure 12-5, it would appear on your screen as illustrated in Figure 12-6.

This is what happens each time you view a page on the WWW; your browser reads a file written in HTML and converts it into what you see on your computer screen. To demonstrate this, all you have to do is to open up any page on the WWW with your browser and you can view the HTML code used to develop that page.

If you use Netscape Navigator, go to the menu item called "View" and select the item "page source". This will open up the HTML file used to create the page you were just viewing. If you use Internet Explorer, go to the menu item called "View" and select the item "source." You will see HTML code similar to what you find in Figure 12-5.

Figure 12-5.
An example of HTML (HyperText Mark-up Language).

Figure 12-6.
What the information in Figure 12-5 looks like when it is read by a web browser such as Netscape.

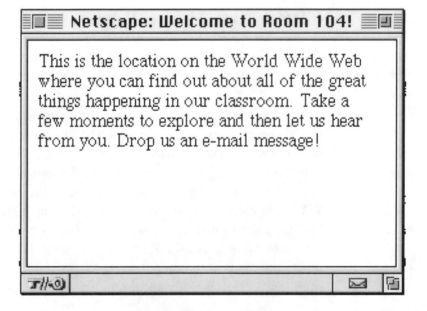

Internet FAQ

I have heard that people often "borrow" code after viewing the HTML source code at a page they admire. They say they "borrow" images, animations, pictures, and other elements from several pages by copying and pasting and add these to their own. Is this illegal?

This, unfortunately, is all too common. Copyright issues are still being defined in this new world of the Internet. Still, it appears that web page owners possess copyright to all of the elements at their location, as long as it is original work. This means you need to request permission from a web owner before "borrowing" original text, images, or anything else. If you wish to read more about copyright issues on the WWW, you may wish to pay a visit to the **U.S. Copyright Office Home Page** (http://lcweb.loc.gov/copyright/), or **Copyright Internet Resources** (http://lcweb.loc.gov/copyright/resces.html). Finally, you may wish to read **Copyright Basics** (http://www.loc.gov/copyright/circs/circ1.html), available online from the U.S. Copyright office.

The easiest way to develop a home page for your classroom is to use an HTML editor. This will allow you to develop your page using a program similar to a word processor.

There are two strategies for developing a classroom home page in HTML. The easiest way is to simply begin using an HTML editor. If you are the adventurous type, or simply wish to save time, locate an HTML editor and just begin. Your explorations will teach you all you need to know.

HTML editors are very similar to a word processor. With an HTML editor, you need not even see the underlying HTML code. What you see in your window is pretty much what you will get when you post your page to the Internet. There are several fine programs that enable you to do this.

If you are using Netscape 4.0 (or later), or Internet Explorer 5.0 (or later), your program comes with an HTML editor already built in. The editor in Netscape is called Netscape Composer. Figure 12-7 shows an image of this program as a teacher quickly developed an initial version of a home page in just ten minutes.

To begin using Netscape Composer, you simply click on the pencil icon in the bottom right hand side of the Netscape window.

To begin using Netscape Composer, you simply click on the pencil icon in the bottom right hand side of the Netscape window. This editor, like all HTML editors, requires little explanation. It works similarly to a word processor. Just begin typing away and exploring the formatting tools to design your page the way you wish it to look. You can type text, format text, insert a graphic, make a link to another page, set text to blink on and off, add color, and use many additional functions as you design your page. Simply explore each of the editing tools at the top of the Composer window and in the menu items.

You might also wish to use a word processor containing an integrated HTML editor. The latest versions of most word processors now come with an HTML editor. Separate HTML editors such as **FrontPage Editor** (http://www.microsoft.com/frontpage/) or Adobe's **PageMill** (http://www.adobe.com/products/pagemill/main.html) are also available. You may also wish to see if one of these programs is supported by your district. Copies may already be available for teachers in your district to use.

Figure 12-7.
The beginnings of a home page being developed with HTML editor **Netscape Composer**.

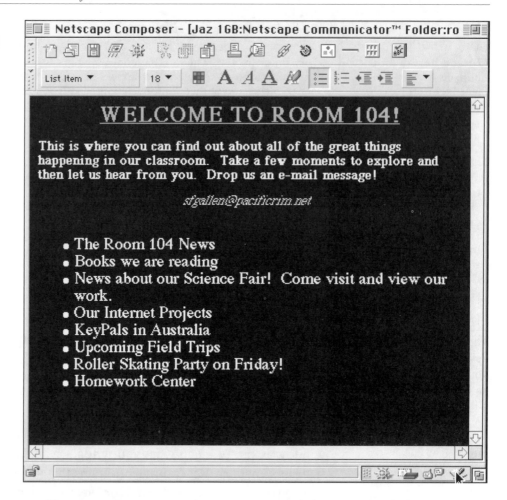

If you are the more cautious type, you might want to take a second approach for developing a classroom home page–spend a little time going through one of several fine tutorials that exist on the Internet.

If you are the more cautious type, you might want to take a second approach for developing a classroom home page—spend a little time going through one of several fine tutorials that exist on the Internet. These take you step-by-step through everything you need to know to develop a classroom home page. Some of these tutorials show you how to use a web editor. Examples include:

- **Six-Step Netscape Composer Tutorial**—
  http://www.msubillings.edu/tool/tutorial/index.htm

- **Tutorial on Creating Web Pages with FrontPage Editor**—
  http://www.siec.k12.in.us/~west/online/website/index.html

- **Building Web Pages with Composer**—
  http://home.netscape.com/browsers/using/newusers/composer/index.html

Others will take you into the world of HTML coding. These are very easy to follow and get you immediately into the world of HTML without assuming any prior knowledge. The best tutorial we have found for teachers who wish to learn HTML code is **Writing HTML: A Tutorial for Creating WWW Pages** (http://www.mcli.dist.maricopa.edu/tut/index.html). Others also exist, including:

- **A Beginner's Guide to HTML**—http://www.ncsa.uiuc.edu/ General/Internet/WWW/HTMLPrimer.html
- **Introduction to HTML**— http://www.cwru.edu/help/introHTML/toc.html
- **Web66: Classroom Internet Server Cookbook**— http://web66.coled.umn.edu/Cookbook/

If you decide to use an HTML editor, we also encourage you to work your way through one of these fine tutorials. Understanding the language of HTML will enable you to easily spot problems in your HTML code should these ever arise. It also permits you to individually modify elements in your home page in a way that might not be possible with an HTML editor.

Internet FAQ	
I want to build a web page for my class but our school doesn't yet have a server to host our web pages. What can I do?	Many teachers in your situation are using the free space available to them with their home Internet Service Provider (the company that provides you with Internet service). Others are using sites on the Internet that will provide you with free web space in return for an ad for their company or a rotating series of pop up or banner ads. They include **Geocities** (http://geocities.yahoo.com/home/), **Tripod** (http://www.tripod.lycos.com/), **Angelfire** (http://angelfire.lycos.com/), and others. This should be your last resort, given concerns we have raised in earlier chapters about commercials in the classroom. It is always better to encourage your school to provide this space for you or to use free space (without ads) available through your Internet service provider.

Which Elements Should I Include in My Classroom Home Page?

The design elements you include in your classroom home page will inevitably reflect your teaching style, your goals, and the culture you hope to develop for your classroom.

The design elements you include in your classroom home page will inevitably reflect your teaching style, your goals, and the culture you hope to develop for your classroom. You may, however, wish to consider elements such as the following:

- A location where parents and others viewing your pages can send you and your class an e-mail message.
- A location where students may publish their work.
- A location where due dates for major assignments are posted.
- A location for organizing links to sites in various thematic units.
- A location where students can publish a newspaper of classroom events and opinions.

It is important to think of your home page as a window through which the rest of the world may see your class. Thus, you will want to provide an opportunity for others to communicate with you and your students. This is easily done on a home page. You can quickly make a link that will open up an e-mail message window containing your address. This makes it easy for parents and others to get in touch with you and your students.

E-MAIL FOR YOU

To: Our Colleagues
From: Terry Hongell <hongell@pocantico.lhric.org>
        Patty Taverna <taverna@pocantico.lhric.org>
Subject: Classroom Web Sites

Classroom web sites present an incredibly authentic showplace for children's work. Our biggest fear is that teachers will create the world's largest bulletin board with their school web sites. We can do so much more. It is difficult to marry good technology use with sound instructional practice but it can be done.

We try to make our web site unique with student created content. The activities that we have created provide numerous opportunities for children to demonstrate what they've learned. In order to write a multiple-choice question where all of the answers have some relationship to the topic, the children must understand the subject thoroughly. Students use what they have learned and decide how to teach that information to other children. They have to make choices about what parts of their knowledge they share. They have to verify the information that they're teaching to make sure it is accurate. They also have to think about the best way to teach it (simple multiple choice questions, multiple choice questions with text reference clues, timelines, picture books, ABC books, crossword puzzles, etc.). Our goal is to make the web site a tool for our student learning and a resource for others to use. The work involved in creating each site generates excitement and a genuine commitment on the students' part.

We get many visitors and the children are often asked questions about what they post on their web sites. The communication from middle school, high school and university students in particular brings us a tremendous sense of satisfaction and motivation to continue to produce the kind of work that is recognized for its quality and usefulness. It is so exciting for us to hear from high school students who say, "Wow, I can't believe second graders had something to teach me!" Everyday we get E-mail from people across the country and around the world. We have made many interesting and helpful connections to authors, historians and university professors, like Dr. Leu. We think the Internet has brought a more global way of thinking to our children at a much younger age. With mail from Australia, Canada, England, Poland, Russia and Hong Kong, the world arrives here at Pocantico regularly.

Please visit us and see our work at:

A Children's Guide to Vietnam—http://www2.lhric.org/pocantico/vietnam/vietnam.htm

Charlotte's Web—http://www2.lhric.org/pocantico/charlotte/index.htm

Harriet Tubman—http://www2.lhric.org/pocantico/tubman/tubman.html

Pocantico Hills School Home Page—http://www2.lhric.org/pocantico/pocantic.html

Terry Hongell.<hongell@pocantico.lhric.org> and Patty Taverna <taverna@pocantico.lhric.org>

You should also consider using your home page as a location where students may publish their work. This allows others to see what you are doing. It also makes material and information available for others to read and enjoy. Stories, poetry, descriptions of classroom events, responses to literature . . . your home page will provide countless opportunities to allow your students to show off their best writing and art. And, an HTML editor makes this very easy as just a few clicks will enable you to copy and paste student work on your home page.

You might also wish to have a bulletin board listing due dates for major classroom assignments. Often, parents appreciate knowing when assignments are due. This is especially important in the older grades.

Another important function for your home page may be to organize links on the WWW for the various thematic units you cover during the year. You can save students much time by placing these at a single location where they are easy to access.

Finally, if you teach in the elementary grades, think about including a student newspaper on your home page. This can be a wonderful source of many writing activities. You may wish to appoint an editor for each two-week period and make this person responsible for soliciting articles and seeing that they are revised and edited to meet the standards of your home page. You might also wish to follow Fred Roemer's example from the previous chapter and make one student responsible each day for writing a log entry, describing the events of that day. These provide students, parents, and others with a real understanding of all the great things that take place in your classroom.

Of course, these are just the beginning elements to consider. As you work with your home page you will develop many more ideas that will be most appropriate for your individual needs. We hope the outstanding classrooms we have featured in these pages will provide you with many new ideas and the inspiration to develop an outstanding home page for your classroom.

The End of Your Journey

No. This isn't the end of your journey. It is really just the beginning as you discover new resources on the web, new friends around the world, and new sources of inspiration for the important work you do with the students in your classroom. We are firmly convinced the world awaiting our students is one where each of them has more potential to grow and to learn. We also believe your role in this will be central to their success, especially with these new technologies. As we indicated in the first chapter, Internet resources will increase, not decrease, the central role you play in orchestrating learning experiences for your students. Each of us will be challenged to thoughtfully guide students' learning within information environments that are richer and more complex, presenting richer and more complex learning opportunities for both us and our students. We hope you have found the ideas we have to

We are firmly convinced the world awaiting our students is one where each of them has more potential to grow and to learn.

E-MAIL FOR YOU

To: Colleagues

From: Jodi Moore, math teacher <Jmoore@ms.spotsylvania.k12.va.us>

Subject: Our Journey on the Internet

Hi!

The Internet has invaded our homes, schools, and lives. Just as the world and our lives change constantly so must the way we use the Internet. It is necessary to learn to integrate this resource while enriching our daily lessons. The connection is there, but the challenge is to transform our existing curriculum to most effectively utilize this awesome tool.

The vastness of this resource can be frightening to some, but to me it provides an avenue to motivate and involve all types of learners. I rely on the Internet to provide real-life data to interpret. One site students enjoy visiting for weather data is http://www.weather.com. This data is then used to graph, make predictions, and devise arguments for developing trends. No longer is it a walk to the library, but now with a few keystrokes we have access to current data. When students work with fraction operations I have discovered they really get excited when they use recipes. Each student or student group visits http://www.allrecipes.com/ and chooses a dessert. Next they must plan how many times that recipe must be prepared to feed the class, the grade level, and the entire school, and then provide the appropriate ingredient measures for each. This encourages students to problem-solve as well as apply their understanding of fractions.

I use the Internet to communicate with my students and their parents. Not only does our school improvement plan call for increased communication, I believe informed parents and students are more involved. Each day I post homework, upcoming projects, tests, and information about my class at http://www.schoolnotes.com. Also posted at this site, I include links to Internet sites, which might be helpful for students to investigate at home. Using schoolnotes.com enables students who are absent the ability to review homework from that day, as well as to provide a venue for parents and students to easily contact me.

I cannot imagine my life as a professional educator without the Internet. It is my responsibility to develop the talents of my charges and provide them with the skills necessary to journey into an ever-changing world. This road can be easily traveled using the Internet. I will continue to trek in that direction!

Jodi Moore, math teacher

Jmoore@ms.spotsylvania.k12.va.us

Battlefield Middle School
11120 Leavells Road
Fredericksburg, VA 22407

share useful in the important work you do to prepare children for their tomorrow's. Best wishes!

Instructional Resources on the Internet

Animated Images Archives—
http://www.aphids.com/susan/imres/anim.html
Looking for great animations to put on your web pages? Here you go!
This central site has links to a host of sites with wonderful animations.

Guides to HTML—http://www.hypernews.org/HyperNews/get/www/html/guides.html
A useful central site, but only if you have some familiarity with HTML.
An extensive set of resources.

How Do They Do That With HTML?—
http://www.nashville.net/~carl/htmlguide/
Have you ever seen a great web page and wondered how they were able
to use a special background pattern, animations, background sounds, or
other tricks? Here is the page that explains everything and shows you
how to include these and many other useful features in your classroom
home page. Set a bookmark!

Internet in the Classroom Tutorial—
http://www.indirect.com/www/dhixson/class.html
See the section "Design and Post Your Classroom Home Page". This is
a great place with useful ideas and useful templates for your home page.

Resources for Icons, Images, and Graphics—
http://www.aphids.com/susan/imres
Another nice location to obtain great visual elements for your classroom home page.

The Backgrounds Archive—http://www.pixelfoundry.com/bgs.html
A great collection of visually appealing backgrounds for use on your
classroom home page.

The Free Site—http://www.thefreesite.com/
The soup to nuts location for everything you might want to put on your
web page: graphics, Web page counters, trackers, freeware, E-mail, free
E-mail, Web pages, Webmaster tools, fonts, etc.

Web Clip Art—http://webclipart.miningco.com/internet/webclipart/
An extensive collection of art for your home page including alphabets,
backgrounds, and all kinds of clip art and animations. Set a bookmark!

webreference.com—http://www.webreference.com/
This is a great site to learn about creating web sites. Information rages
from the very beginner to the expert.

WebTools: Essential Tools for Web Weavers—
http://schmidel.com/webtools.htm
An extensive collection of images, animations, and other resources and
tools for your web building work.

Web66—http://web66.coled.umn.edu/

This is a great general source of information for developing a classroom home page. The section on technology contains step-by-step instructions for setting up a WWW server, HTML templates you may wish to copy for your use, and much more. Set a bookmark!

Listservs/Mailing Lists for Developing a Classroom Home Page

Follow the usual subscription procedures to join as seen in Chapter 3.

WEB66—WebMaster@web66.coled.umn.edu

A discussion group for teachers preparing web pages in schools.

Glossary

acceptable use policy A written agreement signed by parents/guardians, students, and teachers which specifies the conditions under which students may use the Internet, defines appropriate and unacceptable use, and defines penalties for violating items in the policy.

bookmark The feature used in Netscape Navigator to mark a location on the Internet so that you might quickly be able to return to this location at a later time.

browser A browser is a software program on your computer allowing you to connect to locations on the Internet. There are several different browsers: Netscape Navigator, and Internet Explorer. Each comes in at least two flavors: Windows and Macintosh.

central site A central site is a location on the Internet with extensive and well-organized links about a content area or important subject. Most are located at stable sites which will not quickly change. Examples include: **History/Social Studies Web Site for K-12 Teachers** (http://www.execpc.com/~dboals/boals.html), **Children's Literature Web Guide** (http://www.ucalgary.ca/~dkbrown/index.html), or **The Math Forum** (http://forum.swarthmore.edu/)

central site strategy Often teachers find a central site strategy effective for locating useful instructional resources. Rather than using a search engine, they will locate a central site in a subject area, set a bookmark, and then use this location to find useful resources.

chat-rooms Locations on the Internet where you may engage in simultaneous e-mail correspondence with other people.

classroom home page A classroom home page is a location on the Internet where you can display the work your class is doing and organize links to useful resources for your students.

Content Advisor A feature on Internet Explorer enabling you to block student access to web sites with inappropriate content. Like other software filters, this also ends up blocking access to useful sites, making it somewhat problematic.

cookies Cookies are requests for information from web site administrators who may record and request information about you whenever you visit their site. Sometimes this is information they collect to direct you to locations you visit most often. Sometimes web sites gather information about you for statistical purposes in order to determine how many people visit their site.

favorites The feature used in Internet Explorer to mark a location on the Internet so that you might quickly be able to return to this location at a later time.

home page location   A home page location is the page that shows up first on your screen each time students connect to the Internet. You may set the home page location to a site your prefer to see first by setting the preferences in your browser.

HTML (HyperText Mark-up Language)   HyperText Mark-up Language, or HTML, is the programming language used to design web pages on the Internet.

HTML editor   An HTML editor is a software program that allows you to design a web page they way you wish it to appear while automatically converting your design into HTML code. Netscape's Composer and Adobe's PageMill are examples.

hypertext link   Words or objects that take you to the site on the Internet linked to that item(s) when you click on it. A key navigational element for Internet use.

Internet Inquiry   An instructional practice using the Internet in a more student-directed fashion. Usually, it consists of five phases: question; search; analyze; compose; and share.

Internet Project   A collaborative approach to instructional use of the Internet. Generally, Internet projects follow these procedures: plan a collaborative project for an upcoming unit in your classroom and write a project description; post the project description and timeline several months in advance at one or several locations, seeking collaborative classroom partners; arrange collaboration details with teachers in other classrooms who agree to participate; complete the project, using Internet Workshop as a forum in your own class for working on the project and exchanging information with your collaborating classrooms.

Internet Workshop   An instructional practice often used by teachers getting started with using the Internet. It often includes these steps: locate a site, or several sites, on the Internet with content related to a classroom unit of instruction and set a bookmark for the location(s); develop an activity requiring students to use the site(s); assign this activity to be completed during the week; have students share their work, questions, and new insights at the end of the week during a Workshop session.

Internet Workshop activity page   An activity page often used by teachers to organize the activities in Internet Activity. Students complete the activities in this page and then bring it to Internet Workshop for discussion about what they learned and new questions they have.

Java   Java is a programming language often used at Internet locations to provide animations and other interactive and multimedia features. A plug-in for Java is in both Internet Explorer 4 and Netscape Navigator 4.

plug-in   A small software program you can download from the Internet allowing you to read, view, or play multimedia elements at a web page.

pourquoi tales   Pourquoi tales are creation myths that exist in every traditional culture. Pourquoi tales explain sources of natural phenomena such as how people obtained fire, why mosquitoes buzz in people's ears, where the moon came from, or why rivers run into the ocean. Gathering and exchanging pourquoi tales over the Internet is a wonderful way for students to discover the wider world around them.

RAM (Random Access Memory)	A type of memory stored on chips in your computer. Each application you use requires a certain amount of RAM. The amount of your computer's RAM determines how many programs you can run at once. It will also determine whether or not your computer can run the latest versions of Internet browsers which require more RAM than earlier versions.
RealAudio technology	This technology permits streaming audio, a way to continuously send audio signals over the Internet to your computer. This permits you to listen to audio sources of information including radio programs broadcast from stations around the world. RealAudio has recently applied their technology to RealVideo, and developed RealPlayer a free plug-in available at their web site (http://www.real.com/products/player/index.html).
scientific thinking	Thinking scientifically involves developing and evaluating best guesses about why things are the way there are. This can be an important part of Internet Project in science as students question one another, decide upon appropriate ways of evaluating competing hypotheses, gather information, and evaluate that information to reach conclusions that are agreed to by all parties. Thinking scientifically is an important part of the new national standards for science education.
search engines	Computers on the Internet that search for sites containing words or phrases you specify. These include Yahoo, InfoSeek, HotBot, Lycos, and others.
server	A server is a computer in a network, containing information or programs that are often shared with others. A web page on the Internet is always located on a server.
software filters	These filters deny access to locations where certain words appear. Teachers and parents may edit the list of words used in the blocking software. They include: **Cyber Patrol**—(http://www.cyberpatrol.com/), **Net Nanny**—(http://www.netnanny.com/), and **SurfWatch**—(http://www.surfwatch.com/)
Student-to-Student	During a Student-to-Student activity, students first identify a useful web location related to their studies. Then they develop a learning experience using the web site for other students to complete. This is often done for a culminating activity for Internet Inquiry or thematic units.
text-to-speech technology	This technology allows a computer to read aloud, written text. It is available for both Windows and Macintosh systems, supporting visually challenged children as well as our very youngest readers.
toolbar	A row of objects on your browser with labels underneath each object. Items in the toolbar let you do things with your browser. The toolbar often includes items such as "Back", "Forward," "Reload," "Home," "Search," "Guide," "Images," "Print," "Security," and "Stop."
Uniform Resource Locator (URL)	The address of a location on the Internet. For example, the URL of Quill Net is: http://www.quill.net/
web-site Internet Project	A web-site Internet Project is a more permanent Internet Project, coordinated by an individual at a web site.

Index

Note: Bolded items are web site locations, mailing lists, or newsgroups on the Internet.